# A GEOGRAPHY OF THE CANADIAN ECONOMY

IAIN WALLACE

OXFORD

UNIVERSITY PRESS

# OXFORD
UNIVERSITY PRESS

70 Wynford Drive, Don Mills, Ontario M3C 1J9
www.oup.com/ca

Oxford University Press is a department of the University of Oxford.
It furthers the University's objective of excellence in research, scholarship,
and education by publishing worldwide in

Oxford New York

Auckland Bangkok Buenos Aires Cape Town Chennai
Dar es Salaam Delhi Hong Kong Istanbul Karachi Kolkata
Kuala Lumpur Madrid Melbourne Mexico City Mumbai Nairobi
São Paulo Shanghai Singapore Taipei Tokyo Toronto

with an associated company in Berlin

Oxford is a trade mark of Oxford University Press
in the UK and in certain other countries

Published in Canada
by Oxford University Press

Copyright © Oxford University Press Canada 2002

The moral rights of the author have been asserted

Database right Oxford University Press (maker)

First published 2002

National Library of Canada Cataloguing in Publication Data

Wallace, Iain, 1946
A geography of the Canadian economy

Includes bibliographical references and index.
ISBN 0-19-540773-3

1. Canada – Economic conditions, 1991-   2. Economic Geography.
I. Title.

HC113.W28 2001      330.971      C2001-903188-2

Cover Design: Joan Dempsey
Cover Image: Roy Ooms/Masterfile
Text Layout, Maps and Graphics: Paul Sneath/free&Creative

1 2 3 4 - 05 04 03 02
This book is printed on permanent (acid-free) paper ∞.
Printed in Canada

# Contents

*List of Tables* / vii
*List of Figures* / viii
*Acknowledgements* / xi
*Preface* / xii


PART I    CONTEXT

1    Canada in the World Economy / 3
        Introduction / 3
        Global Economic Restructuring and Its Implications for Canada / 4
        Canada and the Global Economy / 7
        Canadian Industrialization in a Continental Context / 10
        The Pattern of Canada's International Economic Linkages / 13
        Conclusion / 15
        Further Reading / 18

2    The Role of Culture and Political Economy / 19
        Historical Introduction / 19
        The Political Economy of Regionalism: Background / 21
        The Era of 'Regional Policy' and Its Impact / 22
        Regional Political Economy at the Start of the Twenty-First Century / 28
        Society, Culture, and the Economy / 34
        Conclusion / 39
        Further Reading / 40

3    The Natural Environment and the Economy / 41
        Introduction / 41
        Environmental Parameters / 45
        Staple Industries and the Environment / 46
        From Consumer Society to Conserver Society? / 51
        Climatic Change and Environmental Hazards / 53
        Conclusion / 56
        Further Reading / 57

4    Structural Change in the Canadian Economy  /  58
         Introduction  /  58
         Globalization  /  58
         Situating Canada in the Capitalist World Economy  /  60
         National Competitive Advantage: Porter's Model  /  62
         Economic Restructuring at the National Scale  /  66
         The Region as a Key Economic Environment  /  68
         Conclusion  /  71
         Further Reading  /  71

5    Economic Dimensions of the Canadian Urban System  /  72
         Introduction  /  72
         Urban Systems  /  73
         The Canadian Urban System  /  76
         Metropolitan Concentration  /  80
         Metropolitan Economies  /  82
         Canada's Largest Metropolitan Regions  /  84
         Strategies of Adjustment  /  89
         Beyond the Metropolitan Areas  /  90
         Conclusion  /  92
         Further Reading  /  93

PART II    **SECTORS**

6    The Service Sector  /  97
         Introduction  /  97
         Distributive Services  /  102
         Producer Services  /  103
         Public, Non-market Services  /  104
         Personal Services  /  106
         Tourism  /  106
         Conclusion  /  108
         Further Reading  /  109

7    Post-Staples Manufacturing  /  110
         Introduction  /  110
         Manufacturing Overview  /  112
         Canada's Place in the North American Auto Industry  /  114
         The Aerospace Industry  /  118
         Telecommunications, Computer Equipment, and Related Industries  /  119
         Other High-Technology Sectors  /  121
         Conclusion  /  122
         Further Reading  /  122

8    Agriculture, Agri-Food, and the Rural Economy / 123
         Introduction / 123
         Farm Characteristics / 128
         The Policy Framework / 129
         Regional Patterns / 133
         Beyond Agriculture / 137
         Conclusion / 138
         Further Reading / 139

9    The Forest and Minerals Industries / 140
         Introduction / 140
         The Forest Sector / 142
         The Minerals Sector / 145
         Conclusion / 149
         Further Reading / 150

10   The Energy and Chemical Industries / 151
         Introduction / 151
         The Geopolitics of Energy / 152
         Interfuel Competition and Industrial Location / 156
         Energy Projects as Means of National and Regional Development / 160
         Issues of the Early Twenty-First Century / 163
         Conclusion / 164
         Further Reading / 164

11   Transportation / 165
         Introduction / 165
         The Role of Technological Change / 170
         Changes in Transportation Networks / 172
         Major Traffic Flows / 174
         Conclusion / 176
         Further Reading / 176

PART III    REGIONS

12   Atlantic Canada / 179
         Introduction / 179
         Regional Challenges / 181
         Newfoundland / 183
         Nova Scotia / 186
         New Brunswick and Prince Edward Island / 187
         Conclusion / 189
         Further Reading / 190

13   Central Canada / 191
        Introduction / 191
        Contrasts in the Core / 193
        Recent Economic Performance of Central Canada / 194
        Regional Economic Structure / 198
        Quebec Subregions / 199
        Ontario Subregions / 205
        Challenges of Economic Restructuring / 207
        Conclusion / 210
        Further Reading / 210

14   Western Canada / 211
        Introduction / 211
        The Character of the Prairie Economy / 212
        The Character of the British Columbia Economy / 215
        Economic Restructuring in Western Canada / 216
        Regional Economy of the Western Provinces / 220
        Conclusion / 228
        Further Reading / 229

15   Northern and Aboriginal Canada / 230
        Introduction / 230
        The Northern Economy / 234
        Conclusion / 238
        Further Reading / 239

        *Conclusion: Continuity and Change* / 240
        *Glossary* / 243
        *References* / 246
        *Index* / 258

# List of Tables

1.1     Canadian Merchandise Trade, by World Region, 1999 / 7

1.2     Canadian Merchandise Trade, by Commodity Group, 1999 / 14

2.1     Equalization Payments to Six Provinces, 1957–1995 / 24

2.2     Equalization Payments to Quebec, 1957–1995, Selected Years / 24

2.3     Canada's Casinos: Revenue and Attendance, 1996 / 38

3.1     The PEP Framework: Components / 43

3.2     Economic Impact of Selected Natural Disasters in Canada / 55

5.1     Census Metropolitan Areas, 1996 Population / 78

5.2     Metropolitan Specialization (Location Quotients), 1991 / 81

5.3     Employment Structure: Montreal and Toronto, 1991 and 1996 / 86

5.4     The Structure of Urban Competitive Advantage:
        Representative Capital Stocks and Systems / 91

6.1     The Structure of the Service Sector / 98

6.2     North American Industry Classification System / 101

6.3     Foreign Tourism in Canada, Selected Statistics, 1999 / 109

7.1     Share of GDP and Employment by Industry Group, 1966–1996 / 113

8.1     Farms in Canada, 1996 / 129

9.1     Lumber Production, 1995 / 143

9.2     Canadian Mineral Output, 1978 and 1998 / 146

10.1    Electricity Supply in Canada, 1998 / 159

11.1    Leading Commodities Transported by Railways within Canada, 1997 / 169

11.2    Principal Canadian Domestic Airline Routes, 1997 / 173

12.1    Employment Structure: Atlantic Canada, 1996 / 182

13.1    Employment Structure: Quebec and Ontario, 1991 and 1996 / 195

14.1    Employment Structure: Prairie Provinces, 1996 / 214

14.2    Employment Structure: British Columbia, 1986 and 1996 / 226

# List of Figures

1.1  Foreign Direct Investment in Canada, 1999 / 16

1.2  Canadian Direct Investment Abroad, 1999 / 17

2.1  DREE Designated Regions and Special Areas, 1973 / 25

2.2  Canadian Forces Bases and Military Personnel, 1991 / 27

2.3  Interprovincial Trade Flows, Ontario as Origin, 1998 / 30

2.4  Interprovincial Trade Flows, Other Regions as Origin, 1998 / 31

2.5  Canada–US Trade, Main Ontario Trade Flows, 1998 / 32

2.6  Canada–US Trade, Main Trade Flows, Other Regions, 1998 / 33

2.7  Average Annual Rates of Interprovincial Migration, 1989–1998 / 35

3.1  Population–Environment Process Framework / 44

3.2  Canada's Forests / 48

3.3  Decline in Newfoundland Groundfish Stocks, 1982–1993 / 49

3.4  Projected Changes in Forest and Grassland Boundaries, Doubled $CO_2$ Scenario / 54

4.1  National Determinants of Competitive Advantage: 'The Diamond' / 64

5.1  Evolution of Settlement System / 75

5.2  The Canadian Urban System, 1996 / 77

5.3  Employment Rates in the Montreal CMA, 1989–1999 / 88

6.1  Distribution of Visits to the Top 10 Tourism Regions, 1997 / 108

7.1  Canadian Auto Industry Locations, 1993 / 116

8.1  Value-Added in Canada's Agri-Food Industry, 1997 / 126

8.2  Income Variation on Canadian Farms, 1996 / 127

8.3  Predominant Farm Type, 1991 / 130

8.4  Typology of Rural Regions in Canada / 134

9.1  Canadian Mineral Property Portfolio Abroad, 1997 and 1998 / 147

10.1    Crude Oil Production and Movements, by Source, 1998  /  154

10.2    Natural Gas Sales and Movements, by Source, 1998  /  155

10.3    Regional Variations in Energy Consumption, 1991  /  157

10.4    The Canada Lands, 1980  /  161

11.1    Canadian National and Canadian Pacific Railway Networks, 1999  /  167

12.1    Fish-Processing Plants Affected by Cod Moratorium  /  184

13.1    Size and Structure of Provincial Economies, 1998  /  192

13.2    Average Per Capita Income, Quebec Regions, 1996  /  200

13.3    Sectoral Distribution of Economic Activity, Quebec Regions, 1989  /  201

14.1    Prairie Railway Network, 1931  /  213

14.2    Wheat, Barley, Canola Production, 1966–1998  /  217

14.3    Provincial Labour Productivity, 1989 and 1999  /  219

15.1    Modern Treaties and Political Units in the Canadian North  /  231

15.2    Hamelin's 'Nordicity' Index  /  232

15.3    Typology of Socio-Economic Well-Being
        among First Nations Communities, 1996  /  237

TO GILLIAN

# Acknowledgements

'The press is patient—after all, 500 years of publishing has taught us something.'

When I received this reassurance from Brian Henderson, then College and Trade Publisher at Oxford University Press, Toronto in 1992, I had no idea how much I would push the envelope! The contract for the book had been signed with Oxford in 1989, for delivery (admittedly, over-optimistically) in 1991. So I am 10 years overdue, and very grateful for the confidence maintained by editors in the intervening decade that they would ultimately have a product that confirmed the press's original interest. This project would not have seen the light of day but for the tolerance and encouragement of Richard Teleky, Euan White, and Laura Macleod. The publisher's patience has been a necessary but not sufficient condition, however. Without loving but firm pressure latterly from my 'benevolent dictator', constructive critic, and fan to bring things to a finish, I might still be trying to justify procrastination. The book is deservedly dedicated to my wife, Gillian.

I am also glad to acknowledge the interest and support of Joel Yan, Co-ordinator, University Liaison Program, Statistics Canada, and I strongly encourage users of this volume to become familiar with the relevant data resources available at http://www.statcan.ca/english/edu/researchers.htm.

# Preface

This book analyses the forces shaping the geography of the Canadian economy at the start of the twenty-first century. It recognizes that change is being driven by many different agents, operating at a variety of geographical scales. The starting point for analysis is the reality of *globalization*, the fact that there is now effectively a single dominant world-scale economic system, within which events make their effects felt rapidly and pervasively. The forces of change, such as the workings of unregulated international financial markets and the economic consequences of global environmental change, have markedly different effects in different places. As a result, countries, regions, and specific local communities exist within an overarching dynamic environment that presents often unpredictable challenges and opportunities. The capacity to respond effectively to economic change is thus a primary measure of the sustainability of societies and their capacity to promote the welfare of citizens, or residents, in a turbulent world. Nationally and locally, Canadians are facing these economic challenges.

The varied challenges originate partly from differences rooted in the physical geography of the biosphere. But each society has also been shaped by a history of human activity, whether over centuries or of more recent origin. This 'human environment' incorporates the resources that societies, defined at various geographical scales, bring into the present. It includes their settlement and cultural history, the legacy of past economic activity, and the political and institutional means by which national or local communities have managed their collective endeavours. The Canadian economy, as a whole and in its regional components, encounters the present with the opportunities and constraints provided by its geography and accumulated from its past.

This book is structured in three sections designed to unravel the interplay of forces shaping the contemporary economic geography of Canada. These forces involve developments linking various scales—the global and the local, the national and the regional—as well as those involving different contexts—the biophysical and the human, the ones that structure geographical space and those that define the character of places.

The chapters in Part I, Context, start by situating the Canadian economy within the global and continental spheres of activity, tracing how Canada's experience as a major industrialized nation continues to be structured by its global location and by its history of human interaction with the country's biophysical environment. Whether they like it or not, Canadians are situated next door to the world's largest and most powerful nation. Both passively (just by being there) and actively (in pursuit of its own national interest), the United States influences the economic circumstances that Canadians face. Much of Canadian economic and political history involves the tension between pursuing policies aligned with influential forces originating in the United States and, conversely, other policies that set out in some way to oppose those forces in the interests of a distinctively Canadian agenda.

Similarly, the exploitation of natural resources has shaped the economic geography of Canada and reveals a counterpoint between the pursuit of comparative advantage and a struggle against allowing opportunities to be too readily constrained by an often harsh environment. That different peoples have been drawn in different ways and at different times into the encounter with the Canadian environment explains much of the cultural geography within which economic activity is embedded. But the context of the modern Canadian economy is increasingly an urban one. The majority of the population lives and works in its principal metropolitan areas, where the largest sector of the economy, service activities, is distinctively localized.

The chapters in Part II, Sectors, analyse the geography of the different principal subdivisions of the Canadian economy and the sources of change within each one. Accessibility to information, and to the skills that can profit from it, are central to the 'knowledge economy' of higher-level service employment in Canada's metropolitan centres. The manufacturing sectors that have been expanding fastest are those whose basis in research and innovation also attracts them to this milieu. At the same time, the Canadian economy retains its historic connection to the natural resources of the world's second-largest country. A number of chapters document changes in the global markets for Canadian staple resources and in the structure of the industries that extract them. The transportation sector, which provides services to all other sectors of economic activity and has been central to maintaining the widely dispersed nation that is Canada, is also reviewed.

The final section of the book, Regions, acknowledges an enduring logic to conventional macro-regional divisions of the Canadian economy. Issues of economic development differ across the country, as do the responses they have invoked from people, firms, and governments. The sectoral focus of the second section of the book needs to be balanced by a consideration of how different elements of economic activity combine *in places* (defined at varying geographical scales) to produce the national mosaic that is Canada's economic geography.

Finally, a concluding chapter looks at both continuity and change as these relate to the interplay between the country's economy and geography.

# PART I

# CONTEXT

# Canada in the World Economy

## INTRODUCTION

The beginning of the twenty-first century is a good time to take stock of Canada's economic geography. Forces that change the spatial and sectoral distribution of economic activity are continually at work, but some developments have greater long-term impact than others, and the past few decades have seen some significant turning points. In other words, the economic geography of the early 2000s differs in important ways from that of the early 1970s, only a generation ago. This can be seen, for instance, in the following three contexts.

First, the 1970s will likely prove to have been the last decade in which the exploitation of natural resources played a major role in shaping the geography of Canada's national economy. The resource-based industries remain extremely important, but their expansion will no longer change the map of settlement or significantly change the regional political balance, as it has in the past. The continuous postwar expansion of the mining frontier effectively came to an end in that decade; the last major commercial stands of softwood lumber were identified for exploitation; and the revolution in global energy markets associated with the OPEC price rise and its aftermath resulted in resource revenue-based shifts in domestic geopolitics on a scale that is unlikely to be repeated (see Chapter 10).

Second, during the 1980s, steps were taken to cement a deeper integration of the Canadian and American economies. While this move, culminating in the signing of the Canada–United States Free Trade Agreement (FTA) in 1988, had parallels in other parts of the world, it marked a significant departure from century-old Canadian policies of economic nationalism. These had long been justified to maintain Canada's independence from its powerful southern neighbour, but by the 1980s the forces of globalization in the world economy were rendering nationalist policies increasingly ineffective. Powerful voices in the Canadian business community and in government and academia argued that free trade with the United States was the best choice available to Canadians if they were to prosper in the new international order (Macdonald Commission, 1985). The expansion of the FTA into NAFTA (the North American Free Trade Agreement) in 1993, through the inclusion of Mexico into a continental free trade zone, has situated the Canadian economy within an institutional framework whose full implications are still in the process of being discovered.

Third, by the end of the 1990s, most commentators were recognizing that Canada's economic future was tied to the 'knowledge economy' and the quality of its human resources, much more so than to its traditional natural resource staples. As a result, in Canada as in other advanced industrial nations, those large metropolitan regions that are the centres of corporate and government decision-making, research and development (R&D) facilities, and institutions of higher education are gaining prominence as the key spatial units of economic dynamism, more so even, some have claimed, than national or provincial economies as a whole (see Chapter 4).

These changes and others involve shifts within the global economy that are given particular form domestically by their interactions with features of Canada's historical and geographical evolution. The Canadian economy has always been particularly 'open' to the wider global economy, so we will look first at that broader geographical context.

## GLOBAL ECONOMIC RESTRUCTURING AND ITS IMPLICATIONS FOR CANADA

The late twentieth century was marked by the widespread recognition that a qualitative change is taking place globally in the nature of economic, political, and cultural systems. Despite considerable disagreement as to what, precisely, is bringing about change and how novel the changes are, the term 'globalization' has become widely, although often carelessly, used to capture these processes and their effects (Scholte, 2000; Castells, 1996, 1997, 1998). They comprise changes in the structure of the global economy, in the political and cultural contexts of economic activity, and in the ways that individuals and societies experience their involvement in the economy. Scholte (2000) identifies 'supraterritoriality' as the critical distinguishing feature that sets contemporary changes apart from some of those developments that have a longer history. What is new is the pervasiveness of transborder connections, facilitated by the ongoing growth of transnational corporations, continual innovation in the technologies of transportation and communication, and the spread, through these means, of cultural values and communities of interest that make the world an increasingly integrated, though by no means homogeneous, social system. The vastly accelerated movement of goods, information, and financial resources around the world, at falling real cost, has resulted in what Harvey (1989b) terms 'time-space compression'. In advanced industrial states such as Canada, the ability of citizens to have almost instant access to an enormous range of material goods, personal and business services, and information is changing how people view the world and hence how markets operate.

The socio-political context of contemporary globalization is the emergence of capitalism as a truly worldwide mode of organizing economic activity and as the most powerful basis for allocating resources. Its form reflects the changing balance of power and influence between territorially-bounded states, such as Canada; international institutions, such as the United Nations and the World Bank; and transnational corporations, such as General Motors and Alcan, which, not being confined to one territorial state, have a strategic flexibility in their worldwide use of geographic space. As markets have become increasingly global and deregulated by governments to facilitate the expansion of international business, individual states have lost many of their powers to exercise control over national economies and to influence the domestic impact of external developments. At the same time, individuals, firms, and many metropolitan communities have gained a greater capacity to interact directly across a range of geographical scales within the global arena, as telecommunications, travel, and the Internet provide unprecedented access to distant opportunities. This can increase the ability of corporations or regional communities to exploit trends in the global or continental economy to their advantage; but it can equally increase their vulnerability to these trends, in ways that national governments may be hard-pressed to protect them from. The intense debates within Canada, as in other countries, about the merits of globalization and the distribution, both domestically and in the wider world, of its costs and benefits point to the fundamental importance of the issues at stake.

The reduced capacity of national governments to direct or manage economic forces reflects both systemic and ideological trends. The advanced industrial societies of the capitalist world (collectively, 'the West') have not found it easy to adjust to the pressures of globalization, despite the fact that these states, including Canada, benefit more from them than do poorer nations. The dominant social order that emerged in the West after the World War II and flourished in the period 1945–72 was based on a Fordist production regime. This took the form of leading industries (of which the auto industry was the archetype), organized primarily for national markets, achieving productivity gains through innovation and mechanization, and negotiating a sharing of the wealth they created with their unionized workers. Large firms and their workers contributed to the well-being of the wider society through a taxation system that provided the basis for expanded government investment in public health, education, and other benefits (pensions, etc.) of the welfare state. Canada's rapid economic growth in the 1950s and 1960s rested on this foundation, with the added contribution of steady immigration from Europe and the growing demand of US industries for Canadian natural resources.

In contrast to the postwar Fordist regime, the current era of globalization is characterized by intensified international competition, with national economies much more open to the dynamics of change in world markets. These pressures have forced firms to become much more *flexible* (see Chapter 4) in their capacity to respond to changes in technology, in the nature of demand for their output, and in the competition offered by firms in newly industrializing countries (NICs). Western governments have proven considerably less able to respond rapidly to major changes in the world economy, especially when these impose costs (particularly higher unemployment) on their citizens. During the 1980s Canada, more than most other industrialized countries, went heavily into debt by maintaining patterns of government spending no longer being supported by tax revenues. By the mid-1990s the consequences of a large accumulated debt, and an ideological backlash against the political philosophies that had allowed it to reach such proportions, came together to create a *neo-liberal* political environment in which 'deficit reduction' and the 'downsizing' of government and the institutions of the welfare state became pressing policy objectives.

Contradictory currents have been shaping the global economy since the early 1970s. Since then, the postwar economic dominance of the United States has given way to a more complex pattern of international economic power. This reflects the consolidation of Japan's status as a major economic actor; the emergence of an increasingly integrated Western Europe (the European Union, or EU) as an economy to rival that of North America; and the resilience of the US economy itself (on which the prosperity of the Canadian economy has become increasingly dependent) (Table 1.1). Challenging the global hegemony of these core industrial regions has been the growth in the competitiveness of firms in the NICs and, since the 1980s, of China. The growth of manufactured exports from these countries has been encouraged by the steady multilateral reduction of tariffs and other barriers to international trade, promoted by the World Trade Organization (WTO) and its predecessor, the General Agreement on Tariffs and Trade (GATT). Yet at the same time that Western governments and transnational firms have championed the benefits of 'free trade', they have also been active to limit its scope in contexts where particular domestic political interests appear threatened. Both Canada and the United States have been guilty on this score, usually at the expense of less-developed nations.

Within each of the three global core regions (North America, Europe, and Japan and Southeast Asia), there have been moves towards greater *regional* economic integration, with institutional arrangements giving preferential treatment to firms in member states (Stallings, 1995). The signing of NAFTA by Canada, the United States, and Mexico, the ongoing expansion of the European Union to include members from the former state-planned socialist economies of Eastern Europe in the near future, and the considerable functional economic integration brought about within ASEAN (the Association of Southeast Asian Nations) by the workings of the Japanese economy can all be seen as marking the emergence of trading blocs that fragment the global market. Moreover, even within these regional trading systems, forms of protectionism remain active. Where sensitive domestic interests are threatened, governments act to keep foreign competitors at bay, and the more powerful states can do so most effectively. Nowhere is this more apparent than in the history of trade disputes between Canada and the United States since the signing of the FTA. Canadian softwood lumber exports to the US have been a particularly contentious issue (see Chapter 9). Governments' ambivalence towards freer trade arises out of the fact that it invariably brings both costs and benefits. The economic benefits are usually more diffuse, sectorally and regionally, than the costs of adjustment, giving those who stand to lose a louder voice in the domestic political arena than those who gain. Canada is certainly not unique in this respect.

The changing profile of the world economy, as it affects the economic geography of Canada, goes well beyond shifts in the competitive position of the various core nations and their industries. The persistent and, in most places, widening gap between living standards in the global North and the South (it needs to be remembered that at this scale 'the North' is essentially synonymous with 'the West') and the flow of refugees from regions of conflict or repression influence Canada's international trade, development

**Table 1.1    Canadian Merchandise Trade, by World Region, 1999 (Current $)**

| Imports $ million | % change 1989–99 | Region | Exports $ million | % change 1989–99 |
|---|---|---|---|---|
| 220,662 | 246 | North America | 286,798 | 282 |
| 10,789 | 394 | Central America | 2,779 | 175 |
| 9,521 | 558 | Mexico | 1,523 | 239 |
| 4,057 | 163 | South America | 2,372 | 198 |
| 41,941 | 224 | Asia | 17,237 | 111 |
| 1,632 | 183 | Oceania | 1,141 | 86 |
| 35,846 | 199 | Western Europe | 16,177 | 116 |
| 1,480 | 261 | Other Europe | 664 | 69 |
| 1,513 | 194 | Middle East | 1,943 | 121 |
| 1,990 | 172 | Africa | 1,298 | 138 |
| 319,910 | 237 | Total | 330,410 | 238 |

NOTE: Statistics Canada, in source document, includes Mexico as part of 'Central America'; 'North America' includes the US and the French territory of St Pierre et Miquelon.
SOURCE: Statistics Canada, *Canadian International Merchandise Trade*, Dec. 1999, Cat. no. 65–001.

assistance, and immigration policies. They also have domestic repercussions. The influx of people and capital from Hong Kong in the early 1990s, for instance, helped to shape both the housing market and the business climate in the Lower Mainland of British Columbia. The uncertain outcome of political and economic transformations still underway in China, Russia, and the Middle East will undoubtedly affect the markets for Canadian resources and the business opportunities for Canadian firms.

## CANADA AND THE GLOBAL ECONOMY

Since the collapse of state socialism in the former Soviet Union and Eastern Europe and with the decision of China's leaders to pursue economic integration into world markets, the global economy has become truly integrated on the basis of capitalism. The essence of this economic system is that, in a world divided territorially into numerous independent political units (*states*), economic transactions are regulated by relatively autonomous mechanisms of exchange (*markets*) that operate internationally and are in principle independent of any state's political control. In practice, the theoretical construct of neo-classical economics, which portrays markets as abstract regulators of the prices and quantities of traded goods, obscures the power both of the few dominant (*oligopolistic*) corporations in any particular industry and of governments, by a wide variety of measures, to influence market conditions. Among the tensions that have persistently characterized the capitalist world economy is the degree to which a country's government (often identified as *the state*) can and should intervene in the market system to achieve specific goals, whether these are narrowly economic or expressive of broader societal interests. In Canada, such questions have formed the basis of the ideological differences between 'economic nationalists', who advocate varying degrees of state intervention, especially in the face of dominant American influences, and neo-liberal 'free traders', who favour giving individuals, firms, and market forces maximum freedom of action, even if this does involve a loss of Canadian control or cultural identity.

The capitalist world economy is inherently dynamic, being driven by the profit-seeking actions of individuals and firms in their role as producers of goods and services. This dynamism is expressed in time, in space, and in the economy's structural composition. Particularly since the start of the Industrial Revolution in England in the late eighteenth century, the evolution of leading national economies has been subject to cycles of faster and slower growth. These *Kondratieff waves* capture the effects of periods of rapid economic expansion, maintained by the exploitation of profitable new business opportunities, in part based on the diffusion of technical innovations, followed by periods of more limited growth (including major recessions) as excess productive capacity results in lower profitability—the resource-saving benefits of innovative technologies gradually tail off, and institutions find difficulty in responding to a more demanding operational environment (Wallace, 1990). The global economy, and Canada with it, enjoyed its most recent sustained expansionary period from 1945 to 1972. Foreign demand for Canadian resources and the domestic demand of a rapidly growing and increasingly productive population led to major investments in all sectors of the economy, including public services and private housing. Slower growth from the mid-1970s to the mid-1990s resulted from a variety of causal factors. These included a decade of greatly increased world oil prices and related inflation (1973–85); the sharp growth of competition from the NICs, which captured markets and displaced jobs in North America and Western Europe; and significant institutional rigidities affecting the performance of labour, business, and governments in mature industrial economies such as Canada. The cycle of Kondratieff waves suggests that a new economic upswing may well be getting underway at the start of the twenty-first century, and the performance of the North American economy during the 1990s certainly gave substance to that expectation. It appears that the 'Fifth Kondratieff' (Hall, 1985) will be driven by innovations in telecommunications, information handling, and biotechnology.

The geographical evolution of the capitalist world economy has been marked by its areal and structural differentiation. From the time of the Industrial Revolution, the centre of greatest economic power and vitality, the *core*, has shifted from Britain and northwestern Europe (in the early nineteenth century) to the northeastern United States (in the late nineteenth century), to the west and southwestern US (in the mid-twentieth century), and on to the Asia-Pacific region, which includes Japan, China, and the western United States, by the turn of the twenty-first century. There is no uniform explanation for these spatial shifts, and eclipsed core regions do not usually cease to be major centres of economic power (Knox and Agnew, 1998). Nevertheless, the westward movement of the global economy's 'centre of gravity' has been both very noticeable and very significant in its consequences for Canada.

Canada entered the capitalist world economy as an exporter, on the economically undeveloped global *periphery*, of crude natural resource products (*staples*—initially fish, furs, and lumber) to the European core. The axis of the St Lawrence channelled trade with Europe and became the region within which an incipient Canadian core economy developed. After the mid-nineteenth century, the larger core economy of the northeastern United States began to exert its pull on Canadian resources and stimulated the westward expansion of the sawn lumber industry through the Great Lakes region. Confederation (1867) led to the nation-building policies of tariff-protected industrialization, which further strengthened the economy of the Canadian core, and of prairie settlement, which revitalized staple trade with Europe, this time in wheat. Meanwhile, economic development on Canada's Pacific coast was already being stimulated by the emergent markets of California. Construction of the Panama Canal by the US government (1917) furthered this process by making the resources of British Columbia much more accessible to Europe and the Atlantic coast of North America. With the relaxation of US tariffs on newsprint imports (1911), pulp and paper became the leading staple industry in eastern Canada.

The expansion of Canadian industrial capacity to meet the demands of World War II was primarily concentrated in the core region of southern Ontario and Quebec. This spatial pattern was dramatically reinforced, especially with respect to central and southwestern Ontario, by the vigorous expansion of manufacturing that followed in the 1950s and 1960s, in which branch plants of US firms played a prominent role (Ray, 1965). This growth, together with the dynamic expansion of the US economy, triggered demand for a significant expansion of the Canadian forest and mining industries, especially across the Shield, from northern Manitoba to Labrador. The most important new staple, however, was the emergent oil and gas sector in Alberta. These resources were developed to provide the industrialized core of Ontario with Canadian petroleum products (see Chapter 10) and to meet demands in the closest US core regions (the Pacific states and the western end of the Manufacturing Belt in the US Midwest). By the late 1960s, western Canada began to feel the stimulus of Japan's growing resource needs, particularly with respect to copper and coal. The 'Northeast Coal Project', opened in 1983 near Tumbler Ridge, BC, and the pulp and paper mills established in northern Alberta in the late 1980s continued this pattern of Canadian staples attracting investment to provision the leading global core economy of the day. Renewed interest in Arctic Canada's natural gas reserves to supply primarily US markets will likely constitute the next round of such development.

This brief history of staple resource development should not be read to imply that Canada is still *only* an economy of 'hewers of wood and drawers of water', although natural resources and their immediate processing do loom large in the nation's industrial structure. Rather, it points to the fact that the changing geography of the global economic system has had geographically regionalized impacts within such a large country as Canada. As the dynamic core of the world economy shifted from the European shores of the Atlantic to the Asian shores of the Pacific, the accessibility of the Maritime provinces to that core has declined, whereas that of British Columbia has increased. This shift has had direct consequences for the respective levels of prosperity of the two regions today. Not only does the natural axis of the Great Lakes–St Lawrence open out towards the North Atlantic, but the grain-handling infrastructure of the Prairies was also built to funnel traffic eastward (see Figure 14.1), yet the largest markets for grain currently lie across the Pacific. Similarly, from the time that a core industrial region first emerged in the northeastern United States, and as the US economy expanded westward, adjacent regions of Canada have felt the pull of larger markets for their resources south of the border. The tariff provisions of the 1879 National Policy were explicitly designed to offset that pull and to promote an east-west integration of the Canadian economy. But in the era of continental economic integration facilitated by NAFTA, those north-south linkages have mushroomed in size and scope. This is straining the viability of many Canadian institutions and the infrastructures that have been developed over the past century or more (see Chapter 2).

## CANADIAN INDUSTRIALIZATION IN A CONTINENTAL CONTEXT

Historically, the emergence of global core economies has been marked by their growing and increasingly diversified manufacturing output and the decline in relative importance of their agricultural and other primary resource production. For a country such as Canada, entering global markets as a peripheral producer of resource staples, the development challenge has been to avoid getting stuck in a *staples trap*. The danger of creating an economy, whether national or regional, almost entirely dependent on the export of raw or relatively unprocessed resources is that it is vulnerable to a range of predictable setbacks sooner or later. A non-renewable resource, or a 'renewable' one that is exploited destructively, will eventually give out, as did the white pine of the Ottawa Valley and as the conventional oil reserves of Alberta are doing today. Demand for the staple may be undermined by changing technology, changing markets, or the emergence of competitive suppliers, the latter two developments being particularly linked to shifts in the geographical configuration of global production. The threat that newsprint recycling poses to remote Canadian paper mills, the shrunken market for Quebec asbestos that has followed greater concern about the health hazards associated with its use, and the problems that 'grain subsidy wars' between the European Union and the United States have created for prairie farmers since the 1980s all demonstrate the limited control that staples producers have over their markets and the limited options that face them when demand or prices decline.

The principal avenues for diversification within a staples economy have been identified as the development of *backward*, *forward*, and *final demand* linkages. These imply, respectively, exploiting the expertise and market power that accumulate within the staples sector to manufacture the capital goods that it requires; initiating resource-based manufacturing industries; and, at the same time, developing a widening range of construction, service, and consumer goods industries to service the general population. There is plenty of evidence of such activity in the economy of Canada from the mid-nineteenth century onward. The relatively prosperous agriculture of southern Ontario provided an environment in which food processing, farm equipment production, and a broadening array of engineering capabilities became established. Railway building to promote the grain trade supported the emergence of indigenous locomotive and rolling stock works. The forest-based industries generated a market for implements and subsequently for specialized machinery. The building of the country's expanding urban fabric, and equally the scattered settlement that characterized the opening of the Prairies, provided markets for a whole range of firms and products. Clothing, furniture, and equipment of all sorts of specifications were added to the domestic supply capabilities of the Canadian economy (Gentilcore, 1993).

All peripheral economies have faced the challenge of diversifying their output in the face of competition from established producers in core regions. In Canada's case, industrialization took place in the very strong shadow of a nearby American core that was established earlier and was more technologically sophisticated. It was also larger in size and generated larger pools of venture capital, and its citizens frequently showed more entrepreneurial initiative than did their Canadian contemporaries. Thus, both before and after 1879, when tariff protection gave increased security to domestic firms, US interests figured prominently in Canadian industrial development. US firms found little difficulty in creating and keeping markets north of the border, and US technology was imported when no Canadian equivalent was available. Philemon Wright, founder of the lumber industry in Ottawa–Hull, and Francis Clergue, creator of the multi-sectoral manufacturing complex in the wilderness of Sault Ste Marie, were but two of the Americans who made a lasting contribution to the industrial geography of Canada. One clear result of the tariff was the opening in Canada by US manufacturing firms of some of the world's first branch plants. This locational strategy allowed them unhindered access to growing Canadian markets. Foreign ownership, mainly by parent companies in the United States, but also in Britain, became pervasive within the Canadian economy, more so than in any other nation at a comparable level of development.

By the early 1960s, the weaknesses of Canada's predominantly 'branch-plant economy' were becoming increasingly evident. This was the heyday of Fordist production systems. Rising incomes and levels of material consumption were based on the manufacture of standardized, mass-produced goods assembled in large, mechanized factories with a unionized and generally well-paid labour force. Economies of scale and rising labour productivity kept the real price of goods down and made them increasingly affordable. However, within Canada's relatively small and tariff-protected market, many of the potential benefits of Fordist production were lost. Foreign firms tended to operate 'miniature replica' factories that produced small quantities (at high unit cost) of each of the wide range of goods that could be produced more efficiently (usually in separate plants) within their larger home markets. This constraint on Canadian economic growth was particularly damaging in the auto industry. Fortunately, the sector's tightly oligopolistic structure (the 'Big Four' of General Motors, Ford, Chrysler, and American Motors) and these firms' dominance of the North American market created conditions in the mid-1960s in which the Canadian and US governments, together with the Big Four, were able to agree on a cross-border rationalization of production. This allowed Canadian assembly plants, like US plants, to specialize in particular models of car, obtaining all the benefits of economies of scale, and it allowed new automobiles to cross the border in either direction duty free. The 1965 Auto Pact thus represented a retreat from economic nationalism, although with the Big Four providing safeguards that guaranteed a minimum level of production in Canada, it represented a move to 'managed trade' rather than to 'free trade'.

The diseconomies of scale are not the only adverse consequences of a branch-plant economy. Transnational firms normally retain the higher-level corporate functions, including research and development, in their home country, so that the activities and occupations their operations support elsewhere are truncated (Britton and Gilmour, 1978). This limitation on most Canadian subsidiaries has become increasingly detrimental, as ongoing structural change in the global economy has increased the significance of high-level *producer services* and their separation, even within the same firm, from the site of manufacturing. These non-routine, knowledge-intensive functions, involving such roles as design, consulting, market research, strategic planning, etc., are critical to maximizing the value-added of products and to maintaining corporate flexibility in responding to an increasingly dynamic global market. Firms whose Canadian operations are truncated create fewer demands for producer services in Canada than do domestically owned firms (Britton, 1976). Moreover, the limited R&D (both in scope and amount) conducted in Canada by all but a few foreign firms accentuates the country's underperformance in this area compared to other industrialized nations, as evidenced in Canada's substantial trade deficit in high-technology goods and services.

Large Canadian-owned manufacturing firms have thus tended to be confined to the resource-processing industries or to have emerged in a small number of industrial sectors that have grown in response to specific opportunities of the Canadian environment. Alcan (now merged with a European partner), Inco, Domtar, and McCain Foods are representative of the first group; Nortel (in telecommunications) and Bombardier (in transportation equipment, initially the snowmobile) best exemplify the second group, which has grown with additions such as JDS Uniphase (a Canadian/American fibre optic telecommunications transnational) and Magna (auto parts). In contrast, firms in most of the other engineering subsectors, including both capital and consumer goods, are substantially foreign-owned. Even the potential backward linkages from mineral and forest resource exploitation have been less developed in Canada than in Scandinavia, for instance, whose leading mining and forest industry equipment manufacturers show what might have been possible.

Given the intensity of R&D in today's dynamic manufacturing sectors, especially the high-technology fields such as microelectronics, biotechnology, and composite materials, and equally the competitive pressures to apply advanced technology across the entire range of traditional sectors, from sawmilling to garment production, the way in which Canada's manufacturing sector has evolved presents particular problems of adjustment to globalization, as Chapter 4 reveals. On the other hand, the greater contemporary advantage of smaller-scale, flexible producers of 'niche' products provides market opportunities in which Canadian manufacturers and producer service firms need not be disadvantaged vis-à-vis established transnationals with large domestic sales.

## THE PATTERN OF CANADA'S INTERNATIONAL ECONOMIC LINKAGES

Despite being overshadowed in the global arena by the neighbouring US economy, which is almost 14 times larger in terms of gross national product (GNP), Canada ranks ninth in the world (at US$581 billion in 1998), just ahead of Spain (World Bank, 2000). That Canada's economic significance is often underestimated stems from more than simply its being the junior partner in the North American core, however. For all its indisputable credentials as an industrialized country, it remains, like Australia, more dependent on natural resource products and relatively weaker in advanced manufacturing compared to nations with a comparable standard of living. To some extent, these structural characteristics merely reflect Canada's low population/resource ratio: only 30 million people occupy the territory of the second-largest country on earth. But these features also signal some of the constraints on diversifying the national economy beyond its resource-dependence, which have been imposed both by domestic policy choices and by pressures arising from Canada's position within the global economic system.

Canada's strong linkages to the American economy, seen in the volumes of bilateral trade, patterns of corporate ownership, and the importance of the monetary exchange rate to Canadian firms, mean that Canadians are bound to take a keen interest in what happens south of the border. Since 1988, the two economies have become even more closely tied by free trade agreements—first between themselves, and since 1994 including Mexico also, within NAFTA. But Canada remains a distinctive and significant component of the world economy in its own right. Its domestic economic geography reflects very clearly a long history of openness to the currents of international trade, as well as of government attempts to channel or resist them. These currents have shifted significantly since the 1970s, as developments in Europe and the Asia-Pacific region in particular have created new challenges to the established economic order in North America, and as transnational firms (including those based in Canada) have become increasingly adept at integrating global systems of production. In the process, Canada has become even more dependent on the performance of the US economy.

By 1999, the United States provided 67 per cent of Canada's merchandise imports and purchased fully 87 per cent of Canadian merchandise exports (Table 1.1). In the decade from 1989, which also marked the first decade of the Canada–United States Free Trade Agreement, Canada's dependence on trade with its southern neighbour increased. The steady growth of the US economy during this period certainly worked to Canada's advantage, but the narrow concentration of Canadian exports on the US market will prove a handicap whenever its expansion slows relative to that of other parts of the global economy. The extension of the free trade area in 1993 to include Mexico shows up in the very rapid growth of Canadian imports from that country, but it has not been as marked in the rate of increase of Canadian exports. With respect to trade flows beyond North America, the Asia-Pacific region has become Canada's

**Table 1.2   Canadian Merchandise Trade, by Commodity Group, 1999**

| Commodity Group | Imports $ million | Exports $ million |
|---|---|---|
| Agricultural & fish products | 17,639 | 25,614+ |
| Energy products | 10,646 | 30,310+ |
| *Crude petroleum* | *7,098* | *11,014+* |
| Forestry products | 2,741 | 38,903+ |
| Industrial goods & materials | 62,142 | 56,940 |
| Machinery and equipment | 108,230 | 84,959 |
| *Industrial & agricultural* | *27,775* | *16,665* |
| *Aircraft & other transport* | *13,291* | *17,337+* |
| *Office machinery* | *16,895* | *8,701* |
| *Other machinery* | *50,270* | *42,256* |
| Automotive products | 75,903 | 96,142+ |
| *Passenger autos* | *19,584* | *51,488+* |
| *Motor vehicle parts* | *45,673* | *25,168* |
| Other consumer goods | 36,962 | 13,591 |
| Special & unallocated | 12,399 | 14,141 |
| Total | 326,662 | 360,600 |

+ = Canadian trade surplus.
NOTE: Italicized data are included within the relevant group heading/total.
SOURCE: Statistics Canada, *Canadian International Merchandise Trade*, Dec. 1999, Cat. no. 65–001.

second most important partner, having displaced during the 1980s the historic role of Western Europe. Western Europe's standing as a source of imports would have slipped further had Norwegian North Sea oil not largely displaced Canadian purchases from the Middle East. The absolute decline in Canadian exports to the rest of Europe mainly reflects the economic difficulties of Russia and other states of the former Soviet Union.

The composition of Canada's merchandise (or *visible*) trade reveals the importance of three major components—natural resources, automobiles and auto parts, and machinery and equipment. The first four major commodity groups listed in Table 1.2 are essentially resource-based commodities, in which Canada has long enjoyed a comparative advantage. Note that the first three groups all generate a trade surplus, and that the forest sector stands out as the greatest contributor to Canada's balance of payments. The fourth category, 'Industrial goods and materials', includes minerals and metals, together with chemicals, plastics, and various basic fabricated products. The second component is the two-way trade associated primarily with the Canada–US Auto Pact. Note that Canada has run a substantial trade surplus on automobiles, which is partially offset by imports from the US of vehicle parts (see Chapter 7). The third component is the large volume of trade, both imports and exports, consisting of a very wide range of machinery and equipment. Canada has run a trade surplus on aircraft and parts in recent years (see Chapter 7), but has a proportionately large deficit on trade in computers and other office machinery.

Canada's overall involvement in the global economy extends far beyond its visible trade, which normally produces a surplus. International trade in services has grown rapidly and it consistently results in a deficit (Statistics Canada, 1998). Canada's trade in commercial services is dominated by cross-border flows with the United States, which in 1998 took 71 per cent of Canadian payments and provided 63 per cent of Canadian receipts. Those commercial service sectors in which Canada has developed a surplus include architectural and engineering services, research and development, and computer services. These provide evidence of the growing role of knowledge-based exports in Canada's international trade. The commercial service transactions in which Canada runs the largest deficits are for royalties and licence fees, management services, and tooling services. The first two categories point primarily to the large element of foreign ownership in Canada's economy, as they represent primarily payments to parent companies. The third points to the weak development of a domestic capital goods industry and of the skills that it nurtures (see Chapter 5). Another deficit sector is travel and tourism. Canadians' foreign spending regularly and substantially exceeds domestic tourist receipts from visitors, with the imbalance in Canada–US tourist traffic accounting for over 60 per cent of the deficit (see Chapter 6).

Foreign direct investment (FDI), especially from the United States, has long played a major role in the evolution of the Canadian economy (Burgess, 2000). In 1999, US firms owned 72 per cent of the FDI assets in Canada, with Western European firms owning another 19 per cent and Japanese firms 5 per cent. Finance was the largest single sector of foreign ownership, but otherwise investments were widely spread across the economy (Figures 1.1 and 1.2). In recent years, FDI by Canadian-owned firms has been increasing at a considerably faster rate than foreign investment in Canada. In 1970, the FDI assets of Canadians amounted to only 23 per cent of the value of FDI in Canada, but by 1999 the ratio had risen to 107 per cent. The geographical distribution of Canadian direct investment differs from that of the source countries of FDI in Canada in that a smaller percentage of Canadian assets are held in the United States and a considerably larger percentage is held in less-developed countries, especially in Latin America and the Caribbean.

## CONCLUSION

The openness of the Canadian economy to international trade has traditionally reflected its position as a staples-based economy whose global location has given it easy access to large and dynamic core markets. Canada remains a major exporter of natural resources, but this is no longer its defining characteristic in the global economy. The growing diversity and sophistication of its manufactured products and of its commercial service exports suggest that many of the handicaps associated with its previous dependence on staples and branch-plant production are being overcome.

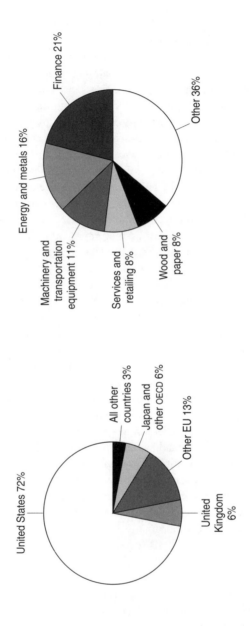

**Figure 1.1    Foreign Direct Investment in Canada, 1999**

*SOURCE:* Statistics Canada, Cat. no. 67–202, Chart 6.

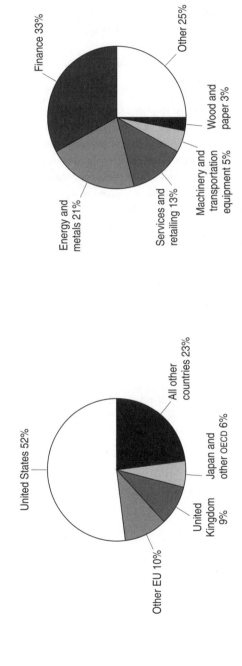

**Figure 1.2   Canadian Direct Investment Abroad, 1999**

SOURCE: Statistics Canada, Cat. no. 67–202, Chart 8.

On the other hand, the country's very high, and still rising, dependence on the United States as its principal trading partner is problematic. Certainly, Canada's proximity to the largest and most innovative national economy in the modern world works to its advantage in many respects, giving its firms access to capital, advanced technology, and demanding customers. The flip side, however, is that the United States has enormous power to pursue its national economic interests. The rhetoric of US government and corporate interests that extols the universal benefits of globalization and free trade frequently masks narrower agendas promoted at the expense of weaker parties, including Canadian government and corporate interests. Attempts to deepen Canada's economic linkages with other parts of the world to offset the pull of US markets have shown little success in the face of the trading opportunities so close to home. Moreover, the domestic political and cultural climate in Canada is not the same as that in the United States, and Canada's economic history and public policy priorities reflect values and circumstances that differ in some important respects from those south of the border. In the context of the increasing economic integration of the North American economy through NAFTA, it is important to identify the distinctiveness of Canada's political economy and its links to the country's economic geography. This is the focus of the next chapter.

## FURTHER READING

Britton, J.N.H., ed. 1996. *Canada and the Global Economy: The Geography of Structural and Technological Change*. Montreal and Kingston: McGill-Queen's University Press.

Burgess, B. 2000. 'Foreign direct investment: facts and perceptions about Canada', *Canadian Geographer* 44: 98–113.

Helliwell, J.F. 1999. 'Canada's national economy: there's more to it than you thought', in H. Lazar and T. McIntosh, eds, *How Canadians Connect*. Montreal and Kingston: McGill-Queen's University Press, 87–100.

Merrett, C.D. 1996. *Free Trade: Neither Free Nor About Trade*. Montreal: Black Rose.

Norcliffe, G. 2001. 'Canada in a global economy', *Canadian Geographer* 45: 14–30.

# The Role of Culture and Political Economy

## HISTORICAL INTRODUCTION

The 'Canada' that became a self-governing part of the British Empire in 1867 was neither a European-style nation-state nor a US-style republic. It was a political creation by the British Crown designed to unite the two 'founding peoples' of British and French origin who had settled the Maritime provinces, the St Lawrence Valley, and southern Ontario. The presence of Aboriginal peoples was recognized, but they were not deemed worthy of inclusion in the institutions of government. The Confederation was explicitly a *British* North America, although one in which it was hoped that the interests of the French minority were sufficiently protected so as to remove causes of friction between them and citizens of British origin. However, the creation of Canada was also to provide a framework for consolidating a British Dominion 'from sea to sea' (Vancouver Island already being the nucleus of *British* Columbia), secure from the northwestward expansion of the United States. The federal political structure provided for a strong central government, with constitutional authority to regulate the national economy in fulfilment of this vision. The National Policy of 1879 formulated the principal mechanisms designed to achieve it: a transcontinental railway, a policy of land settlement fed by European immigration, and a national tariff to protect infant Canadian manufacturing industries from the competition of established firms in Britain and the United States.

The Canada that took shape between the 1880s and the 1920s was geographically extensive and culturally and environmentally diverse. Settlement spread across the Prairies and into the southern perimeter of the Canadian Shield. In both regions, temperate agriculture encountered unfamiliar and limiting environments. Immigration to the West brought large numbers of ethnic groups from Eastern and Central Europe, sharing neither the language nor, often, the religious traditions and political ideologies of the 'founding peoples'. Across much of the country, the transcontinental railways linked small pockets of communities, which remained relatively remote from each other and from the more densely settled heartland of southern Ontario and Quebec. By the early twentieth century, the growing economy of Ontario, particularly its extensive resource-based sectors (hydro power, forest products, and mining), provided the basis for policies of 'province-building' by provincial élites, whose economic interests did not always align with those in power in Ottawa (Nelles, 1974). In contrast, in Quebec, the leaders of the francophone majority left economic development to the Montreal-based anglophone élites and concentrated their efforts on preserving the cultural identity of their society through control of the institutions of the Roman Catholic Church, the legal system, and the provincial state.

As a hinterland economy with a dendritic transportation and trading system funnelling towards Winnipeg and the St Lawrence (Figure 14.1; Burghardt, 1971), the Prairies experienced the powerlessness of remote staples producers dependent on markets and infrastructures controlled in central Canada, Chicago, or Europe. The hinterland status of the Maritime provinces was also accentuated during the early twentieth century, as the geographically polarizing effects of a National Policy that benefited central Canadian manufacturers became more pronounced. Maritime firms found it difficult to adjust to changing markets and the impact of new technologies. When Depression and drought hit Canada after 1929, neither Ottawa nor the provincial governments were ideologically or materially equipped to intervene in the economy to much good effect.

The 'modern' Canada that experienced dramatic economic growth during World War II, and for nearly 30 years following, was shaped by some major cultural and political transformations. Compared to the United States, Canada has, for much of its history, been a country in which the active intervention of the state in economic affairs (at first the federal government alone, but by the 1970s the provincial governments also) has been accepted or even welcomed, rather than treated with suspicion and minimized (Hardin, 1974). (The significant shift in this political sentiment that has taken place in recent years is examined below.) By the 1970s, Canadian governments were involved to an unprecedented degree in the functioning and orientation of the economy. This role had developed cumulatively from the experience of meeting the state's wartime requirements for increased industrial output, followed in the 1950s and 1960s by the implementation of Keynesian policies of macroeconomic management, the gradual but comprehensive introduction of welfare state social services, and the adoption of a culture of social and urban planning. By many yardsticks, the country had come to resemble a Western European social democracy more than it did the US, the land of 'free enterprise' and ideological home of global capitalism.

Within this broad social and political transition there were some particularly significant developments. First, provincial governments became much more prominent than before in shaping the daily lives of Canadians, through their growing expenditures on health, education, and social and physical infrastructures. As a result, popular loyalties to, and political claims upon, the state have for many Canadians become more immediately defined in provincial rather than in national (federal) terms. Moreover, during this period, the size and competence of provincial bureaucracies increased relative to that of the federal public service, so that provinces became better equipped to pursue policies independently of, and even in opposition to, Ottawa. (Saskatchewan's nationalization of foreign-owned potash mines in 1976, despite Ottawa's disapproval, was a notable example.) Second, the emergence of the 'provincial state' took a distinctive form in Quebec, where the Quiet Revolution of the 1960s saw the dramatic reorientation of francophone society towards a modern, secular, and politically self-conscious project of becoming '*maîtres chez nous*', not least in the sphere of business and the economy. The active role of institutions of the Quebec state in 'nation-building' has had economic and technological thrusts (epitomized by the corporate mission of Hydro-Québec) as well as cultural and linguistic ones. Finally, the position of Aboriginal peoples within Canada has shifted profoundly since the 1950s, when the federal government finally implemented more actively its responsibilities, such as for health care and education. With fuller recognition of the rights of Aboriginal peoples to participate actively in the political and social evolution of Canada have come major changes in their rights and their capacity to be involved in shaping the economy, especially in the North (see Chapter 15).

## THE POLITICAL ECONOMY OF REGIONALISM: BACKGROUND

The interaction of physical geography and settlement history has made Canada one of the most highly regionalized countries in the developed world. This has both cultural and economic dimensions, and the two come together in the practical politics of making the federal system work. Harris (1987) has likened Canada to an 'archipelago'— a string of regional societies that differ significantly in ethnicity, political culture, and economic orientation. As a consequence, federal policies rarely attract the same level of support in different regions, and in the economic sphere they rarely impact the various parts of the country uniformly. The federal political arrangements adopted in 1867 reflected the experience of a society more geographically compact and culturally homogeneous (despite the French/English divide) than exists today. It was expected that 'national' political parties would find nationwide support, leading to a regionally representative federal cabinet that would ensure that the interests of each part of the country had a voice. But by the last decades of the twentieth century it became clear that such an assumption is no longer tenable. Between 1972 and 1984, support for 'national' parties became so geographically polarized that some regions (notably the West) were largely excluded from the circles of power in Ottawa. Provincial governments, seen as 'closer to home' and more consistent in protecting regional interests than the distant and frequently 'unsympathetic' Ottawa, grew in power and legitimacy vis-à-vis the federal government. Then, following the general election of 1993, new political parties strongly identified with particular regional interests (western-based Reform [now Canadian Alliance] and the Bloc Québécois) began to reshape the federal electoral map. Moreover, with the election of an Ontario government in the mid-1990s that has been ideologically disposed to challenge the long-standing assumption that the country's richest province should bankroll redistributive policies that favour poorer regions, the economic balkanization of Canada has increased, at least rhetorically.

Because external influences and domestic policies invariably have different economic implications for the various regions of Canada, the federal government is necessarily involved in an elaborate set of balancing acts. But the geographical location of Ottawa, the constitutional protection of francophone interests, and the electoral arithmetic that results in the national dominance of the Ontario and Quebec heartland have all contributed to the widespread perception in hinterland regions, particularly in the West, that the federal system essentially favours central Canada.

Western alienation has been a feature of Canadian politics since the late nineteenth century. Initially it expressed frustration with the dominant, exploitative role of central Canadian businesses, notably the chartered banks and the Canadian Pacific Railway. It was fed in the 1970s and 1980s by federal energy policies that were viewed as depriving the West (Alberta in particular) of the revenues and economic development prospects to which its fossil fuel resources entitled it (see Chapter 10), and by agricultural and trade policies that never did enough to satisfy the concerns of prairie farmers. Federal pro-heartland, especially pro-Quebec, bias was perceived in other policy areas, including airline regulation (favouring Montreal-based Air Canada over western carriers) and the awarding of defence contracts (one notorious case favouring a Montreal firm over a Winnipeg aerospace firm that made a better and lower contract bid). Alberta has tended to be more active and creative in challenging federal policy than has BC, partly because its oil and gas industries have been more directly affected by federal regulation than has the west coast forest sector. In recent years, the province's growing wealth has increased its capacity for independent action.

Maritime alienation began soon after Confederation, with complaints about the Upper Canada (Ontario) bias of national policies and institutions. But since the 1950s, residents of Canada's poorest provinces (with Newfoundland contributing its economic hardship to Atlantic Canada) have been more equivocal. While remaining critical of central Canada's dominance, they have sought to offset their region's disadvantages primarily by attracting federal largesse in a variety of forms, including industrial subsidies, preferential employment insurance regulations, and compensation for lost livelihoods in the Atlantic fishery (see Chapter 12).

Since the Quiet Revolution, governments of Quebec have added to the national discourse of alienation, primarily by accusing federal policy-makers of favouring Ontario. However, such examples as the disproportionate employment benefit that Ontario has gained from the Auto Pact and the increasing displacement of Montreal by Toronto as Canada's financial centre have owed at least as much to forces beyond Ottawa's control as to forces within it. Nevertheless, by engaging in policies that have deliberately sought to stimulate the economies of less prosperous regions, including that of Quebec, federal governments have regularly attracted criticism from one region or another over their role in attempting to shape Canada's economic geography.

## THE ERA OF 'REGIONAL POLICY' AND ITS IMPACT

Almost every government policy has regionally differentiated effects, but this fact is rarely acknowledged. 'Regional policies' are those with an explicit geographical dimension, intended to improve the economic prospects of selected parts of the country. It was only in the context of postwar Keynesianism that regional policy, as such, became a widely used tool of government, and in Canada such policies were first introduced in the early 1960s. But the geographical extent and regional diversity of the Canadian economy had, as noted above, prompted the adoption of de facto regional policies from a much earlier date. The Crow's Nest Pass Agreement, which between 1897 and 1995 gave prairie farmers reduced rail freight rates for shipping export grain, can be interpreted as Canada's first major regional policy, despite the fact that, over time, it hindered diversification of the Prairie provinces' regional economy away from the grain staple. The Maritime Freight Rate subsidy (1927) was introduced to make it easier for Maritime industries to compete in central Canadian markets. These transport provisions, attempting to offset the consequences of the distance between producers and their markets, were followed in 1935 by legislation that attempted to compensate for regional environmental conditions. The Prairie Farm Rehabilitation Act (PFRA) was a response to the 'dust bowl' conditions of the early 1930s, as well as the wheat farm cash crisis of the Depression years. The Maritime Marshland Rehabilitation Act (1948) sought to improve land-use practices and farm incomes in the East.

By the late 1950s, the provincial governments faced a growing need to finance expansion of everything from roads to education and health services. But with regional economic inequalities persisting (accentuated by the addition of impoverished Newfoundland to eastern Canada), the federal government was prompted to inaugurate a system of 'equalization payments'. This was designed to bring the government revenue of poorer provinces up to a level that would allow 'an acceptable level of public service' to be offered throughout the country. Since the early 1960s, Ontario, Alberta, and British Columbia, the richest provinces, have been the only ones not eligible to receive these federal transfers (Tables 2.1 and 2.2). The per capita assistance has obviously been greatest to the poorest provinces (over $1,100 throughout Atlantic Canada in 1995, compared to $533 in Quebec), but because of its population size Quebec has received 49 per cent of the cumulative payments over the 1957-95 period. These payments, together with other federal fiscal transfers to provinces and federal payments to individuals (pensions, employment insurance, family and senior citizen benefits, etc.), have gone a long way towards reducing disparities in household income and levels of public service provision across the country.

The most visible elements of regional policy in the 1960s and 1970s sought to assist poorer areas in achieving a higher rate of economic growth. An early set of programs, associated particularly with the Agricultural Rehabilitation and Development Act (ARDA, 1961) and the more spatially focused Fund for Rural Economic Development (FRED, 1966), addressed problems of farm poverty and stagnant rural economies. But by focusing on mitigating limitations of the land resource base for agriculture rather than addressing the social and economic challenges of modernizing the agri-food production system, these measures had little long-term impact (see Chapter 8). A second policy thrust explicitly targeted the Atlantic provinces as the region most in need of development assistance. The Atlantic Development Board was established in 1962, but beyond funding overdue improvements to the region's physical infrastructure (roads, electricity supply, water and sewage systems), it suffered from a lack of strategic planning. The Cape Breton Development Corporation (DEVCO) was created in 1967 specifically to manage the phasing out of the totally uneconomic coal industry of the Sydney/Glace Bay region, while finding alternative industrial employment for its 3,500 workers. It achieved neither objective (see Chapter 12).

**Table 2.1   Equalization Payments to Six Provinces, 1957–1995**

| Province | Total Payments, Current Dollars ($ million) | Per Capita Payment (1995) | Percentage of National Total |
|---|---|---|---|
| Nfld | $ 14,224.6 | $ 1,647 | 11.10 |
| PEI | 3,071.9 | 1,516 | 2.40 |
| NS | 15,240.9 | 1,162 | 11.90 |
| NB | 13,846.9 | 1,285 | 10.81 |
| Man. | 13,055.1 | 934 | 10.19 |
| Sask. | 5,884.4 | 616 | 4.59 |

SOURCE: *Globe and Mail*, 13 July 1995, A15.

**Table 2.2   Equalization Payments to Quebec, 1957–1995, Selected Years**

| Year | Annual Payments, Current Dollars ($ million) | Per Capita Payment | Percentage of National Total |
|---|---|---|---|
| 1957 | $ 46.3 | $ 9.75 | 33 |
| 1961 | 72.7 | 13.82 | 35 |
| 1971 | 453.3 | 75.20 | 48 |
| 1981 | 2,489.9 | 349.31 | 57 |
| 1991 | 3,464.1 | 505.90 | 45 |
| 1995 | 3,845.3 | 532.90 | 44 |
| Total, 1957–95 | $ 62.7 billion | | 48.9 |

SOURCE: *Globe and Mail*, 13 July 1995, A15.

The third element of regional policy consisted of offering financial incentives to manufacturers to locate in less prosperous regions or those with high levels of unemployment. The Area Development Agency (ADA, 1963) began this program, but it expanded considerably following the creation of the Department of Regional Economic Expansion (DREE) in 1969 to co-ordinate the whole range of federal regional development initiatives. Canada's industrial incentive program faced problems common to similar programs elsewhere. Questions of how extensive the 'designated regions' should be; of whether to devote resources to the least prosperous localities or to those with more obvious growth potential; of whether to favour large, foreign- (or at least non-locally) owned, and relatively more capital-intensive plants or to support small and medium-sized, often locally based, firms; indeed, of whether exclusive targeting of manufacturing employment was sensible in light of more promising alternative sources of potential employment in many peripheral regions (such as tourist services): these important considerations were never consistently or satisfactorily addressed. By the early 1970s, the designated regions covered most of the country

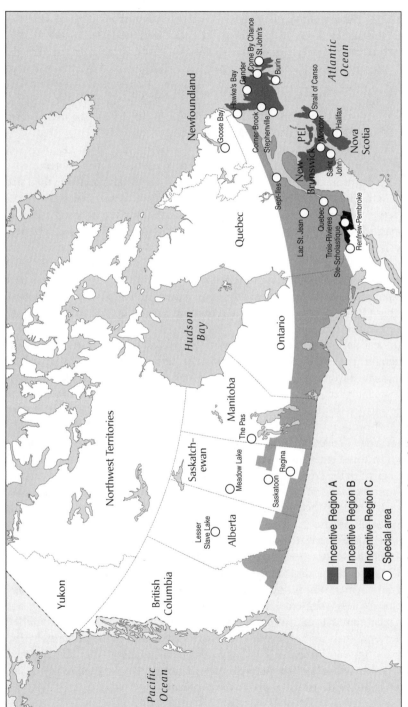

**Figure 2.1  DREE Designated Regions and Special Areas, 1973**

*SOURCE:* Department of Regional Economic Expansion.

south of 60° N and east of the Alberta border, except for southern Ontario (Figure 2.1). Although the highest levels of investment incentive were restricted to the Atlantic provinces and the Montreal region was eligible for the least generous support, the regional development impact of the program was clearly diluted by its widespread availability. It was argued that much of the funding went into projects that would have proceeded anyway, and some spectacular failures of high-profile but ill-considered ventures (such as the Bricklin auto plant in New Brunswick) further undermined confidence in the effectiveness of the program.

Following a policy review in 1973, an increasing proportion of DREE funds was channelled into General Development Agreements (GDAs), which represented a much closer co-ordination of federal and provincial development efforts than had prevailed in the past. GDAs permitted support for a wider range of projects than those eligible under existing programs, although this flexibility often entailed a lack of spatial specificity in the impacts. By the early 1980s, however, the federal government had clearly become dissatisfied with the political and economic payback of its regional policies. DREE was disbanded and residual regional commitments were folded into the sectoral mandates of the Department of Industry. New agencies were created to maintain a federal profile in the development of Atlantic Canada, the West, and northern Ontario, but their status and funding were reduced as part of Ottawa's downsizing in the mid-1990s.

The 30-year period of the federal government's formal commitment to regional policy remains extremely difficult to evaluate in terms of its overall effectiveness (Cannon, 1989; Savoie, 1992). Not only is it impossible to factor out the regionally differentiated impacts of such powerful forces as fluctuations in the Canadian dollar exchange rate or the Bank of Canada's interest rate, but the scale of designated regional expenditures was extremely modest when measured against the total volume of federal government spending, all of which contributes to regional differentiation. In some cases this is clear to see, as in the compensation paid to grain farmers caught in the crossfire of international 'subsidy wars' in the 1980s or to fishing communities suffering from the disappearance of the Atlantic cod in the 1990s. But often the localized patterns of economic impacts of government decisions are not immediately apparent. For instance, Canada's defence expenditures are small in comparison to those of its North Atlantic Treaty Organization (NATO) partners, but their geographical pattern has been very significant. Military considerations have resulted in bases being disproportionately concentrated in hinterland regions, so that the employment impact of a major round of closures in the early 1990s was a severe blow to less prosperous areas (Figure 2.2). The award of production and maintenance contracts has also traditionally been shaped by regional political considerations, such as how naval orders are distributed between yards in BC, Quebec, and the Maritimes. In sum, all government spending—not just 'regional' programs—has spatially differentiated outcomes; of course, so, too, do the investment and spending decisions of private-sector firms.

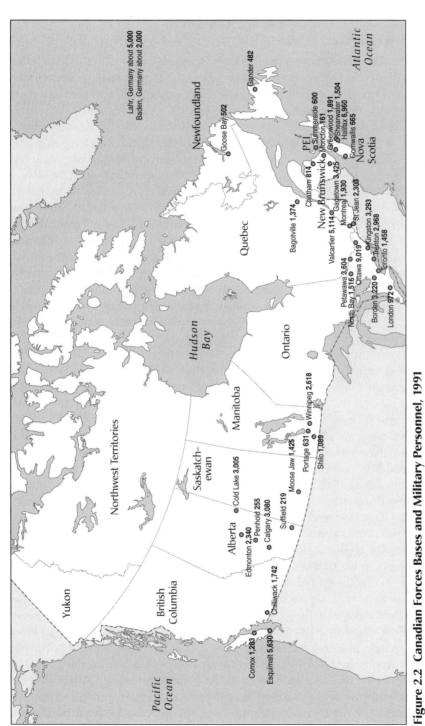

**Figure 2.2  Canadian Forces Bases and Military Personnel, 1991**

*SOURCE:* Department of National Defence, in *Globe and Mail*, 20 July 1991, A2.

## REGIONAL POLITICAL ECONOMY AT THE START OF
## THE TWENTY-FIRST CENTURY

The processes of globalization have created increasingly competitive conditions for Canadian firms and have forced Canadian governments at all levels to reassess their capabilities. Provincial economies are considerably smaller, and most are much more narrowly based, than the national economy. In particular, Canada's history as a supplier of resource staples has left most provinces, even today, vulnerable to the cyclical insta-bility of global commodity markets. The federal government, therefore, set out to manage Canada in the postwar era much like a giant mutual insurance company, trans-ferring revenues from parts of the country that were prospering to soften the blow in those parts that were experiencing hard times (Savoie, 1992). During the 1970s and 1980s, however, it chose to run continuous deficits, rather than to balance its books over the course of macroeconomic cycles, as John Maynard Keynes had recommended. By the early 1990s, a time of deep recession, most provincial governments, including Ontario's, had similarly opted for deficit-financing. The growing burden of debt serv-ice payments and the steady weakening of the Canadian dollar that resulted eventually prompted a change in the prevailing political culture. By the end of the 1990s, all senior levels of government in Canada had adopted policies to eliminate their deficits, notably by reducing their expenditures. (Downloading responsibilities to municipal govern-ments, without granting them the financial resources to fulfil these responsibilities, has been one dysfunctional but politically effective strategy: see Chapter 5.) Public-sector downsizing and the privatization of many services previously provided by governments are evidence of a significant change in the dominant political ideology in Canada. But within this overall move towards a neo-conservative outlook that sees the state more as an economic 'problem' than a 'solution', there have been clear regional differences.

The federal government has almost completely dismantled the formal regional policy programs of the 1970s and thereby put a greater onus on governments and communities in poorer regions to restructure their own economies and promote indigenous growth. This has undoubtedly been more in tune with popular sentiment in the West than in the East. Despite their provincial economies' resource-dependence, westerners have long tended to regard Ottawa more as an obstacle to regional pros-perity (because it is seen as reflecting the economic interests of central Canada) than as a source of economic security. Many westerners share cultural traits with their counterparts on the US Plains, more confident in individual initiative or communal self-help than in the operations of 'big government', and so more ready than many Canadians to embrace the uncertainties as well as the freedom of market forces. The Reform Party emerged in the 1990s to represent this growing constituency. The popu-lation of the Atlantic provinces, in contrast, has generally been much more eager to see federal agencies and programs assume a lead role in improving regional prosperity, and only recently have the problems of a culture of dependency become widely recog-nized within the region (see Chapter 12). The political culture of Quebec since the Quiet Revolution has been supportive of the provincial state playing a strong role in economic development, in this reflecting the philosophy and experience of governments in France. Especially with Parti Québécois governments in power, Ottawa's policies have frequently been portrayed as thwarting a potentially sovereign Quebec's national ambitions.

Ontario governments, in contrast, throughout the postwar period until the recession of the early 1990s, invariably found their interests compatible with federal policy priorities. With the largest concentration of manufacturing—especially high-technology industry—in the country, Ontario has benefited from federal policies aimed at strengthening national technological capacity and the market for Canadian manufactured exports. The Auto Pact, benefiting the predominantly Ontario-based auto industry, was particularly significant in maintaining the prosperity of the province. But following the election in 1995 of a provincial Conservative government committed to a neo-conservative 'revolution' and an agenda of tax cuts, Ontario's role as the motor of the Canadian economy, and therefore the prime source of federal revenues that are disproportionately channelled to other parts of the country, has been cast in a more confrontational perspective. This has contributed significantly to the stresses the political economy of the Canadian federation currently faces.

One of the features of the current era of globalization is the emergence of prosperous subnational regions as politically self-conscious entities that can position themselves within the global arena relatively independently of their national governments. This has been true especially in Europe, where the overarching institutions of the European Union provide a congenial environment for greater regional autonomy. The Parti Québécois has argued that an independent Quebec could enjoy a similar position within the North American free trade area (although this is a very different macro-environment than the EU). Recently, however, the Ontario government seems to have been drawing most strongly on these ideas.

Courchene and Telmer (1998) explore in detail the circumstances that support the repositioning of Ontario as a 'North American regional state', rather than as the 'Canadian heartland'. The geographical reorientation of the Canadian economy promoted by continental free trade has had its strongest expression in Ontario. During the 1980s, and even more so during the 1990s, Ontario's trade with the United States has steadily increased relative to its trade with the rest of Canada (Figures 2.3-2.6). Courchene and Telmer argue that, consequently, the Ontario government is acting to position itself as a competitive jurisdiction within 'middle America' rather than within Canada. And part of this strategy is to adopt the 'lower taxation, business friendly' policies that certainly are aligned with the political philosophy of the Conservatives under Premier Harris. But ideology aside, as Courchene and Telmer point out, in the past Ontario's support for hinterland provinces in Canada tended to benefit the Ontario economy, as most of the goods and services they purchased came from heartland industries. In the context of NAFTA, there is a greater probability that spending in hinterland provinces will benefit suppliers outside of Canada. Ontario's postwar role within the Canadian economy and federal system is clearly changing, therefore, and this requires careful political handling of the threat to federal policies of East-West equalization that have held the country together for the past half-century.

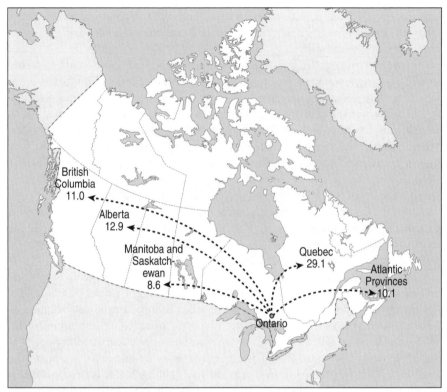

**Figure 2.3  Interprovincial Trade Flows, Ontario as Origin, 1998** *(billions of dollars)*

*SOURCE:* Transport Canada (2000: 66)

There are, of course, other unresolved issues that impact on federal priorities and Canada's economic performance. Although the probability of Quebec's separation from Canada appears to be extremely low, the provincial government consistently challenges a federal structure that it argues does not adequately recognize the province's distinctive status. Federal attempts to devise constitutional solutions that are acceptable both to Quebec and to the other provinces have so far proved unsuccessful. Similarly, giving political and constitutional expression to the enhanced status that Aboriginal people have gained within Canadian society over the past generation has proved too great a challenge so far to the status quo, other than in the Far North (see Chapter 15).

Meanwhile, in parallel with the experience of most European-style social democracies, Canadian governments, especially Ottawa, have found the transition to a less generous pattern of welfare-state spending politically difficult to negotiate. Popular support for neo-conservative policies that focus on combatting the 'stifling of initiative' by an 'over-regulating state' and show limited sympathy for the socially and economically disadvantaged (who are portrayed as having abused an overly-generous safety net) is associated, geographically, with the increased voice of the West in

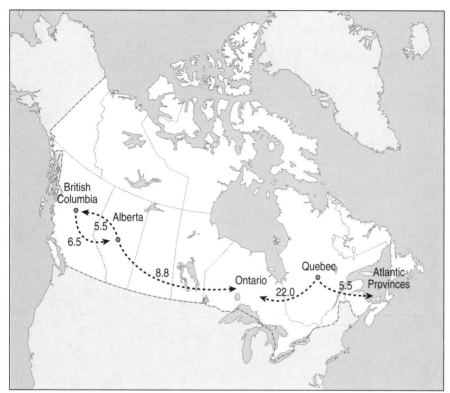

**Figure 2.4  Interprovincial Trade Flows, Other Regions as Origin, 1998** *(billions of dollars)*

SOURCE: Transport Canada (2000: 66)

national affairs and the emergence of 'suburban values' as an important electoral force in metropolitan politics (see Chapter 5). On the other hand, the central cities of Canada's largest metropolitan areas are places where the continuing need for welfare-state policies is very apparent. Food banks, school breakfast programs, shortages of affordable housing, the demand for immigrant reception services, and the needs of those released into the 'community' by downsized psychiatric institutions are concentrated in those heavily populated municipal jurisdictions whose governments have least power within the Canadian constitution. If the urban quality of life is a significant component of a region's economic attractiveness, as many recent studies claim, growing social polarization is detrimental to it, as well as being a challenge to notions of social justice (Bourne, 2000).

   The internal stresses that appear to be fragmenting Canada are reinforced by trends in the continental and global economies. During the mid-1980s, the pros and cons of Canadian participation in a free trade agreement with the country's dominant neighbour were fiercely debated. The FTA was initially promoted by the federal government as enhancing Canadian competitiveness, and hence prosperity, in an era

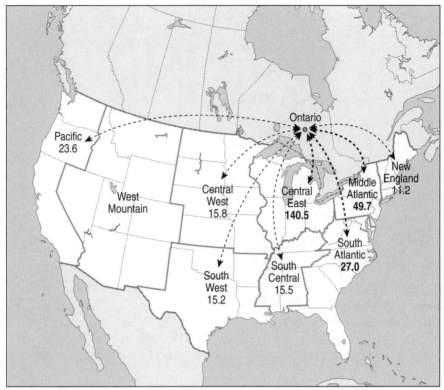

**Figure 2.5  Canada–US Trade, Main Ontario Trade Flows, 1998** *(billions of dollars)*

SOURCE: Transport Canada (2000: 69)

of globalization. Opponents stressed the loss of control by Canadians of their economic future and the threat of job losses to US jurisdictions that offer less protection to the interests of workers and the economically disadvantaged. Freer movement of goods and services across the border fitted well with traditional sentiment in the export-dependent West, where Canadian tariffs on imported manufactures have always been resented and where many farmers, ranchers, loggers, and oil and gas producers saw promising new markets south of the border. However, one of the surprises and paradoxes of the 1988 federal election, which was fought essentially on whether to sign the Free Trade Agreement or not, was the support of the Quebec electorate for a policy seemingly at odds with the prevailing Québécois belief in the state's rightfully key role in the economy, and apparently counter to the interests of many of the province's low-productivity manufacturing industries.

The early years of the FTA were ones of intense and painful restructuring in the Canadian economy. How far this resulted from the FTA itself and how far it would have resulted anyway from the international recession of the early 1990s is an open

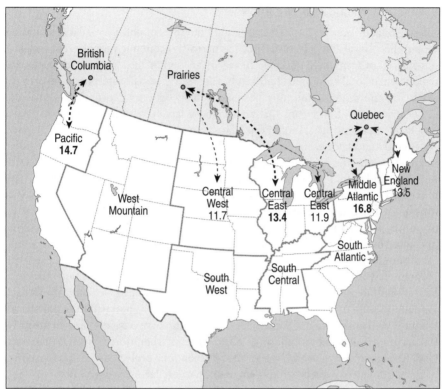

**Figure 2.6  Canada–US Trade, Main Trade Flows, Other Regions, 1998** *(billions of dollars)*

SOURCE: Transport Canada (2000: 70)

question. The fact is, of course, that firms were responding to both contexts. The typical diversity of regional economic experience in Canada was once again illustrated, however, as the branch-plant economy of central Canada underwent severe contraction at a time when the economy of British Columbia enjoyed steady expansion on the basis of its growing integration into what was, at the time, the dynamic Asia-Pacific region. By the late 1990s, the situations were reversed. British Columbia suffered reduced export markets as a result of the financial crisis and check to economic growth in Asia. Ontario, on the other hand, was enjoying an economic resurgence based on its increased integration into the strongly expanding economy of the United States. Yet, despite some of the more alarmist warnings of the impact of free trade, there is still a significantly 'tighter weave' to Canada's 'economic fabric' than might be expected (Helliwell, 1999: 95). A gravity-model analysis of Canadian merchandise trade found that in 1988 interprovincial flows were 20 times stronger than cross-border flows: in 1998 that had dropped to 12 times, but it still indicated that the Canadian–US border separates distinct national economies.

## SOCIETY, CULTURE, AND THE ECONOMY

Interregional differences in prosperity, and in the sorts of policies available to address them, reflect social and cultural as much as narrowly economic variables. For instance, out-migration (especially of single males) is an option that has long characterized regions where local economic opportunities are restricted. The interprovincial propensity to migrate varies significantly, however, notably between francophone and anglophone Canadians, for reasons that appear to be largely related to the much greater linguistic barriers a francophone faces in relocating outside of Quebec. Newfoundlanders, for example, are noticeably more mobile (Figure 2.7). International migration continues to have a geographically differential effect also, both between provinces and within the urban size hierarchy. Since World War II, immigrants have moved overwhelmingly into major metropolitan areas. In 1996 over half of Canada's immigrant population lived in Toronto, Montreal, and Vancouver. Although the impact of wealthy business people from Hong Kong who settled in the Vancouver area in the mid-1990s may have been more immediate than that of refugees from East Africa establishing homes in Toronto or Montreal, the net effect of immigrant arrivals on the urban economy has tended to be positive. However, there are wider implications that may have economic consequences. The concentration in 1996 of 88 per cent of Quebec's immigrants in Montreal and the preference of the allophone population (whose native tongue is neither English nor French) for using English have certainly affected the political geography of Quebec and, some claim, lessened the priority given by the Parti Québécois government to tackling Montreal's economic problems (see Chapter 13).

Demography may not be prominent as a topic at federal-provincial first ministers' meetings, but it shapes the economy in significant ways. The combined effects of differential patterns of interprovincial and international migration, and of underlying regional variations in fertility, have gradually changed the population and electoral maps of Canada. In contrast to the situation in 1867, when Quebec constituted 32 per cent of the Canadian population, by 2000 it accounted for about 24 per cent of the population, which should be compared to the 22 per cent of Canadians resident in Alberta and British Columbia combined. In the 1980s the Quebec government indicated its concern about the province's proportional population decline and attempted to combat it with a more generous program of family allowances, though without noticeable success. Despite federal institutions that entrench a disproportionate voice for eastern Canadians in national affairs, the 'weight' of western interests within the federal system is bound to increase relative to that of other parts of the country, and, as noted above, this is already bringing shifts in economic philosophy and policy preferences. The aging of the population implies shifting patterns of consumer demand and public expenditure, which have spatial implications in themselves, but it is also associated with identifiable migration streams of retirees seeking congenial environments, including both coastal and inland southern BC. At the same time, however, the notably more youthful profile of the Aboriginal population, as compared to the Canadian average, makes the challenge of economic development and job creation for this segment of society all that more urgent (see Chapter 15).

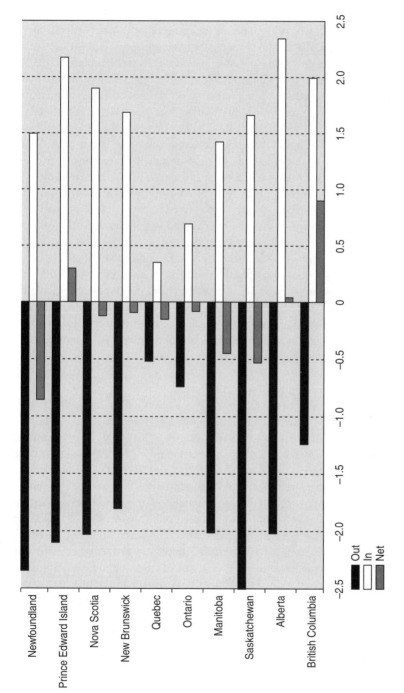

**Figure 2.7  Average Annual Rates of Interprovincial Migration, 1989–1998** *(per cent of population)*

*SOURCE:* Transport Canada (2000: Figure 2.6).

Since the early 1970s, Canadian society has become increasingly diverse, both in substance and in public perception. The largest immigrant flows have been from Asia rather than Europe, and the federal government has endorsed a 'multicultural' rather than a US-style 'melting pot' vision of Canadian identity. It was estimated in the mid-1990s that by 2001 members of visible minorities would represent a consumer market of over $300 billion. The ethnic Chinese population alone is now approximately 1.25 million, and the growing appeal of this market was reflected in the start-up of Chinese-language editions of *Maclean's* and *Toronto Life* magazines in the mid-1990s (*Globe and Mail*, 28 Aug. 1995). Yet these developments have had a quite focused geographical impact. Immigration, as already noted, has been overwhelmingly concentrated in the largest metropolitan areas; and the West, with its many links to the Asia-Pacific region, has received much more of an economic stimulus than have the Atlantic provinces and Québec. Greater Vancouver is home to over 250,000 ethnic Chinese, including a stream of entrepreneurial immigrants from Hong Kong who obtained Canadian citizenship in advance of the British colony's return to Chinese rule in 1997. Their attempts to establish careers in Canada have not always been as smooth as was predicted (Ley, 1999), but their wealth and business experience have led to investment in property (such as the large Pacific Place development in downtown Vancouver), hotels and tourist facilities, and trading organizations. The emergence of suburban shopping centres geared to the ethnic Chinese market, in places such as Richmond, BC, and Richmond Hill, Ontario, is one of the more visible manifestations of Canada's broadening cultural mosaic (*Globe and Mail*, 23 Aug. 1995; Wang, 1999; Preston and Lo, 2000).

Culture is a source of regional economic variation in all sorts of ways, however. The distinctiveness of Quebec society vis-à-vis anglophone Canada stems partly from its different legal system and from a stronger tradition of corporatist, as opposed to individualistic, philosophies of social life. This is true even in comparison with the Prairies, where farmers' co-operatives and other institutions of collective provision (notably the Canadian Wheat Board and Canada's first public health insurance scheme) have been distinctive elements of the economy. Yet only in Quebec are farmers *required* to be union members (of the Union des producteurs agricoles). The Quebec government has promoted public ownership of a wide variety of business ventures and has attempted to direct the development of the provincial economy through 'indicative planning', aimed at fostering expertise and competitiveness in particular industries. Communal organizations, exemplified by the caisse populaire (credit union) movement, have a strong presence, and collaboration between the public sector and provincial trade unions has often been much closer than in other provinces.

In Canada as in other industrialized societies, however, the political and business climate at the beginning of the twenty-first century is less tolerant of many forms of collective enterprise. Some co-operatives, such as the Saskatchewan Wheat Pool, have transformed themselves into private-sector corporations, with shares trading on the Toronto Stock Exchange, in order to raise the amounts of capital needed to compete with agribusiness transnationals such as Cargill. But the former public sector has seen the greatest changes. Many former federal Crown corporations, including Air Canada and Canadian National Railways, have been privatized, and operations formerly controlled by federal public servants, such as major ports and airports, have been handed over to locally based management agencies. Many provincial agencies and government functions (including liquor sales in Alberta, toll-road operation in Ontario, and various construction and maintenance operations in most provinces) have also devolved to the private sector. The geographical implications of these developments vary. Greater scope for local initiative and decision-making allows communities with the human and financial resources to exploit profitable opportunities. On the other hand, the assurance of minimum levels of service provision in rural or remote areas normally associated with the public sector may be forgone. The element of partisan political geography traditionally associated with government-controlled spending, at all geographical scales, is also reduced—for good or ill!

At the same time, there has been an increase since the early 1970s in the number of employee buyouts of firms or factories about to be closed by their usually distant owners. These initiatives, not all of which have been successful, have attracted the strongest support in resource-based towns in the hinterland, where a single employer dominates the local economy. Examples include Temiscaming, Quebec (Tembec), Pine Falls, Manitoba, Sault Ste Marie, Ontario (Algoma Steel), and Prince Rupert, BC. While not confined to single-industry towns, this form of economic restructuring seems to have thrived best in relatively peripheral areas, where local knowledge and community support have been tapped effectively and provincial governments have felt obliged to assist in retaining jobs (Quarter, 1995).

The influence of corporate structure on regional economic prospects poses some interesting questions in Atlantic Canada. In New Brunswick, it was estimated in the mid-1990s that one in every 12 jobs, and one in three in Saint John, was tied to the business empire of the Irving family (*Globe and Mail*, 24 Feb. 1996). It has been argued that this degree of concentrated corporate influence, extending into sectors ranging from food-processing to shipbuilding, real estate, and the mass media, has stifled competition and encouraged social conformity, resulting in a less dynamic and innovative regional economy. On the other hand, the success of large family-owned businesses in peripheral regions can be seen as bringing opportunities and economic stability that would not likely come about without locally committed management. A comparable New Brunswick firm, McCain Foods, the frozen-food industry transnational, has been criticized for the power it wields over contract potato growers; but the firm has brought prosperity to a marginal rural area, and the extension of its influence by vertical integration into trucking, machinery production, and other businesses can be seen as a strategy to provide needed services that non-local firms showed little interest in supplying (Glover and Kusterer, 1990).

Geographical differences in household spending are another sign of the interaction between culture and the economy. The distinctiveness of the Québécois compared to other Canadians is evident, for instance, in their much greater propensity to rent

### Table 2.3   Canada's Casinos: Revenue and Attendance, 1996

| | Gross revenue | | Attendance | |
|---|---|---|---|---|
| | Annual $ million | Monthly $ million | Annual million | Daily |
| Casino Halifax, Halifax | $ 43.2[1] | $ 3.6[1] | 2.0 | 5,400 |
| Casino Sydney, Sydney | 21.4[1] | 1.8[1] | 1.1 | 2,930 |
| Casino de Montréal, Montréal | 336.7 | 28.1 | 4.2 | 11,450 |
| Casino de Charlevoix, Pointe-au-Pic | 24.5 | 2.0 | 0.8 | 2,150 |
| Casino de Hull, Hull[1] | 119.9 | 10.0 | 3.2 | 8,820 |
| Casino Windsor, Windsor | 562.2 | 43.8 | 5.4 | 14,900 |
| Northern Belle Casino, Windsor[1] | 178.8 | 14.9 | 2.6 | 7,040 |
| Casino Rama, Orillia[1] | 366.1 | 30.5 | 4.6 | 12,600 |
| Casino Niagara, Niagara Falls[3] | 650.0 | 54.2 | 6.0 | 16,400 |
| Crystal Casino, Winnipeg[2] | 19.6 | 1.6 | 0.4 | 1,200 |
| Club Regent, Winnipeg[2] | 36.0 | 3.0 | 1.4 | 5,000 |
| McPhillips, Winnipeg[2] | 42.9 | 3.6 | 1.8 | 3,800 |
| Casino Regina, Regina[1] | 36.6 | 3.1 | 1.3 | 3,550 |
| Saskatchewan Native, 4 casinos[1] | 29.3 | 2.4 | 1.5 | 4,140 |
| Diamond Tooth Gertie's, Dawson City[4] | 1.9 | 0.5 | 0.1 | 510 |
| Alberta, 15 casinos | 48.9[2] | 4.1[2] | 4.1[1] | 13,180[1] |
| British Columbia, 17 casinos | 88.8 | 7.4 | 5.2[1] | 16,490[1] |
| Total[5] | 2,606.8 | 217.7 | 45.5 | 129,560 |

[1] *Canadian Casino News* estimate.
[2] For the 1994–5 fiscal year.
[3] Government estimate.
[4] Open for four months each year.
[5] Totals may not add due to rounding.
Source: *Globe and Mail*, 24 Feb. 1997, A10.

urban homes or to purchase classical music CDs. The disproportionate appeal of Florida as a place for Quebecers to escape winter may suggest elements of environmental determinism, but it is part of a broader pattern of America's cultural pull on francophones (Hero, 1988). Regional differences across Canada in preferences for food, drink, automobiles, and the like are to be expected; but they should not be overlooked as elements of the country's economic geography.

A final and contemporary example of the interaction of culture, politics, and the economy in shaping Canada's geography is the distribution of legalized gambling. Government lotteries were legalized in Canada in 1969 and soon became popular sources of revenue, initially for specific causes, such as the 1976 Montreal Olympics. But more recently, in a climate of fiscal constraint, provincial governments across the country have found the appeal of gambling receipts as a general revenue source overwhelming. In particular, geographically localized casino gambling developed rapidly during the 1990s (Table 2.3). Ontario opened a casino in Windsor in 1994 to tap the Detroit market (where legislation prohibited such operations until 1999), and Quebec opened one in Hull in 1996 to tap the growing tourist potential of the Ottawa area. In both cases, the provincial treasury attracts revenues primarily from non-residents. Although Montreal has a casino and the Toronto tourist industry has access to a large provincially operated casino in Niagara Falls and to an Aboriginal-managed one at Rama, near Orillia, so far the residents of Vancouver have rejected this latest icon of urban tourist appeal.

## CONCLUSION

Canadians' experience of contemporary globalization forces them to try to resolve some major tensions. On the one hand, there is widespread support for the universalistic neo-liberal ideology that gives primacy to market mechanisms and international free trade. On the other, the political traditions and cultural values represented in modern Canada are more varied than that single dominant perspective, and these sustain a greater sense of national political identity, one that validates a more active role for the state in shaping economic life. In particular, the distinctiveness of Québécois political culture within Canada is not simply that it is embodied within the French language, but that it consistently articulates its vision of a society in which market forces are best not left to be essentially autonomous, but are to be appropriately harnessed to a broader social purpose.

From the 1950s to the 1980s, the federal government pursued policies that continued the post-Confederation tradition of Canadian economic nationalism. Creation of the modern welfare state and the adoption of such geographically explicit initiatives as equalization payments and regional policy gave Ottawa a significant redistributive role, promoting the economic well-being of individuals and regions less favoured by market forces. Since the 1980s, however, the mechanisms of globalization, acting internationally and within Canada, have made these government interventions to channel or deflect market forces much more difficult to pursue, both practically and ideologically. Canada's commitment to continental free trade through NAFTA and the proposed Free Trade Area of the Americas (FTAA), and its participation in the global movement towards greater trade liberalization through the World Trade Organization represent the external face of these shifts. The election of a neo-conservative government in Ontario in 1995, together with the growing influence of an increasingly rich and ideologically similar administration in Alberta, has significantly changed the regional dynamics of Canada's political economy. An Ontario that acts as a 'North American regional state' and an Alberta that challenges a federal 'national welfare' culture that seems traditionally to have benefited primarily eastern and central Canada are creating a more complex and potentially more fragmented national economy than existed in the twentieth century. These tensions find expression in many specific contexts reviewed in later chapters. First, however, the next chapter addresses the human use of Canada's biophysical environment as another source of the geographical particularity of the Canadian economy.

## FURTHER READING

Harris, R.C. 1998. 'Regionalism and the Canadian archipelago', in L. McCann and A. Gunn, eds, *Heartland and Hinterland: A Geography of Canada*, 3rd edn. Scarborough, Ont.: Prentice-Hall Canada, 395–421.

Ley, D. 1999. 'Myths and meanings of immigration and the metropolis', *Canadian Geographer* 43: 2–19.

Ray, D.M. 1971. 'The location of United States subsidiaries in southern Ontario', in R.L. Gentilcore, ed., *Geographical Approaches to Canadian Problems*. Scarborough, Ont.: Prentice-Hall Canada, 69–82.

Shields, R. 1992. 'The true north strong and free', in Shields, *Places on the Margin*. London: Routledge, 162–99.

Weller, G.R. 1977. 'Hinterland politics: the case of northwestern Ontario', *Canadian Journal of Political Science* 10: 727–54.

# The Natural Environment and the Economy

## INTRODUCTION

The development of the Canadian economy has in many respects been a story of successful efforts to overcome natural environmental constraints. For instance, the east-west transcontinental railways that bound the country together were constructed, at considerable cost, across the north-south grain of the western Cordillera and the southward extension of the Canadian Shield in Ontario and Quebec. The successful settlement of the Prairies was made possible by the breeding of Red Fife wheat, a variety that matured in the short prairie growing season. The invention of the snowmobile was prompted by the need to improve winter mobility across landscapes of ice and snow. Certainly, Canada has proven to be well endowed with economically valuable resources, but their exploitation has required human creativity in coping with the challenges of the country's biophysical environment. This remains true today, for although the relevant knowledge and infrastructures for natural resource development are much more available than they were in the nineteenth century, international competition from other producers, many of them with richer or more accessible resources, is much more intense.

Moreover, attitudes towards the human conquest of nature have changed, in ways that make contemporary resource development a more ambiguous undertaking. Compared to the 1960s, let alone the 1860s, among non-Aboriginal Canadians today there are significantly different understandings of the *values* that should govern human use of the earth and of the *scale* of exploitation that nature can sustain (Wallace and Shields, 1997). The philosophical reappraisal of nature, which has become widespread within Western culture, has undoubtedly been reinforced in Canada by greater respect for the environmental values and traditional knowledge of Aboriginal peoples (Inglis, 1993). Instead of seeing forests simply as so much marketable timber, or rivers simply in terms of their hydroelectric potential, most people have come to appreciate the multi-dimensional relationship that humanity has with the natural environment (Mitchell, 1995). To varying degrees, this involves appreciating that nature has intrinsic value, beyond its obvious utilitarian value as a storehouse of marketable commodities. It has involved recognizing, too, that the biosphere not only produces economic resources but also provides services (such as the ozone layer's protection of the earth from harmful ultraviolet radiation), the economic value of which has too often been discounted in the past.

Some newly recognized environmental values are themselves economic resources, for instance, when the recreational value of wild rivers provides a basis for tourism. But in some other contexts, Canadians (and foreigners making their views known in Canada through the market or the media) have chosen to put a premium on preserving nature from consumptive use or from the threat of despoliation. In these situations, sharp conflicts can develop between the priorities of the general public, as measured in opinion polls; of environmental activists, pursuing campaigns focused on specific issues; and of the particular interests of hinterland communities or firms whose livelihoods are based on resource exploitation. The clashes that erupted over the proposed logging of old-growth forest in Clayoquot Sound, BC, in the early 1990s exemplified this.

Although concern about the growing environmental impact of economic activity is worldwide, Canadians face a particular challenge. The vast size of the country and of its resource endowment, particularly when measured on a per capita basis, has until recent times encouraged a sense of limitless potential. This was certainly true of forest exploitation. The history of lumbering in eastern Canada, from the early nineteenth to the mid-twentieth century, was one of a moving frontier of resource depletion: there were always more trees further on, so forest regeneration was generally viewed as uneconomic and unnecessary (Swift, 1983). Only in the 1970s did a sense that the commercially valuable forest was finite, and that its limits had been reached, really come home to the industry and the provincial governments that control Crown land.

The east coast fishery is another example. The dangers inherent in the exploitation of an open-access resource, where there is no effective control of harvesting levels, have long been established in economic theory. But such was the historic richness of the Grand Banks, and so limited did the economic options for the population of Newfoundland appear to successive governments, that the industry was encouraged to expand until the 1980s, when the damage done to fish stocks became too obvious to ignore (Fisheries and Oceans Canada, 1993). A similarly depressing scenario threatens the once-abundant salmon stock of the west coast fishery. Less stark but still significant issues of the scale of environmental impact are those arising from the loss of productive agricultural land to the continuing expansion of urban areas and to the degradation of soils associated with mechanized monoculture (Canada, 1984).

Responding to the value and scale dilemmas that constantly expanding economic activity in a finite world create for contemporary societies, Canadians have taken up the concept of 'sustainable development' (Manning, 1990). There is considerable ambiguity in this term, however, and in the willingness of consumers, firms, and governments to pursue its implications in depth. Attempts to better understand and document the relationship between the natural environment and the economy are illustrated in Figure 3.1 and Table 3.1. Statistics Canada has traditionally concentrated on documenting population and capital, and such related processes as migration and industrial output. Now, data on the quantity and quality of environmental variables, and on interactions between them and the functioning of the socio-economic system, are increasingly being

**Table 3.1    The PEP Framework: Components**

| Component | Variable Type | Examples |
| --- | --- | --- |
| *Stocks* | | |
| Population | State | Number of people. Number of households. Health status. |
| Capital | State | Stocks of capital for pollution abatement and control, by sector, by material controlled. Built-up area. Transportation infrastructure including energy transport. |
| Natural assets | State | Quantity and quality of minerals and energy. Quantity and quality of living resources. Air quality. Water quantity and quality. Amount and quality of wilderness. |
| Wastes | Stock | Quantity of wastes. Number of landfill sites. |
| *Processes* | | |
| Population | Activity | Growth, migration. |
| Socio-economic | Activity | Outputs by sector. Production and consumption of environmentally dangerous substances. Energy consumption. Operation of transportation stock. |
| Natural | Activity | Rates of geochemical cycles. Natural events (storms, earthquakes, fires, pest infestations). |
| *Interactions* | | |
| Socio-economic processes with population | Flow | Contaminants in food and other goods. |
| Natural assets with population | Flow | Air quality in populated areas. Sport fishing and hunting. Groundwater withdrawals. |
| Natural assets with socio-economic processes | Flow | Extraction of minerals and energy. Water use. Harvest of forests, fish, and wildlife. Agricultural production. |
| Population with natural assets | Restructuring | Impacts of visits to wilderness and protected areas. Impacts of extracting local environmental resources (e.g., firewood). |
| Socio-economic processes with natural assets | Restructuring | Physical restructuring through development of agriculture, mines, dams, and transport infrastructure. Biological restructuring through harvesting activities. |
| Wastes with natural environment | Flow | Release of pollutant emissions and wastes, breakdown of wastes. |
| Socio-economic processes with wastes | Flow | Generation of waste materials, recycling. |

SOURCE: Statistics Canada (1991: 215).

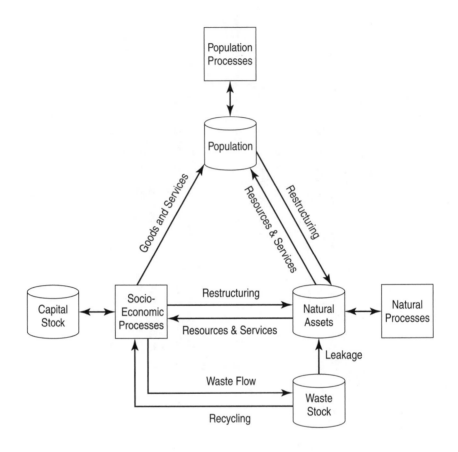

**Figure 3.1  Population–Environment Process Framework**

*SOURCE:* Statistics Canada (1991: 215).

added (Statistics Canada, 1991, 1995). Meanwhile, following the initial report of the National Task Force on Environment and Economy (CCREM, 1987), which brings together representatives of government, industry, environmental organizations, and universities, a variety of multi-stakeholder groups are working to improve the sustainability of the Canadian economy and the competitiveness of firms facing more stringent demands to limit adverse environmental impacts of their operations.

Notable advances in ameliorating environmental pollution have been achieved in recent years, as witness the improved water quality of Lake Erie and the reduction of sulphur emissions from smelters at Sudbury (Wallace, 1998). Canadian autos and industrial processes are much more energy-efficient than they were in the 1970s, and 'green technologies' are a growing segment of the high-technology industry. Yet despite many signs that prevailing patterns of economic activity are not sustainable indefinitely (ironically, especially those involving so-called 'renewable resources'), the dominant values and institutions of our society are generally resistant to radical change (Clapp, 1998). Human well-being is still measured primarily in terms of command over material goods, and corporate success hinges on expanded production and profits. Provincial governments have found it hard to agree on modest measures to curb carbon dioxide emissions because some (notably fossil fuel-rich Alberta) have so far seen the direct economic costs outweighing the less tangible social and environmental benefits.

## ENVIRONMENTAL PARAMETERS

Canada is the world's second-largest country, yet it contains only 30 million inhabitants, giving it one of the lowest national population densities in the world (3.1 persons per km²). This is compelling testimony to the limited availability of agricultural land. The biophysical obstacles to permanent settlement channelled the streams of European immigrants that arrived from the seventeenth century onward into the relatively confined spatial corridor of the St Lawrence Valley and the lower Great Lakes, leaving the majority of the land mass sparsely peopled. Settlement of the Prairies, once transcontinental railways made them accessible to mass immigration, greatly expanded the agricultural ecumene, but climatic and soil conditions exercised major influence on the geography of potential prosperity. So, on the one hand, the national economy has been characterized by a low population/resource ratio, which has given Canada a comparative advantage in many forms of primary production, including forest products and extensive agriculture. On the other, the population is heavily concentrated in a southern strip close to the US border. This has assisted the cross-border forces of economic and cultural integration, which Canadians have traditionally resisted through tariffs and regulation of the media industries, but which have become much stronger in recent years.

Yet there can be no doubt that Canada is a northern, high-latitude nation. 'The True North Strong and Free' does differ significantly, biophysically as well as culturally, from its neighbour to the south (Shields, 1992). Only Russia, the Scandinavian nations, Greenland, and the American state of Alaska share the particular challenges to economic activity that come from Canada's arctic and sub-arctic location and climate (see Chapter 15). Among the direct consequences of the global location of the Canadian land mass are the costs of adapting southern technologies to conditions of permafrost and extreme cold; the comparative disadvantage of slow-growth forests and frost-limited crop options in mid-northern areas as compared to warmer regions closer to the tropics; and the extra energy consumed in maintaining life and economic activity in Canada as opposed to most other countries of the world. There are some offsetting economic benefits to a high-latitude location, such as freedom from many agricultural pests and diseases that afflict regions with warmer climates; the earnings of winter sport-based tourism; the ability to use low-cost ice roads to supply remote northern locations in winter; and lower summer cooling costs than in hotter environments. But the balance of economic advantage, especially with respect to renewable resources, seems to lie with industries and nations situated in lower latitudes than Canadians occupy, and globalization has increased competition from these sources.

In a world of continuing rapid population growth and increasing pressure on land and water supplies, however, Canada's generous natural endowment grows in value. The availability of large areas of 'wilderness' relative to other countries, and to the crowded metropolitan areas at home, is increasingly an asset for recreation and tourism (see Chapter 6). At the same time, it has become apparent that the majority of Canada's national parks, which are supposed to be environmentally protected areas, are themselves in danger of being overwhelmed by the impacts of the people who visit them or land-use changes adjacent to them. The danger is that, locally, pressures of use can threaten the environment that is valued, as in Banff National Park or on the Pacific Coast Trail. Part of the solution to excessive human loading of particular sites, however, can come from the better marketing of comparable opportunities for experiencing the natural environment in less frequented areas.

Canada's plentiful supply of fresh water is another appreciating asset. Growing pressure on water resources, particularly in arid parts of the western United States, has led to a number of proposals over the years for large-scale water transfer from Canada. These have not materialized because of a variety of economic, environmental, and political objections. The same is true of proposed supertanker shipments of fresh water from coastal BC to southern California. But although politicians have announced that Canada's water is 'not for sale', exported electricity, generated by harnessing Canadian rivers, has been an important element in the economic development strategy of Quebec, Manitoba, and British Columbia (see Chapter 10). Too often, however, the environmental damage resulting from damming and flooding river systems has imposed severe and rarely compensated damage on the health and livelihoods of the Aboriginal communities affected.

## STAPLE INDUSTRIES AND THE ENVIRONMENT

On the Prairies, in the boreal forest of the Canadian Shield, in the forests of BC, and in the fishing grounds off the Atlantic and Pacific coasts, the staple industries exploiting Canada's renewable resources are all confronting the demands of long-term sustainability. In each case, the challenge is essentially one of institutional and attitudinal change, but this involves a better appreciation of what the biophysical environment can (and cannot) support, as well as of the potential benefits of scientific and technological advances. Clapp (1998: 130) argues that 'all wild populations [such as natural forests and fisheries] under commercial use sooner or later pass through a resource cycle—that is, a pattern of overexpansion followed by ecosystem disruption and economic crisis.' The initial richness of the resource base declines as the scale of exploitation increases, and the push for economic efficiency in the face of shrinking marginal returns leads to exploitation practices that undermine the sustainability of the resource at former levels of ecological productivity. A decline in fish stocks or forest fall-down (the transition to a lower output-level harvesting regime, see Chapter 14) becomes inevitable, although its timing, severity, and the social and economic consequences will vary with its history of exploitation. Agricultural production systems are not immune from the resource cycle, as the experience of the 'dust bowl' conditions of the 1930s made clear on the Prairies.

Soil erosion, salinity, and the decline of natural fertility resulting from a century of cultivation were estimated in the mid-1980s to be costing prairie agriculture over $1 billion per year (Science Council of Canada, 1986). Although summer fallow (alternate-year cropping) was adopted as a moisture conservation response to dryland conditions in the early 1900s, it has proved to promote salinity, and the area of summer fallow shrunk by 38 per cent between 1981 and 1996 (Statistics Canada, 1999b). Continuous cultivation with limited or zero tillage, to conserve moisture and organic matter, has become more popular, and was applied to almost half of the area seeded to crops on the Prairies in 1996, made easier by newer and cheaper herbicides that do little damage to the soil and groundwater. There is a rising demand for water for agricultural use in the Prairie provinces, where 90 per cent of Canada's irrigated land is found. As in the western United States, farmers' use of water has been heavily subsidized by government. In eastern Canada, the costs to agriculture of soil degradation (particularly erosion in Ontario and the Atlantic provinces, and compaction in Quebec) were estimated in the mid-1980s to amount to $228 million annually (Science Council of Canada, 1986).

The intensification of agricultural production, and especially the emergence of large production units, has brought increasing concerns about the environmental and health hazards of such operations. Water pollution that resulted in fatalities in Walkerton, Ontario, in 2000 was linked to the density of intensive cattle farming in Bruce and Grey counties. Intensive hog operations, such as one planned to produce 150,000 pigs a year west of Lethbridge, have been rejected, despite their economic benefits, because of fears that the manure handling would negatively impact air and water quality. In the Beauce region of Quebec, which has the highest concentration of hog producers in the country, Canada's first exclusively animal waste-treatment plant has been constructed as a response to such concerns (*Globe and Mail*, 31 May, 12 July, 3 June 2000). A tenfold increase in pesticide usage between 1970 and 1985 (Statistics Canada, 1991) was another result of agricultural intensification, and one that in recent years has given a boost to sales of organic produce (Chapter 8).

The management of Canadian forests (Figure 3.2), which until fairly recently had been characterized by an unsatisfactory division of responsibility between provincial governments (as landlords) and the industry (as tenants), is belatedly coming to grips with the requirements of sustainability. Forest restocking was grossly inadequate in the past, but performance has improved considerably since 1980, rising from 68 per cent to 82 per cent of the harvested area by the mid-1990s (Natural Resources Canada, 1996). Softwoods comprise three-quarters of the national annual allowable cut (227 million cubic metres in 1993), and 44 per cent of this component is found in BC. There, the transition from exploitation of old-growth stands to harvesting sustainably managed forests may require a 16 per cent reduction in allowable cut by 2050 (see Chapter 14). In addition, growing public interest in non-consumptive uses of the forest, fuelled by evidence of destructive industry practices in the past (such as

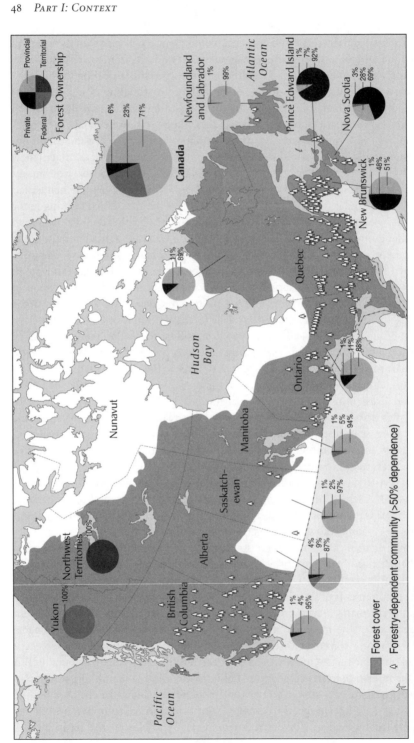

**Figure 3.2  Canada's Forests**

SOURCE: Natural Resources Canada, Canadian Forest Service: <www.nrcan.gc.ca/cfs/proj/ppiab/sof/maps/map98.pdf>

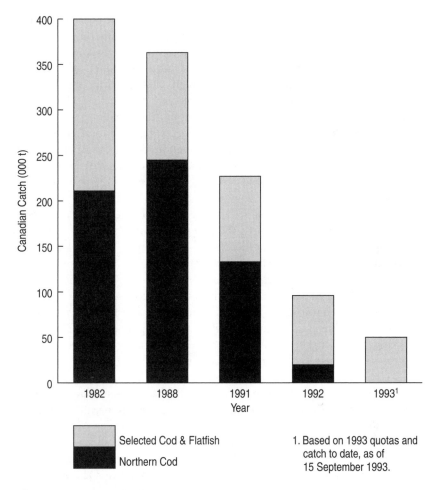

**Figure 3.3  Decline in Newfoundland Groundfish Stocks, 1982–1993**

SOURCE: *Report of the Task Force on Incomes and Adjustment in the Atlantic Fishery* (Ottawa: Ministry of Supply and Services, 1993: 30).

clear-cutting on coastal mountain slopes), has forced the major companies to curtail their operations and employment (see Chapter 9). In eastern Canada, where commercial exploitation is already into the second or third generation of the resource base, closer integration of the pulp and paper and lumber sectors is improving forest utilization. Moreover, research into new processing technologies has broadened the market for hardwoods, notably aspen and poplar, which form the basis of oriented strandboard (OSB). This product has increasingly replaced plywood, as large-tree 'peeler logs' have become scarce.

The medium-term outlook for Canada's ocean fishery is bleak on the east coast and worrisome on the west. Overfishing of cod on the Atlantic coast so reduced stocks by 1992 that the federal government imposed a moratorium on the industry (Figure 3.3). The annual catch off Newfoundland plummeted almost 90 per cent in five years between 1988 and 1993. Responsibility for this disaster has been attributed to a combination of government mismanagement, destructive practices by the industry (both Canadian and foreign), and ecological change (including cooler water and shifting predator-prey relationships among seals, capelin, and cod). The timetable and scale of recovery of the resource base are highly uncertain (Fisheries and Oceans Canada, 1993). Both the ecology and economics of the inshore fishery in Atlantic Canada are on a firmer footing: indeed, revenue from shellfish (mainly crab and shrimp) in Newfoundland in 1994 exceeded the income of the entire offshore fishery at its peak in 1988.

Although not as immediately catastrophic as the collapse of the Atlantic cod fishery, the Pacific coast salmon fishery has been showing signs of stress since the early 1980s, when the third-largest salmon run (at Rivers Inlet, on the central BC coast) was closed for four years (*Globe and Mail*, 2 Mar. 2000). By the late 1990s, the decline in stocks returning to spawn led to the first-ever closure of the Fraser River fishery (which generates over half the industry's revenue) in 1999. The collapse of the west coast salmon stocks has been attributed to a combination of overfishing, environmental degradation of the spawning grounds (resulting from logging practices), and from climate change that has raised water temperatures to harmful levels. Management strategies have been complicated and rendered less effective by conflicts of interest associated with the fact that the salmon runs cut across the Canada–US offshore boundary. As on the east coast, salmon farming in BC has developed significantly in recent years, but there are fears that escaped captive species are negatively affecting wild salmon stocks.

The sustainability of non-renewable staple industries, notably in the mining and energy sectors, is a function of two variables: (1) the continued availability of the resource in economically viable forms; (2) the ability of producers to comply with increasingly stringent regulation of their environmental impacts. Despite its long history of production, Canada is in no danger of running out of mineral resources. The discovery in the 1990s of one of the richest nickel deposits in the world at Voisey's Bay, Labrador, and major diamond finds in the Northwest Territories are illustrative of the still-to-be-discovered potential of the nation's vast land mass. In addition, known large deposits of many minerals exist whose extraction is not currently profitable. Conventional oil reserves are less abundant, although they are proving to be more extensive than predicted in the 1970s (see Chapter 10). Coal and gas reserves are relatively plentiful, and the vast fuel potential of the Athabaska tar sands has barely begun to be tapped by existing extraction plants (of which the largest is Syncrude at Fort McMurray, Alberta). The principal environmental constraint on expansion is likely to come from stronger international efforts to limit carbon dioxide ($CO_2$) emissions from fossil fuel combustion.

The ecological impact of mineral production raises more immediate concerns. A record of environmental damage, caused particularly by acid drainage from mine tailings (waste rock dumps), use of toxic substances in mineral processing (such as cyanide in the gold industry), and atmospheric pollution by smelters has provided the industry's critics with compelling arguments for opposing new projects, despite major technological advances and stronger legislation to reduce negative environmental impacts in recent years. The British Columbia government's ban in 1993 on exploitation of the large Windy Craggy copper deposit, however, reflected growing public unwillingness to take risks with sensitive environments. This factor, more than physical exhaustion of the resource base, is likely to define the economic sustainability of mineral production in Canada. During the 1990s many Canadian mining firms shifted the focus of their exploration and mine development expenditures towards opportunities in other countries, notably in Latin America.

Environmental degradation is more effectively controlled at source rather than at 'the end of the pipe'. This has prompted research and development into new production technologies in many industries since the 1970s, accelerated by the threat or implementation of government regulation. In Ontario, for instance, progressive tightening of permissible sulphur dioxide ($SO_2$) emissions stimulated research by Inco that resulted in a less polluting non-ferrous smelting process that also proved to have significant economic advantages over existing methods. Similarly, both federal and provincial regulations to reduce or eliminate the discharge of chemicals from pulp mills have forced the pace of technological change—towards chlorine-free bleaching of pulp, for instance—while imposing significant costs on firms retrofitting existing mills. Relatively 'clean' high-technology industries have also had to respond to fuller knowledge of their environmental impacts. Following Canada's acceptance of international commitments to protect the atmospheric ozone layer, a Nortel innovation eliminated the need to use chlorofluorocarbons (CFCs) in manufacturing printed circuit boards, while achieving substantial cost savings. The Canadian chemical industry has been steadily pursuing a strategy of voluntary reductions in its environmental impact.

## FROM CONSUMER SOCIETY TO CONSERVER SOCIETY?

Resource exploitation and processing are not the only sources of environmental degradation. Household consumption creates an ecological impact that has been increasingly recognized. Pollution of the Great Lakes is an instructive example, for it resulted primarily from the routine functioning of the North American urban-industrial system. Although some of the degradation of the Great Lakes ecosystem can be attributed to primary industries (nitrate runoff from agricultural fertilizers, for example), most contaminants have derived from substances used in the homes and workplaces of the metropolitan areas bordering the lakes. Certainly, the pollution of these water bodies resulted from activity in the United States as well as in Canada, but the type, if not the severity, of impact has been similar on both sides of the border. Remedial action has improved some measures of water quality (e.g., phosphate loading) since the 1970s, but has been less successful in other respects (such as nitrate loading) (Canada, 1991).

The reuse or recycling of materials has become increasingly significant in reducing the environmental impact of economic activity. In various forms, the practice has long characterized many resource-transforming industries, as in the use of scrap by the steel industry to feed electric furnaces (the basis of all steel production in western Canada) and the burning of mill wastes to generate steam in the pulp and paper industry. Extending recycling to the household level, through government-subsidized 'blue-box' schemes, was the major innovation of the 1980s. The economic viability of municipal collection systems depends on developing markets for recycled materials and on the institution of charges for residual garbage disposal that fully reflect the social costs incurred (Statistics Canada, 1995). By 1996, approximately 75 per cent of Canadian households had access to municipal recycling, and the tonnage of materials handled (2.2 million) was three times greater than it had been in 1988. The economics of recycling are least favourable in remote areas, where unit collection costs are higher, markets for recycled materials are more distant, and local disposal costs are lower than in metropolitan areas. This has limited the adoption of municipal recycling in Nova Scotia, for instance. The (former) City of Toronto estimated that its cost per tonne for recycling waste was only two-thirds the cost of landfill disposal in 1996 ($59 versus $87), but a larger national study found that recycling still involved a net cost to municipalities of $109 per tonne (*Globe and Mail*, 6 Feb. 1998, 1 Aug. 2000).

Disposal of solid wastes has become strongly contested in some metropolitan areas, particularly in southern Ontario. Disputes over the most suitable technologies (notably incineration versus sanitary landfill) and optimum facility locations have been protracted and ideologically charged. In the early 1990s, the NDP government of Ontario refused to permit the establishment of a garbage disposal system for Metropolitan Toronto that would have involved shipping 1.5 million tonnes of waste per year by rail to an abandoned mine at Kirkland Lake, a site that was claimed to be environmentally secure and had the approval of many in the local community. Instead, the government required that new dump sites be found within the Greater Toronto region. By 1995, when the Conservative government rescinded that legislation, $81 million had been spent on the site selection process (*Globe and Mail*, 6 July 1995). Finally, in 2000, the (new amalgamated) City of Toronto confirmed the decision to ship the waste to Kirkland Lake; but this then met with such strong opposition from environmentalists and groups in Kirkland Lake and communities en route that the provincial government banned the project. The immediate result was to increase the flow of Ontario solid waste into Michigan. Edmonton, in contrast, has developed a highly successful metropolitan solid waste recycling and management operation.

Newsprint has been an obvious candidate for recycling, and in 1993 it represented 46 per cent of the material collected in blue-box programs (16.3 kilograms per person). But the integration of used newsprint into the production process of the pulp and paper industry was delayed by instability in the supply and price of recycled material and by the need for investment in de-inking plants (see Chapter 9). Regulations by metropolitan governments (including Toronto and many US cities), setting out minimum levels of recycled fibre contained in newspapers sold in their jurisdiction, has been a necessary catalyst to change. Regulation was also necessary to initiate the recycling of beverage containers. Aluminum is the most valuable material per unit weight handled in municipal recycling systems. Its role in generating recycling revenues was used by the leading soft drink producers to gain approval for the wider use of cans (in growing demand by consumers), rather than reusable glass bottles (favoured by many provincial governments on environmental grounds and to protect jobs in bottling plants). The addition of PET (polyethylene terephalate) plastic bottles to the recycling stream has also reflected the interests of the soft drink industry.

## CLIMATIC CHANGE AND ENVIRONMENTAL HAZARDS

The expectation that Canada will experience significant climatic change during the twenty-first century has prompted a wide range of assessments of the potential economic consequences. Warmer winters in the Arctic are already degrading permafrost, thereby dislocating pipelines and the footings of buildings. Warmer temperatures further south are predicted to increase extreme climatic events, notably droughts and severe storms, both of which can impose major losses on agricultural producers. Although a warmer climate would theoretically extend the physical limits of cultivation northward, neither soil properties nor the available economic infra-structure will necessarily support viable agricultural expansion. The soils of the Canadian Shield, for instance, are patchy and poor. Reduced runoff in the Great Lakes–St Lawrence drainage basin is predicted to reduce its hydroelectric potential and, because of shallower draughts in shipping channels, the freight capacity of vessels using them. Shorter and milder winters in southern Canada will extend the golfing season, but the economic benefits are unlikely to match the reduced earnings of ski resorts. As the dominant national land use, forestry stands to be most severely affected by climatic change. Figure 3.4 indicates the degree to which the geography of the boreal forest could eventually change, possibly leading to its eventual elimination west of Hudson Bay. Other species could be expected to invade from the south, but the existing infrastructure of forest-based industries is geared to current resource avail-ability, and the adaptation costs would be considerable.

Estimates of the costs and benefits of long-term climate change are based, in part, on the recent and historical experience of extreme climatic events (Table 3.2). For instance, the 1988 prairie drought is estimated to have cost $1.8 billion in lost output and to have cut the value of Saskatchewan's farm production by 38 per cent compared to the previous year (Smit, 1993). The 1997 Manitoba flood inundated the Red River Valley but Winnipeg's floodway protected the city from major damage. The 1998 ice storm in eastern Ontario and southern Quebec is estimated to have been Canada's most costly environmental disaster to date, inflicting costs of $3 billion. Even year-to-year fluctuations in temperature or precipitation have significant economic conse-quences, especially for power utilities. Other natural disasters that have inflicted localized economic costs (let alone loss of life) include tornadoes (e.g., Edmonton, 1987, $300 million), landslides (notably on the leda clay of the former Champlain Sea,

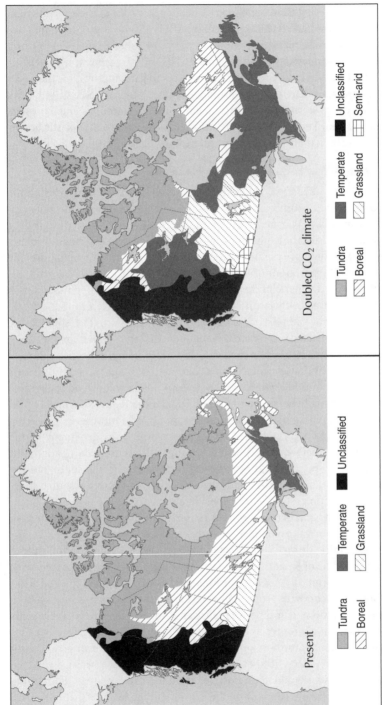

**Figure 3.4 Projected Changes in Forest and Grassland Boundaries, Doubled CO₂ Scenario**

NOTE: Much of BC and Yukon is unclassified because ecological transitions, vertically and horizontally, within the Western Cordillera are too complex to be meaningfully mapped at a regional scale.

SOURCE: Environment Canada (1991: 44).

**Table 3.2   Economic Impact of Selected Natural Disasters in Canada**

| Date | Natural Disaster | Location | Economic impact |
|---|---|---|---|
| 9–12 September 1775 | hurricane | Grand Banks, Nfld | UK £140 000 |
| 30 June 1912 | tornado | Regina | $4 million |
| 18 November 1929 | tsunami triggered by submarine landslide and earthquake | south coast of Newfoundland, the Burin Peninsula, and Nova Scotia | $1–2 million |
| Summer 1936 | drought and heat wave | entire country | $514 million (1989 dollars) |
| Spring 1950 | flood | Red River, southern Manitoba | $125.5 million (1957 dollars) |
| 14–16 October 1954 | hurricane | greater Toronto area | $25 million |
| Summer 1961 | drought | Prairie provinces | $668 million (1989 dollars) |
| Summers 1979 and 1980 | drought | Prairie provinces | $2.5 billion (1989 dollars) |
| 28 July 1981 | hail storm | Calgary | $100 million (1989 dollars) |
| Summer 1984 | drought and heat wave | western provinces | $1 billion |
| 31 May 1985 | tornado | southern Ontario | $100 million |
| July 1985 | forest fires | British Columbia | $300 million (1989 dollars) |
| 14 July 1987 | flood | Montreal | $229 million |
| 31 July 1987 | tornado | Edmonton | $250–300 million (1989 dollars) |
| Summer 1988 | drought and heat wave | Prairie provinces and Ontario | $1.8 billion (1981 dollars) |
| 7 September 1991 | hail storm | Calgary | $343 million |
| Spring 1993 | flood | Winnipeg | $175 million |
| 1–30 May 1995 | forest fires | Saskatchewan | $122 million |
| 6 September 1995 | flood | Alberta and British Columbia | $100 million |
| 16 July 1996 | hail storm | Calgary | $150 million |
| 16 July 1996 | hail storm | Winnipeg | $105 million |
| 19–21 July 1996 | flood | Saguenay region, Que. | $1.5 billion |
| 22 December 1996 to 3 January 1997 | winter storms | British Columbia | $200 million |
| May 1997 | flood | Red River, southern Manitoba | approximately $300 million |
| January 1998 | ice storm and subsequent cold wave | eastern Ontario and southern Quebec | at least $3 billion |

NOTE: The main criterion for inclusion of a natural disaster in this table is a significant impact on people.
SOURCE: Statistics Canada (2000: Table 6.10.1).

as at St-Jean-Vianney, Quebec, 1971), avalanches, and tsunamis (both primarily in British Columbia) (*Canadian Geographic*/Geomatics Canada, 1996).

Of Canada's most densely urbanized areas, the one most vulnerable to severe economic disruption by natural disasters is the Lower Mainland of BC. Together with all the economic benefits that Vancouver derives from its Pacific Rim location goes at least one cost—sharing the belt of seismic instability that has inflicted damaging earthquakes on San Francisco (1989) and Kobe, Japan, where the 1995 earthquake resulted in losses of US$150 billion. Expert opinion suggests that the Lower Mainland is due for a major seismic event 'soon'. Following the San Francisco quake, which caused US$7 billion of damage, the BC government introduced a 10-year, $125 million program to reinforce structurally the Vancouver region's 12 major bridges. But by 1996, as a result of budget cuts, the program was years behind schedule and only one project had been completed. Securing the city's fresh water supply against destruction of the pipelines bringing it from the surrounding mountains also lagged. And disaster response in the Lower Mainland has been made more difficult by the relocation of the Canadian Forces from the base at Chilliwack, BC, to Edmonton as a federal cost-cutting measure (*Globe and Mail*, 6 Aug. 1996). Meanwhile, suburban expansion to low-lying islands in the Fraser delta has been rapid. Richmond (with a population of 149,000) relies on 10 pumping stations to sluice out seepage through its surrounding dikes. Real estate developers have not been forced to comply with ordinances requiring the 'flood-proofing' of new housing (*Globe and Mail*, 18 Nov. 1995). One needs to recognize, nevertheless, that neither potential disaster nor damage to environments that serve valuable ecological functions is confined to the Vancouver region: they remain a cost of urban and economic growth at many locations across Canada.

## CONCLUSION

Environmental determinism, the belief that geographical variations in the pattern of human activity result directly and necessarily from variations in natural environmental conditions, has a long history (Livingstone, 2000). In the nineteenth and early twentieth centuries, however, its use as an 'explanation' for distributions of economic activity was frequently spurious or crude. It is not surprising, therefore, that it had almost no impact on the development of mainstream economics, in which 'land' (representing society's natural endowments), as a 'factor of production', has figured very little in analyses of economic growth and development. Today, however, this neglect of biophysical variables in explaining patterns of production and prosperity, whether globally or more regionally, is being remedied (Mellinger et al., 2000). Even in advanced industrial countries such as Canada, where the majority of employment and GDP comes from service activity in urban areas, environmental and resource concerns are commanding increased attention. The consumption patterns of affluent societies create constant demands for natural resource exploitation, and they also impose increasing loads on the assimilative capacity of the biosphere.

With a per capita endowment of forests, minerals, and fresh water greater than nearly every other nation on earth, and with an economy built on the export of natural resource staples, Canada is still regarded by many foreigners as essentially a resource-based economy. Global financial markets discount the Canadian dollar when world commodity prices fall. Canadians themselves have too long acted as though their natural resources were inexhaustible, yet in recent years the forestry and fishing industries in particular have had to confront the fact that this is not so. What is new since the 1960s is growing public recognition that, even in an urbanized society, economic success and the quality of life are intimately related to the quality of the environment. In this sphere, as in other aspects of Canada's economic development, issues and processes at the global level (e.g., atmospheric $CO_2$ concentration) are linked to those at the local level (e.g., energy consumption and air quality).

## FURTHER READING

Clapp, R.A. 1998. 'The resource cycle in forestry and fishing', *Canadian Geographer* 42: 129–44.

Mitchell, B., ed. 1995. *Resource and Environment Management in Canada: Addressing Conflict and Uncertainly*, 2nd edn. Toronto: Oxford University Press.

Statistics Canada. 2000. *Human Activity and the Environment*. Ottawa: Statistics Canada, Cat. no. 11–509.

Wallace, I., and R. Shields. 1997. 'Contested terrains: Social space and the Canadian environment', in W. Clement, ed., *Understanding Canada: Building on the New Canadian Political Economy*. Montréal and Kingston: McGill-Queen's University Press, 386–408.

# Structural Change in the Canadian Economy

## INTRODUCTION

The first three chapters of this book have identified important socio-economic and biophysical characteristics of contemporary Canada. These represent conditions and trends that have a strong influence on, but do not ultimately determine, the trajectory of economic development the country is experiencing in the early years of the twenty-first century. Those circumstances that the current generation inherits from the past may become assets that can be applied to exploit new economic opportunities, but equally they may prove to be constraints on the capacity of individuals or institutions to adjust to economic change. Whether one considers regional economies based on natural resource staples or metropolitan areas undergoing industrial restructuring, past prosperity is no guarantee of continuing economic success. In an era of profound economic transformation involving the scale and pace of globalization, the structure and dynamics of markets, and the shifting technological and occupational composition of the workplace, new combinations of factors are proving to be critical for economic success. This is true for Canada as a whole and for its constituent regions and places. To understand what these factors are and how they combine to produce different effects in different places, we need to review some of the topics that have been previously introduced.

## GLOBALIZATION

The term 'globalization' includes the recognition that the contemporary world economy is so structured that change in any one part of the globe may well have impacts that are felt throughout the entire system, and hence may directly or indirectly affect any other place. For instance, when German environmentalist NGOs succeed in persuading local retailers to boycott timber that comes from clear-cut forests, specific BC sawmills may quickly lose customers and have to lay off employees. In this sense, the links between the 'global' and the 'local' are becoming much stronger and more immediate than in the past. And although the Canadian government may engage in diplomatic activity in Europe to counter ignorance or misleading impressions of Canadian forestry practices among governments and the media, in the end there is not much it can do to prevent consumer boycotts (Collins, 1998; Hayter and Soyez, 1996). For this sort of reason, many scholars argue that globalization represents a significant reduction in the power and reach of the state.

Moreover, the industrial economy of Fordism was essentially built on the regulation by the state of *national* markets. The social compact among governments, large firms, and the trade union movement delivered a relatively secure and widely shared prosperity during the 1950s and 1960s. But the undermining of Fordist regulation in the 1970s and 1980s by changes in the international economy and in domestic political ideology meant that the capacity and inclination of national governments to protect their citizens (and even their businesses) from the adverse impact of globalization were significantly reduced. Hence, the post-Fordist era has been widely presented as one in which the national state does not have much real economic influence. The wave of closures of US branch plants that followed the implementation of the Canada–US trade agreement in 1989 can be seen in part as a consequence of the dismantling of regulations that protected Canada's national market from unfettered international competition.

The demise of the national state as an economically significant institution, and hence of the nation as a useful scale for geographical analysis of the economy, has been greatly exaggerated by some commentators. But there is no doubt that in recent years the 'region' has returned to prominence as a key spatial unit for understanding economic change (Storper, 1997; Scott, 1998). In particular, analysts of the 'new' economy of knowledge-intensive services and high-technology manufacturing have noted the pronounced regional-scale territorialization of these sectors. Their argument, which is explored in greater depth below, is that some of the factors most critical for the growth of these metropolitan-focused regional complexes are the 'untraded interdependencies' that can be shared by firms and individuals clustered within easy reach of each other. The current dynamics of growth in Canada's largest metropolitan areas are reviewed in these terms below.

For the sake of clarity, then, it is good to establish the hierarchy of geographical scales used in the following discussion. Canada participates in a *global* economy. Different places in Canada participate in different subsystems of that worldwide set of interactions and so feel (and sometimes influence) global economic forces in different ways. Although the Canadian economy is open to the world, one of the country's distinctive features is the dominance of its bilateral economic ties with the United States. Since the early 1990s, Canada's economic geography has been shaped by the dynamics of an increasingly integrated *continental* economy, providing both new opportunities and new challenges to domestic firms. NAFTA has not eliminated the distinctiveness of Canada as a *national* economic system, however, partly because, as we have seen, national economies have distinctive resource endowments and are embedded in distinctive cultural and political institutions. Conventionally, the national Canadian economy is divided into six *macro regions* (the North, BC, the Prairies, Ontario, Quebec, and Atlantic Canada). Some of these are provinces, others are multi-provincial/territorial jurisdictions, but because of the federal constitution of Canada and the economic significance of provincial governments, *provinces* are meaningful units of analysis for many purposes. With the possible exception of PEI, all provinces are large enough and diverse enough as geographical units to justify *sub-regional* analysis. The very largest metropolitan areas, certainly Toronto, Montreal, and Vancouver, attain a spatial scale that easily constitutes such a sub-region; and it is at this level of analysis that some of the most recent theorizing about the determinants of economic growth has been focused. Remember that the essence of globalization is that many of the important forces at work within modern economies cut across and selectively link these different geographical scales.

One aspect of globalization is how the development and application of academic ideas unfold. In developing his theory of economic staples, which provides powerful insights into Canada's economic history and geography, Harold Innis set out quite deliberately to provide an interpretation of how the Canadian economy functioned that differed from the reigning orthodoxy of neo-classical economics (Barnes, 1999). He recognized the power of economically and culturally powerful societies, notably the global metropoles of Britain and America, to present their experience and perspectives as essentially ahistoric universals. In particular, he argued that the equilibrium dynamics at the core of neo-classical theory ignored the realities of how core-periphery economic interactions are actually structured—by institutions and technology, and by geography itself. He wanted to explain the actual experience of Canada as an economy on the global periphery.

We need to recognize that a comparable situation still exists, in that the dominant ideas and key examples within the literature of economic geography and related disciplines tend to reflect the experience of the economically most advanced nations or regions. In recent years, California, often seen as the place where the shape of the future first becomes evident, has been an important focus for theorizing, whether based on analysing the emergence of Silicon Valley or the complex economic structure of the Los Angeles metropolitan area (Saxenian, 1996; Scott, 1993). Similarly, the transformations of metropolitan economies brought about by the globalization of finance and the growth of producer services as engines of economic growth have been most thoroughly explored and conceptualized in studies of London, New York, and Tokyo (Sassen, 1991). These and many other areas of theorizing about the geography of economic change at the start of the twenty-first century have much to offer the student of Canada's economic geography. But it is important to recognize the differences that may exist between the national or regional context in which theories or examples originate and the Canadian situation to which they may be applied. Naturally, Canadian-based geographers are those most likely to show awareness of these differences and to situate their own thinking accordingly. The study by Norcliffe (1994), which is reviewed in detail below, provides an excellent example of how 'international' concepts are evaluated against the specific spatial configuration of the Canadian economy.

## SITUATING CANADA IN THE CAPITALIST WORLD ECONOMY

At the global scale, three major core regions account for a large proportion of all economic activity, however that is measured. These are the United States, Europe, and East Asia. The goods and services demanded in these centres of consumption largely account for the structure and geographical pattern of economic activity throughout the world, whether in the 'developed' North or the 'less-developed' South . Explaining how these regions gained their dominant position is beyond the scope of this volume, but we can invoke many of the same mechanisms of core-periphery relations working at a global scale that are used to explain the core-periphery, or heartland-hinterland, structure of Canada itself. Since the collapse of the former Soviet Union in the early 1990s, the capitalist world economy (Wallerstein, 1976) has extended its reach to encompass the entire globe. A complex web of interdependent elements, including the quasi-hegemonic power of the United States (measured by its economic, military, and cultural power to impose its national agenda on the world), the workings of multilateral institutions such as the International Monetary Fund and the World Bank, the profit-seeking strategies of transnational corporations, and the unco-ordinated but powerful currents of global financial flows maintain a polarized world order of core-periphery relations. Neither the global core nor the global periphery is a homogeneous region. Canada is certainly a core nation, as its standard of living and pattern of economic linkages with the rest of the world confirm (see Chapter 1). But its economy reflects in a number of ways its secondary status within the global core.

Canada's less than dominant position among global core nations is dramatically highlighted by its geographical position as the continental neighbour, and largest trading partner, of the world's largest and richest economy, the United States. At the continental scale, Canada's economy is in many respects a hinterland of the US heartland. Throughout much of the twentieth century this was evident in the large role played by natural resources and processed products in Canada's exports; by high levels of US corporate ownership and control of Canadian industry; by Canada's low level of research and development spending compared to its neighbour, and hence its large bilateral trade deficit in advanced-technology goods (not unrelated to the level of foreign ownership); and by Canada's continuing sensitivity to US monetary policy and the US/Canadian dollar exchange rate (Britton and Gilmour, 1978).

The debate within Canada in the 1980s that preceded the signing of the FTA was largely cast in terms of the desirability of continentalist versus nationalist economic policy. The continentalist arguments were based on neo-classical economic theory, especially its view of the benefits of specialization and scale economies within large, unregulated markets. The nationalist case was based primarily on theories of political economy, which argue that without supportive state intervention peripheral economies will remain truncated and ill-equipped to develop domestic innovative capacity and competitive advanced technologies. In more recent years, ideological interpretations of globalization that present the reduced powers of the national state as both inevitable and desirable have formed the principal argument in support of a continentalist stance towards Canada's economic relations with the United States. But some of the most consistent frictions in the bilateral trade relationship, such as the softwood lumber dispute (see Chapter 9), have come about precisely because the United States regularly acts nationalistically to protect its domestic industries from the consequences of free trade when it is politically expedient to do so. (See also the discussion of 'voluntary' export restraints in US/Japan auto trade relations in Chapter 7.)

Our theoretical understanding of the economic significance of the national scale has been advanced considerably in recent years. The arguments of the classical economists, notably Adam Smith and David Ricardo, focused on the benefits to a nation of exploiting its *comparative advantage*. This involves economic specialization in those activities in which its national endowment of the factors of production provides the basis for the most efficient use of resources relative to the production opportunities of its trading partners. In the case of nineteenth-century Canada, this implied specialization in natural resource products, which gave rise to an economy based on exports of lumber, fish, grain, and subsequently pulp and paper and minerals, and to a national dependence on imports of machinery and other advanced manufactures from the core economies of Britain and the United States.

The theoretical assumptions underlying the case for comparative advantage were steadily undermined by the course of developments during the nineteenth century. Factors of production (investment finance, resource commodities, and particular categories of labour) became increasingly mobile internationally, and the dynamics of *circular and cumulative causation* consolidated the leadership advantages of core economies at the global scale (Britain and the US) and at the continental scale (notably, in North America, within the US manufacturing belt) (Pred, 1965). To promote diversification away from the potential 'traps' of an economic dependence on staples, the federal government enacted the National Policy of tariff protection in 1879 to encourage broadly based industrialization in Canada. (Other nations seeking to break out of their economic and technological dependence on the core economies in this era, notably Germany and Japan, pursued similar nationalistic policies.)

From then until the present day, arguments about the costs and benefits of state intervention to shape the structure of national markets and of flows of international trade and finance have continued. The mainstream (neo-classical) economic argument has usually been framed in terms of the greater efficiencies that can be obtained by increasing the size of the market, ideally to a global scale, and by encouraging firms and (by implication) nations to specialize within it. Conversely, nationalist political economists have pointed to the persistent economic and geographical polarization inherent in capitalist markets and have justified a significant role for state policies to ensure that less than dominant nations have the capacity to build up a significant mass of advanced and globally competitive industries of their own. Clearly, however, the dominant thrust of international policy-making since 1945, driven by American hegemony has been to reduce national tariffs and to promote a global arena for trade and investment that is increasingly free of national controls. The creation of the World Trade Organization (1995) has institutionalized this perspective.

## NATIONAL COMPETITIVE ADVANTAGE: PORTER'S MODEL

New ways of thinking about the importance of the national scale in a world of globalization have moved away from the simplicities of neo-classical analysis. The work of Michael Porter (1990) is widely cited in this context, and has been used specifically in an analysis of Canada's economic strengths and weaknesses (Porter, 1991). Porter's concept of 'national *competitive* advantage' gives attention to a much wider range of variables than those traditionally used to measure comparative advantage. The distinctiveness of a nation's attributes include not only its resource endowments, but also its institutional structure, aspects of its human geography, and explicit consideration of the role of government policy. He defines a 'diamond' of four sets of variables that together constitute the basis of national competitiveness in today's globalized economy (Figure 4.1). They are chosen on the basis of their contribution to fostering a climate of ongoing innovation and the constant upgrading of sources of national advantage, both natural and socially constructed.

- *Factor conditions* include natural resource endowments, well-developed infrastructure, and localized pools of skilled labour.
- *Demand conditions*, particularly the presence of sophisticated firms, i.e., demanding customers, challenging their suppliers to be constantly in the forefront of innovation.
- *Related and supporting industries*, i.e., the presence of national clusters of related industries that promote and transmit innovation among themselves, especially through links between the producers and the users of machines and specialized services.
- *Firm strategy, structure, and rivalry* emphasize the management culture and regulatory environment of corporate activity and the presence of strong domestic inter-firm competition (Porter, 1991: 24).

Conversely, the absence of one or more of these variables handicaps a country's competitiveness. Chance and the formative role of government policy are also recognized as influencing how these elements combine in the evolution of a national economy. Porter argues that interactions among all of them work to establish the distinctive strengths and weaknesses of national competitiveness, and in particular to promote (or inhibit) the emergence of clusters of successful industries. Moreover, geographical concentration tends to intensify synergistic effects among these variables, accelerating the growth of favoured regions and cumulatively retarding the performance of regions that lack them. Hence, in this analysis, interregional disparities in economic growth are to be expected.

Porter's diamond focuses attention on four salient features of Canadian economic development (ibid., 28-32). First, the heavy dependence on natural resources need not be a liability in the high-technology era. The benefits of a rich resource endowment will only materialize, however, if firms are committed to product and process innovation and to constant improvements in productivity. For instance, the declining reserves of conventional oil fields in Alberta have stimulated major technological advances in 'secondary recovery' and horizontal drilling, which have cut production costs and expanded the resource base: but they have been made possible only by sophisticated geophysical prospecting and complex computer modelling. Canadian commitment to R&D in the forest products and mineral industries has not in the past been outstanding, given the size and wealth of the resource base. But in

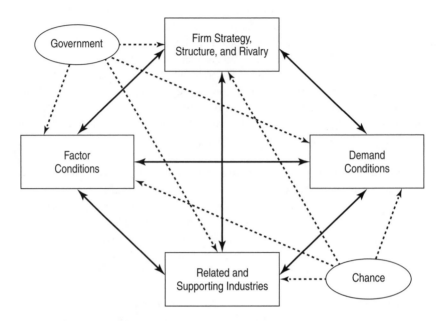

**Figure 4.1  National Determinants of Competitive Advantage: 'The Diamond'**

SOURCE: Porter (1991: 25).

these sectors also, increased productivity and product innovation now rely primarily on advanced technology (see Chapter 9). It follows from this that popular distinctions drawn between 'new (or knowledge) economy' and 'old economy' industries can be quite misleading.

Second, the extensive amount of foreign direct investment in Canada's economy has traditionally been attracted to tap into either the country's natural resources or else the domestic consumer market. Until very recently, relatively little FDI has come to tap into (but invariably to enlarge in the process) pools of highly trained expertise in Canada as the basis for carrying out internationally competitive production in this country. In the past, some of that expertise has been located in government agencies and Crown corporations, such as Atomic Energy of Canada Limited and Hydro-Québec, which have, as a matter of policy, promoted the development of domestic innovation capacity over reliance on imported technologies. But since the early 1990s the advanced expertise of Canada's human resources has become apparent in some areas, notably in the world-class telecommunications and computer software industries, thereby attracting investment by leading foreign firms keen to establish operations and recruit staff in regional high-technology clusters in Canada (see Chapter 7). At the same time, of course, the increasing international mobility of skilled professionals in these and other knowledge-intensive sectors has given rise to concern about the 'brain drain' of Canadian talent to the United States.

Third, for a variety of reasons, including the branch-plant character of much Canadian industry and the effects of government policy, inter-firm rivalry in most sectors of the economy has been relatively weak. The competitive structure of some new industries, notably the advanced technology sectors just mentioned, has improved the overall situation, but Canada has not benefited (as has Switzerland or Italy, let alone the United States) from the presence of a group of large domestic firms in particular industrial sectors actively competing with each other to develop leading-edge innovative products and, with them, clusters of technologically advanced suppliers.

Finally, the close proximity and strong influence of the US economy, with its own patterns of national competitive advantage and its power to project them sometimes at its neighbours' expense, mean that Canadian firms and industry clusters are forced to position themselves within not only a national but also a continental market. This context can create distinctive weaknesses, as well as strengths, for Canadian firms and institutions. For instance, the visibility of most Canadian firms in the vastly larger US market is very low, whereas many large US firms have high visibility and market power in Canada.

International competitiveness involves not just comparability with leading industries in other advanced economies. Since the early 1970s, Canadian producers have had increasingly to reckon with export-oriented manufacturing sectors in newly industrialized countries (NICs), primarily in Asia, and more recently (with NAFTA) also in Mexico. The competition may take the form of overseas operations established by the same transnational corporation that has (or had) manufacturing facilities in Canada, or it may involve unrelated suppliers selling into the Canadian market. Canada has not been alone in attempting to limit the disruptive domestic impact of competitive NIC products through tariffs and international 'agreements' to restrict exports, especially (though not exclusively) of items such as clothing and footwear that compete with labour-intensive, low value-added production at home. The political pressure to protect low-wage employment in Canada, rather than to facilitate its shrinkage in favour of expanding higher value-added sectors, has much to do with the geographical and occupational concentration of the jobs at risk. Clothing, for instance, provides employment (mainly for women) in inner districts of Montreal and, to a lesser extent, Toronto that can be taken up by recent immigrants who have few alternatives. This industry is also a major employer in some smaller urban centres in both Ontario and Quebec for people who lack the skills or linguistic ability for job mobility. With freer trade and declining tariff protection, those Canadian firms that respond successfully to increased global competition in these sectors do so on the basis of increased productivity, product differentiation, and/or reduced labour costs. Adoption of flexible, advanced-technology garment assembly and increased exploitation of home-working (characterized by low-wage piecework) are two contrasting strategies that are evident in this sector (Cannon, 1996).

## ECONOMIC RESTRUCTURING AT THE NATIONAL SCALE

Although globalization has reduced the leverage of the nation-state, Porter recognizes that it has by no means eliminated the important role that a country's social, cultural, and political characteristics play in distinguishing it from others and in contributing to, or detracting from, its economy's competitiveness. These institutional features have been most fully explored by the French school of *regulation theorists*, whose work has been applied in Canada by writers such as Gertler (Drache and Gertler, 1991) and Norcliffe (1994). Of particular interest to regulationists is how governments and other groups in society strive to balance the priorities of capital accumulation by business with the maintenance of reasonable standards of living and social services for the country's population. This was easier to achieve in industrialized countries such as Canada in the 1960s, under a Fordist 'regime of accumulation', than it is today in a globalized economy that sharpens competitive pressures internationally and tends to increase interpersonal and interregional disparities within national economies.

Norcliffe (1994) argues that economic restructuring in Canada is shaped by the extensiveness of the country's resource hinterland and its history of staples production. Even trends that southern Ontario and Quebec may share with other industrialized heartlands are modified in the Canadian context. Norcliffe suggests, for instance, that whereas Fordist *labour relations* within firms did develop quite strongly in major branches of Canadian industry, the full expression of Fordist *technologies* (large, inflexible machines and the development of vertically integrated production complexes) was hampered by the small size and wide dispersal of the national market. The adoption of more flexible production systems by firms in the post-Fordist era of globalization may offer them greater scope to derive advantages from the particular characteristics of Canada's economic geography. Norcliffe's analysis of the major restructuring of industrial employment in the closing years of the twentieth century involves five principal features: labour market segmentation, labour market bifurcation, cyclical sensitivity, labour supply and demand, and the situation in single-industry towns.

*Labour market segmentation* addresses the emerging distinction between a firm's *functionally* flexible core workforce and its *numerically* flexible peripheral one. The former segment usually enjoys relative job security, in exchange for abandoning the rigid work rules and hierarchies typical of unionized Fordist manufacturing. The latter segment comprises employees engaged on a part-time or contract basis; but its fluctuating size points to a third segment, a 'marginal work world', where people combine 'seasonal and part-time jobs with informal work, black market work, and welfare' (Norcliffe, 1994: 9). This last group is particularly evident in *single-industry towns*, where alternative formal employment opportunities are very limited and often shrink when the major employer downsizes. As resource-based industries close, so do the primarily male institutions associated with the workplace, notably the union local. In these circumstances, initiatives developed by women in the community often become critical to its sustainability as a place to live (Mackenzie, 1987). Mining towns, especially those in remote, inhospitable locations, tend instead to be rapidly depopulated once the resource-based jobs have disappeared (Bradbury and St-Martin, 1983).

*Labour market bifurcation* refers to polarization of the workforce, which is central to contemporary economic restructuring. It involves a significant shrinkage in that large range of middle-income, blue-collar jobs that were the mainstay of Fordist industrial employment in the postwar era. The job categories that are expanding, on the other hand, are either well-paying knowledge-intensive professional and managerial positions ('good jobs'), particularly in high-technology industry and producer services, or low-paying service-sector jobs, most of them by nature insecure, and disproportionately filled by women or young people ('bad jobs' or, colloquially, 'McJobs') (Economic Council of Canada, 1991). In Canada, the high proportion of foreign-owned branch plants in the manufacturing sector exacerbated the impact of blue-collar job losses in the late 1980s and early 1990s. With the coming of continental free trade, many Canadian factories closed and their production was transferred to lower-wage plants in 'right-to-work' states (hostile to unionism) in the southern US or to Mexico (Merrett, 1996). In addition, the truncated nature of Canadian subsidiaries has meant that fewer management positions remain to cushion the loss of production workers. Suburbs such as Scarborough, in Toronto, as well as Ontario manufacturing centres such as Brantford and Cornwall suffered severe job loss as a result. The geographical distribution of good jobs is highly concentrated within large metropolitan areas, which means that most of Canada's resource hinterland has not shared in their growth.

The *cyclical sensitivity* of employment in Canada has traditionally been most obvious in the periphery, as a result of the large role of externally traded natural resource products. Global markets for minerals, forest products, and even agricultural staples are marked by cycles of considerable price fluctuations, which are transmitted to the regional economies dependent on them. In contrast, the industrial heartland of southern Ontario and Quebec enjoyed relative employment stability during the era of Fordist regulation. But under globalization, the growing orientation of Canadian manufacturing to export markets could increase the volatility, particularly of Ontario's labour markets. As firms in the auto and engineering industries cut their core workforces and increasingly outsource production to subcontractors, these flexible arrangements quickly transmit fluctuations in demand. Although the economies of Canada and the United States enjoyed steady growth from the mid-1990s into the start of the new century, the next major recession, whenever it comes, is likely to reveal the wider geographical impact of some of these changes.

Moreover, restructuring for survival in a more competitive environment has also brought job losses to service industries (notably finance and insurance) disproportionately located in heartland metropolitan centres (see Chapter 5). In terms of *labour supply and demand*, one outcome of restructuring across the country is that laid-off middle-income workers, from both blue- and white-collar jobs, have had to accept lower-paying work, 'thereby remaining employed, but earning lower aggregate incomes and making little use of the[ir] human capital' (Norcliffe, 1994: 12). The number of long-term unemployed, discouraged workers tends to increase over the duration of major recessions such as that of the early 1990s, especially in regions with a narrow industrial base. The steady growth of the Canadian economy at the end of the 1990s saw an overall reduction in unemployment, to a level (6.8 per cent in December 1999) that had not been equalled since April 1976 (Statistics Canada, 2000b). But, as always, the national rate masks considerably higher rates in peripheral regions. At the end of 1999, the provincial unemployment rate in Newfoundland was 14.1 per cent, despite faster than average employment growth in the three preceding years.

## THE REGION AS A KEY ECONOMIC ENVIRONMENT

Focus on the globalization of economic activity has been accompanied, as noted above, by renewed interest in the *region* as a key spatial unit for economic analysis (Storper, 1997). Much of this literature seeks to explain the nature and dynamics of geographically clustered industrial growth in regions that have developed specialized expertise in a particular sector of production. Markusen's (1996) typology, described below, indicates some of the forms of reasoning used to identify key variables. But in keeping with the broad theoretical basis of contemporary economic geography, regional analysis has extended beyond the confines of the firm, or the network of link-ages forming the industrial production system, to explore the significance of the cultural and institutional environment within which these are situated. Gertler's (1999) research, most of it undertaken in Canada, into the importance of cultural differences between the region in which machinery is made and the regions in which it is put to use is a notable contribution to this theme. In the process, he shows that national-scale conventions and institutions, such as policies towards apprenticeship and skills training (or their absence), have not been eclipsed in analytical importance by global-local or global-regional relationships.

Almost by definition, clustered industrial activity is situated in urban regions. The advantages of agglomeration and urbanization economies have long been recognized in the industrial location literature (Hayter, 1997). But contemporary interest in the economies of metropolitan regions draws a number of new strands into the argument about regional dynamics (Scott, 1998). As the modern economy has become increasingly knowledge-based and the division between 'manufacturing' and 'services' has become more fluid (e.g., the interface between a machine's 'hardware' and 'software', or the interdependence of product design and marketing), so the long-standing metropolitan orientation of professional occupations, which are those associated with the 'new economy', has intensified. The growing economic importance of sectors such as financial services and the cultural industries (see Chapter 6) has accelerated this trend. As a result, regional economic growth in the early twenty-first century is seen to be principally associated with a complex mix of factors, which include: firms with leading-edge technologies or cultural products (which are, of course, combined in the growth of the Internet and e-commerce); institutions (such as universities and government laboratories) that are sources of innovation and advanced training; a cultural, social, and natural (recreational) environment conducive to a good quality of life, as defined by a labour market dominated by professionals; and easy transportation and communications access to the global or continental set of similar dynamic regions with which business links are the most critical. These elements essentially characterize the environment of large metropolitan areas. Consequently, there has been a convergence, theoretically and empirically, between the study of metropolitan-centred regions and studies of industrial growth and location (Castells and Hall, 1994). The significance of these developments for Canada's metropolitan areas is explored more fully in Chapters 5 and 6.

Canada did not develop any of the regional-scale concentrations that dominated the industrial geography of Western Europe and the northeastern United States from the late nineteenth to the mid-twentieth centuries. (At a highly localized scale, industrial Cape Breton was Canada's nearest equivalent to these regions built around coal and steel production—see Chapter 12). This lack can be explained on the basis of Canada's small and scattered market; the branch-plant character of much manufacturing investment, which hampered the development of local industrial linkages; policies that favoured importing advanced technology over promoting domestic innovation in capital goods manufacturing and the development of the skilled labour force associated with such activity; and the simple fact that there were no coalfields in the St Lawrence Valley and southern Ontario in the era when coal was the basis of the industrial system. Thus, the industrial restructuring of the closing decades of the twentieth century did not create a Canadian 'rust belt' to match that which emerged south of the Great Lakes (Wallace, 1999a). Certainly, many of Montreal's economic difficulties in recent decades have stemmed from the decline of its traditional manufacturing sectors, inviting comparisons with cities such as Baltimore or Cleveland. But Hamilton's steel and engineering complex remained considerably more prosperous than most of its US equivalents, partly because of better management at the local steel firms and partly because, as the only industrial concentration of its type in Canada, it lost proportionately fewer manufacturing plants (Anderson, 1987).

Research on the contemporary dynamics of industrial regions tends to be based on key foreign examples from economies that are larger than Canada's. Its applicability to the Canadian context therefore needs to be judged carefully. Markusen (1996) identifies a fourfold typology that serves as a useful starting point:

1. *'Marshallian' industrial districts*, made up of a dense network of small firms that interact intensively with each other;
2. *hub-and-spoke districts*, structured by one or more major corporations surrounded by linked suppliers;
3. *satellite platform districts*, primarily made up of major branch plants of distant foreign transnationals;
4. *state-centred districts* anchored by major government facilities (e.g., in research or the defence sector).

In applying this typology to the industrial geography of Canada, two points are worth making. First, there are very few industrial regions in the country. Most resource-processing plants (smelters, pulp mills, petrochemical producers, etc.) ship their output to distant fabricators; and it is only in the Montreal region and in southern and southwestern Ontario (approximately from Oshawa to Windsor and from Niagara Falls to Barrie) that one finds large and long-established concentrations of diversified manufacturing. West of Ontario, industrial development other than in the resource-based sectors was very limited before the 1950s, although Winnipeg became the home of a diverse set of manufacturing plants serving western Canada. The geography of metropolitan-focused industrial regions that is now emerging does include the Ottawa high-technology cluster and the more diversified industrial economies of Vancouver, Calgary, and Edmonton.

The second point is that these Canadian industrial regions are hybrids, containing elements of different types of structuring. Southern Ontario's manufacturing sector is dominated by the Canadian operations of the integrated, foreign-owned, North American automobile industry. The distinctive geography of this manufacturing complex is described in Chapter 7, but its spatial distribution can be summarized as an extended hub-and-spoke pattern, shaped by the demands of closely regulated subcontracting and 'just-in-time' delivery systems. Montreal's two major high-technology clusters, aerospace and pharmaceuticals, have both been essentially satellite platform districts, with governments playing a significant role in attracting foreign firms through contracts, financial assistance, or policy inducements (e.g., drug patent legislation). The consolidation of a major portion of the aerospace sector by locally owned Bombardier since the 1980s, however, has brought a local 'hub' firm into being. The emergence of Ottawa's computer and telecommunications complex (see Chapter 7) was promoted by state-centred action and a major 'hub' firm (Northern Telecom, now Nortel Networks), but it is taking on some of the character of a 'Marshallian district', with growing numbers of independent small and medium-sized firms contributing to the region's dynamism.

The flexible specialization of production that is emerging as the best strategy for firms to meet the competitive demands of globalization involves adopting leading-edge technology, but also business practices that foster flexible and productive collaboration with other firms. Marshallian industrial districts, such as the much-cited clusters of small firms in Emilia-Romagna (the so-called 'Third Italy'), are held up as regional environments that promote this. Gertler (1993, 1995a) has researched some of the distinctive issues facing Canadian firms in emulating these characteristics, and, specifically, how well southern Ontario functions as a post-Fordist industrial district. He identifies a number of handicaps, which are deeply rooted in Canada's industrial history. Government policy and corporate priorities have not favoured the emergence of a strong infrastructure of worker training or a domestic machine-building industry. The success of regions such as 'Third Italy' appears to derive significantly from close interaction between firms that build and those that use advanced machinery. High productivity comes from the exchange of know-how between makers and users. In Ontario, in contrast, many firms, especially smaller ones, report difficulties in achieving the expected benefits of sophisticated capital equipment. It is predominantly imported, and the 'cultural' distance between machine user and its maker seems to be at least as important as geographical distance in hindering Canadian manufacturers from getting the best results from their purchases. There is less recognition that technology involves a learning process: it is not something one can simply 'buy off the shelf'. Significantly, some of the most successful engineering firms in southern Ontario have strong links (through immigration) into Central European industrial culture. The sustained growth of industrial output since the mid-1990s in the Kitchener–Waterloo and Guelph area owes something to that tradition.

## CONCLUSION

The purpose of this chapter has been to situate Canada's experience of industrial restructuring within theoretical perspectives derived from international research. Insights and categories from other places help us to see more clearly what forces are at work nationally; but it is also important that we recognize the distinctiveness of the Canadian context. The concepts discussed above are used in the interpretation of the more empirically focused material in the later chapters that review specific industrial sectors.

## FURTHER READING

Courchene, T.J. 1995. 'Globalization: the regional/international interface', *Canadian Journal of Regional Science* 18: 1–20.

Norcliffe, G. 1994. 'Regional labour market adjustments in a period of structural transformation: an assessment of the Canadian case', *Canadian Geographer* 38: 2–17.

Porter, M.E. 1991. *Canada at the Crossroads: The Reality of a New Competitive Environment.* Ottawa: Business Council on National Issues and Minister of Supply and Services Canada.

# Economic Dimensions of the Canadian Urban System

## Introduction

Despite its vast physical extent, contemporary Canada is an overwhelmingly urban nation. Almost one-third of the total population resides in the three largest metropolitan areas (Toronto, Montreal, and Vancouver); half the population lives in the top 10 census metropolitan areas (CMAs); and just over three-quarters of Canadians in 1996 resided in the 137 urban places of 10,000 inhabitants or more (McCann and Simmons, 2000). Not only do the majority of Canadians live and work in towns and cities, a growing percentage of national economic output is sourced there. It is true that the resource-based staple industries, which were the basis of Canadian economic development until the mid-twentieth century, continue to contribute significantly to the value of goods production and sustain populations in the agricultural, forest, and mining hinterlands. But as in other advanced economies, the growth of manufacturing and now even more so the growth of the service sector have geographically concentrated Canada's employment and economic output in large urban centres and their regional commutersheds.

It is highly significant that Canada's metropolitan areas are concentrated in regions very close to the United States border, particularly in southern Ontario and Quebec and in southern British Columbia. As a result, from the mid-nineteenth century onward, Canada's urban system has, at some levels, functioned as part of the larger North American urban system (ibid.). Urban places have been the nodes for institutions controlling and channelling patterns of economic development in North America since European commercial exploitation of the continent's natural resources began. In Canada, successively, Montreal came to dominate the fur trade, the merchants of St John's took charge of the east coast cod fishery, Winnipeg took control of the prairie wheat economy, Vancouver became the control centre of the west coast forest industry, and Toronto consolidated its position as the financial and management centre of the Canadian mining industry. But at the same time, cities such as New York and Chicago were powerful centres of influence on the Canadian economy.

Stimulated by the tariff protection of the National Policy, the growth of manufacturing increased the urban orientation of the economy in the last decades of the nineteenth century. Montreal, Canada's pre-eminent 'gateway city', financial centre, and railway hub, emerged as the largest manufacturing centre in the country (Lewis, 2000). Toronto's industrial growth was promoted by the network of railways that fanned out from the city into southern Ontario, where numerous small towns developed industrial capabilities, initially in response to the needs of their surrounding agricultural economy (Kerr and Spelt, 1965; Gilmour, 1972). The early decades of the twentieth century were a time when the expansion of the pulp and paper and mining and smelting industries across much of the southern rim of the Shield and in southern BC led to the widespread creation of single-industry towns (McCann, 1980). In the years following World War II, a number of powerful forces contributed to the accelerated growth of metropolitan areas. Agricultural mechanization intensified rural-urban migration, especially on the Prairies; renewed immigration from Europe now brought people primarily to cities rather than to farms; and the 'baby boom', together with the expansion of government services and the institutions of the welfare state, favoured the rapid expansion of urban populations. Regional differences in growth rates resulted from such developments as a new round of branch-plant investment by US-based corporations, which disproportionately benefited cities in the greater Toronto region and southwestern Ontario (Ray, 1971a), and the development of Alberta's oil and gas reserves, which gave a boost to urban growth in that province (Smith, 1987). Subsequently, with the Pacific Rim increasing in importance from the early 1970s as a focus of Canada's trade and immigration streams, the urban population of the Lower Mainland of BC underwent accelerated expansion.

The economic transformations of the late twentieth century have, as noted in the previous chapter, heightened the significance of metropolitan regions, not only as centres of population but as engines of economic growth. The service sector, which comprises a very wide range of economic activities, now accounts for approximately three-quarters of all employment and two-thirds of Canadian GDP. To a far greater extent even than manufacturing, services are urban-based, and there is a strong correlation between a city's population and the size and range of its service sector. At the same time, particularly among the 'business services' category (see Chapter 6), there are important functional links between the health of a city's manufacturing sector and that of its service economy.

## URBAN SYSTEMS

Geographers' theoretical understanding of the evolution of urban economies has tended until recently to follow a 'bottom-up' logic. Christaller's (1966) original insights, derived from research in southern Germany in the early 1930s, identified the role of 'central places', from the size of a hamlet up to that of a large city, as fulfilling the needs of consumers located within their surrounding area. The diversity of goods and services offered at each level of the settlement hierarchy was found to be a reflection of the volume of purchasing power necessary to ensure that the given set of goods could be made available profitably at that place. Outlets for frequently purchased necessities, or 'low-order goods', such as groceries, were distributed widely, being found in communities at all levels of the settlement hierarchy. In contrast, 'high-order goods', those purchased infrequently because of their expense or the nature of the demand (e.g., specialized medical services) were available only in large urban centres,

with correspondingly wide market areas. Lösch's (1954) theory of manufacturing location also focused principally on market-area analysis. Especially in their simplified
textbook versions, both theories have been interpreted as producing landscapes of
hexagonal market areas surrounding urban centres of differing size, an equilibrium
pattern of implied universality.

However, two important publications in the early 1970s questioned that textbook
version (which itself was coloured by the positivist epistemology of geography's 'quantitative revolution'). Vance (1970) and Burghardt (1971) developed alternative conceptual models based on insights that grew out of their study of the settlement history of
North America. Whereas the regional and historical setting of Christaller's work
inclined him to underline the dependence of central places on the surrounding
regional population and its economic activity that gave rise to their growth, Vance and
Burghardt both recognized that in countries of European settlement, long-distance
trade gave the first impetus to urban development. In particular, *gateway cities*, such as
Montreal and Winnipeg developed at strategic points (usually break-of-bulk locations) along the routes that linked core economies (initially overseas) to resource
hinterlands (Burghardt, 1971). The filling-in of a regional central place hierarchy
followed later, as population grew (Figure 5.1). Not only were the spatial pattern and
historical sequence of urban development along these dendritic transportation
networks different from those proposed by central place theory, so, too, was the
implicit geographical distribution of economic and political power. The full social and
political context of different spatial patterns of regional and urban system formation
has been most fully articulated by Smith (1976). Her work is highly complementary to
Innis's studies of Canada's staple economies with respect to explaining the urban and
transportation infrastructures and heartland/hinterland power relations that evolved
in nineteenth- and early twentieth-century Canada.

The core-periphery dimension of the Vance and Burghardt models is all the more
pronounced in contemporary studies of the global urban system. The integration of
national economies, which has been accelerated by reduced barriers to trade, the
greatly expanded number of transnational corporations, and the emergence of an
essentially unregulated global financial market, has been achieved through a hierarchy
of control centres or 'world cities' (Knox and Taylor, 1995). From these concentrations
of financial and corporate power, most prominently New York, London, and Tokyo,
resources are channelled and decision-making is delegated in ways that significantly
shape the economies of cities in lower tiers of the worldwide system of metropolitan
areas. As the articulation points of the global economy, world cities transmit forces and
shocks from the international arena into the national sphere and, to a lesser degree,
transmit national developments into the wider global system. But their success in these
roles is very much influenced by variables reflecting their national and regional
context. Globalization means that, to understand the economic forces at work in
Canada's metropolitan areas today, we need to recognize that the cities function within
the dynamics of this wider system of continental and global proportions. The factors
contributing to Vancouver's emergence as Canada's gateway to the Asia-Pacific

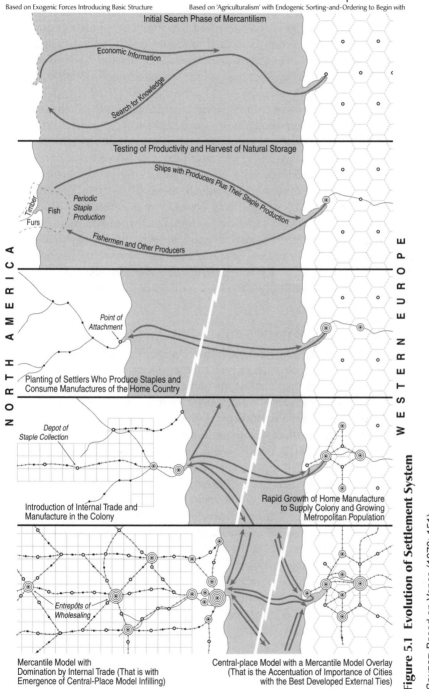

**The Mercantile Model**
Based on Exogenic Forces Introducing Basic Structure

**The Central-place Model**
Based on 'Agriculturalism' with Endogenic Sorting-and-Ordering to Begin with

Initial Search Phase of Mercantilism

Economic Information

Search for Knowledge

Testing of Productivity and Harvest of Natural Storage

Ships with Producers Plus Their Staple Production

Timber
Fish
Furs

Periodic
Staple
Production

Fishermen and Other Producers

NORTH AMERICA

WESTERN EUROPE

Point of
Attachment

Planting of Settlers Who Produce Staples and
Consume Manufactures of the Home Country

Depot of
Staple Collection

Introduction of Internal Trade and
Manufacture in the Colony

Rapid Growth of Home Manufacture
to Supply Colony and Growing
Metropolitan Population

Entrepôts of
Wholesaling

Mercantile Model with
Domination by Internal Trade (That is with
Emergence of Central-Place Model Infilling)

Central-place Model with a Mercantile Model Overlay
(That is the Accentuation of Importance of Cities
with the Best Developed External Ties)

**Figure 5.1  Evolution of Settlement System**

SOURCE: Based on Vance (1970: 151).

region—for example, its transportation terminals, Asian demand for resources from its hinterland, the arrival of a large Asian immigrant community, its role as a tourist destination—typify the range of issues involved. The prosperity of metropolitan areas may not always reflect the economy of their immediately surrounding region, especially in poorer parts of the country such as Atlantic Canada, but it will certainly be affected over time by the relative strength of the macro-regional economy in which they are situated.

There is no unanimously recognized world city hierarchy, but Toronto, together with US cities such as Chicago and San Francisco, and European equivalents such as Paris and Zurich, can claim the status of a second-rank world city, at least judged by economic criteria. The characteristics that give substance to this label are discussed below, as is the relationship between Toronto and its formerly dominant rival, Montreal, which, since the 1960s, has gradually declined to the next level of the metropolitan hierarchy, where (depending on how status is measured) Vancouver currently sits also. Vancouver's rapid emergence as a Pacific Rim metropolis was hastened in the 1990s by the movement of entrepreneurs and financial resources to Canada that preceded the transition of Hong Kong from British to Chinese control (Hutton, 1998). In particular economic sectors, smaller Canadian cities such as Calgary (energy) and Winnipeg (grain) play significant decision-making roles within global production systems.

## THE CANADIAN URBAN SYSTEM

Canada's urban system (Figure 5.2) is dominated by the Windsor–Quebec City corridor (Yeates, 1975, 1991), which contains half (12 of 25) of Canada's census metropolitan areas and over half of the national population (Table 5.1). Within this core region, Toronto and Montreal each anchor a network of subsidiary cities to which they are connected by strong functional linkages. Beyond the central Canadian corridor, metropolitan areas in the national periphery function to a greater extent as free-standing centres, reflecting their origins as nodes within long-distance trading systems (e.g., Winnipeg, Thunder Bay), as regional central places (e.g., Saskatoon), or as sites of resource exploitation (e.g., Sudbury, Chicoutimi). However, faster population and economic growth in the West in recent decades has brought about the consolidation of functionally integrated urban corridors (Vancouver–Nanaimo–Victoria, Edmonton–Calgary–Lethbridge) as provincial core regions. There is a much smaller and more fragmented set of cities in the Maritimes, although Moncton is emerging as the key node in an emerging regional system linking Halifax, Saint John, Fredericton, and (with the bridge to PEI) Charlottetown.

Economic and spatial change within the Canadian urban system since 1971 has been extensively researched and documented by Coffey (1994, 2000). In his study of all urban centres of over 10,000 inhabitants in 1991, Coffey notes that, broadly speaking, growth rates have reflected the gradually shifting balance within the national space economy. Places in faster-growing regions have grown faster. Of the 10 urban areas that showed the most rapid population increase between 1971 and 1991 (from

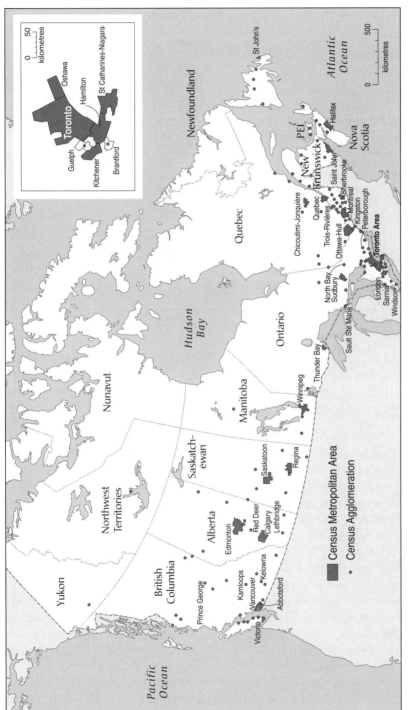

**Figure 5.2 The Canadian Urban System, 1996**

SOURCE: Bourne (2000: 27).

Table 5.1   Census Metropolitan Areas, 1996 Population

| City | Population (000s) |
|------|------------------|
| Toronto | 4,264 |
| Montreal | 2,921 |
| Vancouver | 1,832 |
| Ottawa | 1,010 |
| Edmonton | 863 |
| Calgary | 822 |
| Quebec City | 672 |
| Winnipeg | 667 |
| Hamilton | 557 |
| London | 399 |
| Kitchener | 383 |
| St Catharines | 372 |
| Halifax | 333 |
| Victoria | 304 |
| Windsor | 278 |
| Oshawa | 269 |
| Saskatoon | 219 |
| Regina | 194 |
| St John's | 174 |
| Sudbury | 160 |
| Chicoutimi–Jonquière | 160 |
| Sherbrooke | 147 |
| Trois-Rivières | 140 |
| Saint John | 126 |
| Thunder Bay | 126 |

SOURCE: *Census of Canada*, 1996.

Fort McMurray, Alberta, at 414 per cent to Fort St John, BC, at 153 per cent), nine were west of the Saskatchewan/Alberta border (Lloydminster, one of the nine, lies on it), many of them benefiting from expansion in the energy sector. The pattern of the 10 slowest growing (or declining) urban areas was less regionally concentrated, largely because it reflected the experience of single-industry, forest sector, or mining communities, from Port Alberni, BC, to Sydney, NS; but only two of them were west of Ontario (Coffey, 2000: Table 6.3).

Urban economic specialization is generally inversely associated with population size. Single-industry towns based on resource extraction and processing tend to be found in the 10,000–20,000 range (Labrador City, Newfoundland, and Kitimat, BC, were the most specialized urban communities in 1991), as do towns, such as Hawkesbury, Ontario, and Magog, Quebec, most dependent on other branches of manufacturing employment. At the other end of the spectrum, the five least specialized, or most economically diversified, urban areas in 1991 were all CMAs (although not the very largest). Calgary, Edmonton, Vancouver, Regina, and Saskatoon, in that order of increasing specialization, shared the characteristic of being in the West, as were eight of the next 10 most diversified urban areas (ibid., 6.5). This may point to the typical importance of diverse central place functions in the more widely scattered urban centres of western Canada.

The city size distribution within each province varies significantly, and this has economic implications. Manitoba is an extreme example, with the Winnipeg metropolitan area (667,209 in 1996) containing 60 per cent of the provincial population and the next largest city, Brandon (40,581), less than 4 per cent. The urban population of most other provinces except Ontario and Quebec is heavily concentrated in just two cities, leaving a dearth of medium-sized centres. In Nova Scotia, for instance, this involves Halifax (332,504) and the Sydney/Glace Bay agglomeration (135,601); in Saskatchewan, Saskatoon and Regina; in Alberta, Edmonton and Calgary; and in BC, Vancouver and Victoria (see Table 5.1). Outside of the Windsor–Quebec City corridor the relative absence of intermediate-sized centres (the relevant thresholds vary somewhat, but generally between 75,000 and 150,000) has tended to discourage the dispersion of manufacturing and higher-order services and thereby to accentuate core-periphery contrasts between the metropolitan and hinterland regions of each province. This has been the case even in Quebec, where Montreal has long dominated the distribution of population and industrial employment. Quebec City (645,550) and three centres of approximately 150,000 (Sherbrooke, Trois-Rivières, and Chicoutimi) are the only other large cities (discounting here the Quebec portion of the Ottawa–Hull CMA). In contrast, Toronto is situated within a regional urban system that includes six cities between 200,000 and 600,000 (Hamilton, St Catharine's, Kitchener–Waterloo, Oshawa, London, Windsor) together with five of 75,000 to 100,000 (Brantford, Guelph, Sarnia, Barrie, Peterborough). South-central British Columbia (the Okanagan Valley and Kamloops) is one of the few parts of the country where recent rapid population growth has created a diversified urban system of significant size remote from an established metropolis.

The flows of goods, people, and money that bind the Canadian urban system together reflect the distribution of economic and political power. The headquarters of business corporations and banks, controlling the allocation of funds and resources throughout the national space economy, are overwhelmingly concentrated in Toronto. By these measures, Montreal has increasingly lost its national role and become principally a regional capital for Quebec, although it retains a significant number (second only to Washington in North America) of headquarter offices of international institutions, such as the International Civil Aviation Organization (Germain and Rose, 2000). The exodus of corporate headquarters from Montreal in the years following the initial electoral victory of the Parti Québécois in 1976 worked principally to the benefit of Toronto. But since the 1980s, the westward shift of economic potential in Canada has continued, primarily to the benefit of Calgary and Vancouver. Their formerly relatively small and narrowly focused control functions, in the energy and forest sectors respectively, have increased in size and scope. By the late 1990s, Calgary had emerged as the second-largest centre of corporate head offices in Canada, ahead of both Montreal and Vancouver. However, the failure of Alberta and BC-based banks to break the stranglehold of the 'eastern' banking oligopoly in the early 1980s revealed the degree to which 'initial advantage' continues to shape the geography of power in the Canadian urban system.

Although the highest personal incomes are earned in the largest metropolitan areas, the urban size hierarchy is not completely congruent with the income hierarchy. In Canada, some of the highest median incomes are found in resource-based single-industry communities where high-paying mining or forest industry jobs are dominant. In 1996, Nanisivik, the location of a zinc mine on northern Baffin Island, reported an average income of $52,300, the fifth highest in the country. (Note, however, that as is common throughout the North, this is matched by a high cost of living. See Chapter 15.) Among metropolitan areas, Ottawa–Hull and Oshawa (which has often headed the overall ranking when the auto industry has been doing well) had the highest median incomes (*Globe and Mail*, 26 July 1996). And just as wealth tends to be concentrated in the biggest cities, so, too, is poverty. Changes in the job market and in the funding priorities of the welfare state have tended to shift the greatest incidence of poverty from the elderly and from rural areas to young persons, particularly in single-parent households, in metropolitan centres. Cities in Quebec tend to have higher percentages of people living below the Statistics Canada low-income cut-off level (in 1991, Montreal was highest with 22 per cent), whereas smaller metropolitan areas in southern Ontario have lower percentages (Oshawa was lowest with 9 per cent) (*Globe and Mail*, 1 July 1996).

## METROPOLITAN CONCENTRATION

In 1991, Canada's 10 largest CMAs together contained 49 per cent of the national population and 52 per cent of all employment (Coffey, 1994). Their contribution to total economic output has been rising as the contribution of services to GDP increases. Although these cities have been responding to many common economic and social trends, they each retain distinctive characteristics, as reflected in sectoral employment location quotients (Table 5.2). Calgary's role as the headquarters of the Canadian oil and gas industry makes it the only CMA with a sizable localization of employment in the primary sector. Hamilton stands out clearly as the CMA most specialized in manufacturing, anchored by its steel and engineering industrial complex. Toronto, Montreal, and, marginally, London also show above-average dependence on this sector. Winnipeg and, to a lesser extent, Vancouver show the highest relative specializations in transportation services, reflecting their gateway functions. But in this context, wholesaling is less locationally concentrated: among the largest CMAs only the 'government cities' of Ottawa–Hull and Quebec City have a location quotient of less than 100 in this sector.

At the heart of the growing metropolitan service economy are the producer services and financial services categories (Coffey, 1994). The former constitute the sector whose distribution most closely mirrors the metropolitan size hierarchy, and since 1971 its relative concentration in the largest of the large CMAs has increased. By 1991, Toronto, Calgary, and Ottawa, in that order, had roughly similar degrees of specialization in this

**Table 5.2  Metropolitan Specialization (Location Quotients), 1991**

| | Primary Sector | Manufacturing | Construction | Transportation | Communications | Wholesale | Retail | Finance, Insurance, Real Estate | Producer Services | Education | Health | Accommodation | Public Services | Other |
|---|---|---|---|---|---|---|---|---|---|---|---|---|---|---|
| Toronto | 16 | 120 | 96 | 87 | 114 | 120 | 98 | 161 | 168 | 90 | 81 | 82 | 71 | 108 |
| Montreal | 12 | 127 | 83 | 112 | 118 | 126 | 100 | 118 | 129 | 94 | 105 | 90 | 72 | 107 |
| Vancouver | 40 | 76 | 111 | 132 | 109 | 138 | 99 | 132 | 141 | 92 | 96 | 118 | 65 | 124 |
| Ottawa-Hull | 20 | 41 | 86 | 63 | 128 | 62 | 89 | 86 | 158 | 108 | 96 | 89 | 308 | 98 |
| Edmonton | 74 | 60 | 118 | 114 | 123 | 125 | 100 | 98 | 103 | 110 | 110 | 107 | 115 | 109 |
| Calgary | 141 | 57 | 108 | 118 | 104 | 120 | 95 | 115 | 164 | 94 | 93 | 104 | 69 | 114 |
| Winnipeg | 23 | 92 | 81 | 151 | 123 | 117 | 97 | 115 | 82 | 111 | 122 | 104 | 113 | 103 |
| Quebec | 23 | 62 | 81 | 71 | 82 | 81 | 102 | 127 | 95 | 117 | 127 | 113 | 204 | 101 |
| Hamilton | 32 | 151 | 103 | 71 | 78 | 109 | 106 | 104 | 97 | 112 | 102 | 85 | 65 | 99 |
| London | 43 | 109 | 96 | 66 | 96 | 102 | 107 | 125 | 92 | 120 | 134 | 105 | 66 | 98 |

NOTE: Index of specialization comparing the degree of concentration of a given economic sector in a given CMA to the national average. Values below (above) 100 indicate a lesser (greater) degree of specialization than in the national economy.

SOURCE: Coffey (1994: Table 2.5).

fastest-growing set of services, which includes computing, consulting, legal, and other business services. Toronto's dominance of Canada's financial, insurance, and real estate sector is reflected in a location quotient that well exceeds that of any other large CMA. Montreal's relative specialization in this sector dropped significantly during the 1970s but held steady during the 1980s. Vancouver's specialization in financial services held fairly steady between 1971 and 1991, whereas Calgary's fell noticeably after 1981. More recent data would undoubtedly show a reversal of fortunes between the two cities, not least because of Calgary's success in capturing corporate head office employment (see Chapter 14). Quebec City and London owe their high location quotients to the finance and insurance sectors respectively.

## METROPOLITAN ECONOMIES

The population growth and physical expansion of Canada's largest metropolitan areas have involved changes to their internal economic geography. While variations in size, regional setting, and economic base necessitate care in making generalizations, the suburbanization of economic activity has been a common feature. This has been going on for decades, particularly in the manufacturing sector, as existing plants have sought less cramped and congested sites in the suburbs and new plants have been attracted there. Lower taxes in suburban municipalities and cheaper housing than in the central city have also become increasingly significant advantages. The rise of office employment after 1960 saw a concentration of service jobs in the central city and the development of transportation systems in most cities to handle commuting between centre and suburb (Bourne, 1989).

Since the late 1980s, however, new economic pressures have profoundly affected both central cities and inner (pre-1960) suburbs. The restructuring of office employment associated with the widespread diffusion of new technologies has resulted in significant downsizing among middle managers and especially among predominantly female support staff. Toronto alone lost 70,000 clerical jobs between 1990 and 1993, or 40 per cent of its employment decline in that period (*Globe and Mail*, 14 Nov. 1994). Simultaneously, the unprecedented degree of restructuring in the manufacturing sector, associated specifically with the FTA, 'hollowed out' Toronto's inner-city manufacturing. Most of the jobs lost were in industries that traditionally provided employment for recent immigrants (especially women) and for males with limited educational qualifications. Together, these developments have been a major contributor to the greater polarization of urban incomes and job opportunities in Toronto since the 1990s (Bourne, 2000).

The advantages of maximum accessibility and ease of interpersonal contact that have traditionally attracted high-order functions to the central business district (CBD) persist, but they are weaker than they were. Office construction booms in the 1980s changed the downtowns of Toronto, Vancouver, and other metropolitan areas and accommodated the expansion of business services in particular. But the growing size of the service sector has led to increased functional specialization, which, with advances in office technology, favours the decentralization of routine work that does not require face-to-face transactions (*back-office* activity). High CBD occupancy costs (rents plus taxes), road congestion, and inadequate parking are among the 'push' factors. Greater availability of 'suitable' labour (suburban women, most with families, generally regarded as reliable and rarely militant employees), lower rents, and better accessibility by car are among the 'pull' factors (Gad, 1991). Moreover, although not as developed a phenomenon as in the 'edge cities' of the United States (Garreau, 1991), outer suburban clusters of headquarters and other high-level offices have developed in the Toronto area, for example, at Markham. Montreal has experienced significant decentralization of financial and insurance back offices to the outer suburbs, but the corporate head offices in the central city have tended to anchor business services (Coffey and Drolet, 1994). In Vancouver, decentralization of public-sector offices (BC Telephone Company to Burnaby, a federal Regional Taxation Centre to Surrey) was part of the planning strategy of the 'Livable Region' concept in the mid-1970s (North and Hardwick, 1992).

The increasing use of cellular phones, laptop computers, and fax/modems has begun to erode demand for some types of office space. IBM was an innovator when, in the early 1990s, it switched 900 of its service and sales employees to work from their homes, cars, or small local offices. This allowed it to save $40 million per year in real estate costs, chop its use of office space in Metro Toronto by one-third, and shrink its CBD office from 14 floors to 2 floors of a Toronto-Dominion Centre tower (*Globe and Mail*, 14 May 1993). Such changes have become part of a larger shift towards the growth of home-based employment. In 1991, there were 743,000 paid, non-agricultural workers based at home, one-third of whom were self-employed. The total includes traditional and relatively low-paying jobs such as child care, but there is a growing proportion of information-based activity, both routinized and professional (*Globe and Mail*, 14 Mar. 1996). The trend was given added impetus in the 1990s by the downsizing of large organizations in both the public and private sectors and their increased use of outsourcing. New higher-income subdivisions in the Toronto and Ottawa regions are featuring homes designed with 'information highway' infrastructure (i.e., wired for intranets and high-speed Internet access) to appeal to home-based professionals.

The growth of Canada's metropolitan areas has prompted administrative reorganization to better manage the provision of infrastructure and services. In the 1970s, the creation of unitary cities in Calgary and Winnipeg and of regional municipalities (such as Niagara and Ottawa-Carleton) in Ontario enabled those large urban centres to undertake major investments in transit and sewage provision. Canada's three largest metropolitan areas, however, have encountered more difficulty in adapting to the different pressures facing them. Metropolitan Toronto, which was a model of effective urban administration when it was created in 1953, became stranded by the relentless expansion of settlement and industry into its immediate hinterland in the following decades. Attempts by various governments of Ontario to co-ordinate regional-scale planning in the variously described Toronto-Centred Region (in the 1970s) or Greater Toronto Area (in the 1990s) have generally been half-hearted at best. The Conservative government's amalgamation of the constituent municipalities of Metropolitan

Toronto into a single city in 1998 brought some benefits, but at the broader regional scale it exacerbated inner/outer metropolitan area conflicts about equitable service provision and revenue-sharing (Sancton, 2000).

The situation is considerably less promising in Montreal, where administration of the metropolitan area has been chronically fragmented (until 2001 there were 29 municipalities on the Island of Montreal alone). A 1993 task force recommendation that would have established a comprehensive regional authority was shelved (Sancton, 2000). Yet the inner-city/outer-city contrasts are much sharper than in Toronto. In the 20 years to 1991, the Island of Montreal lost over a quarter of a million inhabitants, while the outer suburbs gained half a million, but the infrastructure to support the 400,000 daily commuters on to the Island remains largely the responsibility of the inner-city municipalities. The provincial political context is relevant to this impasse (see below and Chapter 13).

Strategic planning for the Vancouver area, which has been under tremendous growth pressures since the 1970s, is even less co-ordinated at the metropolitan level than in Toronto and Montreal. Having put some region-wide planning functions in the hands of the Greater Vancouver Regional District (GVRD), the provincial government subsequently took back responsibility for physical and transportation planning (Ley et al., 1992). Until the early 1990s, the province gave priority to development interests that supported municipal parochialism and promoted suburban sprawl. The need for metropolitan-scale co-ordination of zoning and transportation system planning has gradually been accepted by the outlying municipalities, but in many respects metropolitan Vancouver is institutionally under-equipped to handle the challenges of its ongoing economic and social transformation.

## CANADA'S LARGEST METROPOLITAN REGIONS

### Toronto

However it is precisely defined, the Toronto-centred metropolitan area is the largest in Canada. The CMA population in 1996 was 4.3 million and that of the wider Greater Toronto Area (GTA) planning region was 4.8 million. In other words, the Toronto region contains almost one-sixth of the Canadian population—but it is responsible for approximately *one-quarter* of national economic output. As noted above, the city is Canada's principal node within the global network of world cities: it houses by far the largest concentration of corporate head offices and domestic and international banking headquarters in the country and is the home of the major national stock exchange. As the experience of the 1990s made clear, however, Toronto's economic strengths are not immune to changing circumstances at either the global or the local scale. (And in this, it reflects the experience of every other metropolitan regional economy, in Canada and around the world.) Its ranking among world cities is influenced by the changing geography of forces of globalization, especially as these affect the North American urban system. So, for instance, the role of the Toronto Stock Exchange, despite being strengthened domestically by its incorporation of the stocks formerly traded on the Montreal Stock Exchange, is being eroded by the rising number of Canadian firms obtaining a listing on the New York Stock Exchange or raising capital on the NASDAQ (the New York-based exchange specializing in 'new economy' stocks). With respect to local-scale challenges, the continuing growth of the metropolitan area has been accompanied by increasing inner-city/outer-city tensions, which provincial government policies have accentuated rather than resolved.

As Table 5.3 indicates, the total number of people employed in the Toronto CMA was almost identical in 1991 and 1996. What these census data do not show is that employment had increased by fully 25 per cent during the 1980s, but by early 1994 had dropped 11 per cent below its pre-recession peak in 1990. In the last half of the 1990s, economic growth was once again strong, but certainly not uniform, either spatially or across sectors. This roller-coaster experience, more normally associated with hinterland single-industry communities, was abnormal in the economic capital of Canada, and it points to the radical nature of the restructuring that was going on during that time. Between 1991 and 1996, the region lost 19,000 jobs in manufacturing and 32,000 in construction; but it also lost 20,000 in retailing, 12,000 in finance and insurance, and 38,000 in government services. The sectors where Toronto gained substantial numbers of jobs were wholesaling (29,000), business services (23,000), health services (19,000), accommodation and food services (13,000), and 'other services' (23,000, half of them in the 'amusement and recreational services' category). To be sure, employment growth was concentrated in services, many of them strongly associated with a city at the top of the metropolitan hierarchy; but equally clearly, service employment was no guaranteed solution to the ongoing loss of manufacturing jobs, for many services also were retrenching (see Chapter 6). And among the manufacturing losses were 6,000 jobs in the electrical and electronics products sector, a drop of 15 per cent, at a time when the sector grew by 12 per cent in the rest of Ontario.

How do we interpret these changes? Manufacturing employment in Toronto peaked in 1981, but the sector's share of all jobs had been declining since the early 1950s (GTA Task Force, 1996). Its postwar growth was heavily dependent on expansion by (principally American) transnational corporations operating 'miniature replica' branch plants (see Chapter 2). But declining tariffs in the postwar period, culminating in the Canada–US Free Trade Agreement and the reorganization of corporate production systems on a continental scale, left many of Canada's inefficiently small, aging, Fordist manufacturing plants very vulnerable to closure. The Toronto region bore the brunt of this restructuring. Many workers made redundant by the closure of older industrial plants were not, in terms of their education or skills, in a position to gain employment in expanding industries, and the number of persons registered as long-term unemployed or no longer seeking work increased noticeably. The established manufacturing areas in the GTA core, in the current City of Toronto (former Metro), were all the slower to recover from the early 1990s recession because of the strong attraction for new plants of lower-tax municipalities beyond its perimeter. Moreover, with the Ontario economy deteriorating, the city was subjected to intensified efforts by US states to 'cherry-pick' local firms, encouraging them to expand or relocate in the US (ibid.). Meanwhile, Toronto was losing routine

Table 5.3   Employment Structure: Montreal and Toronto, 1991 and 1996

| | Montreal | | Toronto | |
|---|---|---|---|---|
| Sector | 1991 | 1996 | 1991 | 1996 |
| Agriculture | 10,130 | 10,040 | 14,810 | 12,410 |
| Fishing | 140 | 70 | 235 | 175 |
| Logging | 1,115 | 780 | 1,605 | 635 |
| Mining | 2,080 | 1,610 | 4,380 | 2,830 |
| Manufacturing | 311,555 | 283,370 | 385,340 | 366,565 |
| *Food* | *25,740* | *22,915* | *31,290* | *32,850* |
| *Textiles & Clothing* | *63,620* | *56,740* | *24,765* | *24,610* |
| *Wood* | *5,950* | *5,030* | *6,540* | *7,220* |
| *Paper* | *10,445* | *8,255* | *13,505* | *13,515* |
| *Metal* | *8,970* | *6,275* | *10,665* | *6,230* |
| *Machinery* | *9,605* | *8,585* | *14,395* | *14,210* |
| *Transportation equip.* | *29,155* | *28,510* | *48,625* | *46,180* |
| *Electrical* | *26,385* | *25,590* | *41,475* | *35,280* |
| Construction | 92,555 | 67,075 | 139,390 | 107,235 |
| Transportation | 76,330 | 69,300 | 78,105 | 78,850 |
| Communication | 66,225 | 60,355 | 84,720 | 81,215 |
| Wholesale | 89,890 | 101,455 | 113,945 | 142,445 |
| Retail | 215,110 | 202,425 | 276,185 | 256,125 |
| Finance | 84,825 | 68,890 | 149,460 | 137,880 |
| Real estate | 26,570 | 29,595 | 52,170 | 56,595 |
| Business | 119,535 | 134,650 | 208,810 | 231,890 |
| Government | 93,370 | 78,880 | 121,440 | 83,410 |
| Education | 106,700 | 112,330 | 135,425 | 137,485 |
| Health | 157,460 | 162,195 | 159,860 | 179,200 |
| Accommodation | 95,860 | 96,090 | 115,720 | 129,005 |
| Other service | 117,705 | 130,710 | 157,255 | 180,495 |
| Total | 1,715,765 | 1,692,555 | 2,268,610 | 2,232,470 |

Source: Statistics Canada, Cat. no. 93F0027XDB96008.

service-sector jobs, some (as in banking) to the impact of automation; others (particularly 'back-office' functions) to relocation to lower-cost communities; and yet others to the nationwide downsizing of government employment.

Despite all these negative trends in the early 1990s, the Toronto region retained its national leadership in the infrastructure and human resources for knowledge-intensive, 'new economy' industries, and these have enjoyed strong growth in recent years. Ottawa's claim to be 'Silicon Valley North' (see Chapter 7) masks the fact that high-technology employment is numerically (but not proportionately) considerably greater in the Toronto area. Over one-quarter of Canada's industrial R&D is undertaken by Toronto firms (Britton, 1999). In 1999, the city's top three manufacturing employers were de Havilland (aircraft), Celestica (computers), and Xerox (electronic equipment). At the same time, the Web page of the business development group for the information technology and telecommunications (IT&T) industry in the GTA (www.sto.org) was claiming that 155,000 people were employed by firms in this sector. It claimed that the region's 300 'new media' firms ranked it second only to Los Angeles in this field, and pointed, for instance, to the important training and incubator role of programs in this field at Sheridan College. A segment of the Toronto economy that flourished less sustainably in the mid-1990s was the theatre industry—the cultural entrepreneurship that was principally behind Toronto's rise to third rank worldwide in English-language live theatre (with clear spillovers in the tourism sector) collapsed in scandal and bankruptcy at the end of the decade, showing again the critical role of local variables in the economic fortunes of world cities.

## Montreal

The complex set of factors that have contributed to Montreal's economic decline, beginning gradually in the 1930s and accelerating after the 1960s, are reviewed in Chapter 13. By 1996, the Montreal CMA contained just over 11 per cent of the Canadian labour force, or 75 per cent of the Toronto total, and in aggregate had lost jobs slightly since 1991 (Table 5.3). The sectors showing the greatest change during this period were quite similar to those in Toronto, but with some interesting differences. Manufacturing job loss (28,000) was almost half as much again as in Toronto, from a smaller base. Losses of 25,000 in construction and 13,000 in retailing were proportionately close to those experienced in Toronto. But, both absolutely and relatively, Montreal suffered a more severe reduction in finance and insurance employment (16,000), yet a very much lighter one in government services (14,000). Montreal's growth sectors generally corresponded with those in Toronto, but in every case the increase was proportionately weaker: business services (15,000), 'other services' (13,000, almost half in amusement and recreation), wholesaling (12,000), and health (5,000) fell into this category. In contrast to Toronto, employment in the accommodation and food services sector was essentially static, whereas in the education sector it increased slightly (5,000).

The structural weaknesses of the Montreal manufacturing sector in recent decades have stemmed from the strong presence of traditional, low value-added industries, notably clothing and food-processing. The former, despite various forms of protection, has been particularly vulnerable to competition from developing-country exports and from higher-productivity plants in the US. Food-processing employment has contracted as a result of increased automation, hastened by corporate concentration and plant rationalization. Both sectors have been essentially oriented to the domestic Canadian market, which grew more slowly than Canada's international trade during the 1990s. The transportation industries of this gateway city were also shedding labour steadily during that decade. Nearly all of Montreal's traditional sectors of employment are situated in the inner areas of the CMA, where the employment rate throughout the 1990s was 10 percentage points below that in the outer suburban ring (Figure 5.3).

At the start of the 2000s, however, there are signs that the manufacturing sector in the Montreal economy is emerging from this long period of restructuring (Germain and Rose, 2000; Ville de Montréal, 2000). The clothing sector, though still probably

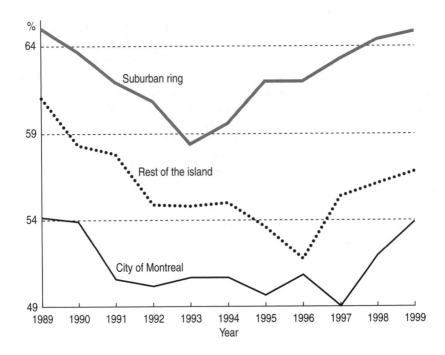

**Figure 5.3  Employment Rates in the Montreal CMA, 1989–1999**

SOURCE: Ville de Montréal (2000: 3).

contracting in employment (the use of subcontracting to organizers of recently immigrated female homeworkers makes precise data hard to come by), has increased its level of automation and its orientation to higher-value fashion items. It has also increased its level of exports, mainly to the United States. But the largest contribution to employment growth is coming from high-technology sectors that appear to have reached a critical mass in the Montreal region. Numerically these are led by the transportation equipment industry, which in Montreal is dominated by the aerospace sector (the local automobile assembly plant has a very uncertain future, see Chapter 7). The commercial success of the Bombardier series of 'Regional Jet' aircraft and of the aero-engine sector (notably Pratt & Whitney Canada) has resulted in steadily rising employment in the region. The electrical and electronic products sector has also prospered (note its marginal job loss between 1991 and 1996, compared to the Toronto figure quoted above: Table 5.3). Nortel, which employed around 7,000 people in the Montreal region at the end of the 1990s, has major telecommunications and fibre-optics R&D and production facilities.

Montreal's modest growth in service employment in the 1990s, certainly compared to Toronto, reflected the reduced role of the city as a business centre of national importance and its ties to a provincial economy that has been growing more slowly than the Canadian average. But the seepage of corporate jobs and influence away from the city towards centres in Anglophone Canada (see Chapter 2) has now largely run its course. Since the start of 2000, the Montreal Stock Exchange has been recast as Canada's centre for trading financial derivatives, and the city has attracted a Canadian satellite trading centre for the NASDAQ. Although in 1996 Montreal had only half the number of computer industry professionals as Toronto, the knowledge-based economy is expanding in a number of areas. Employment in the IT&T industry was claimed to have reached 83,000 in 2000, with multimedia and animation software a specialty. The city's long-time strength in medical research, aided by federal and provincial support for R&D by transnational drug firms, has been the basis of significant expansion in the pharmaceuticals and biotechnology sectors (Germain and Rose, 2000).

## STRATEGIES OF ADJUSTMENT

The long period of economic expansion that developed through the late 1990s has opened up new possibilities in most of Canada's metropolitan economies. But the forces of economic globalization and the consequences of continuous technological change mean that the challenges of economic restructuring will reappear in new forms in the future. Moreover, although all levels of government in Canada acted in the 1990s to reduce or eliminate their indebtedness (at the cost of many thousands of public-sector jobs), continuing support for neo-conservative political agendas suggests that fiscal constraint will continue to limit public-sector spending at all levels. In recent years, Canada's cities have faced major challenges in maintaining their prosperity and appeal as places to live, and growing socio-economic polarization is likely to create new problems. These difficulties are shared in other advanced industrial societies, and Harvey (1989b) has identified four strategies of response by city governments and other institutions.

The strategy most widespread in Canada has been for cities to increase their appeal as *centres of consumption*. This has prompted all the largest metropolitan areas to ensure, for instance, that they acquire a convention centre and related hotels to attract conferences and trade shows. Investment in cultural capital, such as galleries, museums, concert halls, and theatres, and in sports arenas and other crowd-drawers (including theme parks, and more recently, casinos) was particularly evident in the late 1980s and early 1990s. Toronto's Skydome and restored Pantages Theatre; the new National Gallery and Museum of Civilization in Ottawa–Hull; the Winter Olympic facilities in Calgary; Canada Place in Vancouver; and the West Edmonton Mall: these are all embodiments of the strategy to attract high-income residents and tourists. The restoration of distinctive heritage environments to provide an appealing ambience for affluent resident and visitor alike, as in Old Montreal, has been implemented at every level of the urban hierarchy. Waterfront redevelopment, made possible by the decline of conventional shipping and port-dependent industries, has been a particular focus, from St John's to Victoria and in communities of all sizes along the Great Lakes shoreline.

Two other strategies identified by Harvey have been less in evidence in Canada than in other countries. *Inter-metropolitan competition* to capture key managerial control functions in the public and private sectors is limited by the small number of cities realistically in contention and by the significance of provincial governments and their agencies as centres of power. Locational shifts in the distribution of corporate headquarters have more to do with global and national forces (notably affecting Montreal) than with the relative attractiveness of cities as urban environments. Rivalry between Calgary and Edmonton, for high-level service jobs and for air transport connections, has come closest to this form of competition. And *creation of a favourable business climate* is not a strategy by which Canadian urban centres can meaningfully distinguish themselves, primarily because so many of the relevant powers used by cities in the United States (such as tax abatement and bond issues) are restricted to the provincial level in Canada. But there is undoubtedly scope for local government and other institutions to earn a reputation for being proactive in support of economic development, as has been the case, for example, in Moncton in recent years.

Harvey's fourth strategy, which involves *urban centres exerting direct political pressure* to channel government spending into their locality, has declined in significance as public-sector budgets have shrunk. Cities facing high levels of unemployment, as Sudbury did in the early 1980s and as Sydney, NS, has done persistently, have successfully lobbied for government jobs. Other cities have benefited (not always permanently) by attracting government support for their dominant employer, as was the case in Brantford (formerly site of Massey-Ferguson's agricultural machinery production), Thunder Bay (maintaining what is now Bombardier's railcar plant), and Sault Ste Marie (orchestrating the survival of Algoma Steel Co.). In the 1990s, one of the 'prizes' that some cities fought for was the location of government-regulated casinos.

The multi-faceted nature of urban competitive advantage at the start of the twenty-first century is well summarized by the wide range of variables listed in Table 5.4. Some of the key attractors of economic activity, such as existing agglomerations of high-level service functions, research-intensive universities, and international air links, are confined to cities at the top of the metropolitan hierarchy, where Canadian cities compete with US rivals and not just with each other. But many aspects of urban communities are relevant at all levels of the hierarchy in influencing a city's economic appeal. Local institutional cultures of governance and in business, education, and environmental conservation, for instance, are important in creating an atmosphere open to economic initiative while valuing accumulated social and physical capital.

## Beyond the Metropolitan Areas

The 34 metropolitan centres in Canada with populations of 100,000 or greater (in 1996) contain approximately 66 per cent of the national population. The total urban population (in centres of 10,000 or more) constitutes 78 per cent of the national total. This still leaves almost one in four Canadians resident in rural or remote areas. Across a country as large as Canada, there is considerable variation in the economic health of these non-urban regions. Figure 8.4 reflects one typology that attempts to distinguish

**Table 5.4   The Structure of Urban Competitive Advantage:
Representative Capital Stocks and Systems**

| | |
|---|---|
| Environmental capital | Locating and siting |
| | Integrity of environmental capital stock |
| | Supply/quality of land |
| | Environmental amenity |
| Economic capital | Stock of production capital (factories, offices) |
| | Propulsive sectors, industries, and firms (including advanced services) |
| | Agglomerative clusters |
| | Indigenous multinational corporations and firms |
| | Supply of commercial and industrial land |
| | Local market conditions (efficiency, openness) |
| | Local income levels and saving rates |
| Physical capital (infrastructure) | Roads, railways, and other transportation systems |
| | Seaports and airports |
| | Public buildings |
| | Quality of the housing stock |
| Technological capital | Quality of local technological base |
| | Costs of technology |
| | Technology diffusion mechanisms |
| Human capital (labour force) | Labour productivity |
| | Embodied skills and expertise (including literacy and numeracy) |
| | Entrepreneurship |
| | Adaptability and attitudes |
| Social capital (population and community as a whole) | Quality of social organization (tolerance, equity, etc.) |
| | Community networks (socio-cultural agglomeration) |
| | Culture (beliefs, values, behaviours, and cultural capital) |
| | Leadership capital |
| | Strength of non-governmental organizations (NGOs) |
| | Health indices |
| Connectivity and communications | Air connections to international business centres |
| | Niche within trade networks (commodities, services) |
| | Diaspora networks |
| | Communications infrastructure and systems |
| | Internal metropolitan circulation (efficiency of transit systems) |
| Institutions, governance, and policy systems | Quality of educational institutions |
| | Efficiency of public institutions and agencies |
| | Integrity and openness of public institutions |
| | Responsiveness of policy systems |
| | Condition of local democracy |
| Quality-of-life and amenity capital | Access to health services |
| | Access to cultural and recreational amenity |
| | Personal security and safety |
| | Vitality of urban/community life |
| Identity capital and image | International image |
| | Uniqueness/distinctiveness of local culture, identity |
| | Community self-image and confidence |

SOURCE: Hutton (1998: 165).

their prospects. Many rural areas that lie within an hour's commuting distance of large cities have seen their population grow, as more urban residents move to cheaper housing and a preferred lifestyle in the country. More remote agricultural areas have generally suffered population decline. Resource-based communities in the hinterland have had mixed experiences; but whether positive or negative in terms of growth, instability has been typical. Fort McMurray, Alberta, is notable (and unusual) in seeing steady expansion associated with the development of the nearby oil-sands deposits. At the other extreme, places such as Schefferville, Quebec, and Uranium City, Saskatchewan, have closed down almost entirely as their profitable mineral resources have been exhausted. The collapse of the east coast fishery has left the economy and social fabric of many isolated communities in Atlantic Canada in a precarious state. On the Prairies, the rural-urban migration so evident in the 1950s and 1960s is no longer as prominent, but the concentration of agricultural and other service functions in a few favoured locations continues.

Demographic and cultural shifts are working to change the geography of settlement. The generation of Canadians that most benefited from the secure employment and reasonable earnings of the long postwar boom years have reached retirement age, and many are choosing to relocate to favoured environments, particularly in southern British Columbia, but also in pleasantly situated small towns in Ontario and Quebec, such as Bobcaygeon, on the Kawartha Lakes, and Nicolet, across the St Lawrence from Trois-Rivières (Bollman and Biggs, 1995). At the same time, many younger people, of a generation more identified with modern environmental values and more willing to find employment in non-traditional contexts, are also choosing to live in small communities. Telecommunications technology has given to certain categories of self-employed service workers (e.g., editors, software developers) the locational freedom to move to pleasant rural environments, such as Nova Scotia's South Shore or small-town southern Ontario (e.g., Elora). Overall, between 1986 and 1991, Canada's rural areas experienced a net influx of 289,000 people from urban areas (Bourne and Olvet, 1995). (Urban growth was thus significantly dependent on foreign immigrants, who tend to concentrate in the largest metropolitan areas.) But plenty of rural poverty still exists in hinterland regions of Canada, its economic effects accentuated by the out-migration of the better-educated members of the younger generation. Poverty exists, too, in parts of rural heartland Canada, sometimes in close proximity to high-amenity communities, such as in Ontario's Muskoka region. The influx of a considerably more affluent population tends to inflate real estate prices and push up the cost of living, creating economic hardship for local residents in low-income occupations (*Globe and Mail*, 22 May 2000).

## CONCLUSION

Worldwide, metropolitan regions are growing in importance as arenas of economic organization and governance in the era of globalization. This focuses the question of how well Canada's largest cities are equipped to fulfil their role. The constitutional framework allots metropolitan governments very limited powers, leaving them dependent on the unpredictable policy agendas and funding priorities of higher levels of government (primarily at the provincial level). Unfortunately, there is no immediate prospect of Canada's metropolitan areas gaining an increased capacity to govern themselves effectively as motors of the national economy, and so to better position themselves strategically with respect to their global competitors.

Nevertheless, Canada's economic output is increasingly originating from urban areas. More than anything else, this reflects the relative decline of the resource-based goods-producing industries and the rising contribution of knowledge-intensive service activities, which are disproportionately attracted to metropolitan communities. For example, between 1989 and 1998, the two fastest-growing industrial sectors were 'professional, scientific, and technical services' and 'management, administrative, and other support', which were together responsible for 41 per cent of net employment growth. Whereas census metropolitan areas attracted 66 per cent of net job growth nationally during this period, they accounted for 77 per cent of the increase in these two sectors (Statistics Canada, 1999a). Similar trends towards the localization of economic activity in urban areas are evident at lower levels of the settlement hierarchy, despite the potential of modern telecommunications to distribute earning opportunities in knowledge-based industries more widely. The following chapter analyses the geography of the service sector in more detail.

## FURTHER READING

Coffey, W.J. 2000. 'Canadian cities and shifting fortunes of economic development', in T. Bunting and P. Filion, eds, *Canadian Cities in Transition: The Twenty-First Century*, 2nd edn. Toronto: Oxford University Press, 121–50.

McCann, L, and J. Simmons. 2000. 'The core-periphery structure of Canada's urban system', in T. Bunting and P. Filion, eds, *Canadian Cities in Transition: The Twenty-First Century*, 2nd edn. Toronto: Oxford University Press, 76–96.

Randall, J.E., and R.G. Ironside. 1996. 'Communities on the edge: a geography of resource-dependent communities in Canada', *Canadian Geographer* 40: 17–35.

PART II

# SECTORS

# The Service Sector

## INTRODUCTION

Employment in the service sector of the Canadian economy surpassed that in the goods-producing sectors as long ago as the late 1950s. By 1996, almost three-quarters of all jobs and two-thirds of national GDP were generated by service-sector activity. This historic shift in the structure of the national economy parallels that experienced by other advanced industrial nations. The relative decline in the importance of the primary and secondary industries does not reflect a reduction in their overall output, but rather it points to the enormous increases in labour productivity that have been achieved by the application of technology to production processes in these sectors. In thousands of specific contexts—the mechanization and increased chemical-intensity of agriculture, the efficiencies of bulk mining and of modular building construction, the consequences of micro-processor applications throughout the manufacturing sector, the improved performance of transportation vehicles—the economy has been undergoing continuous transformation on a per-unit-of-output basis, enabling Canadians to 'do more with less', and particularly with fewer goods-production workers. Some of these gains have come at the expense of environmental externalities, which are now having to be accounted for (see Chapter 3), but most of them represent the benefits of applying new knowledge gained from investments in higher education, skills training, and scientific and industrial research and development (R&D).

Nevertheless, recognition of the importance of the service sector has been slow to develop, partly because of difficulties in deciding what it represents. Whereas the commodities produced in the goods-producing sector are readily identifiable and measurable (tons of wheat, numbers of cars or houses, etc.), the output of many services (e.g., primary education, police work, or nursing care) is much harder to tally. Moreover, computers, and the embedded intelligence they and their software represent, have greatly blurred the distinction between tangible and intangible commodities. This definitional problem is also emerging in the field of biotechnology, as genetic modification results in new organisms that incorporate the knowledge gained through research. As a result of these challenges to our understanding of how the economy is changing, the categories used to subdivide the service sector are not yet as consistent as those classifying the goods-producing sectors. The division into distributive, producer, public, and personal (or consumer) services has been widely used to capture basic differences in the character and orientation of activities, and is the one adopted

**Table 6.1   The Structure of the Service Sector**

| Dynamic Services |
| --- |
| Transportation, communications, and utilities |
|   Air, rail, and water transport |
|   Ground transportation |
|   Pipelines |
|   Storage and warehousing |
|   Broadcasting—radio, television, cable |
|   Telephone systems |
|   Postal and courier services |
|   Utilities—electricity, gas, water, and sewage systems |
| Wholesale trade |
| |
| Finance, insurance, and real estate |
|   Banks and trust companies |
|   Credit unions and mortgage companies |
|   Insurance companies |
|   Investment dealers |
|   Real estate operators |
| Business services |
|   Employment agencies |
|   Advertising services |
|   Architectural, scientific, engineering, and computing services |
|   Legal services |
|   Management consulting |

| Traditional Services |
| --- |
| Retail trade |
|   Food stores |
|   Drug stores and liquor stores |
|   Shoe and clothing stores |
|   Furniture, appliances, furnishings, and stereo stores |
|   Car dealers, gas stations, and auto repair shops |
|   Department stores |
|   Jewellery stores and photographic stores |
| Accommodation, food, and beverages |
|   Hotels, motels, and tourist courts |
|   Camping grounds and travel trailer parks |
|   Restaurants |
| |
| Amusement and recreation |
|   Motion picture, audio, and video production and distribution |
|   Motion picture exhibition |
|   Sports and recreation clubs and services |
|   Bowling alleys and billiard parlours |
| Personal services |
|   Barber and beauty shops |
|   Laundries and cleaners |
|   Funeral services |

**Table 6.1   The Structure of the Service Sector** *continued*

| Non-market Services | |
|---|---|
| Education services | Social services |
| Schools, colleges, and universities | Day care, meal services, and crisis centres |
| Libraries, museums, and archives | Psychologists and social workers |
| Health services | Religious organizations |
| Hospitals | Public administration |
| Doctors and dentists | |
| Medical laboratories | |

NOTE: This classification scheme is organized according to Statistics Canada's Standard Industrial Classification (1980).
SOURCE: Economic Council of Canada (1991: 9).

in this chapter. An alternative distinction between 'dynamic', 'traditional', and 'non-market' services is valuable in acknowledging differences in growth rates among subsectors of the service economy, their varying scope for being non-locally traded, and the varied nature of the management challenges they present (Table 6.1).

In the late 1990s, Statistics Canada, together with its counterparts in the United States and Mexico, introduced a new industrial classification system, the North American Industry Classification System (NAICS). One of the incentives to do so was that the categories of the existing Standard Industrial Classification (SIC), which had maintained its fundamental structure for decades, were increasingly unsatisfactory, primarily because they did not allow for an adequate representation of the now dominant and highly diverse service sector. At the time of writing, it is too soon for the results of this change to be apparent. The 1996 census, and analyses based on it, used the 1980 revision of SIC codes. Discussion here is therefore framed in terms of these categories. However, it is worth noting the structure of the NAICS division of the service sector (Table 6.2). Some elements are relatively unchanged, for instance, the Wholesale Trade (42) and Retail Trade (44–5) codes. But the newly defined Information sector (NAICS Code 51), which recognizes the importance of knowledge production and dissemination in the modern economy, brings together activities formerly found in many different parts of the SIC. For instance, among the industries it includes, newspaper and book publishing were coded as part of the manufacturing sector (where printing is still found); database publishing was coded under 'business service industries'; radio and television broadcasting were coded under 'communication and other utility industries'; film and video production were coded under 'other service industries'; and libraries were coded under 'educational service industries'.

There are many reasons why it is important to understand the evolution of the service sector. First is its sheer size, as measured by the proportion of all employment and output that it generates. Second, it is clear that different segments have very different characteristics, notably in terms of the qualifications they require and the incomes they generate, reflected in a 'good jobs, bad jobs' polarization (Economic Council of Canada, 1991). Third, a large proportion of service employment has traditionally been in the public sector. This component is undergoing profound change, as governments respond to fiscal pressures and shifting ideological currents, and so reshape the size, structure, and geography of their operations. Fourth, private-sector services also are changing rapidly, as national and global competition develops in industries that formerly enjoyed substantial spatial or regulatory protection in local, regional, or national markets. The role of technological innovation is paramount here, opening up entirely new opportunities such as e-commerce and Web-based education.

Underlying all these forces of change are two fundamental developments working themselves out within society and the economy. On the demand side, the growth of the service sector reflects the set of spending choices an affluent society makes. Having for the most part achieved security in meeting their basic material needs, people focus increasingly on goods and activities given value by their embodied human, rather than material, content. The shift from the mass-production economy of Fordism to the

**Table 6.2    North American Industry Classification System (NAICS)**

| | |
|---|---|
| 11 | Agriculture, forestry, fishing, and hunting |
| 21 | Mining |
| 22 | Utilities |
| 23 | Construction |
| 31–3 | Manufacturing |
| 41 | Wholesale trade |
| 44–5 | Retail trade |
| 48–9 | Transportation and warehousing |
| 51 | Information |
| 52 | Finance and insurance |
| 53 | Real estate and rental and leasing |
| 54 | Professional, scientific, and technical services |
| 55 | Management of companies and enterprises |
| 56 | Administrative and support, waste management, and remediation services |
| 61 | Educational services |
| 62 | Health care and social assistance |
| 71 | Arts, entertainment, and recreation |
| 72 | Accommodation and food services |
| 81 | Other services |
| 91 | Public administration |

*Source*: Statistics Canada <www.statcan.ca/english/Subjects/Standard/index.htm>.

differentiated and flexible economy of post-Fordism gives heightened value to features such as style, symbolism, and other expressions of cultural value. Hence, goods production requires an increasing array of knowledge- or information-intensive service activities. Increasing knowledge-intensity also characterizes employment in large sectors such as health care, education, and social and personal services, together with rapidly expanding financial, cultural, and recreational services. At the societal level, the *time-space convergence* of contemporary global capitalism puts an increasing premium on monitoring the current condition of global systems (economic, political, technological, cultural, etc.) and having the capacity to predict, or at least respond rapidly to, their constant shifts. Service employment that responds to these needs is at the core of the 'new economy'.

On the supply side, the rapid expansion of service employment has been fuelled by the increasing importance of expert knowledge, embodied in people and in the computer systems that they work with, in all sectors of the economy. A major contribution has resulted from the widespread horizontal and vertical disintegration of production by manufacturing firms. In pursuit of flexibility, corporations have outsourced not only many goods-producing activities but also a vast range of ancillary functions, from product design, personnel recruitment, and market research to transportation, office-cleaning, and catering. Jobs, therefore, that would formerly have been coded as belonging to the manufacturing sector if performed by the firms' own employees now are recorded within a 'service' category.

Geographical analysis of the service sector has traditionally drawn heavily on central place theory, which provides an appropriate but partial perspective. Much of the activity in the distributive, consumer, and social services is indeed closely tied to the distribution of population. Producer services, however, are disproportionately concentrated in the upper levels of the urban hierarchy. This is evident in Table 5.2, which indicates sectoral specialization in Canada's major cities. Among Canada's 10 largest metropolitan areas, retailing, education, and accommodation employment is approximately proportional to population, yet business service industries are clearly concentrated at the very top of the urban size hierarchy and financial and related services are only slightly less so. The distinctiveness of Ottawa–Hull and Quebec City as specialized centres of government is very clear; likewise, Winnipeg continues to specialize as a transportation gateway (more so, relatively, than does Montreal). The specializations of Calgary as administrative centre of the oil industry, of Hamilton as a manufacturing-oriented city, and of London as a major centre of health services are also apparent.

## DISTRIBUTIVE SERVICES

Retailing is the largest service subsector (11 to 13 per cent of all employment) in nearly every part of Canada except the territories (Tables 12.1, 13.2, 14.2, 14.5). Nevertheless, it shrank absolutely (by 50,000) and relatively (dropping from 12.9 to 12.0 per cent nationally) between 1991 and 1996, and in Manitoba was overtaken as the largest subsector by health services. The structure and spatial distribution of retailing have changed primarily at the regional and metropolitan levels as a result of population shifts and the dynamics of competition within different market segments (Jones, 2000). Half the nation's retail sales take place within the 10 largest metropolitan areas (Jones and Simmons, 1993). Within these, the geography of retailing has changed to reflect the increasing suburbanization of population and the power of the dominant retailing chains. Automobiles alone account for over one-third of the value of retail sales (or approximately half of non-food transactions).

Until the 1990s, the major retail chains grew by clustering their outlets in planned shopping centres, where they came to generate almost a quarter of all retail sales in Canada from only 8 per cent of store locations. Writing at that time, Jones and Simmons (1993: 55) noted that, 'Most of Canada's retail sales are carried out by a small number of chains (less than 200), operating in a small number of locations (less than 500), that are designed and controlled by a small number of developers (less than fifty).' The 1990s saw the end of that phase of retail expansion, however, and the emergence of the 'big-box' retailer (such as Home Depot and Future Shop), with large, free-standing stores at strategically accessible locations, primarily in outer suburban areas. Despite the overall dispersion of retailing from city cores, Canadian metropolitan centres retain substantial downtown shopping areas that in most cases have been developed or redeveloped as part of a tourist- and recreation-oriented extension of the inner urban economy (see Chapter 5). So far, Web-based retailing has captured only a very small share of the Canadian market and will impact different segments of the industry differentially.

Stores selling relatively intangible items, such as recorded music and travel services, will be threatened long before those marketing fashion clothing or general hardware.

In contrast to retailing, employment in the wholesale trade subsector grew between 1991 and 1996, increasing its share of all employment from 4.3 to 4.8 per cent. Relatively, it is slightly more important in the western provinces than in Atlantic Canada. Location quotients show that wholesale trade is concentrated in large cities (with some exceptions, such as Ottawa), but its relative importance is highest in more remote subregional centres such as Corner Brook, Newfoundland, and Brandon, Manitoba (Economic Council of Canada, 1991). The nature of wholesaling is changing as manufacturers and retailers in many subsectors streamline their operations to eliminate unnecessary goods handling. The supermarket chains that dominate food retailing and have become the most powerful shapers of this consumer market increasingly organize their own warehouse and distribution systems (Wallace, 1992). Big-box retailers have developed similar ways of minimizing the number of steps in the manufacturer-to-consumer delivery chain. The growth of e-commerce for tangible items, such as books, may reduce the importance of retail outlets, but it puts a premium on efficient wholesaling logistics.

Transportation-related service employment in Canada (4.0 per cent of all jobs) is predominantly associated with use of the road network. The trucking industry has steadily increased its share of the domestic freight market for non-bulk commodities, while the 1990s saw accelerated attrition of the railway workforce (see Chapter 11). Restructuring by the major oil companies has significantly reduced the number of service stations, but those remaining have become more multi-functional, adding small food and convenience stores, banking machines, etc. to their gas and oil sales. In many less densely populated areas, service stations have become the 'one-stop shopping' central place.

## PRODUCER SERVICES

There is no consistent definition of 'producer services', but their core is undoubtedly the knowledge-intensive 'business services'—the fastest growing component of the service sector in Canada since the 1970s. As noted above, some of this growth has come from the contracting out of specialized professional services by large manufacturing firms. But even more important are the close links between producer services and high-level corporate decision-making in every sector of the economy. The requirement for financial, legal, and communications specialists is growing, partly as a reflection of the increasingly wide-ranging scope of business decisions in a globalizing marketplace. Despite all the advances in telecommunications and Web-based linkages, the majority of high-level business service transactions involve regular face-to-face meetings, which help to establish networks of trust and shared understandings among the participants. This explains the geographical concentration of the business services sector in Canada's largest metropolitan centres.

In 1996, producer services provided 1,725,435 jobs in Canada, or 11.6 per cent of all employment. Business services accounted for just over half of these (54 per cent), having grown by almost 350,000, or 60 per cent, since 1986. In 1991, Toronto alone accounted for 26 per cent of business service employment, and that city, together with Montreal, Vancouver, and Ottawa, contained over 55 per cent of the national total (Coffey, 1994). The concentration of activity in these cities reflects more than simply the fact that they cluster around decision-makers at the highest levels of business and government in Canada. Economic globalization means that the expertise of Canadian management consultants, systems integrators, and project engineers is increasingly marketable around the world, so that access to major international airports, branches of foreign banks, and the community of foreign diplomatic and trade representatives in Canada becomes more critical (see Chapter 1).

The finance, insurance, and real estate (FIRE) sector is the other most commonly recognized component of producer services. This group differs, however, in that its operations span a broader range of markets, from financing corporate takeovers and undertaking major property developments to servicing student loans and assisting individual homebuyers. The FIRE sector thus combines elements of high-order business services and of lower-order retailing, and its geographical characteristics reflect this. Two-thirds of all employment in the sector is found in the 10 largest metropolitan areas (Toronto alone accounts for 25 per cent), but it is less concentrated in the top four, and the specialization of London in insurance and Quebec City in finance (caisses populaires) is apparent. At the other end of the central place hierarchy, many bank branches in rural areas have been closed, to be only partially replaced by ATMs (automatic teller machines) in gas stations or supermarkets. Much FIRE-sector employment is associated with routine data-processing (bookkeeping, claims handling, etc.) not requiring the central city location of experts and decision-makers. It represents back-office activity that has increasingly been located in the suburban areas of Toronto, Montreal, and Vancouver (which provide lower office and wage costs than the CBD and are more easily accessible by the typical workforce). With the spread of advanced telecommunications, this routine work is beginning to spread to small towns in rural areas where most operating costs are even lower.

## Public, Non-market Services

Definitions are not uniform for the public sector, which is here taken to comprise health, education, and social services, as well as public administration. In Canada (but not, for instance, in the United States) nearly all these activities are funded almost entirely from the public purse, although privatization and the encouragement of greater cost recovery from users means that the 'non-market' designation (Table 6.1) is not as applicable as formerly. Because of the centrality of these services to the functioning of the Canadian welfare state, they are large employers, with a tendency to expand as the population grows. In addition, Canada's demographic structure is such that health-care expenditures and employment are growing as the baby-boom population ages. On the other hand, the political and fiscal climate of the 1990s favoured reducing government expenditures and employment. These considerations underlie the different trajectories of employment in different subsectors. Despite the squeeze on health-sector spending, employment has continued to increase—by 1996 health services employment was the second-largest services category, after retailing, with 1.4 million jobs (9.5 per cent of the total). Education followed a similar pattern, but with a considerably slower growth rate between 1986 and 1996. Government services employment, however, having increased strongly between 1986 and 1991, shrank by 20 per cent in the next five years, to a total of 887,450 (6.0 per cent of all jobs). By 1996, only at the local government level was employment higher than a decade earlier.

Much of the work undertaken in the public services sector involves close contact with the population served (in schools, clinics, local government offices, etc.) and hence is geographically dispersed. Location quotients for teachers reflect this, varying relatively little within the central place hierarchy. But in rural areas with fairly stable or declining populations, there are ongoing pressures to close and consolidate small and scattered institutions, such as schools and hospitals. Higher-order services (such as colleges and universities, specialist medical treatment, and regional offices of higher levels of government) are more concentrated in larger urban centres, but not as markedly as are producer services. For instance, occupational data for health professionals indicate location quotients (where 100 would match the national average) in the 80–120 range among the largest metropolitan centres, and generally between 55 and 140 among smaller urban communities. Some of the highest location quotients for social service occupations are related to non-governmental organizations. Church-based institutions in small towns such as Prince Albert (Anglican Diocese of Saskatchewan) and Campbellton, New Brunswick (various Roman Catholic agencies) result in quotients of 246 and 408, respectively, for professional religious employment, compared to 83 in Montreal, for example (Economic Council of Canada, 1991).

Government administration at the federal and provincial levels includes a wide range of functions that correspond in character to those in the private sector. Many involve routine office jobs that do not demand close contact with the public, whereas others involve policy formation and strategic decision-making. Until the 1970s, there was a tendency for both types of activity to be concentrated in Ottawa and the provincial capitals, with additional employment in Montreal and Vancouver and some regional agencies in smaller centres. Improved telecommunications and networked office management systems, however, have enabled both levels of government to decentralize their operations and transfer jobs to less prosperous regions. The Maritimes benefited, for instance, from Ottawa's relocation of the Department of Veterans Affairs to Charlottetown and of routine functions associated with Employment Insurance to Bathurst, New Brunswick, and with the establishment of the Goods and Services Tax administrative centre at Summerside, PEI (see Chapter 12). Relocation of higher-level functions from Ottawa, motivated in part to bring government decision-makers closer to their private-sector counterparts, lay behind the Farm Credit Corporation's move to Regina and the National Energy Board's transfer to Calgary. At the provincial level, the Ontario government has used its power to locate public-sector employment in northern centres, such as Sudbury and Sault Ste Marie, to relieve regional unemployment and to support economic diversification (see Chapter 13), although privatization of some agencies has seen a net loss of such jobs in hinterland areas. In contrast, when the Manitoba government attempted to decentralize some of its operations from Winnipeg to smaller communities in the province, the plans had to be scaled down in the face of employee resistance to relocation. As noted in Chapter 2, employment by the Department of National Defence has always involved significant concentrations in peripheral regions, at locations with much less attraction to private-sector business, which is why base closures have always been politically charged decisions (see Figure 2.2).

## PERSONAL SERVICES

The services grouped under this heading include *personal* services per se, such as beauty salons and funeral homes, as well as the recreation and hospitality (hotels and restaurants) subsectors. As noted above, the SIC categories include quite heterogeneous activities, which should become better defined now that the NAICS codes are being adopted. Many of the businesses in this sector are associated with a retail environment, and have a geographical distribution to match. Others, such as hotels with convention facilities, merge into business services. What gives some conceptual unity to this group is that the majority of the services are purchased with discretionary income. Overall, the sector has seen rapid growth since the 1950s as a result of a rise in the living standards of Canadians. Despite the stagnation of real incomes for many people in the 1990s, the spending power of higher-income earners and the growing volume of retirement income becoming available have meant continued expansion of leisure-market services, especially those related to recreational travel and tourism.

In aggregate, personal and leisure services are broadly distributed across the country and throughout the urban hierarchy. Of the top 10 metropolitan areas, only Vancouver showed a mild specialization in 1991. But the markets for some of these services are certainly more geographically concentrated, even if this is not always easy to demonstrate from available data. Both at a regional scale (e.g., the communities servicing the Banff National Park, Prince Edward Island, and the Muskoka region in Ontario) and at a local or urban scale (e.g., Peggy's Cove, Nova Scotia, and Ontario's Stratford and Niagara-on-the-Lake) there are economies in which employment is primarily or significantly dependent on tourist-related activity. Much of this exhibits pronounced seasonal variation, with associated problems of underutilized capital and many temporary jobs. Where resources and imagination permit, development of year-round business provides greater economic stability, as in the Magog/Mount Orford, Quebec area, with its winter skiing, summer water-based recreation and arts festival programs, and its fall foliage attractions.

## TOURISM

Tourism as a major industry draws together a wide range of services. It continues to grow rapidly in Canada, as it does globally. Analysis of its characteristics is complicated by the intensely varied and fragmented nature of its components (including hotels, restaurants, car rental, retailing, museums, etc.) and by its multi-functional attributes (sales, for example, are rarely confined to the travel and tourism sector). Statistics

Canada (2000d) has begun to compile satellite tourism accounts in an effort to better chart the dynamics of the sector. In 1999, tourism receipts in Canada totalled just over $100 billion and the sector employed 524,300 people. Transportation accounts for 44 per cent of domestic tourism expenditures (over one-third of this amount consists of vehicle fuel) and the food and beverage sector 34 per cent. Accommodation accounts for under 8 per cent of expenditures but 27 per cent of tourist sector employment, equal to the size of the food and beverage labour force.

Recreational travel and tourism are forms of discretionary spending, and so their level of activity tends to reflect broad trends in consumer confidence. Canadians have habitually been active as international travellers, reflecting their general affluence by world standards and hence their capacity to travel for recreation abroad, and also their high level of immigrant origin, which specifically promotes travel to visit friends and relatives overseas. At the same time, Canada's dominant travel and tourism flows, in both directions, are with the United States. Many Canadians regularly travel south to escape some or all of the winter, a practice that helps to explain the perennial deficit on Canada's international travel account. Although the falling value of the Canadian dollar in recent years has moderated growth in Canadians' cross-border travel, it has had the predictable effect of encouraging more rapid growth in visits from the US (Statistics Canada, 2000d, 2000e).

Domestic recreational travel (measured as a minimum of one overnight non-business trip) is engaged in by two-thirds of the Canadian population, with the highest rate (in 1997) by residents of Saskatchewan (84 per cent) and the lowest by residents of Quebec (58 per cent). Canadian residents generate 79 per cent of all overnight trips, Americans 16 per cent, and overseas visitors 5 per cent. The 10 most popular destination regions together account for just under half of all trips (Figure 6.1). They include major metropolitan areas (Toronto, Montreal, Quebec City), areas close to major urban centres noted for their rural and cultural attractions (Festival Country, which includes Niagara Falls and Stratford in Ontario), and areas such as southwestern BC, which offers both urban attractions (Vancouver) and the seasonal recreational opportunities (especially skiing) of Whistler.

Visitors from the United States constitute between 70 and 80 per cent of foreign visitors in every province, except for Quebec and Alberta, where they make up approximately 60 per cent. Among overseas visitors, there are some distinct variations in the geography and institutional structure of travel (Table 6.3). The United Kingdom is the origin of the largest group of travellers, among whom visitors of friends and relatives are prominent. This helps to account for the particularly large share of visits attracted to Ontario. Visitors from Germany, on the other hand, while visiting Canada for a similar length of time and spending a similar amount per day as the British, are considerably more attracted to Atlantic Canada and Quebec. They are also much more interested in visiting the Yukon (where the territory's tourism Web site includes pages in German). The regional distribution of German visitors reflects the particular appeal of the Canadian outdoors to tourists from this market. Alberta and British Columbia together account for just over 40 per cent of both British and German tourist visits,

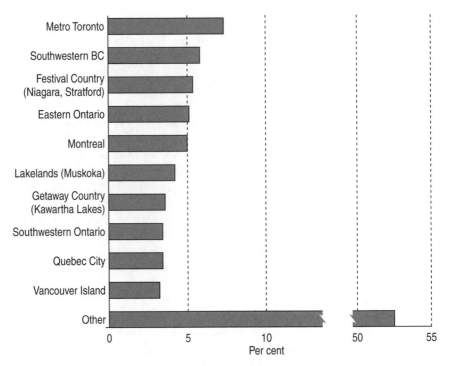

**Figure 6.1  Distribution of Visits to the Top 10 Tourism Regions, 1997**

SOURCE: Statistics Canada (2000e: 68).

testifying to the wide international appeal of the Banff–Vancouver–Whistler tourist regions. This is the regional focus to an even greater extent of visitors from Japan, whose tourism in Canada is highly organized by the travel industry. Six-day package tours taking in Vancouver, Banff, and Toronto/Niagara Falls are dominant for Japanese tourists, the second-largest nationality group of visitors to Canada after the British (Edgington, 1998).

## CONCLUSION

As the largest sector in the Canadian economy, services are commanding increasing attention from geographers. Applications of geomatics play a crucial role in the analysis of most issues facing service providers. It is true that in many respects, both spatially and hierarchically, the distribution of service activity conforms to that of the national urban system. However, significant variation exists between communities of similar size in the relative importance of particular activities, and we need to understand better what factors account for this. Moreover, as tourism illustrates well, service activities are by no means confined to urban settings. Much of hinterland Canada has been associated traditionally with a single dominant goods-producing industry,

**Table 6.3    Foreign Tourism in Canada, Selected Statistics, 1999**

|  | UK | Germany | Japan |
|---|---|---|---|
| Visits (000) | 780.3 | 392.5 | 516.1 |
| Average length of stay (nights) | 11.2 | 13.1 | 6.2 |
| Average spending per day ($) | 101.2 | 93.3 | 179.1 |
| *Regional share of visits (%)* | | | |
| Atlantic | 9.7 | 16.7 | 2.0 |
| Quebec | 8.3 | 12.4 | 9.1 |
| Ontario | 36.7 | 23.0 | 30.5 |
| Manitoba/Saskatchewan | 3.7 | 3.2 | 1.9 |
| Alberta | 17.1 | 18.8 | 20.5 |
| British Columbia | 23.7 | 22.1 | 34.3 |
| Yukon | 0.6 | 3.8 | 1.7 |

SOURCE: Calculated from Canadian Tourism Commission data at <www.canadatourism.com/en/ctc/tourismresources/research/researchms.cfm>.

such as agriculture or forestry, but as various pressures are reshaping employment in these sectors, household 'pluriactivity' (involving a mix of service and/or goods-producing activities) is becoming more widespread.

For many years, academic thinking and government regional policy favoured manu-facturing over service employment (see Chapter 2). This reflected a sense that manu-facturing production was 'basic' to a local economy, for its products were shipped away and brought income into the community, whereas service employment was 'non-basic', in that it supplied local needs and essentially circulated income within the community. This had some validity when applied to remote, resource-based, single-industry towns, of which Canada has many. But the capacity to bring income into a community is in fact a feature of a wide range of services, whether provided by individuals from their homes over the Internet or by specialized businesses that attract a national or interna-tional clientele (including educational establishments, tourist and conference facilities, and non-local government agencies). Whether in metropolitan or hinterland settings, therefore, the service sector is as much capable of linking the global economy to the local as is manufacturing industry, the focus of the next chapter.

## FURTHER READING

Coffey, W.J. 1996. 'The role and location of service activities in the Canadian space economy', in J.N.H. Britton, ed., *Canada and the Global Economy: The Geography of Structural and Technological Change*. Montreal and Kingston: McGill-Queen's University Press, 335–51.

Janelle, D.G. 2001. 'Globalization, the Internet economy, and Canada', *Canadian Geographer* 45: 48–53.

Jones, Ken. 2000. 'Dynamics of the Canadian Retail Environment', in T. Bunting and P. Filion, eds, *Canadian Cities in Transition: The Twenty-First Century*, 2nd edn. Toronto: Oxford University Press, 404–22.

# Post-Staples Manufacturing

## INTRODUCTION

Canada's natural resource staples have given rise, as noted in previous chapters, to the emergence of major resource processing industries, such as pulp and paper production, food processing, and steel manufacturing. These forward linkages have increased the value-added derived in Canada from natural resource exploitation and have contributed to spreading the availability of manufacturing employment beyond the largest metropolitan centres. Because of the generally close association, geographically and functionally, between manufacturing and the resource base in these industries, their locational characteristics are analysed together in the sectoral chapters that follow (Chapters 8–10). The principal focus of the present chapter, therefore, is those sectors of Canadian manufacturing that represent the 'post-staples economy', sectors that became prominent during the second half of the twentieth century on the basis of Canada's strengths as a high-income country (and therefore a major market) or as a centre of highly educated labour (and hence a source of technological innovation). The growth of the automobile industry, and more recently of the telecommunications and aerospace sectors, typifies these expressions of Canada's contemporary industrial dynamism. Such sectors have contributed most to diversifying the country's manufactured exports beyond those of its traditional staples-based industries.

Outside of the export-oriented, resource-processing sectors, the growth of Canada's manufacturing industries took place behind the protective tariffs of the National Policy. As noted in Chapter 1, this promoted a technologically dependent branch-plant economy rather than one characterized by internationally competitive domestic firms (Britton and Gilmour, 1978). Even in the agricultural, forest products, and minerals sectors, where the growth of staple commodity production might have been expected to encourage the emergence of innovative domestic suppliers of capital equipment (backward linkages), US or European firms generally captured the market. As a result, until the 1960s, most Canadian manufacturing outside of the resource-processing industries was characterized by relatively small-scale, low-productivity operations producing relatively little that was internationally competitive. The few Canadian transnational manufacturing firms that had become established, such as Massey-Harris in farm equipment, engaged in direct investment and production in foreign markets more than in sourcing exports of machinery from Canada.

The growth of international trade in the 1950s and 1960s, stimulated by reductions in tariff barriers between industrialized countries, revealed the weakness of an economy structured like Canada's (Australia faced comparable challenges). One strategic response undertaken by the federal government was to negotiate the Canada–United States Auto Pact, which took effect in 1965. The essence of the Auto Pact and its related agreements was that, in return for guaranteeing a given amount of industrial activity in Canada, the major North American auto manufacturers would be able to rationalize their production systems on a continental basis. Instead of operating 'miniature replica' plants in Canada that turned out a full range of models to satisfy Canadian consumer demand almost entirely from domestic sources, but in uneconomically small numbers, the Big Four auto manufacturers were permitted to specialize production at each auto plant and to ship different models across the border in either direction duty-free. As a result, the volume of auto trade (including exports from Canadian assembly plants) expanded enormously.

Increasing globalization of the world economy in the 1970s and 1980s put a premium on the manufacture of internationally competitive products, and for a high-wage economy such as Canada that meant goods that captured markets on the basis of their advanced technology rather than their low prices. One difficulty of adapting to these new conditions was that a truncated branch-plant economy was relatively lacking in the knowledge-intensive research and development, design, and strategic marketing functions that are the contemporary sources of innovation and that transnational corporations habitually maintain in their home country. This 'weakest link' (Britton and Gilmour, 1978) had resulted in the technological underdevelopment of Canadian industry and, together with corporate policies that sometimes restricted the export of Canadian goods (Williams, 1983), it threatened a steady increase in Canada's trade deficit in high-technology manufactures.

However, a number of developments since the early 1980s have resulted in a better record of innovation and international competitiveness in Canadian industry, both in manufactured products and in the important knowledge-intensive producer services that are increasingly associated with them. In this respect, Canada can be said to have been relatively successful in negotiating the transition from 'Fordist' to 'post-Fordist' manufacturing (see Chapter 4). But in the context of debates about the power of the national state in an era of globalization (see Chapter 1), it is worth noting that in Canada the role of the federal government has been very important. More than in other advanced industrial countries, R&D spending in Canada has depended on government sources (Britton, 1996). The government's role in creating institutional arrangements that have encouraged the expansion of manufacturing has also been crucial, as evidenced in the automotive sector (through the Auto Pact), the aerospace sector (through technology-sharing 'offset agreements' with US firms supplying military equipment in the 1970s and 1980s), and in telecommunications equipment manufacturing (through government-supported R&D). By the beginning of the twenty-first century, many of these supportive mechanisms had become problematic, as the international trade regime promoted by the WTO increasingly limits the scope for national governments to act in ways that are deemed to subsidize their exporters.

The federal government's pursuit since the mid-1980s of expanded free trade agreements, globally and especially within North America (NAFTA), has been presented as a step towards stimulating Canada's more competitive industrial sectors or firms and accelerating the decline of less competitive ones. The impact of free trade has, of course, been selective. Given the branch-plant character of so much of Fordist-era manufacturing in Canada, a lot has depended on how transnational corporations have treated their subsidiaries. Some have encouraged product specialization and a reduction of 'truncation' by allocating 'world product mandates' that have given the Canadian subsidiary exclusive responsibility for developing and producing certain lines of equipment for global distribution (e.g., Pratt & Whitney: aero engines; Black & Decker: small appliances). That same strategy, in other instances, has led to the closure of Canadian operations in favour of supplying domestic demand with products from foreign plants. But the dominance of large transnational firms has been reduced by the emergence of many smaller Canadian firms that have developed international markets for knowledge-intensive products and services created at home. Some of these firms have grown to be major players in their respective business sectors globally and they represent the leading edge of Canadian manufacturing in the 'post-Fordist' era.

Examples are especially evident in the telecommunications and computer software industries (firms such as Nortel Networks, JDS Uniphase, and Cognos), but they are also found in the transportation sector (e.g., Magna: auto parts; Bombardier: aircraft and railway equipment). Even in cases where successful Canadian high-technology firms have lost their independence to larger corporations (e.g., the takeover of Ottawa-based Newbridge by the French transnational Alcatel), the Canadian operation has invariably retained its research and innovation capacity, and in that respect the consequences have been much more positive for employment and national innovative capacity than was the case when truncated Fordist branch plants were the norm. Data from the 1990s suggest that firms that are active exporters, whether Canadian-owned or foreign subsidiaries, have similar propensities to be involved in R&D, and that in mature industrial sectors, such as food-processing and textiles, foreign-owned firms tend to have a stronger record than domestic ones (Baldwin and Hanel, 2000).

## MANUFACTURING OVERVIEW

Since the mid-1960s, the goods-producing sectors of the Canadian economy have shrunk in relative importance, in line with those in other advanced industrial countries. Whereas in 1966 they accounted for 45 per cent of GDP and 43 per cent of total employment, their share had dropped to 35 per cent and 26 per cent, respectively, in 1996 (Table 7.1). The top half of Table 7.1 groups those industries that harvest, extract, or process natural resources. These may be regarded as the 'staples-based' elements of the modern Canadian economy, although their output is by no means totally committed to export markets, as will be evident from the discussion in the following chapters. The agri-food and minerals and mineral-processing industries have seen quite a pronounced decline in their national economic importance, with their share of both GDP and employment shrinking by almost one-half during the 30-year period to 1996.

**Table 7.1   Share of GDP and Employment by Industry Group, 1966–1996**

| | 1966 | | 1976 | | 1986 | | 1996 | | Change in share, 1966–96 | |
|---|---|---|---|---|---|---|---|---|---|---|
| | GDP | Employment | GDP | Employment | GDP | Employment | GDP | Employment | GDP | Employment |
| Agri-food | 9.0 | 10.8 | 6.4 | 7.0 | 5.4 | 6.5 | 4.5 | 5.5 | 50.0 | 50.9 |
| Forest products | 5.6 | 5.2 | 4.8 | 4.4 | 4.5 | 3.8 | 4.9 | 3.5 | 87.5 | 67.3 |
| Mineral products | 7.6 | 5.4 | 5.6 | 4.5 | 4.4 | 3.3 | 3.9 | 2.8 | 51.3 | 51.9 |
| Fuel & energy | 4.3 | 1.0 | 6.4 | 1.1 | 7.2 | 1.3 | 6.9 | 1.2 | 160.5 | 120.0 |
| Chemical products | 2.3 | 1.6 | 1.8 | 1.6 | 2.1 | 1.5 | 2.5 | 1.4 | 108.7 | 87.5 |
| *Subtotal* | *28.8* | *24.0* | *25.0* | *18.6* | *23.6* | *16.4* | *22.7* | *14.4* | *78.8* | *60.0* |
| Textiles & clothing | 2.1 | 3.3 | 1.5 | 2.5 | 1.2 | 1.8 | 0.8 | 1.2 | 38.1 | 36.4 |
| Electrical products | 1.8 | 1.7 | 1.3 | 1.4 | 1.2 | 1.1 | 1.1 | 0.8 | 61.1 | 47.1 |
| Machinery & equipment | 1.8 | 1.6 | 1.3 | 1.4 | 1.3 | 1.3 | 1.3 | 1.3 | 72.2 | 81.3 |
| Transportation equipment | 2.4 | 2.1 | 2.2 | 1.9 | 2.4 | 2.0 | 3.3 | 1.9 | 137.5 | 90.5 |
| Misc. goods | 0.7 | 0.9 | 0.6 | 0.9 | 0.5 | 0.8 | 0.6 | 0.7 | 85.7 | 77.8 |
| *Subtotal* | *8.8* | *9.6* | *6.9* | *8.1* | *6.6* | *7.0* | *7.1* | *5.9* | *80.7* | *61.5* |
| Construction | 7.7 | 9.0 | 8.4 | 8.3 | 6.1 | 6.2 | 5.0 | 5.9 | 64.9 | 77.8 |
| GOODS PRODUCING | 45.3 | 42.6 | 40.3 | 35.0 | 36.3 | 29.6 | 34.8 | 26.2 | 76.8 | 61.5 |
| SERVICES | 54.7 | 57.4 | 59.7 | 65.0 | 63.7 | 70.4 | 65.2 | 73.8 | 119.2 | 128.6 |

SOURCE: Compiled from Statistics Canada (2000c: Tables 4.2.1 and 4.2.2).

The fuel and energy sector, in contrast, has experienced significant relative growth on both measures. The forest-based industries have maintained close to 90 per cent of their contribution to GDP while shedding one-third of their share of employment, and the chemical industries show a similar pattern of above-average productivity improvement, increasing their share of GDP while decreasing their share of employment.

The bottom half of Table 7.1 groups those manufacturing sectors that are not based on the processing of Canada's natural resource staples. They include a few traditional industries, such as textiles and clothing, which represented a 'final demand linkage' of the national staples economy, whose share of GDP and employment dropped almost two-thirds over the 30 years to 1996; but they are for the most part sectors that grew significantly during the expansionary period of Canadian postwar Fordism or that have developed more recently on the basis of high-technology innovation. These are the industries that most clearly justify the 'post-staples' label of this chapter. One notes how comparatively limited their overall contribution (as conventionally measured) to the national economy appears to be. Excluding the construction industry and the resource-based industries from the overall goods-producing sector, post-staples manufacturing industries constituted under 10 per cent of national output and employment in 1966, and they provided only 7 per cent of GDP and 6 per cent of employment in 1996.

However, rather than interpreting this as evidence that manufacturing is relatively unimportant to Canada's prosperity in the era of globalization, economic specialization, and the 'knowledge economy', it is good to consider some of the issues that lie behind it. One has to do with the increasing fuzziness of the line between 'manufacturing' and 'services' (see Chapter 4). To what extent does goods production create demands for high-level professional employment beyond the 'manufacturing' sector, and thus have a greater economic impact than the data in Table 7.1 suggest? Another question has to do with Canada's commodity trade balance (Table 1.2). The large deficit on 'machinery and equipment' poses a continuing challenge to a high-wage country, whose comparative advantage must lie in knowledge-intensive production, to increase its capacity to design and manufacture innovative capital goods. The relative lack of a domestic machine-building culture has been shown to handicap many Canadian manufacturers (Gertler, 1995b). A related consideration is the role of the manufacturing sector in providing a broad range of occupational opportunities, especially when a major consequence of the industrial restructuring since the 1980s has been the 'hollowing out' of many semi-skilled blue-collar jobs. The institutional structures of the Canadian labour market, involving the attitudes of corporations, labour unions, and governments towards training and skill formation, have not been as well focused on promoting a dynamic manufacturing sector as they might have been (Rutherford, 1998).

## CANADA'S PLACE IN THE NORTH AMERICAN AUTO INDUSTRY

The Canada–US Auto Pact was not a 'free trade' agreement. (It was phased out in 2001, as its provisions were ruled to contravene WTO regulations by favouring particular corporations.) More accurately, the Auto Pact was an example of 'managed' trade, because it comprised specific commitments by the corporations and governments involved. When it was inaugurated, in 1965, the North American auto market was effectively self-contained—imports from overseas accounted for less than 8 per cent of total sales, so it was feasible for the four dominant firms to restructure their production on a continental basis (Mexico was not functionally or politically part of 'North America' at that time). Ford, General Motors, Chrysler, and American Motors (subsequently absorbed by Chrysler) were thus able to maintain their market dominance while meeting the policy objectives of the Canadian government. These were primarily to ensure that auto production, and the jobs and spinoffs accompanying it, expanded in Canada in proportion to the growth of the Canadian market, and that Canadian consumers reaped the benefits of cheaper vehicles made possible by long production runs of each model.

Ontario has been by far the greatest beneficiary of the Pact, as the vast majority of auto industry plants are located between Windsor and Oshawa (Figure 7.1). Quebec acquired one assembly plant (General Motors at Ste Thérèse, near Montreal) in 1967. Given the comparative cost structures of Canadian and US production, which reflect exchange rate and social benefit (especially health insurance) differentials, the Big Three automakers have invested most heavily in Canada in labour-intensive operations, including final assembly plants and lower value-added parts, rather than in more capital-intensive plants producing engines or drive-train components, which are concentrated south of the border (Holmes, 1992). In 1997, employment in the Canadian motor vehicle and auto parts subsectors totalled almost 163,000, of which 135,000 jobs were in Ontario and only 6,500 in Quebec. The proportion of jobs in vehicle assembly as opposed to parts plants has been shifting in favour of the latter, as the major auto firms increasingly outsource larger components or sub-assemblies to their leading suppliers. Between 1992 and 1997, motor vehicle employment in Ontario dropped by 9 per cent, to 44,000, whereas auto parts employment increased by 17 per cent, to 91,000. Employment in the truck (including trailers) and bus subsector (17,500 in 1997) is more widely distributed across the country, with significant activity in the West, as well as in Ontario and Quebec.

The North American auto market was transformed during the 1970s by the enormous expansion of imports, primarily from Japan. Building on their initial price advantage, these imports soon gained a reputation for better quality and fuel economy than domestic vehicles (in a decade when the world oil price rose by a factor of four). By the early 1980s imports accounted for almost a quarter of new car sales in North America. The Big Three found it hard to adjust to the intensified competition, and Chrysler almost went out of business. Auto industry employment shrank in both Canada and the United States, but more so in the US (by 29 per cent, 1979–82, versus 21 per cent in Canada) (Clark, 1986). The US government responded to the crisis by pressuring the Japanese automakers to accept 'voluntary' export restraints (VERs), but these served to precipitate the strategic decision by the Japanese automakers to secure their future in the North American market by investing in production facilities there (so-called 'transplant' operations). The Canadian government used trade regulations

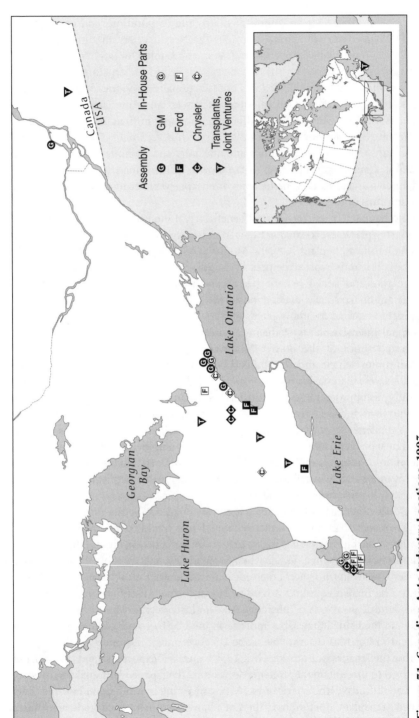

**Figure 7.1  Canadian Auto Industry Locations, 1993**

SOURCE: Holmes (1996: 233).

that were compatible with the Auto Pact to encourage the location of some of these plants in Canada (Holmes, 1992). Significantly, the communities chosen by Japanese firms, while in southwestern Ontario, were ones without a tradition of employment in the auto sector (Alliston: Honda, Cambridge: Toyota, Ingersoll: Cami, a GM and Suzuki joint venture). This matched the locational choice of 'transplants' in the United States and was a geographical expression of the different pattern of labour relations that distinguished the Japanese auto producers from the Fordist model pioneered in Detroit. A prime objective was the recruitment of a younger, non-unionized workforce that could be trained in the more flexible and team-oriented work practices pioneered in Japan's domestic auto sector. A similar non-traditional location (Bromont) was picked by the Korean firm, Hyundai, for the auto assembly plant it opened (with provincial financial incentives) in Quebec in 1987, but that closed within six years after recording disappointing sales.

By the late 1990s the geography of the Canadian auto industry appeared to have stabilized, although it would be rash to claim permanently so. Because the Auto Pact had long permitted the cross-border rationalization of the industry, the signing of the FTA in 1988 had little impact on it. However, the incorporation of Mexico into the functioning of the North American economy, which had been gradually increasing prior to the formal creation NAFTA, does have potentially major implications for the Canadian auto sector. Canada has ceased to be the relatively least-cost location for labour-intensive operations within the continental industry. Many factors suggest the geography of production will not change much in the near future: the close integration of the Canadian and US production systems of the Big Three, the firms' continuing substantial investments in plant modernization in Canada, and the size of the Canadian auto market. However, pressures to be competitive with the cost structure of Mexican production will likely intensify, especially should the Canadian dollar exchange rate strengthen. The most labour-intensive elements of Canada's auto parts sector (items such as seats and wiring assemblies) are particularly vulnerable (MacLachlan, 1992). Some US firms have already moved production from Canada to Mexico, and Magna, the Ontario-based transnational, has opened its first Mexican plant to supply that country's expanding auto assembly operations.

The global restructuring of the automobile industry is not driven only by relative wage levels. Part of the transformation of the corporate culture of the North American Big Three brought about by Japanese competition, and characteristic of the 'transplant' auto plants, has been the adoption of production practices that enhance productivity and quality assurance. One is the preference for co-operative and long-term relationships with major suppliers, on whom more responsibility is placed for research and design of materials and components (Rutherford, 2000). Another is the adoption of 'lean' production, requiring that suppliers provide frequent, 'just-in-time' deliveries directly to the assembly line instead of bulk shipments that require warehousing prior to use. Both of these developments have favoured the clustering of suppliers within easy access of major auto assembly plants. Southwestern Ontario has benefited from these trends, although not as extensively as US regions to the south. But continuing investment in Canada by the Big Three (GM at its Oshawa Autoplex, Ford at Oakville, and Chrysler at Windsor and Bramalea), as well as expansion by the Japanese manufacturers at Cambridge (Toyota) and Alliston (Honda), suggests that there will continue to be a significant market for parts suppliers located in Ontario. A number of parts plants are also located in Quebec and British Columbia. The only major employer associated with the auto industry in Atlantic Canada is Michelin, the tire company that established three plants in Nova Scotia in the 1970s and early 1980s, most of whose output is shipped to the United States. These were attracted by substantial federal regional development incentives and controversial amendments to provincial labour legislation; like the Japanese auto plants, they are located in small towns (Pictou, Bridgewater, Waterville) without a tradition of union activism.

## THE AEROSPACE INDUSTRY

The global aerospace industry has been shaped since World War II by the defence spending of the major military superpowers, each supporting their domestic industry, and the steady concentration of the civilian aircraft market in the hands of a few dominant firms, notably Boeing (US), and Airbus Industrie (France/UK/Germany/Spain). Canadian defence spending since the Korean War has not been adequate to sustain leading-edge military aerospace manufacturing (symbolized by cancellation of the Avro Arrow in 1959). The federal government has endeavoured, instead, to gain access to state-of-the-art technology and production techniques by tying major military purchases, usually from US suppliers, to 'offset agreements' that provide for subcontracting and technology transfer to Canadian firms. For instance, the CF-18 fighter contract in the 1980s was a major source of contracts. Most of the Canadian aerospace industry is oriented towards civilian production (Anderson, 1995). Part consists of branch plants of leading US firms, with mandates to manufacture particular subassemblies of major products, such as the Toronto plant of McDonnell-Douglas (part of Boeing) supplying wings for various McDonnell-Douglas airliners. The Canadian operations of Pratt & Whitney, whose main complex is in Montreal, supply a range of engines. Other firms, both foreign and domestic, specialize in avionics equipment, including the Montreal-based firm, CAE, which is a world leader in flight simulators. Toronto-based Spar Aerospace, whose 'Canadarm' was part of the US space shuttle equipment, was the leading Canadian firm in the space sector in the 1980s, but it left that market when reduced US spending prompted corporate consolidation in the space sector in the 1990s.

The Canadian aerospace industry has been sustained over the years by various forms of state support, including ownership, particularly at times when major foreign firms have proposed closing their Canadian operations. Since 1986, however, Bombardier, which started life in the Eastern Townships of Quebec as a snowmobile manufacturer, has grown into a dominant second-tier global aircraft producer, partly by astute purchases of firms that governments (notably in Canada and Britain) wished to sell as going concerns. Building, for instance, on the STOL (short takeoff and landing) technology embodied in the de Havilland 'Dash' series aircraft, made in Toronto, and on the executive jet developed by Canadair (Montreal), Bombardier has success-fully developed and marketed Canadian products that do not compete with the larger passenger aircraft of Boeing and Airbus and which have met the growing interest of airlines worldwide for short- to medium-distance jets. Employment in the aerospace sector is concentrated in the Montreal and Toronto regions. It is one of the few high-technology sectors in which Quebec has greater employment than Ontario (22,300 versus 13,800 in 1997). Winnipeg is the other major centre of the industry (3,800 employees in Manitoba), and just over 1,200 employees are found in each of Nova Scotia, Alberta, and British Columbia.

### TELECOMMUNICATIONS, COMPUTER EQUIPMENT, AND RELATED INDUSTRIES

Until quite recently, the telecommunications industry was the only high-technology sector in which a Canadian firm had achieved global prominence. Nortel Networks (formerly Northern Telecom) is one of the leading transnational corporations in this industry, a position towards which it grew largely on the basis of being initially a subsidiary of Bell Canada, to whom it was a monopoly supplier of equipment. Bell and Northern both began life as subsidiaries of American firms but, partly in response to antitrust suits in the United States against their parents, they became independent Canadian firms early in the twentieth century. However, Northern remained techno-logically dependent on its former parent until 1956 (Niosi, 1985). In 1958, Bell and Northern established a joint research unit, Bell-Northern Research (BNR), which opened its laboratories in Ottawa in the late 1960s. Innovations in digital technology at BNR provided Northern with leading-edge products that fuelled the company's growth and international expansion in the 1970s. Much of that growth came in the United States, where Northern opened over 20 manufacturing plants and established a major R&D laboratory in North Carolina's 'Research Triangle'. This pattern of expan-sion in large foreign markets, typical of many manufacturing transnationals, meant that Northern's employment growth in Canada did not match its growth in corporate sales, which concerned some nationalist critics of that era. But BNR contributed much more strategically to the expansion of Canada's high-technology sector by serving as an 'incubator' for personnel who left it to start up independent firms in the telecom-munications and computer industries, especially in the Ottawa area.

'Silicon Valley North', as promoters of the National Capital Region's high-technol-ogy complex refer to it, has emerged since the mid-1970s as Canada's most obvious and successful example of a computer and telecommunications industry growth centre. By 2000, employment in advanced technology industrial sectors (broadly defined) in Ottawa had reached 70,000, and while some large firms are responsible for a signifi-cant proportion of the total (Nortel Networks: 14,000; JDS Uniphase: 8,500; Alcatel: 2,900), the complex increasingly contains many small specialist enterprises, some of them spun out of second- or third-generation incubator firms such as Mitel Corporation. Activities range from telecommunications R&D, through software design and information systems integration, to equipment manufacturing. Although sales to government were important to a higher share (25 per cent) of firms than in comparable North American high-technology complexes in the late 1980s (Bathelt, 1991), the high-technology cluster in Ottawa has matured to be steadily less dependent on federal support and purchasing.

A smaller high-tech complex has emerged in 'Canada's Technology Triangle' (CTT) in southwestern Ontario, centred on the University of Waterloo (Bathelt and Hecht, 1990). The incubator role of the university has been the most distinctive characteristic of this region, resulting in a large number of small firms, although establishments of transnational corporations, including Hewlett Packard and AT&T, have also been attracted by the reputation of Waterloo's computer science and mathematics programs. (In the mid-1990s, Microsoft was reported to have placed more co-op students from the university at its corporate headquarters in Redmond, Washington, than from any other institution in the world.) The CTT region has seen the emergence of firms engaged in software development and the production of electronic and scientific instruments, telecommunications equipment, and pharmaceuticals, and the regional complex has developed local input-output linkages. By 2000, such firms as Research in Motion (handheld wireless e-mail devices) and Open Text (business software) had increased the visibility of the region as a successful high-tech environment. As in Ottawa, the local availability of trained personnel is a major attraction for firms in this sector, but skilled labour shortages are still one of the greatest difficulties identified by employers.

The *relative* specialization of these two regional complexes in computer-based high-technology industry should not obscure its growing role in most of Canada's largest metropolitan centres. The Toronto region, for instance, is at least twice as large as the Ottawa area in terms of its employment in the computer and telecommunications sectors (see Chapter 5). It is home to the headquarters and laboratories of IBM Canada as well as many smaller, specialist firms across the whole range of hardware, software, and systems integration production. The attraction of a Disney Corporation computer animation studio to Toronto in 1995 underlined the city's strength in media applications. Vancouver also gained a Disney studio to add to its Microsoft R&D lab and many smaller specialist software and instrumentation suppliers. Montreal is proportionately weaker in computer-related sectors, partly because of the dominance of English in the international software industry, but it has firms active in a wide range of applications. Calgary's petroleum sector has long made the city one of Canada's leading centres of applied computing expertise, supporting related producer-service employment, but specialist instrumentation and software development firms have also emerged.

Overall, Canada's comparative advantage in computer software and system integration may be explained in part by the relatively low entry costs to these subsectors, in a country where venture capital has been in short supply until very recently and where it is still much less readily available than in the United States. Undoubtedly, too, the quality of Canadian talent emerging from post-secondary educational institutions has proven to be high. In contrast, no Canadian computer hardware firm has had the financial resources to support the development and marketing costs needed to thrive as a brand name at the expense of US and Asian competitors. But Canadian labour cost/quality considerations have proven to be favourable for hardware manufacturing within some corporate systems. Until its takeover by Compaq in 1997, Digital assembled personal computers at Kanata (Ottawa) and IBM continues to manufacture computer modules at Bromont, Quebec. By 2000, Toronto-based Celestica had emerged as a leading transnational original equipment manufacturer of hardware for the global computer industry, with two of its 34 manufacturing and design plants in the Toronto region. At the same time, domestic telecommunications equipment transnationals, such as Nortel and Mitel, have tended to increase the foreign share of their manufacturing output as their international sales have expanded and as they have moved more labour-intensive assembly operations to lower-cost countries in Asia.

## OTHER HIGH-TECHNOLOGY SECTORS

Compared to other advanced industrial nations, Canada's spending on research and development historically has been low and disproportionately concentrated in the public sector (governments and universities). Beyond the aerospace and computer and telecommunications industries, clusters of R&D-based producers in Canada can be recognized in the biotechnology-pharmaceutical, advanced materials and chemicals, automation technology, and energy-environmental technology sectors (Britton, 1996b, 1999). The geography of these industries generally corresponds to that of major metropolitan areas, with Toronto, Montreal, and Ottawa standing out. The Toronto region has the greatest diversity of high-technology production, whereas Montreal has developed particular strength in the aerospace and pharmaceutical sectors. The latter, initially based largely on branch operations of the major global drug firms, has expanded considerably since the late 1980s. The federal government has encouraged new investment in biotechnology and pharmaceutical R&D in Canada by granting a lengthier period of patent protection to the industry's products. The Quebec government has helped to channel much of this expansion to the Montreal area through generous R&D tax credits.

Atlantic Canada has relatively little R&D-intensive production. Most of what exists has strong university or government links, for example, firms drawing on the Centre for Cold Ocean Research in St John's, and federal marine science and defence-related contractors in the Halifax area. Public-sector research has also been an important stimulus in western Canada. Saskatoon's high-technology cluster includes firms commercializing agricultural biotechnology originating in University of Saskatchewan and federal government laboratories, and remote sensing and satellite technology related to federal programs, but it has also been stimulated by Nortel's fibre optics facility. The Alberta government has sought to encourage high-technology industry as part of its industrial diversification policy. Spinoffs from the energy and petrochemical sectors have provided a solid basis for this. Edmonton has attracted a growing medical research complex and a joint federal-provincial-corporate research centre for advanced industrial materials run by Westaim. An initial Calgary-based venture in cellular phone technology (Novatel), backed by the Alberta Heritage Fund, did not survive, but the city has since developed as a major centre for wireless communications technologies. There is a varied group of high-technology firms in the Vancouver and Victoria region, some linked to forest and marine applications.

## CONCLUSION

In 1978, economic geographers John Britton and James Gilmour published the *The Weakest Link*, warning of the dangers of Canada's technological backwardness resulting from its truncated branch-plant manufacturing economy. They argued for a nationalist industrial policy that would support Canadian-owned firms, fostering a climate of technological innovation that would enable them to become internationally competitive. Only then, they argued, might Canada benefit from a future commitment to continental free trade. Mainstream economists, however, were uniformly dismissive of their argument that foreign direct investment, because of the sort of industrial structure it generated, had become more of a liability than a benefit to Canada. They argued that what Canadian firms needed were the benefits of freer access to the much larger US market. The (Macdonald) Royal Commission on the Economic Union and Development Prospects for Canada, which reported in 1985, reflected these sentiments and, while acknowledging that there would be adjustment costs for some Canadian industries, clearly supported the negotiation of what resulted as the Canada–US Free Trade Agreement.

So who was right? Both Britton and Gilmour and the researchers working for the Royal Commission prepared their analyses just as the personal computer, and all that it has ushered in, was beginning to appear. The economic structure of Canadian postwar Fordism had cracked, in ways outlined in Chapters 1 and 4: miniature replica branch plants had no future, but it was not fully clear what was going to take their place. Post-Fordist flexible production systems were still in their infancy in North America. A generation later, we can see that the development of Canada's manufacturing sector has been neither as stunted as Britton and Gilmour feared, nor as rosy as the advocates of free trade promised. Post-staples manufacturing in Canada is a smaller element of the national economy than in most industrialized competitor states. Absentee corporate control still limits the extent of high-end management and research functions carried out in Canada (evident in the auto industry, for instance). The limited extent of indigenous machine-building capability remains a weakness. Nevertheless, Canadians need not minimize the successes of domestic firms in the computer, telecommunications, and aerospace sectors and the effectiveness of the network of producer service suppliers and subcontractors that many of them have created. Governments have played a supportive role (as they do in all advanced economies), but more Canadian manufacturers have proven robust competitors, within North America and globally, than many economic nationalists predicted.

## FURTHER READING

Anderson, M. 1995. 'The role of collaborative integration in industrial organization: observations from the Canadian aerospace industry', *Economic Geography* 71: 55–78.

Britton, J.N.H. 1996. 'High-tech Canada', in Britton, ed., *Canada and the Global Economy: The Geography of Structural and Technological Change*. Montreal and Kingston: McGill-Queen's University Press, 255–72.

Holmes, J. 1992. 'The continental integration of the North American automobile industry: from the Auto Pact to the FTA and beyond', *Environment and Planning A* 24: 95–119.

# Agriculture, Agri-Food, and the Rural Economy

## INTRODUCTION

Agriculture and the rural economy continue to pose challenges that policy-makers in Canada and other industrialized countries find difficult to resolve. Those who argue that modern agriculture is just like any other business, best left to evolve as market forces exert their influence on farmers' decisions, are countered by those who claim that agriculture and the communities it supports are too crucial to society's well-being to have their future 'arbitrarily' determined in this way. For much of the past two decades, international trade negotiations have been dragged out and faced with some of the most acrimonious backlash largely because of the difficulty of reconciling these two opposing perspectives. The United States government is the strongest exponent of free markets, which further the interests of its productive agricultural economy and its powerful agri-food transnationals. But despite the free-market rhetoric, protectionist actions and subsidization of particular groups of beneficiaries (peanut farmers, sugar beet growers, etc.) are well entrenched within domestic US agri-politics, sometimes directly at the expense of Canadian farmers. And US federal land-use and irrigation policy has done much to underwrite agricultural production in western states.

At the other end of the ideological spectrum, the Common Agricultural Policy (CAP) of the European Union has embodied a clear political commitment to maintain traditional family farming as a way of life and as a means of sustaining the character and vitality of rural areas. This involves significant economic costs, to governments and to consumers, which have involved the EU in discriminating against lower-cost producers of particular commodities in other parts of the world, including the grain growers of North America. Moreover, the subsidized disposal on global markets of excess European food production has reduced the returns of farmers elsewhere. In the 1980s, the United States retaliated with large export subsidies to its own grain farmers to enable them to match European export prices. This left the farmers and governments of smaller countries such as Canada, Australia, and Argentina, without the financial resources to compete in this contest, caught in the crossfire of the US–EU subsidy wars.

Canada's stance in international agricultural trade negotiations since the 1980s has tended to be ambivalent. This is certainly explicable, although not logically defensible, because of some marked differences within its domestic economic and cultural geography (Chiotti, 1992). Canadian agriculture comprises two very different sets of production environments: one whose output is quite competitive in international markets, notably the grain, oilseed, and beef sectors of the Prairie provinces, and one whose structure of production is not competitive internationally and that operates on the basis of various forms of protective government regulation. Canada's dairy and poultry farmers, who are concentrated in Ontario and Quebec and who operate under a regime of supply management (see below), fall into this category. Note that the competitive exporting sectors are found mainly in the Canadian hinterland; the protected sectors are dominant in the urbanized heartland: this gives a clear regional dimension to Canadian agricultural policy.

As a group, Canadian farmers have adjusted continuously and effectively to changing economic conditions, resulting in a steady rise in agricultural productivity over the past 50 years. Yet with respect to the United States in particular, the disadvantages that many Canadian farmers face stem from both physical and socio-economic factors. A shorter growing season, higher input costs, fewer economies of scale, etc. mean that the playing field on which Canadian and US farmers (and many food processors) compete is far from level. But should governments intervene to 'even things up' and maintain an agricultural economy throughout the Canadian ecumene? This is to a large extent a matter of cultural and political values, and in this sphere the priorities of Québécois and the Quebec government are much more in line with the priorities of France and the European Union, actively concerned to promote agricultural and rural prosperity, than with the more *laissez-faire* attitudes towards farming and rural land use prevailing in Anglo North America (Skogstad, 1998). Public sentiment throughout urban Canada has generally been appreciative of what are perceived as traditional rural values and is still supportive of family farming. Gradually, however, Canadian agricultural output is becoming concentrated in a relatively small proportion of large farm operations, whose commercial orientation or environmental impact have less popular appeal than the 'family farm' image (see Chapter 3). It is no wonder that both internationally and domestically there are ongoing policy tensions within this sector of the economy.

Except in Quebec, agricultural policies in Canada have not exhibited much of a coherent vision of the future of farming, or of the prosperity of rural areas more generally. Federal governments have stepped in with ad hoc support in times of acute financial crisis, particularly to aid Prairie grain farmers (most recently in 2001), and supply management has brought security to most dairy farmers, but in most respects market pressures have been allowed to take their course. This has certainly been true with respect to land. Canada's resource base of high-quality agricultural land is really very limited: it is claimed that one-third of it can be seen on a clear day from the top of the CN Tower in Toronto (Statistics Canada, 1999b)! But, outside of Quebec, the steady erosion of productive land by urban expansion around major metropolitan areas has been met with only patchy attempts to retain it for agriculture. For instance, the distinctive agricultural resources of the Niagara Peninsula, where soils and microclimates support Canada's largest area of soft fruit production, have suffered sustained encroachment (Krueger, 1978). Certainly, the BC government enacted a policy in 1973 to protect agricultural land in the Lower Mainland from further urban sprawl; but only in Quebec has province-wide planning to ensure the maintenance of the agricultural resource base found sustained political support.

Behind this clash of ideological visions are powerful trends in the evolution of modern agriculture. Goodman, Sorj, and Wilkinson (1987) identify two processes through which elements of traditional farm activity have been increasingly taken over by external business corporations. 'Appropriationism' involves the replacement of labour, draft animals, and ecological processes on the farm by industrial products (farm equipment, tractors, fertilizers, etc.) or specialized services (veterinary pharmacists, accountants, etc.). 'Substitutionism' involves the displacement of natural agricultural products or traditional foods by highly processed derivatives (e.g., frozen waffles instead of bread) or manufactured substitutes (e.g., artificial sweeteners instead of sugar). Appropriationism results in farmers spending increasing proportions of their gross income on purchased inputs: substitutionism results in less and less of consumer expenditures on food flowing back to the farmer as income. Together, these two processes result in the farm becoming but one element in a much larger 'agri-food' system. In 1997, the value added by farmers was only one-seventh the value of retail food sales (Figure 8.1). The economic pressures that govern the evolution and integration of the system are the same as those found in other sectors of the economy. As a result, the characteristics that in the past made farming a way of life as much as a business are under pressure.

As the farm supply and agri-food processing and distributing sectors are dominated by large oligopolistic firms with considerable market power, farmers' incomes are caught in a cost-price squeeze. Between 1974 and 1994, Canadian gross farm revenue, in constant 1986 dollars, hovered at around $20 billion, but operating costs rose 40 per cent, to $15.7 billion, cutting total net farm income by almost half (*Report on Business Magazine*, Nov. 1995). Moreover, these overall statistics obscure the fact that within every branch of agriculture, output and income are increasingly concentrated among the larger, well-capitalized farms. Figure 8.2 indicates that, in 1996, half of all farms had a net cash income of less than $4,200 and 39 per cent (mostly smaller farms) were losing money. But in most farm types the upper quartile of farms had a net cash income well above the average. Note that the highest income among poorer farmers (the lower quartile) was gained in the supply-managed dairy sector. Nevertheless the poultry sector, also supply-managed, exhibited substantial income polarization, with many producers suffering losses. Beef, hog, and wheat farms, all exposed to fluctuating international commodity prices, experience greater income variation. In 1996, beef farms of all sizes were suffering financially, whereas low grain prices were hitting some wheat farmers harder than others. To maintain their living standards, farm households have needed to expand the size of their operations and/or to increase their off-farm earnings. Both trends are well established in contemporary Canada.

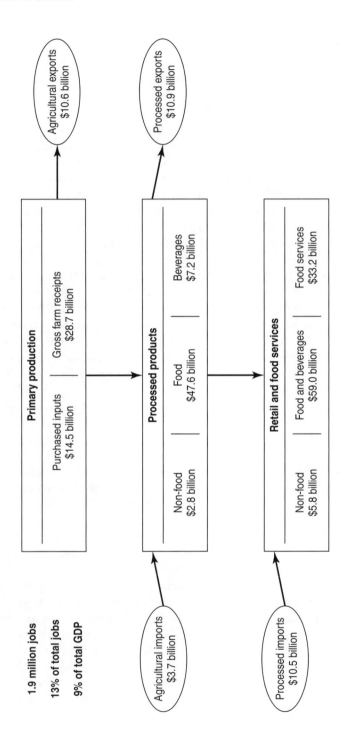

**Figure 8.1  Value-Added in Canada's Agri-Food Industry, 1997**

*SOURCE:* Statistics Canada (1999b: 47).

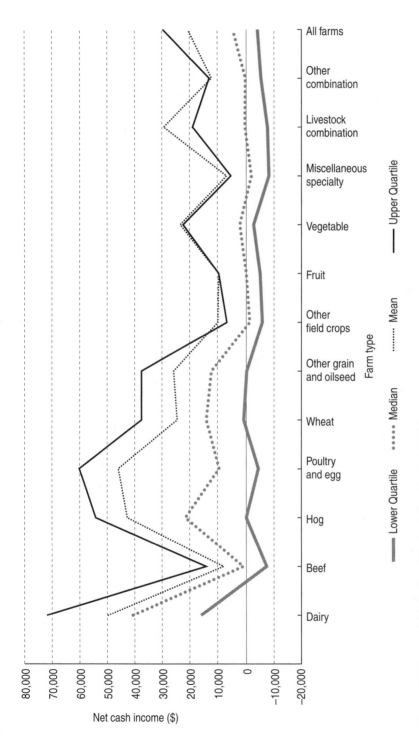

**Figure 8.2   Income Variation on Canadian Farms, 1996**

*SOURCE:* Statistics Canada (1999b: 20).

## FARM CHARACTERISTICS

Between 1941 (peak year for the number of farms) and 1996, the total number of farms in Canada declined by 62 per cent, from 733,000 to 277,000. During the same period, the total farmed area stayed approximately constant, at close to 70 million hectares (ha). As a result, the average farm size increased from 96 to 246 ha. But this national statistic masks the reality displayed in Table 8.1. Grouping the three Prairie provinces, dominated by the grain, oilseed, and beef subsectors, on the one hand, and the remaining provinces, in which the supply-managed dairy and poultry and the more intensive specialty crop subsectors are concentrated, on the other, reveals two very different farm populations, averaging 394 and 94 ha in size, respectively. Contrasting biophysical as well as political-economic conditions underlie this division, although there is much less regional variation in the average capital value of farms ($565,800 in 1996) and in average gross farm receipts ($116,500). Nevertheless, these averages conceal significant differences among farms. The average value of land on Ontario farms in 1991 was $6,200 per hectare, as opposed to $660 in Saskatchewan. The average capital value of a dairy farm in British Columbia was $1 million, and in Ontario $849,000, compared to $397,000 in Quebec. Variations in annual gross farm receipts reflect intensity of production more than regional location. In 1991, they were highest on mushroom ($885,500) and poultry ($357,400) farms, which most closely resemble factory operations, with large investment in buildings and frequent 'batch' production, and lowest on the agriculturally marginal farms specializing in maple syrup.

Among all types of farms there is a continuing trend for output to be concentrated in the largest and best-capitalized holdings. These are the business units that have most successfully integrated themselves into the broader agri-food system, becoming the preferred suppliers to the large domestic food manufacturers and retailers and being those best able to profit from the dynamics of external markets for Canadian agricultural commodities (Smith, 1984). In 1996 there were almost 8,700 farms in Canada with gross receipts of over $500,000. Yet this 3.1 per cent of all farms generated 36 per cent of gross farm receipts and almost the same share of total net revenues. Another measure of inter-farm differentiation by size is in management capacity, as related to the use of computers. Whereas 58 per cent of farms with gross receipts over $500,000 in 1996 used them, only 14 per cent of farms with under $50,000 in gross receipts did so (Statistics Canada, 1997).

In 1991, Canada's 280,000 farms were operated by 241,000 'primary farmers', whose main occupation was agricultural and whose off-farm work averaged 27 days per year, and by 150,000 'secondary farmers', whose principal occupation was off-farm employment, averaging 141 days per year (Statistics Canada, 1994; note that the census definition of 'farmer' now allows for more than one per holding). The incidence of off-farm work by primary farmers was lowest in Quebec and highest in British Columbia. Between 1965 and 1990 the average number of off-farm days worked by a holding's principal operator increased 35 per cent. The extent of off-farm work is highest in the Windsor–Quebec City corridor, and around metropolitan centres elsewhere, where alternative employment opportunities are greatest. The availability of other income

**Table 8.1    Farms in Canada, 1996**

|  | Farms | Total Area (ha) | Average Area (ha) |
|---|---|---|---|
| Canada | 276,548 | 68,054,956 | 246.1 |
| Prairie Provinces | 140,385 | 55,330,428 | 394.1 |
| Alberta | 59,007 | 21,029,228 | 356.4 |
| Saskatchewan | 56,995 | 26,569,062 | 466.2 |
| Manitoba | 24,383 | 7,732,138 | 317.1 |
| Other Provinces | 136,163 | 12,724,528 | 93.5 |
| British Columbia | 21,835 | 2,529,060 | 115.8 |
| Ontario | 67,520 | 5,616,860 | 83.2 |
| Quebec | 35,991 | 3,456,213 | 96.0 |
| New Brunswick | 3,405 | 386,019 | 113.4 |
| Nova Scotia | 4,453 | 427,324 | 96.0 |
| Prince Edward Island | 2,217 | 265,217 | 119.6 |
| Newfoundland | 742 | 43,836 | 59.1 |

SOURCE: Statistics Canada (1997).

sources also seems to facilitate the turnover of farm properties: peri-urban agriculture, especially in southern Ontario, showed the highest proportion of recent entrants to the industry in 1991.

The national agricultural ecumene and principal types of farm operation are identified in Figure 8.3. In recent decades the farmed area in eastern Canada, particularly in Quebec and the Maritimes, has shrunk with the abandonment of physically and economically marginal land. More productive land has also been lost to urbanization, particularly in the commutersheds of Toronto and Montreal. In contrast, modest expansion of the farmed area has continued in Saskatchewan and Alberta, partly encouraged by federal income support programs. These two provinces now account for over 70 per cent of Canadian farmland. There has been a slow increase in the intensity of land use throughout the country, with the proportion of farm area in crops rising from 56 per cent to 61 per cent between 1971 and 1991. The four major farm types—beef, dairy, wheat, and other small grains (corn, barley, etc.)—accounted for 64 per cent of all farms and 61 per cent of gross receipts in 1991. The regional patterns in Figure 8.3 are significant, but they hide complex underlying trends. In general, farm-level specialization has continued to increase since the 1960s, although this is truer of some operations (e.g., pigs) than others (e.g., grain and oilseeds). At the same time, there is evidence of greater sub-regional diversification of production, particularly into specialty field crops on the Prairies.

## THE POLICY FRAMEWORK

Canadian farmers have been no different from their counterparts in other industrialized countries in maintaining a strong presence in policy formation, even as their numbers and role in the national economy have shrunk. The economic vulnerability of the early prairie wheat farmers, dependent on export mono-cropping on the

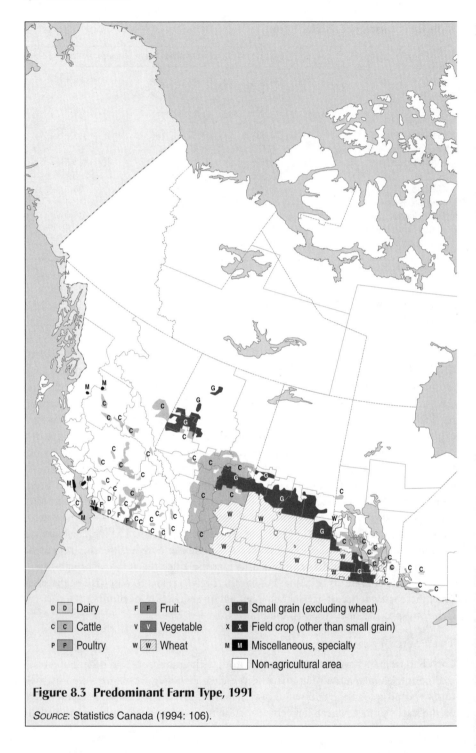

**Figure 8.3 Predominant Farm Type, 1991**

*Source*: Statistics Canada (1994: 106).

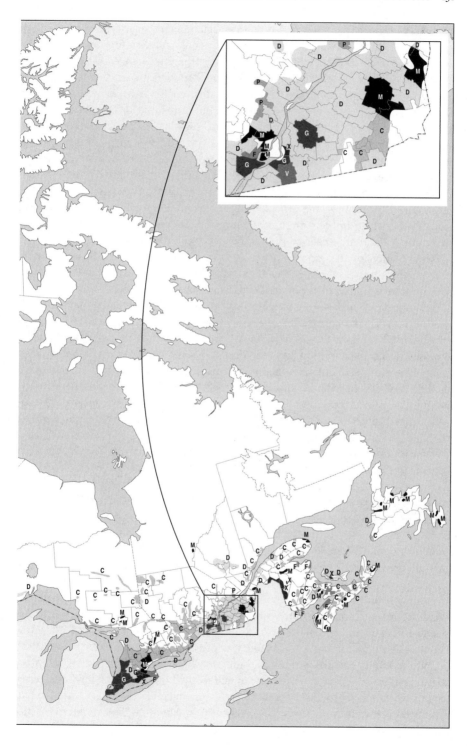

periphery of global markets, moved them to agitate first for government-subsidized freight rates (the Crow's Nest Pass Agreement, 1897), and then for a collective grain marketing agency to bolster their market power (the Canadian Wheat Board, 1935). Together with various other forms of government assistance, such as subsidized crop insurance and income stabilization support, these measures have been the foundation of the prairie grain economy in modern times. But by the mid-1970s it became apparent that the policy of favouring grain production was itself an unhelpful obstacle to economic diversification, both on and off the farm. Moreover, the increasingly costly grain transport subsidies were recognized as becoming counterproductive, inhibiting the emergence of a more efficient grain-handling infrastructure and discouraging the development of regional food-processing industries or the expansion of alternative crops. The dismantling of the Crow subsidy regime in the 1990s has already resulted in significant changes in the pattern of grain movement and has boosted the development of a wider range of agricultural activity on prairie farms.

Continuation of the export monopoly of the Canadian Wheat Board is under considerable threat, as the pressures of globalization in the world grain trade intensify. The US transnationals such as Cargill and Continental Grain that dominate international grain markets have long sought to erode the Board's power, and the worldwide decline in the role of state trading agencies in recent years has intensified their efforts to eliminate competitors (Kneen, 1995). Some Canadian farmers, ideologically opposed to state intervention and well located to sell grain into the US market, have campaigned for the Board's elimination. A federal review panel suggested in 1996 that its monopoly be relaxed but its role maintained. Ownership of other elements of the grain industry is already consolidating in the hands of US transnationals. For example, Archer-Daniels-Midland (ADM) has effectively taken over United Grain Growers (UGG), the third-largest operator of primary elevators on the Prairies, which was a farmers' co-operative until 1993. With federal Competition Bureau approval, it also has become the largest flour miller in Canada by taking over Maple Leaf Mills. Previously, ADM had purchased UGG's interest in a canola crushing plant at Lloydminster, on the Alberta–Saskatchewan border, giving it access to the prairie oilseed market.

The more diversified and domestically focused agriculture of other parts of the country, less exposed to the vagaries of international commodity markets and the power of dominant traders, took longer to consolidate a regulatory framework to provide greater security and stability to farm producers. But the achievement of federal-provincial consensus by the 1960s opened the way to the establishment of marketing boards for many commodities, secured by federal legislation to protect the domestic market from disruptive imports. This regime of *supply management* has been particularly influential in the dairy and poultry sectors (Bowler, 1994). Its advocates present it as a fair and reasonable way of ensuring that domestic demand and supply are kept in balance, without the gluts and shortages that can develop in unregulated markets. It also allows producers to market their output on roughly equal terms (at least within each province), for instance, by pooling milk collection charges so that farms more remote from processing plants are not unduly disadvantaged. Critics argue that by denying consumers access to the cheapest supplies available on open markets, supply management protects existing producers from more efficient competitors and results in higher food prices.

The essence of supply management in the dairy sector has been to establish an overall national target for milk production, subdivided into provincial shares. Within each province, the right to produce milk is regulated by quotas, which farmers can buy and sell. Because they represent an entitlement to an income stream, quotas have market value: in 1994 they represented 27.5 per cent of the capital value of Canadian dairy farms, or almost $250,000 per farm (*Globe and Mail*, 12 Aug. 1995). The milk market is divided into two sectors: fluid (fresh) milk, and 'industrial' milk, which is processed into a range of dairy products, such as cheese and butter. Quota allocations among the provinces reflect historic shares rather than current patterns of demand, with the result that Quebec's share is disproportionately large (37 per cent). Conversely, British Columbia, given its population growth since the 1970s, has a smaller allocation than would be justified today, and this has been openly, but unsuccessfully, challenged by some farmers in the Fraser Valley. In a less regulated market Quebec would still possess a comparative advantage in dairy production, but the extent of the concentration of Canadian dairy output and the related food-processing industries in the province (approximately 75 per cent of the milk produced in Quebec in 1990 was 'industrial') certainly would decline. The Quebec farm movement's strong support for the continuance of the national dairy supply management regime has reflected this reality, although by 1994 only 33 per cent of farm cash receipts in Quebec came from dairying, down from 46 per cent in 1977 (Furtan and Gray, 1991; Skogstad, 1998). The national distribution of poultry quotas conforms more closely to provincial population totals.

## REGIONAL PATTERNS

With the decline of federal government intervention in Canadian agriculture, which, whether by regulation or financial support, has tended to favour a certain pattern and geography of output, there is growing evidence of diversification as farmers identify new market opportunities. On the Prairies, there has been an increase in the variety of wheats grown and a sustained expansion in oilseed (especially canola) production. Cultivation of specialty crops, such as lentils, field peas, and mustard, has also increased, particularly in Saskatchewan, south-central Manitoba, and parts of southwestern Ontario (Statistics Canada, 1994). Over time, crop varieties have been developed that extend the viable area of production in Canada's climatically restricted agricultural ecumene (Joseph and Keddie, 1985). A generation ago, the introduction of corn hybrids permitted the widespread cultivation of that crop in eastern Ontario and southern Quebec: Quebec's corn area expanded from 13,000 ha to 333,000 ha between 1968 and 1998. More recently, the development of soybean varieties that can mature with fewer heat units has changed the map in Ontario, where the area under soybeans has exceeded that under corn since 1992 (Statistics Canada, 1999b). Although still of limited acreage, herbs, spices, and non-traditional vegetables have also expanded in response to the increasing diversity of Canadian food demand.

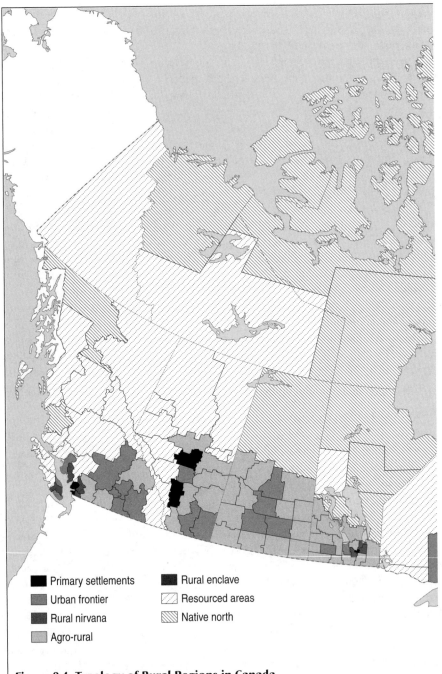

**Figure 8.4 Typology of Rural Regions in Canada**

Source: Statistics Canada (1994: 80).

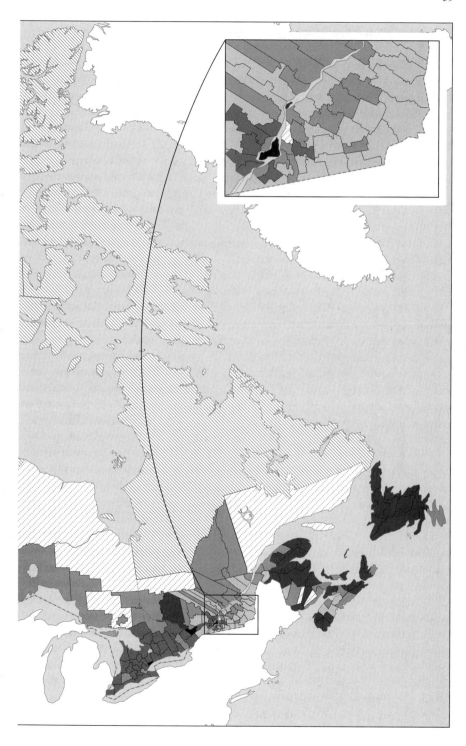

Part of this diversity is reflected in the increasing market for organic products grown without the use of the industrial fertilizers and pesticides that are central to modern conventional farming. Although organic foods represented only 1 per cent of the Canadian retail food market in 1998, sales were increasing rapidly (up to 25 per cent per year) (ibid.). In 1996 there were 1,724 certified organic farms in Canada (not all producers seek certification by a regulatory agency), of which 501 were in Quebec, 365 in Saskatchewan, and approximately 280 each in BC and Ontario (Gagnon, 1999). In Quebec, the majority of organic farms are found in the rural fringe of the largest metropolitan areas (Beauchesne and Bryant, 1999), while those in Nova Scotia are concentrated in the Annapolis Valley (Gagnon, 1999). In both provinces, growers seek access to those metropolitan consumers who are culturally and financially disposed to pay premium prices for organic produce. Consumer concern about genetically modified (GM) foods has recently escalated in Europe and is growing in Canada, to the extent that many food processors are requiring that GM and non-GM crops be segregated throughout the distribution system.

The closer integration of farm production and agri-food processing characteristic of modern industrialized economies has promoted the consolidation of regional production systems (Smith, 1984). For instance, the concentration of Canadian potato growers in Prince Edward Island and the upper Saint John Valley of New Brunswick, which together contain almost half the total hectares under the crop, has been strengthened by the growth of the frozen french-fry market and the spread of contract farming for dominant processing firms such as McCain Foods and Cavendish Farms (Glover and Kusterer, 1990). In southern Manitoba, a more recently established processing industry draws from farms that average 88 ha under potatoes, twice the average size of farms in the Maritimes (Statistics Canada, 1994). Other vegetable production, concentrated in southwestern Ontario and the Montreal plain, is dominated by sweet corn, green peas, and tomatoes. Especially since the signing of the FTA, many older and smaller vegetable-processing operations have closed, but Heinz has expanded its operations at Leamington, Ontario (Wallace, 1992).

Canada's orchard crops have long been concentrated in southern Ontario (especially the Niagara Peninsula), the Okanagan Valley, BC, and smaller areas in the Annapolis Valley, Nova Scotia, and east of Montreal. Loss of land to urban expansion and increased competition from American and Mexican producers have been experienced especially by the first two regions, which have a warmer climate than those further east. On the other hand, the Ontario and BC wine industries, which could easily have been wiped out by Californian and European competitors when protection was reduced in the late 1980s, have instead been transformed by the emergence of new firms that upgraded the varieties of grapes cultivated and focused on quality, rather than quantity, winemaking. More professional marketing has enabled Canadian fruit growers to expand output, from the predominantly Sikh cranberry farmers of Surrey, BC (Ellis, 1993), to the blueberry growers of Lac St Jean and Nova Scotia, who have taken advantage of transportation improvements (containerized shipping and air freight) to expand their sales into Europe.

However, the most important change in recent years in the geography of domestic food production has been the reshaping and relocation of the beef-processing industry. Traditionally, cattle raised on the ranches of Alberta and the BC interior were moved to feedlots in southern Alberta or in southwestern Ontario before being slaughtered in the urban meat plants of Toronto, Hamilton, and Kitchener–Waterloo. Transportation subsidies for prairie grain exports and for feed-grain shipments from the Prairies to central Canada reduced the economic incentive for the beef industry to locate close to its source of feed supply. Moreover, the structure of the meat market was governed by the prevalence of retail butchering close to the consumer. However, with the increased dominance of large supermarket chains and sales of foods in a ready-to-use format, meat-processing in the 1980s became more oriented to sales of pre-cut portions ('boxed beef') than of 'dressed' carcasses delivered to retail butchers. Associated with this trend, which was spearheaded by new entrants to the industry in the United States, was a move away from the urban, market-oriented, aging, and unionized slaughtering plants to new, highly automated, rural and non-unionized plants in the major cattle-rearing regions. In Canada, the phasing out of grain transportation subsidies reinforced the appeal of the Prairies as the lowest-cost location for beef production. So there has been a major shift in the location of the beef industry, away from metropolitan Ontario to small-town Alberta, where the Cargill plant at High River set the trend (Chiotti, 1992; Kneen, 1995). The average annual throughput of cattle at the western (Alberta plus BC) plants in 1996 was 220 per cent greater than that in the Ontario plants (Statistics Canada, 1999), and nationally, the top four processing plants account for almost 75 per cent of the total slaughter. Hog production and processing have also increased on the Prairies, especially in Manitoba, for reasons similar to those for beef production. The expansion of hog production in Quebec, on the other hand, partly reflects provincial measures to encourage greater self-sufficiency in that sector.

## Beyond Agriculture

In 1991, Canada's farm population amounted to 867,000 persons, a mere 3.2 per cent of the total population. In Saskatchewan, the proportion was 16 per cent, and in Manitoba, Alberta, and Prince Edward Island it was around 7 per cent, but elsewhere farm households formed 2 per cent or less of the population. Yet the vast majority of the Canadian ecumene remains non-metropolitan and hence, in popular parlance, 'rural'. Agricultural activity dominates land use, but the nature of the rural economy and the pressures shaping it vary significantly. Figure 8.4 identifies a typology of rural regions, those designated 'resourced areas' and 'Native North' lying essentially beyond the limits of commercial agriculture (Statistics Canada, 1994). The country's most productive agricultural areas—in southern Ontario, the Montreal plain, and southwestern British Columbia—have become increasingly incorporated into the daily urban systems of adjacent metropolitan areas (Bryant and Johnston, 1992). Population migration into this 'rural nirvana' has been rapid, creating pressures to transfer land out of agricultural production. These pressures have been mitigated by planning protection of agricultural zones in Quebec, BC, and, to a limited degree, Ontario and the introduction of 'right to farm' legislation (in the face of attempts by rural newcomers to impose the environmental values of suburbia, such as freedom from farm odours, on agricultural producers). 'Urban frontier' regions are defined by similar but weaker urban influences, mainly outside the agricultural heartlands, as in central Nova Scotia and south-central British Columbia.

'Agro-rural' regions are areas where agriculture is a major employer. They tend to have a stable or declining and older-than-average population scattered in small settlements. The viability of the social service infrastructure in these regions has become increasingly problematic. 'Rural enclave' communities, almost exclusively located in fishing-dependent regions of Atlantic Canada, are nearly all characterized by extreme agricultural marginality, measured both by income and by resource endowment. Isolation from major markets, low activity rates, and high levels of dependence on social transfers make for levels of rural poverty unmatched outside remote Aboriginal communities.

The emergence of these differentiated rural regions reflects broad changes in Canadian society (Fuller, 1994). Notably, the rural economy has become more complex, especially, but not only, where it is within convenient reach (day or weekend trips) of metropolitan areas. The processes of appropriationism and substitutionism have increased the role of non-farm activities in the agri-food production system and hence the variety of employment and occupational opportunities available in rural areas. At the same time, most farm households have to supplement their net agricultural earnings with income from off-farm employment or alternative farm-based businesses (such as agro-tourism). With the growing appreciation of the amenity value of small towns and rural areas and the ability of many people, both of working and retirement age, to choose to reside in favoured localities, in-migration has added further variety and additional purchasing power to these regions. The rural component of the Windsor–Quebec City corridor and its northern recreational fringe on the Canadian Shield display these features most fully, but comparable developments are found in such regions as Nova Scotia's South Shore and south-central British Columbia.

## CONCLUSION

Despite its generally high levels of productivity and demonstrated capacity to adapt to change, Canadian agriculture has entered the twenty-first century facing much uncertainty. The public policy ambivalences that we noted at the beginning of this chapter remain unresolved, and they characterize not only Canadian agriculture but also the international arena. Despite the progress in international trade negotiations towards the elimination of agricultural subsidies, they remain firmly entrenched. OECD data indicate that, in 1999, wheat producers in the US received 46 per cent of their income from subsidies and those in the EU received 58 per cent, while those in Canada received only 11 per cent (*Globe and Mail*, 7 Apr. 2001). While this degree of distortion persists in global markets, the Canadian government and its wheat farmers remain vulnerable to pressures beyond their control. The same issues are present in other agricultural sectors, such as dairy farming, but in many of these sectors Canada's level of producer support is higher than that of its trading partners, and there is no coherent national strategy for adjusting to a less subsidized environment.

Although there are many convincing reasons for eliminating trade-distorting subsidies in global agricultural markets, doing so would not resolve all the deeper policy questions about the future of farming and of rural society more generally. The massive increases in agricultural productivity achieved in Canada and other industrialized nations since World War II have greatly reduced the size of the farm population and, to a lesser extent, the size of the land base needed to produce a given amount of food. What, then, is the desired future for those parts of the country where agriculture has been the foundation of the economy and of social organization? In densely populated regions, such as exist throughout Western Europe, the northeastern United States, and southern Ontario and Quebec, the use and enjoyment of rural areas by urban populations is central to their prosperity. But in this context, the role of farmers as land resource managers can be as important as their role as food producers, especially when intensive agriculture has brought with it a variety of environmentally damaging practices (see Chapter 3). If societies value this function, and the maintenance of rural communities more broadly, they need to devise more intelligent ways to make it economically viable than simply to subsidize the output of agricultural commodities. This is a challenge that Canada and its trading partners need to address together.

## FURTHER READING

Chiotti, Q. 1992. 'Sectoral adjustments in agriculture: dairy and beef livestock industries in Canada', in I. Bowler, C. Bryant, and M.D. Nellis, eds, *Contemporary Rural Systems in Transition*, vol. 1, *Agriculture and Environment*, Wallingford, UK: CAB International, 43—57.

Glover, D., and K. Kusterer. 1990. 'McCain Foods, Canada: the political economy of monopoly', in Glover and Kusterer, *Small Farmers, Big Business: Contract Farming and Rural Development*. Basingstoke, UK: Macmillan, 73—93.

Krueger, R. 2000. 'Trials and tribulations of the Canadian fruit-growing industry', *Canadian Geographer* 44: 342—54.

Smith, W. 1984. 'The "vortex model" and the changing agricultural landscape of Quebec', *Canadian Geographer* 28: 358—72.

Statistics Canada. 1999. *Canadian Agriculture at a Glance*. Ottawa: Statistics Canada, Cat. no. 96—325.

# The Forest and Minerals Industries

## INTRODUCTION

Canada's mineral and forest-based industries are staples sectors that continue to be major players on world markets despite the steady growth of international competition since the 1960s. Globally, Canada is the third largest producer and the largest exporter of minerals, the largest producer and exporter of newsprint, and the largest exporter of softwood lumber. In addition to being major contributors to Canada's balance of trade (Table 1.2), the two sectors are significant domestically for the employment they generate in hinterland regions, as consumers of electrical power, and as purchasers of transportation to ship their bulky output to North American and overseas markets. However, both sectors are characterized by the cyclical fluctuations in earnings typical of all resource commodity producers, and this economic instability can have particularly serious consequences for the remote single-industry communities dependent on them. Moreover, despite rapid growth in world demand for minerals and forest products since the 1950s, global production has more than kept pace. This is partly because of the scale of investment in new facilities, both in less-developed countries and in competing developed countries such as Australia (minerals) and the United States (forest products). It also reflects the systemic trend towards less resource-intensive manufacturing production, whereby new technologies and manufacturing processes economize on the consumption of material inputs. In both sectors, therefore, corporate and workplace restructuring to maintain competitiveness, in terms of cost and product quality, has been an ongoing process that has brought dramatic changes to what are in many respects 'mature' industries. Heightened public concern over the environmental impacts of mineral and forest exploitation has also presented new challenges to firms' conduct.

The Canadian forest products industry is dominated by two subsectors—lumber and newsprint. Other elements include 'market pulp' (sold largely to foreign paper product manufacturers); wood products, such as plywood, particle board, and oriented strand board (the last two having captured many markets from plywood); packaging materials (e.g., corrugated cardboard); and 'fine' papers (for writing, computer printing, etc.). Increasing vertical integration of these various subsectors reflects growing concern on the part of all firms to ensure an adequate supply of wood fibre and to reap the economies that can be obtained by using woodchips as inputs to papermaking or sawmill residues for process heat generation. This has prompted purchases of sawmills and their logging rights by pulp and paper firms. Geographically, the focus of the lumber and related products industry is British Columbia, although production in Ontario and Quebec is growing and there was significant expansion in northern Alberta in the 1980s. Production in New Brunswick and Nova Scotia increased during the 1990s as these provinces have been exempt from the export quota limits established to settle the Canada–US softwood lumber dispute (see below). The greatest concentration of pulp and paper capacity is found across the southern Shield in Ontario and Quebec, where the industry was first established and grew considerably prior to 1950. Mills in Atlantic Canada also date primarily from this period. Expansion in BC, and to a lesser extent in the Prairie provinces, dates principally from the mid-1950s to the mid-1970s.

The mineral industry comprises both mining and mineral processing (the primary metals industry). The range of Canada's resource base is such that all the major subsectors—iron and steel, base metals (nickel, copper, lead, zinc), precious metals (gold and silver), industrial minerals (potash, asbestos, etc.), and solid energy minerals (coal and uranium)—are globally significant producers. The first major developments of mineral production took place in the late nineteenth century with the growth of industrial demand in the United States and the increasing accessibility of Canadian resources as a result of the expanding railway network. A second, prolonged period of growth took place from the early 1950s to the late 1970s, stimulated by rapidly increasing demand in North America and in overseas markets. There are some regional specializations—iron ore in Quebec/Labrador, potash and uranium in Saskatchewan, asbestos in the Eastern Townships of Quebec, coal in BC and the Alberta foothills (and residually in Cape Breton)—but most of the non-ferrous and precious metals have been commercially exploited across a wide arc of the southern Shield, from Flin Flon in the West, through Sudbury, Timmins, and Noranda, to Chibougamau in the East, and also in the western Cordillera (BC and Yukon), the High Arctic, and parts of the Atlantic provinces. Unlike forest resources, minerals are inherently non-renewable, and many sub-regions have seen their reserves depleted, with attendant problems of social and economic adjustment. But the scale of many deposits and the ability of smelters to find accessible replacement feed when initial ore supplies are exhausted have sustained some locations (notably Sudbury and Trail, BC) over a long history of mineral processing.

The forest products and mineral sectors face common, as well as specific, challenges. The adequacy of the resource base for current and future demand is a major concern (see Chapter 3). Sustainable forestry requires changes from past practices and these changes demand a considerable lead-time to take effect. In the short and medium term, some regions will experience a shortage of raw material. Sustainability in the minerals sector implies a business climate (dependent on provincial as much as federal legislation) in which the risks of exploration for new deposits are judged worthwhile. When this confidence is put in question, as it has been notably in British Columbia in recent years, the result has been to accelerate the globalization of Canadian firms, which are increasingly engaged in mineral developments in foreign countries, especially in Latin America. Increased global competition has caused firms in both sectors to restructure production processes and the labour force, resulting in increased capital intensity and changing employment profiles (Hayter, 2000; Wallace, 1996). Both industries have come under much more critical scrutiny of their environmental impacts, and while this has been most obvious in the forest products sector, it is also shaping the geography of mineral development. So, too, is increased attention to Aboriginal land claims. In both industries, firms have traditionally tended to focus on turning out standard commodities (lumber 'two-by-fours', newsprint, 'flat-rolled' steel, etc.) rather than on marketing the special properties and potential uses of their materials. But threats to traditional markets from new materials such as plastics or advanced ceramics, or from substitution (aluminum for steel in autos, steel for lumber in housing), have stimulated greater attention to product differentiation and quality, and a move towards higher value-added manufacturing.

## The Forest Sector

The geography of lumber production has long been dominated by British Columbia (Table 9.1), which accounted for 52 per cent of shipments in 1995. With the more recent expansion of sawmills in western Alberta, 60 per cent of national output is derived from locations west of the longitude of Calgary and Edmonton. Quebec is the centre of eastern production, shipping 24 per cent of national output (1995), principally from mills in the Abitibi and Lac St Jean regions. Sawmills on rail lines in northern Ontario and scattered mills in New Brunswick contributed a further 14 per cent of shipments. The average BC mill ships almost three times the dollar value of lumber as that of the average eastern mill, reflecting both greater size and higher value-added per employee. Within BC there are important differences between the coastal mills, processing larger logs from the old-growth coastal forest, and those in the interior exploiting smaller trees. Two-thirds of Canadian lumber is exported, and the United States has been taking an increasingly large share, although BC mills have also increased their shipments to Asian markets.

The growth of Canadian exports to the United States has triggered opposition from US lumber interests, who complain that Canadian firms paying stumpage to log Crown land are effectively subsidized. Despite the existence of NAFTA, this has resulted in a long-running dispute involving at times the application of US duties on Canadian lumber. Stumpage rates have been raised, notably in British Columbia, partially to deflect this argument; but a range of issues lie behind the cross-border conflict. Protectionist interests in the US continue to challenge the dispute panel ruling that Canada's different institutional arrangements of forest tenure do not constitute a subsidy. Loggers in the US Pacific Northwest are reacting to the marked shrinkage of their own resource base from increased exclusions for forest and habitat conservation and from overcutting. Those in the American Southeast are seeing their costs rise as the regional timber supply declines.

The most common lumber product in Canada is the 'two-by-four' used by the North American construction industry. Revenues from this standard commodity item

**Table 9.1   Lumber Production, 1995**

| Provinces | Production (cubic metres) |
|---|---|
| Newfoundland | 90,262 |
| Prince Edward Island | 110,108 |
| Nova Scotia | 789,262 |
| New Brunswick | 2,709,428 |
| Quebec | 15,416,445 |
| Ontario | 6,098,916 |
| Manitoba | 307,533 |
| Saskatchewan | 565,326 |
| Alberta | 5,445,389 |
| British Columbia | 33,556,369 |
| *Coast* | *8,503,504* |
| *Interior* | *25,052,865* |
| Total | 65,089,037 |

SOURCE: Statistics Canada (1998b: Table 19).

fluctuate with the housing market and the US$ exchange rate. To improve earnings and diversify their markets, Canadian firms have increasingly invested in computerized milling equipment that allows more flexibility and diversity of production. In particular, efforts to popularize North American-style wood-frame construction in the Japanese and other Asian markets, backed by readiness to ship lumber in dimensions popular there, have sustained overseas export growth from BC (Hayter and Edgington, 1997). Workplace restructuring has required acceptance of multi-skilling and teamwork by employees and their unions, which in some locations has involved substantial job loss (e.g., from 654 to 145 at Chemainus, BC, in the early 1980s), but in other places restructuring has meant primarily a reconfiguration of the labour force (e.g., Port Alberni, BC) (Barnes et al., 1990). Although largely captive to the domestic and US markets, leading eastern lumber producers have also invested in flexible mill technology and diversified their product lines.

The pulp and paper industry developed principally to serve export markets, mainly in the United States, but also in Europe and more recently Asia. Foreign ownership of mills, including some vertical integration by newspaper publishers, has always been substantial; Canadian corporations increased their control of the industry in the last decades of the twentieth century, only to lose some of it at the start of the 2000s. Since the 1970s, firms for the most part have increased and modernized their production capacity at existing locations rather than construct mills in new ones, mainly because of the unavailability of new forest cutting rights. The major exception has been the construction of new pulp mills in mid-northern Alberta, based on the release by the provincial government of the last available stands of commercially accessible lumber. Introduction of new pulping technologies that increase wood-fibre utilization and reduce adverse environmental impacts, together with the installation of larger and faster paper machines, has brought substantial change to the workplace. So has the search by most firms for higher value-added products in response to more diversified market opportunities. Increased public support for paper recycling has eroded some of the locational advantages of resource-oriented paper mills (near forests but distant from cities) and favoured mills close to metropolitan markets (far from trees but with easy access to recycled newsprint). American locations have benefited more than Canadian locations.

Regional specialization within the pulp and paper subsector reflects relative accessibility to the North American newspaper market, with Quebec accounting for 42 per cent of newsprint shipments but only 15 per cent of pulp in 1992; BC, on the other hand, is the largest producer of market pulp (41 per cent), most of which is exported overseas, but ships only 18 per cent of newsprint. As with lumber, western newsprint mills are on average larger and more modern than those in the East, but the differences are less marked among pulp mills. Since the 1970s, technological innovations have led to a declining proportion of chemical pulps and an increase in thermo-mechanical pulps (TMPs). The rise in demand for newsprint recycling, and hence of de-inking plants, has been met primarily by investments on the southern edge of the Shield, closest to metropolitan sources of supply. Canada's largest de-inking plant was opened in 1992 at Gatineau, Quebec, as part of the major restructuring of Avenor's newsprint complex (Rose and Villemaire, 1997).

The increased competitive pressures facing pulp and paper producers in Canada have met with varied responses, although all have involved reducing employment. Firms have sought increasingly flexible labour contracts, both regionally and locally. In 1994, the British Columbia Labour Relations Board accepted management's argument that traditional province-wide union contract negotiations should give way to mill-by-mill bargaining, on the grounds that the industry has moved away from generic commodity production and sales on the spot market towards higher-value differentiated products sold under long-term supply contracts (*Globe and Mail*, 20 July 1994). This has weakened the bargaining power of a labour force scattered among remote single-industry (often single-employer) communities. Opening a 'greenfield' paper mill at Whitecourt, Alberta, in 1990, in a newly exploited forest region, allowed the Alberta Newsprint Company to create a flexible, non-unionized workforce of multi-skilled employees drawn from a regional 'oil patch' culture favouring minimum levels of structured workplace supervision (Preston et al., 1997). A number of old mills in central Canada, threatened with closure as uneconomic by their corporate (often originally American) owners, have returned to prosperity following employee buyouts (usually aided by government). This movement was pioneered in the early 1970s at Temiscaming, Quebec, by Tembec, which has since expanded as a pulp and paper producer. The mill at Kapuskasing, Ontario, repeated the success in the late 1990s and is now owned by Tembec.

## THE MINERALS SECTOR

Various measures indicate that the Canadian minerals sector reached its peak activity at the end of the 1970s (Table 9.2). Output and employment then shrank dramatically during the recession of the early 1980s, which ushered in a period of radical restructuring. Many mines ceased to be viable, and Canadian firms maintained their competitiveness only by greatly increased productivity. As a result of these adjustments, the industry was better placed to weather the recession of the early 1990s, but by then two other developments served to limit its growth. One was a less sympathetic political and regulatory climate. Growing public concern over the environmental impacts of mining increased opposition to proposed developments, and more rigorous requirements for impact assessments and decommissioning plans imposed costly delays on mine start-ups. New uranium mines in northern Saskatchewan and the disallowed Windy Craggy copper project in northern BC exemplified these pressures. Moreover, especially in the Arctic, protracted Aboriginal land claim negotiations effectively imposed a moratorium on mineral exploitation for a number of years. The second trend, therefore, was the greater readiness of Canadian firms to invest in exploration and mine development outside Canada, where many deposits of higher grade were becoming attractive, especially in Latin American nations such as Chile (Figure 9.1). Yet the continued promise of Canada's vast resource endowment has been confirmed in recent years by the discovery of diamonds in the Northwest Territories and the world-class nickel deposit at Voisey's Bay, Labrador.

Despite the richness of Canada's resource base, Canadian mineral firms have predominantly remained medium-sized by world standards, many of them long associated with a particular deposit or region. US investment was important in this sector from the very beginning, but its role has declined since the 1970s. European and Japanese investment has increased, the former mainly in Saskatchewan's uranium industry and the latter primarily in coal and copper in BC. Canadian ownership of the industry rose noticeably from the late 1970s to the late 1980s, from around 50 per cent to over 80 per cent (Canada, EMR, 1989). The Saskatchewan and Quebec governments took control of significant portions of their potash and asbestos industries, respectively, and the federal government bought out the major Kidd Creek copper/zinc mine at Timmins, Ontario, from its US owner. These public-sector firms were subsequently privatized, chiefly to Canadian corporations. In addition to changes in ownership, Canadian mineral firms have been involved in the global restructuring of the industry through strategic alliances, technology licensing, and project partnerships overseas.

Response to greater competitive pressures has come primarily in the form of increased automation to reduce mining labour costs and from the introduction of more efficient smelting technologies. The Sudbury basin illustrates this well. Inco and Falconbridge, the two large nickel-copper producers, have cut employment by over 60 per cent since 1971, more than twice the rate of decline in metal output (Saarinen, 1992). They accomplished this by the innovation of bulk mining technology to excavate large caverns of rock in place of the traditional workings of narrow horizontal

**Table 9.2 Canadian Mineral Output, 1978 and 1998**

| Production (by value) | 1978 ($ millions) | 1998 ($ millions) |
|---|---|---|
| Metals | 5,746 | 10,319 |
| Non-metals | 1,481 | 3,277 |
| Structural materials | 1,508 | 2,949 |
| Fuels | 11,578 | 27,770 |
| Total | 20,313 | 44,315 |
| Production (selected minerals) | (000 t) | (000 t) |
| Copper | 659 | 689 |
| Lead | 320 | 152 |
| Nickel | 128 | 201 |
| Zinc | 1,067 | 987 |
| Uranium | 8.2 | 10.0 |
| Iron Ore | 42,931 | 38,908 |
| Asbestos | 1,422 | 320 |
| Gypsum | 8,074 | 8,095 |
| Potash | 6,344 | 8,969 |
| Sulphur | 5,752 | 8,410 |
| Coal | 30,478 | 74,370 |
| Gold | 54 tonnes | 166 tonnes |
| Silver | 1,267 tonnes | 1,115 tonnes |

SOURCE: *Canadian Minerals Yearbook* (1979, 1998: Tables 1 and 2).

drifts. Improvements in smelter technology have been strongly promoted by increasing government pressure since the early 1970s to reduce sulphur dioxide ($SO_2$) emissions. Inco's initial response, to dilute and disperse the smelter gases by means of the 'superstack' (a 381-metre chimney), shifted much of the problem away from Sudbury, but at the expense of downwind forests and lakes subject to increased acid rain. But by 1991, corporate research resulted in new smelting technology that drastically reduced $SO_2$ emissions and also cut energy consumption. Comparable strategies to reduce costs and improve environmental quality were undertaken by Cominco in British Columbia in the 1980s. Its choice of untested technology to upgrade the smelter at Trail proved a commercial mistake, but its logistical rationalization of the large open-pit copper mines at Highland Valley, near Kamloops, achieved considerable cost savings (Wallace, 1996).

Canada's non-ferrous smelting industry has traditionally benefited from cheap electric power. Alcan's aluminum production in the Saguenay region of Quebec and at Kitimat, BC, has been sustained by exclusive water rights that have allowed the firm to control its own power costs. Planned smelter expansion in BC has been stopped by the controversial decision of the provincial government to retract its earlier approval of the 'Kemano Completion' power development because of its threat to fish habitat and its conflict with Aboriginal land claims. But the refining complex in the

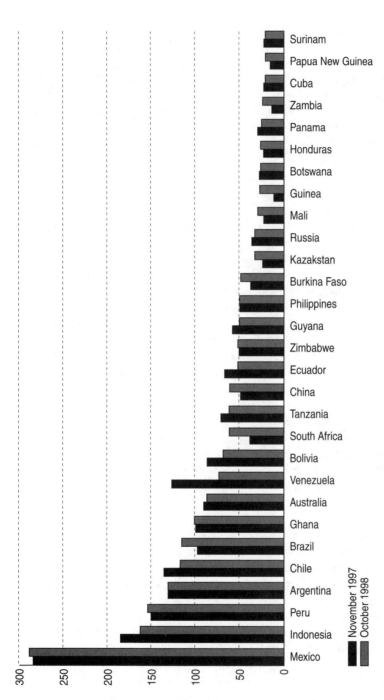

**Figure 9.1  Canadian Mineral Property Portfolio Abroad, 1997 and 1998**

NOTE: Includes companies of all sizes listed on Canadian stock exchanges; does not include holdings in the US. Figure shows 80 per cent of total Canadian holdings outside the US.

SOURCE: *Canadian Minerals Yearbook* (1998: Figure 7).

Chicoutimi–Jonquière region has been steadily upgraded and expanded. The attraction of large-scale foreign investment in electro-metallurgy to the middle St Lawrence Valley in the 1980s, on the other hand, was based on the promise of low energy costs through contracts subsidized by Hydro-Québec. This attracted US opposition and the imposition of countervail measures (import duties) against the producers. As heavy power users, mineral industry firms are sensitive to increases in hydro rates, and in Ontario the sector has lost some of the competitive advantage it had enjoyed prior to the 1980s. The high cost of power in remote regions such as the Yukon is one factor in limiting the development of mining there.

Competitive pressures restructuring the iron and steel industry come from both the supply side and downstream markets. The major innovation since the 1970s has been the diffusion of mini-mill technology, providing the large, vertically integrated steel producers (using blast furnace technology to smelt iron ore) with competition that enjoys the advantages of greater flexibility, both financial (lower break-even volumes of output) and locational (scrap steel is the readily assembled raw material). The geography of steel production has not changed in Canada as much as in the United States because southern Ontario and Quebec remain the dominant domestic markets: indeed, almost half of Canadian steel output is consumed by the auto industry. Stelco and Dofasco have upgraded their plants in Hamilton, and a number of mini-mills have expanded capacity in the Toronto–Niagara region and at sites in the Montreal region. Canadian firms also expanded into the US market following the signing of FTA (which did not remove all US obstacles to imports), particularly by opening mini-mills in the American Midwest. None of many feasibility studies over the years to build a west coast steel mill have come to fruition. And on the east coast, steel production in Sydney, Nova Scotia, was perpetuated from the late 1960s until the opening of the 2000s only with huge government subsidies (see Chapter 12).

On the demand side, the greatest influence on steel producers has been the increasingly stringent quality requirements of the auto industry. Spurred by the exacting demands of Japanese transplants (see Chapter 7), the steel industry has become much more closely associated with auto firms' product research and development. A symbol of this has been the joint investment by Canadian and Japanese steel producers in plants in Windsor and Hamilton that produce specialty steels for the auto sector.

Even more so than the forest sector, the Canadian mining industry is critical to the survival of single-industry communities beyond the agricultural ecumene. In Yukon, mineral revenues were formerly the less-than-secure foundation of the territorial economy and have currently largely disappeared. The major producer, the Faro lead-zinc mine, had a checkered existence in the 1980s and 1990s, closing for a number of periods when world metal prices were low. The threatened future of Lynn Lake, Manitoba, prompted the founding of the Canadian Association of Single Industry Towns in the 1980s, but there is not much future for many isolated mining settlements when the ore is depleted or no longer competitive. Some towns, such as Schefferville, Quebec, and Uranium City, Saskatchewan, have been all but abandoned and others, such as Gagnon, Quebec, have been bulldozed to eliminate corporate liability for upkeep of their infrastructure (Bradbury and St-Martin, 1983). Since the mid-1970s, both governments and mining companies have sought to avoid the problems associated with winding down communities. Hence, nearly all remote mines opened during the past 25 years have been based on a fly-in commuter workforce, housed in a more southerly community offering a good range of social and economic infrastructure to support family life (Shrimpton and Storey, 1992). For instance, the Raglan nickel mine, opened in far northern Quebec in 1998, draws workers from towns in the Abitibi region. At the same time, mining firms in the Arctic have made efforts to ensure that operations are better structured to be attractive to local Aboriginal peoples, whose role in the labour force is slowly increasing.

CONCLUSION

Canada's forest and mining industries are large and important, nationally and internationally. In 1996 they together contributed nearly 9 per cent of GDP and over 6 per cent of national employment, and did so primarily in hinterland regions where their relatively well-paying jobs are the foundation of local prosperity. Although they represent a continuation of Canada's historic role as a producer of natural resource staples, their competitiveness depends increasingly on the application of advanced technologies, and in that respect they, too, are part of the 'knowledge economy'. Both sectors, however, face challenges of sustainability and could be said to be at crossroads. Binkley (1997: 39, cited in Hayter, 2000), argues that British Columbia faces the transition 'between forests provided by providence and those created through human husbandry and stewardship'. In other words, as the natural richness of the forest resource is finally depleted or set aside for posterity in protected areas, the need to manage Canada's forests for sustained yield at a high level of productivity becomes more pressing. This challenge has come earlier to much of eastern Canada, but there is still room for considerable improvement in forest regeneration practices and in achieving maximum value-added from the wood-fibre supply. Hayter (2000) sees the restructuring of corporate policies and labour practices as another challenge facing the BC industry.

The crossroad facing the mineral industry perhaps offers less choice, for the reserves of most base metals have been declining for the past generation. Mineral exploration in Canada has not kept pace with the depletion of mines that were opened when markets were stronger in the 1970s (Wallace, 1996). Rather, as noted above and in Figure 9.1, Canadian mining firms have sought increasingly to develop mineral reserves abroad, where the economic returns are more attractive. Yet Canada has by no means run out of promising mineral geology. Where Aboriginal land claims have been settled, many of the uncertainties that inhibited exploration activity have been resolved and a new round of promising discoveries may result. Certainly, viable mines will be those whose revenues cover the environmental protection costs that are part of doing business in contemporary Canada, as well as the transportation costs of reaching the market; but many opportunities remain.

## FURTHER READING

Edgington, D.W., and R. Hayter. 1997. 'International trade, production chains and corporate strategies: Japan's timber trade with British Columbia', *Regional Studies* 31: 151–66.

Hayter, R. 2000. *Flexible Crossroads: The Restructuring of British Columbia's Forest Economy*. Vancouver: University of British Columbia Press.

Preston, V., J.N. Holmes, and A. Williams. 1997. 'Working with "Wild Rose I": lean production in a greenfield mill', *Canadian Geographer* 41: 88–104.

Wallace, I. 1996. 'Restructuring in the Canadian mining and mineral-processing industries', in J.N.H. Britton, ed., *Canadian and the Global Economy: The Geography of Structural and Technological Change*. Montreal and Kingston: McGill-Queen's University Press, 123–36.

# The Energy and Chemical Industries

## INTRODUCTION

Among the world's industrialized nations, Canada enjoys an exceptionally high level of energy self-sufficiency combined with a wide range of domestic energy sources. Partly as a result, it has the more ambiguous distinction of being the world's most energy-intensive economy in terms of consumption per capita. The geography of domestic energy supplies and of North American energy markets has profoundly shaped the evolution of this sector of the Canadian economy. Significantly, the turbulence of global energy markets in the 1970s was translated directly into domestic geopolitical tensions because of the marked regional contrasts in its consequences. Conflict subsided with the fall in world oil prices in 1985 and the arrival of a less interventionist government in Ottawa, but the energy sector continues to be shaped substantially by political as well as economic influences at the global, continental, and interprovincial levels. This is also true to some extent of those manufacturing industries that process energy raw materials (notably petrochemicals) or that are especially energy-intensive (notably electro-metallurgical processors).

Among the major markets for energy, only the transportation sector is essentially captive to one source (oil) on account of the specific technologies involved. For other uses, such as industrial processing and residential heating, alternative energy sources are usually feasible, and the choice will depend on comparative cost. Because different energy sources have different geographies, at both the supply and distribution stages, and because they face different transportation or transmission costs, patterns of energy consumption are highly expressive of spatial competition. Moreover, one of the most flexible energy sources, electricity, can be generated directly as hydroelectric power or as 'secondary' energy from steam turbines powered by fossil fuels or nuclear energy, and in this case there is considerable freedom in the choice of generating station location.

Since the 1970s, the environmental consequences of energy production and consumption have been recognized as an important policy issue, so that 'cleaner' fuels and technologies have acquired greater appeal, and these considerations have changed the market attractiveness of certain fuels (e.g., favouring natural gas and low-sulphur coal). 'Non-conventional' energy sources, such as wind, biomass, and solar (photovoltaic energy), have begun to make a significant contribution in specific applications, but fossil fuels and hydroelectric power remain the backbone of Canadian energy supply.

## THE GEOPOLITICS OF ENERGY

The overriding feature of Canada's energy map is that the industrial core of southern Ontario and Quebec is almost completely devoid of fossil-fuel resources and has had to secure them from elsewhere or find substitutes. When coal became the principal energy source of this industrializing region in the late nineteenth century, the lowest-cost supplies were (and remain today) the US Appalachian mines south of Lake Erie, readily accessible by rail and/or water. To compete, even in the Montreal market in the 1920s, Cape Breton coal required a federal transportation subsidy. More recently, Alberta coal purchased by Ontario Power Generation (formerly Ontario Hydro) has carried a higher delivered price than coal imported from the United States, but one justified commercially by its lower sulphur content. The development of hydroelectric power in the early 1900s, at sites such as Niagara Falls, Ontario, and Shawinigan, Quebec, provided an indigenous energy source that, in Quebec especially, compensated for the lack of coal. It was harnessed to promote the emergence of an industrial economy weighted towards electricity-intensive resource processing, notably the pulp and paper and aluminum industries (Dales, 1957).

The development of Alberta's oil and gas fields in the 1950s posed new political challenges concerning the relation between Canada's industrialized core and its resource-rich western periphery. At that time, to provide a large and secure market for Alberta's fuels and stimulate the economic development of the province, it was necessary to construct pipelines to link producers to distant Ontario consumers. Arguments were made, comparable to those in the 1870s over the construction of the CPR, for and against making this expensive infrastructure an all-Canadian undertaking or alternatively routing it through the United States and allowing it to serve US markets also. More pointedly, with respect to oil, cheaper imported supplies reaching central Canada via the Portland (Maine)–Montreal pipeline posed a threat that the pipeline from Alberta, once built, would prove a white elephant unless the federal government guaranteed to maintain a substantial market for western oil in central Canada. This commitment was made in 1959, when the 'Ottawa Valley Line' was instituted as a regulatory device to preserve the Ontario market west of Ottawa for Alberta producers, leaving Canada east of that line to be supplied by imported, and then slightly cheaper, oil. In this respect, federal policy discriminated against Ontario consumers for the sake of stimulating Alberta's oil industry.

The impact of the oil price increases in the 1970s induced by the Organization of Petroleum Exporting Countries (OPEC) massively reversed this price discrimination and created a highly charged geopolitical challenge to Ottawa. Although Canada is a *net* exporter of energy, this is achieved only because exports of oil, gas, and coal from western Canada and of electricity, principally from Quebec, exceed imports of oil into eastern and central provinces and coal into Ontario. (Figures 10.1 and 10.2 show Canadian exports and imports of crude oil and natural gas.) The rapid escalation of world oil prices in 1973 and 1979 generated vast resource royalties for the Alberta government, but while it increased energy costs for all Canadians, it hit central and eastern Canada particularly hard. The competitiveness of Ontario's manufacturing sector was threatened, and industries and domestic consumers in Atlantic Canada were even more vulnerable. Because of the lack of alternative cost-competitive energy sources in that region, oil had become the preferred fuel for electricity generation and its cost of production increased dramatically.

The federal government of the day chose to respond to the new global oil price regime by regulating domestic prices. A 'made-in-Canada' oil price, set below world levels with the intention of benefiting Canadian manufacturers (primarily in Ontario and Quebec), was financed by increasing federal taxation of western oil production (at the expense of producers and the Alberta government) and using these funds to subsidize the cost of imported oil consumed in eastern Canada. Yet the still-huge oil revenues of the Alberta government presented Ottawa with a further threat: under the formula for regional equalization payments (see Chapter 2), the federal government was facing massive obligations to transfer funds to the have-not provinces, and by 1977 this group could technically have included Ontario (Courchene, 1980). Ottawa's response was unilaterally to impose new fiscal arrangements that had the effect of ensuring that Ontario would not become eligible for equalization payments. Whatever the merits of the federal government's arguments for moderating the domestic impact of higher world oil prices and protecting the weaker economies of Atlantic Canada (and to a lesser extent Quebec) from their consequences, its policy aroused deeply felt resentment in Alberta. It appeared that, yet again, the interests and prosperity of westerners were being sacrificed for the sake of central Canadians.

The National Energy Program (NEP), instituted in 1980, capped Ottawa's response to the energy crises of the 1970s and reinforced western alienation. Its encouragement of greater Canadian ownership of the oil industry, including an element of state ownership through the creation of Petro-Canada (which was privatized in the 1990s) was philosophically at odds with the outlook of the Calgary business community and was anathema to the oil industry multinationals. The NEP's lavish subsidization of high-cost energy exploration in the Arctic and Atlantic offshore frontiers was seen as undermining continued investment in the oil and gas sector in Alberta and adjacent provinces. Moreover, westerners noted that whereas the federal government was greatly increasing its intervention in, and revenues from, the oil and gas sectors, it was doing little to interfere with the expansion and revenues of provincial hydroelectric utilities, notably Hydro-Québec. Completion of the first stage of the James Bay hydroelectric project in 1981 allowed the Quebec utility to sell large quantities of power into the high-priced market of the northeastern United States at a time when oil and gas exports from western provinces were being curbed.

The return to a lower and more stable world oil price regime after the mid-1980s and the changed political climate in Ottawa, which favoured government deregulation and privatization, reduced the intergovernmental and interregional frictions associated with national energy policy. Concerns about the adequacy and security of Canadian energy supplies have subsided since the 1970s, partly because gains in efficiency of use and structural change in the national economy lowered the growth rate of demand (from 2.6 per cent per year in the 1970s to 0.8 per cent per year in the

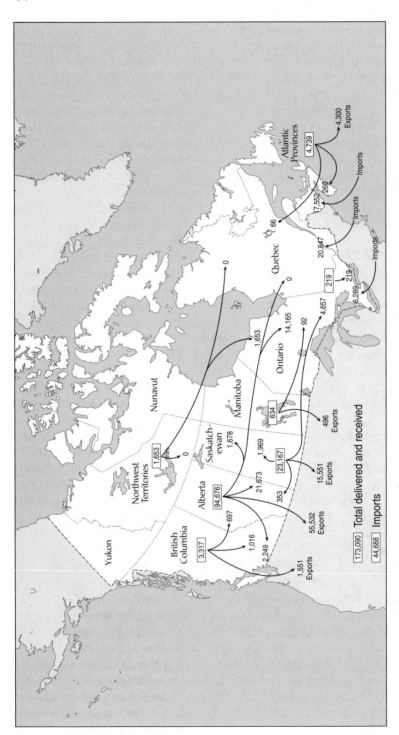

**Figure 10.1  Crude Oil Production and Movements, by Source, 1998**

NOTE: Based on thousands of cubic metres of crude delivered and received.

SOURCE: Statistics Canada, *Oil and Gas Extraction, 1998*, Cat. no. 26–213–xPB, 12.

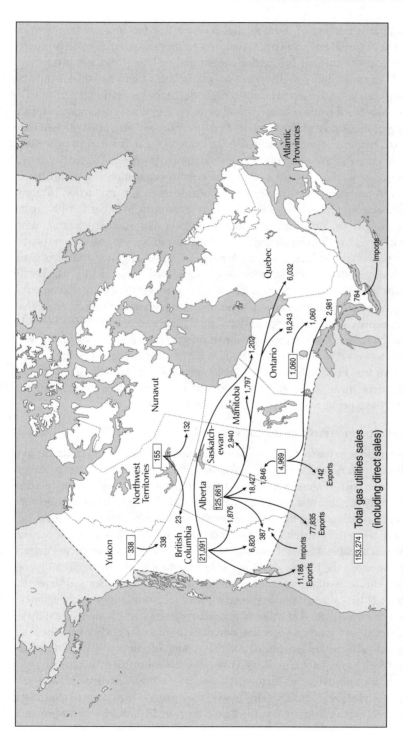

**Figure 10.2  Natural Gas Sales and Movements, by Source, 1998**

NOTE: Based on sales of millions of cubic metres of natural gas.

SOURCE: Statistics Canada, *Oil and Gas Extraction, 1998*, Cat. no. 26–213–XPB, 13.

1980s), and partly because of technological progress that has made more resources available. The National Energy Board (1994), reviewing supply and demand prospects to 2010, anticipated that oil production would gradually increase, gas production would likely expand rapidly, coal production would hold steady, and there would be limited need for major new investments in hydroelectricity generation.

By the late 1990s Alberta's conventional oil output was gradually declining, but since the opening of the Suncor plant near Fort McMurray in 1967 and the larger Syncrude plant in 1978, major efficiency gains have been made in the technology of processing the province's vast oil-sands deposits. These hold out the prospect of a gradual transition taking place in the province's oil industry, from conventional to synthetic oil production. A number of new projects are scheduled to enter production by 2005. Meanwhile, western Canadian gas reserves have continued to expand, with recent sizable discoveries in northeastern British Columbia and southern Yukon. With demand for gas in North America continuing to grow rapidly, proposals were revived in 2000 to build two pipelines from the Arctic. The Alaska Highway and Mackenzie Valley routes would bring supplies from the Alaskan North Slope and the Mackenzie Delta region into Alberta, for onward distribution through the existing continental pipeline network. In eastern Canada, a number of developments have given that region the security of more energy options should there be another crisis in world markets in the future. The interprovincial natural gas grid was extended further east in Quebec in the 1980s, and in 1997 the first barrel of east coast offshore oil was pumped from the Hibernia field. Gas production from fields off Sable Island reached the mainland of Nova Scotia in 2000, a project made financially attractive by the exports that the pipeline will carry to the New England market.

### INTERFUEL COMPETITION AND INDUSTRIAL LOCATION

Regional variations in the fuel composition of demand (here including electricity as a 'fuel') reflect the combined effects of local availability and differential transportation and distribution costs (Figure 10.3). In most non-transportation applications, natural gas is inherently the cheapest energy source, but relatively it has the highest delivery costs. Hence, it dominates the market in regions where it is extracted (the Prairies), but its share declines steadily with increasing distance of shipment. (It is only now becoming available as a fuel in Atlantic Canada.) As a result, oil's share of the energy market is actually lowest on the Prairies, but highest in Atlantic Canada, where its comparative ease and cheapness of transportation (delivered from the North Sea and Venezuela by supertanker) have made it the dominant fuel in a relatively energy-poor region.

Electricity's regional market share is primarily determined by the availability of developed hydroelectric power potential (otherwise, its costs vary in line with the price of the primary fuels used to generate it) and the strength of competition among different types of fuel. Its major role in the Quebec market (almost twice the national average) reflects a combination of factors: the province's large resources of, and real comparative advantage in, cheap hydro power; the relatively high costs of alternative energy sources (although now that natural gas is more widely available in the province

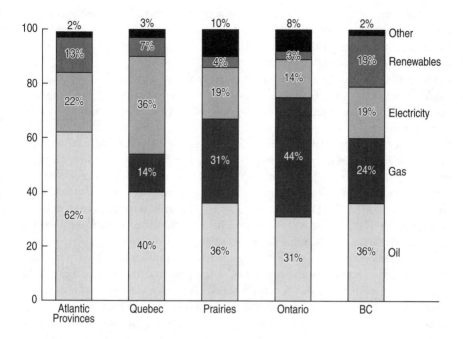

**Figure 10.3  Regional Variations in Energy Consumption, 1991**

*SOURCE*: National Energy Board (1994: Figure 4–10).

it has proved quite competitive); and government policies promoting its use, particularly in the residential sector. 'Renewables' in Figure 10.3 essentially reflects the use of wood residues by the forest products industry; 'other' captures mainly the use of coal and coke, notably by the Ontario steel industry.

Interprovincial variations in the energy input mix of the electricity supply industry augment the preceding analysis (Table 10.1). Hydroelectric generation dominates in Newfoundland (Churchill Falls, Labrador), Quebec, Manitoba (plants on the Nelson River), and British Columbia (on the Peace and Columbia Rivers). These provinces contain sites of large-scale water power potential and are relatively high-cost markets for alternative fuel sources (with the exception of BC, whose coal industry was put on a competitive commercial basis only in the late 1960s). In contrast, Ontario, although generating more hydroelectric power than Newfoundland or Manitoba, is a market where electricity demand outstripped available water power resources by the late 1950s, where relatively cheap coal to fire thermal plants was readily accessible from the Appalachians, and where for a variety of national and provincial strategic reasons governments supported the development of nuclear generating capacity, which supplied approximately 40 per cent of provincial electricity demand in the late 1990s. Alberta and Saskatchewan, with competitive local coal supplies and limited hydro potential, have developed an electricity supply industry predominantly based on mine-mouth thermal generating plants (as at Wabanum, Alberta, and Estevan, Saskatchewan), although the latest additions to Alberta's deregulated energy supply industry have been natural gas-fired.

Whereas Canadian fossil fuels have never been among the very cheapest in the world, significant amounts of Canadian hydroelectric capacity are globally highly competitive and have attracted the development of major energy-intensive industries. The harnessing of Niagara Falls at the beginning of the twentieth century attracted a local cluster of plants in the electro-chemical, electro-metallurgical, and abrasives industries. This region maintained its power cost advantage until Ontario Hydro standardized prices across the provincial electricity grid in the 1960s. Similar activity on a smaller scale grew out of early development of the hydro potential on the St Maurice River at Grand-Mère and Shawinigan in Quebec. The greatest concentration of industry localized by cheap hydro power, however, has been the aluminum processing plants constructed by Alcan in the Saguenay Valley since the 1920s. Here, and also at Kitimat, BC, where the company built a smelter in the 1950s, Alcan has been able to maintain the water rights to a substantial amount of power potential that gives it considerable independence from, and a lower energy cost than, the provincial electrical utilities that have control of the rest of the available water resources. Note, in contrast, that Hydro-Québec's strategy to attract new power-intensive industries (notably aluminum and magnesium smelters) to the St Lawrence Valley in the 1980s involved 'secret' contracts of electricity at a discount from its prevailing rates. These contracts subsequently provoked retaliatory measures under US trade law initiated by competing smelters in the United States.

The Canadian petrochemical industry does not enjoy the global comparative advantage of the aluminum processors, but it has developed some competitive strengths within the continental North American market (Chapman, 1991). Until the 1970s, the industry was concentrated in central Canada, where it relied on naphtha feedstock from oil refineries. The Sarnia area petrochemical complex began as a government-sponsored scheme to produce synthetic rubber during World War II. It expanded with the growth of product markets during the 1960s and the increased capacity of oil pipeline links from Alberta. The smaller Montreal complex developed out of the oil refineries located in that city. The energy crises of the 1970s, however, focused industry attention on the potential of western Canada's gas fields as a competitive source of feedstock accessible to major North American markets and in a politically secure and congenial location. Large, export-oriented ethylene plants, benefiting from economies of scale and from the Alberta government's support for economic diversification initiatives, were opened in 1979 and 1984. These plants were planned at a time when world energy prices were expected to escalate indefinitely and hence, given the price controls of the National Energy Program, were seen to provide an increasing cost advantage to Canadian producers. This scenario did not materialize as predicted, but the Alberta industry was nevertheless much better placed as a source of competitive feedstock than the oil-based producers in Ontario and Quebec, and it established its position as a

**Table 10.1  Electricity Supply in Canada, 1998**

| Energy Source (%) | Canada | Nfld | PEI | NS | NB | Que. | Ont. | Man. | Sask. | Alta | BC | Yukon | NWT |
|---|---|---|---|---|---|---|---|---|---|---|---|---|---|
| Hydro | 60.3 | 97.1 | | 8.4 | 15.0 | 95.6 | 24.9 | 97.0 | 20.3 | 3.7 | 89.8 | 86.3 | 87.3 |
| Wind & tidal | — | | | 0.3 | | — | | | | 0.1 | | 0.1 | |
| Steam | 24.9 | 2.8 | 95.4 | 91.4 | 65.1 | 1.6 | 27.5 | 2.9 | 77.6 | 90.8 | 8.8 | | |
| Nuclear | 12.4 | | | | 19.8 | 2.5 | 42.1 | | | | | | |
| Internal combustion | 2.2 | | | | — | — | — | — | 0.2 | 0.2 | 0.1 | 13.6 | 47.7 |
| Combustion turbine | 2.2 | | | | | | 5.4 | | 1.9 | 5.2 | 1.3 | | 15.0 |
| Total Generated (GWh) | 544,900.0 | 44,947.1 | 2.6 | 10,779.6 | 19,34.5 | 154,955.0 | 142,099.2 | 31,724.1 | 16,961.1 | 55,623.8 | 67,770.3 | 312.9 | 689.8 |
| % of Canada Total | 100.0 | 8.2 | | 2.0 | 3.5 | 28.4 | 26.1 | 5.8 | 3.1 | 10.2 | 12.4 | 0.1 | 0.1 |

— = less than 0.1 per cent.

SOURCE: Statistics Canada (1998a).

significant supplier within the continental market. Plans to develop petrochemical plants oriented towards Pacific Rim markets have proceeded slowly, but a major methanol plant, fed from gas fields in northeastern BC, was opened at Kitimat in 1982. It closed, however, in 1999 as reduced Asian demand, increased international competition, and rising natural gas prices undermined its competitiveness.

## Energy Projects as Means of National and Regional Development

Because most of Canada's energy resources are located in the national hinterland and their development tends to involve large-scale construction projects that stimulate employment (as well as demand in linked capital goods industries), governments have often tended to view energy projects as stimuli to regional economic development. This was all the easier to justify when, in the 1970s and early 1980s, the global energy crisis made state support more defensible on the grounds of security of supply, and revenues from energy projects were being projected to escalate steadily. The NEP gave particular support to oil and gas exploration in the 'Canada Lands' (Figure 10.4), especially those offshore regions of the Arctic and east coast where evidence of potentially commercial deposits was already accumulating. The very high cost and major technological challenges of these frontier energy projects, however, together with the collapse of world energy prices in the mid-1980s (and with it the justification for the NEP), resulted in the abandonment of most of the schemes to access these remote resources. Only the Hibernia oil project survived, promoted as a stimulus to the depressed economy of Newfoundland. However, a number of provincial governments had comparable visions of energy-based regional development: notably Quebec, in the form of the massive James Bay and Great Whale hydro schemes; and British Columbia, with the opening up of the northeast coalfield. In a rather different way, the federal Atomic Energy Canada Limited, Ontario Hydro, and engineering firms in the nuclear supply industry sought to expand the market for Canadian (CANDU) reactor technology as a means of promoting high-technology employment (which primarily benefits heartland urban centres) and exports.

The experience of using the energy sector as a vehicle for regional development in the recent past has been almost universally disappointing, however. The construction of large dams in remote regions provides few permanent jobs and almost no local linkage effects (see Chapter 15). Moreover, as the negative impacts of the James Bay, Nelson, and Peace River projects on ecosystems and Aboriginal communities have shown, there are regionalized losses involved. In addition, government willingness to subsidize frontier energy projects and nuclear technology contributed to the public-sector deficits that have now been recognized as an obstacle to Canadian economic growth. The timing of investment has often been unfortunate in terms of subsequent trends in the global economy, but this is another way of saying that risks were not realistically assessed. This is very clear with respect to the northeast BC coalfield. The Cape Breton coalfield illustrates a different form of failure. Since the late 1960s alone, when the public sector took over the mines of the Sydney region, $1.6 billion have been spent keeping a shrinking number of miners at work

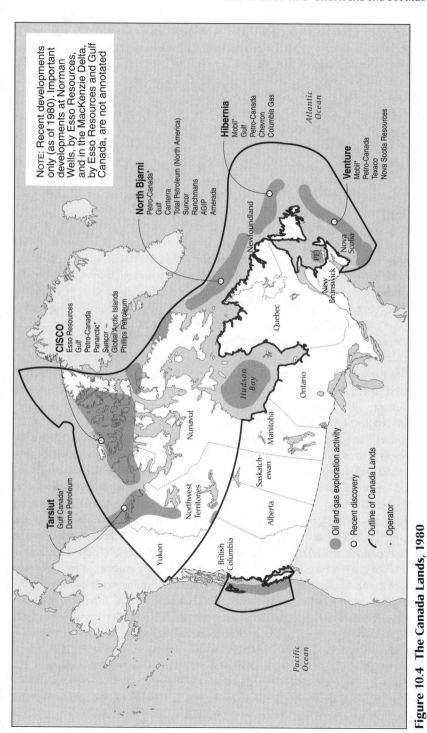

**Figure 10.4 The Canada Lands, 1980**

SOURCE: Energy, Mines and Resources Canada, 1980, *The National Energy Program* (Ottawa, 1980: 43).

(declining from 3,500 to under 500) in a coalfield that was no longer economic, thereby delaying a more productive restructuring of the local economy (see Chapter 12). The same can be said of the low-grade uranium mines at Elliot Lake, Ontario, kept alive until the mid-1990s by expensive price guarantees that Ontario Hydro agreed to at the height of the 1970s energy crisis.

The northeast BC coalfield was developed in the early 1980s as a response to projected demand for coking coal by the Japanese steel industry. The Japanese firms were keen to promote an additional Canadian source of coal supply, and its related transportation system, to provide an alternative to the Kootenay mines and the export shipment infrastructure in southern BC related to them, which was perceived to be prone to interruption by bad weather and strike action. The province, in turn, was keen to see expansion of employment opportunities and economic diversification away from dependence on forestry in the northeast region (see Chapter 14). On this basis, provincial, federal, and private-sector funding went into the construction of two new coal mines, a new rail link, and the townsite of Tumbler Ridge. But not only did the coalfield enter production at a time when many other such projects around the Pacific, targeting the same buyers, were doing so; the contrasting corporate structure and strategies of the Japanese buyers compared to the Canadian producers put the latter in a very weak market position (Parker, 1997). Together, these factors caused the coalfield development to fall short of its projected output and employment targets (and hence of the projected boost to regional economic expansion) and resulted in large financial losses. Moreover, the additional output that the northeast mines brought to a saturated market contributed to the financial difficulties of the Kootenay coal industry. By 2000, coal production from the northeast mines was winding down and modern single-family dwellings were being sold off in Tumbler Ridge for under $30,000.

The concentration of nuclear generating capacity in Ontario (Table 10.1) arose out of decisions taken in the 1960s, when provincial electricity demand was growing exponentially and little hydro power potential remained to be developed. Ontario Hydro embarked on a massive investment program in thermal generating stations and committed itself to diversifying its energy sources. The future costs of atomic energy were seen, over-optimistically, as low and stable; and the environmental costs of the nuclear fuel cycle were underestimated and attracted relatively little concern at the time. An expanded nuclear power industry promised to revive Ontario's uranium mines at Elliot Lake (which had lost the military market they enjoyed in the Cold War of the 1950s) and to support the expansion of high-technology employment in the province's engineering industry (McKay, 1983). The technological, financial, and environmental problems associated with nuclear reactors that have become obvious since the 1980s were not given adequate attention: indeed, CANDU reactors and Ontario Hydro's operational know-how continued to be actively promoted by the federal government as a Canadian high-technology export well into the 1990s. Only New Brunswick Power, with limited fuel options in the 1970s, also commissioned a commercial nuclear power plant, at Point Lepreau. (Hydro-Québec constructed a reactor, mainly for research purposes, at Gentilly, near Trois-Rivières.)

## ISSUES OF THE EARLY TWENTY-FIRST CENTURY

The concerns about security of energy supply that helped to shape Canada's National Energy Program in the 1980s have essentially disappeared. The geopolitics of global energy production are more resilient to disruptive events than they were in the 1970s, and Canada is better equipped to cope with disruptions of supply. On the other hand, the United States has once again become as dependent on imported oil as it was at the height of the 1970s energy crisis, and hence future disruptions in world oil markets are bound to impact it, with immediate repercussions for Canada. For example, in 2001, the new US administration claimed that it was necessary to release protected areas in Alaska for oil drilling to meet domestic needs. This plan has met with opposition in both Canada and the United States on account of its threat to the cross-border migratory caribou herds. Meanwhile, two other issues have gained importance—the link between energy consumption and climate change, and the industrial structure of the energy sector.

The OPEC-induced energy price rises of the 1970s focused world attention on energy conservation. Incentives to innovate for energy efficiency were greatest where energy was most expensive (in Japan and Europe) and less so where it remained relatively cheap (in the United States and Canada, especially under the Canadian oil-price regulation of that period). Most attention since the 1980s has gone into improving energy use in industrial processing, in the transportation sector, and through domestic conservation (Maclaren, 1996). Attempts to develop alternative energy sources in Canada have been limited, attracting nowhere near the level of government support that the nuclear energy industry has continued to receive. Gradually, with improvements in the economics and reliability of wind turbines, commercial wind power generation has been developed in areas with suitable conditions, notably in the foothills of southern Alberta; at Kincardine, Ontario, on Lake Huron; at and on the lower St Lawrence, where Canada's largest windmill farm opened in 1999 near Matane.

During the 1990s, international concern over the buildup of greenhouse gases in the atmosphere and moves to mitigate the threat of global warming added a new dimension to energy policy and conservation concerns. Nuclear energy production trumps fossil-fuel consumption in not contributing to the buildup of atmospheric $CO_2$, but its broader environmental impacts, not to mention its escalating costs, have undermined its appeal. Canada's progress in implementing its international commitments to curb $CO_2$ emissions, made in Kyoto in 1997, has been slow, however (see Chapter 3), and with the subsequent American abrogation of its Kyoto commitments this slow progress cannot be expected to improve. The distinct lack of enthusiasm among most provincial governments (most critically, that of Alberta) and many private-sector interests, including many energy corporations, towards possible measures (regulations or 'green' taxes) that might reduce fossil-fuel consumption has allowed the federal government to procrastinate.

Another feature of contemporary world energy markets is the move by many governments to promote the deregulation and privatization of energy utilities. One result has been to make the sector more open to foreign investment and to the application of innovative supply arrangements. The Canadian government has loosened its regulation of the energy sector, and symbolically indicated this by moving the headquarters of the National Energy Board from Ottawa to Calgary, the corporate home of Canada's oil and gas industry. Provincially owned utilities have been privatized in Nova Scotia (hydro) and British Columbia (gas), and the complex transfer of Ontario Hydro, Canada's largest electrical utility, into the private sector was well underway in 2001. This transition raises particular difficulties because of the 'stranded assets' that Ontario Hydro's nuclear generating stations, and the huge debt load associated with their construction, represent.

Encouraging the separation of ownership between power producers and those who operate the electricity transmission grid allows a much more varied and flexible configuration of electricity supply to emerge than has been typical of large public utilities. Co-generation plants that permit industrial users to meet their own needs and sell excess power through the grid offer lower energy costs to many pulp mills, for instance. Gas turbine technology offers low-cost power in much smaller units than conventional thermal generators, giving suppliers greater locational flexibility. At the same time, energy deregulation has brought problems as well as benefits. Alberta's electricity market was the first in Canada to be extensively deregulated, and the transition has resulted, at least initially, in marked price escalation and instability. A significant stimulus to change in Canada's electricity industry came from federal deregulation in the United States. Of particular importance has been the US move to open transmission grids to any qualified generator of power, which has implications for the cross-border exports of Canadian electricity. The long-running dispute between Newfoundland and Quebec over marketing the power generated at Churchill Falls, which has permitted Hydro-Québec to export large blocks of its own output at a profit while paying Newfoundland only one-tenth the current market price for the energy it receives, may well find a resolution under the rules of the emerging continental regulatory regime (see Chapter 12).

## Conclusion

As the preceding section makes clear, energy-related issues are going to be prominent among the challenges facing Canadian governments, corporations, and consumers in the coming years. The complex geographies of energy that this chapter has considered will ensure that the spatial and environmental implications of energy production and use will figure centrally in the selection and impact of policy choices.

### Further Reading

Froschauer, K. 1999. *White Gold: Hydroelectric Power in Canada*. Vancouver: University of British Columbia Press.

Maclaren, V.M. 1996. 'Redrawing the Canadian energy map', in J.N.H. Britton, ed., *Canada and the Global Economy: The Geography of Structural and Technological Change*. Montreal and Kingston: McGill-Queen's University Press, 137–54.

# Transportation

## INTRODUCTION

Canada is a large country with an open economy. The development of transportation systems has thus been a crucial activity, necessary for tying its regions together and for linking Canadians to foreign markets. During the 400 years or so since commodities began to be shipped out of Canada to markets overseas, the geography of the global economy has undergone major changes and trade flows have become much more complex. It is not surprising, therefore, that traffic flows within Canada, as well as those linking the country to foreign destinations, have shifted their principal geographical orientation a number of times and have become increasingly diverse in their composition.

Trade with Europe was the first set of commodity flows that structured the pattern of transportation systems to and within Canada. Until the mid-nineteenth century, the export of staples (furs, cod, and subsequently lumber) across the Atlantic created axes of shipping down the St Lawrence and from ports in Atlantic Canada. From the 1850s, the accelerating economic growth of the US economy, made possible and geographically configured by the spread of railways, created a new set of commodity flows, demanding different transportation alignments. The movement of Canadian timber into northern states, from New England to Michigan, encouraged the construction of cross-border rail routes (McIlwraith, 1993). Following Confederation, the drive to consolidate a national economy involved the settlement of the Prairies and put the focus once again on east-west routes, notably transcontinental railways, to serve the flows of goods and people linking the regions of Canada. The 1950s and 1960s brought renewed attention to the creation of north-south transportation links within Canada, as the federal government became much more active in developing the Arctic (facilitated by advances in aircraft technology) and as US demand for resources (especially minerals) from the Canadian Shield prompted the construction of new rail corridors northward. The opening of the St Lawrence Seaway in 1959, while clearly facilitating the eastward shipment of Canadian wheat exports, also represented a significant addition to Canada–United States transportation capacity. It linked the recently developed Ungava iron ore deposits at Schefferville, Quebec, via ports on the lower St Lawrence to US steel producers in the Great Lakes region. The expanding oil and gas pipeline networks of western Canada in the 1950s and 1960s further strengthened cross-border transportation infrastructure.

The emergence of the Asia-Pacific region as a focus of Canadian trade in the 1970s prompted the next reorientation of transportation investment, as port and railway bottlenecks limited the movement of natural resource commodities from western Canada to the Pacific Rim. For example, the east-west grain transportation infrastructure had been developed principally to funnel shipments to Europe, not Asia, and terminal elevator capacity on the west coast became inadequate. Growing volumes of coal, potash, and sulphur added to congestion on the rail lines through the mountains to Vancouver. Investment in double-tracking on these routes, and in building the coal export terminal at Roberts Bank, responded to the increasing traffic demands. Moreover, the growing volume of international air traffic at Vancouver airport necessitated a major expansion there.

The most recent switch of trade orientation, in the 1990s, has resulted from the movement towards continental economic integration represented by NAFTA. Canada's heightened dependence on trade relations with the US and Mexico has resulted in heavier cross-border traffic by all modes and the increasing operational integration of transportation systems linking the three countries. Regulatory restrictions on Canada–US air traffic have been eased and Canadian railways have expanded their networks south of the border (Figure 11.1). The cumulative effect of all these changes in the geographical orientation of Canada's international economic ties has been to create transportation bottlenecks in some regions and excess capacity in others, as services and infrastructure have gradually adjusted to new demands.

However, the process of transportation system adjustment to the shifting currents of trade is never smooth. Particularly for modes that require heavy investment in fixed networks, notably railways, there are significant economic barriers to keeping pace with changing demand. Routes become underutilized long before they are abandoned, and investment in new infrastructure usually lags well behind the emergence of the traffic that justifies it. Marine and air transport systems are less tied to a fixed network geography and can be more flexible in responding to changing patterns of demand, although the need for heavy investment in terminals complicates the adjustment process. The ubiquity of road networks and the vast number of vehicles that use them make change in the orientation and volume of highway traffic inherently easier to accommodate. Yet congestion rapidly builds up in areas of high demand, principally within metropolitan regions but also on major freight corridors. As with other modes, new investment in roads invariably follows some time after the demand for it emerges. But this begs the question of what investment priorities are appropriate for a national road transportation system that might be compatible with a sustainable economy.

The share of total traffic captured by each mode of transport (the modal split) has been determined by changes on the supply side—the transportation technologies and operating systems available—and on the demand side, notably by the changing composition of the national economy and rising levels of consumer purchasing power. This has been true both for freight and for passenger traffic. As in other parts of the world, transportation in Canada prior to the development of the railways was almost entirely by water. Natural resource staples (fish, furs, and timber) were the first major

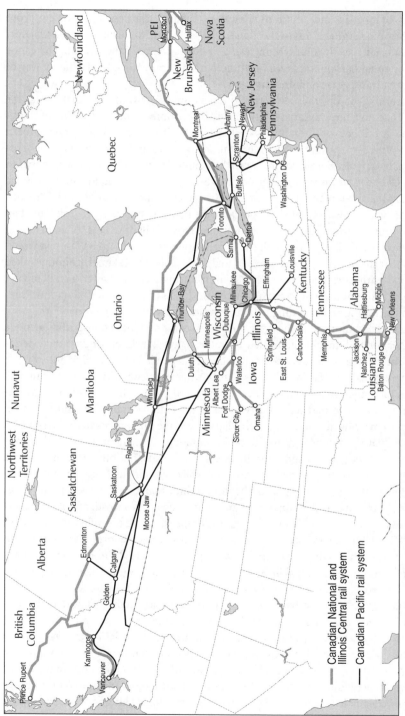

**Figure 11.1 Canadian National and Canadian Pacific Railway Networks, 1999**

*Source: Globe and Mail*, 24 July 1999, B1.

products of long-distance traffic, moving along dendritic transportation systems from interior or outport locations to the 'points of attachment' to Europe (Figure 5.1), port settlements such as St John's, Montreal, and Quebec City (Vance, 1970). The canoe routes or small harbours that serviced most of this traffic produced little by way of permanent transportation infrastructure.

The coming of the railway, a revolutionary mode of transport that broke the dependence on waterways, made possible the development of the interior of North America. A rail network began to take shape in the St Lawrence Valley and southern Ontario after 1850 (Andreae, 1997), linking major cities and allowing them, notably Toronto, to gain economic control over their hinterlands. Rail connections between eastern Canada and the northeastern United States were also built, to handle growing volumes of cross-border traffic stimulated by the dynamic growth of the US 'manufacturing belt'. But with Confederation came the political imperative to link Canadian regions 'from sea to sea' and hence the 'National Dream' (Berton, 1970) of an east-west transcontinental railway. This, with the agricultural settlement of the West that would create the traffic to cover its costs, served to define Canada as a staples economy linked to Europe, with a developing domestic manufacturing sector in Ontario and Quebec, politically resistant to being overwhelmed by the forces of north-south economic integration (including an expanding US rail network just south of the border).

For almost a century, until the 1950s, railways were the dominant transportation mode in Canada for both freight and passenger traffic. Places flourished, or did not, depending on their access to rail service. Manufacturers depended on rail shipment to reach their markets nationwide. Montreal, as Canada's major gateway city, became its railway node and its largest manufacturing centre (Burghardt, 1971). The network of transcontinental railways consolidated the city's role as the national transportation hub, with Winnipeg emerging in a similar but subsidiary role as the gateway city to the West. Water transport played an important role in bulk commodity movements through the Great Lakes/St Lawrence system and coastally in eastern Canada, but otherwise the railways had a monopoly of transportation provision, which soon invited government regulation. The technological monopoly of the steam train was decisively broken in the 1950s, however, by the rapid expansion of road and air transport. The growth of road transport in Canada had been delayed by the Depression of the 1930s and the military priorities of World War II, but the prosperity of the postwar years brought enormous investment in roads and the vehicles that use them. The same period witnessed a revolutionary expansion in the technological capabilities of air transport, which was particularly significant in regions beyond the road and railway networks of southern Canada.

By the 1970s, domestic passenger transportation had become almost exclusively shared between the private automobile and the airline industry, and trucking had captured the vast majority of shipments of manufactured goods. The railways' ability to adjust to new traffic demands was handicapped by regulations that continued to assume that they possessed the economic power of a monopolist and by their own organizational rigidities. As the structure of the Canadian economy moved increasingly away from dependence on natural resources and traditional patterns of producing and

**Table 11.1   Leading Commodities Transported by Railways within Canada, 1997**

| Commodity | Total Freight Traffic (initial haul—tonnes) | % Total |
|---|---|---|
| Bituminous coal | 40,154,624 | 15.5 |
| Iron ore and concentrates | 38,813,197 | 15.0 |
| Wheat | 26,262,176 | 10.1 |
| Containers on flat cars | 17,755,947 | 6.9 |
| Muriate of potassium (potash) | 14,223,131 | 5.5 |
| Pulpwood chips | 13,435,163 | 5.2 |
| Lumber | 9,531,313 | 3.7 |
| Woodpulp | 9,267,435 | 3.6 |
| Sulphur | 5,703,850 | 2.2 |
| Gypsum | 5,390,961 | 2.1 |
| Bauxite ore and alumina | 5,355,113 | 2.1 |
| Newsprint paper | 4,865,446 | 1.9 |

SOURCE: Statistics Canada, Cat. no. 52-216.

distributing manufactured goods, so the technological advantages of fast, flexible, and punctual truck and air freight shipments became more attractive economically, despite the higher average rates per ton/kilometre charged by these modes. Today, the principal commodities moved by rail, as by domestic water transport, reflect the residual strong association of these modes with Canada's resource-based industries (Table 11.1)

As in other industrialized nations, the evolution and functioning of Canada's transportation systems have been significantly shaped by government; but in parallel with trends elsewhere, the period since the early 1980s has seen a substantial decline in state intervention in the sector. Binding the country together from coast to coast required public investment in the Intercolonial Railway (to the Maritimes) and substantial state subsidies for the Canadian Pacific Railway, for distances were great but people and traffic were initially sparse. Once built, however, the railways were effectively transportation monopolists, so calls for government regulation of their tariffs and services were quick to emerge. Subsidized freight rates for prairie grain (the Crow's Nest Agreement of 1897) and traffic from the Maritimes (after 1927) were early expressions of what would later be called 'regional policy'. They came to be regarded as hinterland 'entitlements' or, when they were judged inadequate, as evidence of Ottawa's collusion with rapacious central Canadian interests (Darling, 1980). Regulatory reform in the transportation industries (particularly the railways), to reflect the very different competitive conditions that emerged after World War II, was thus delayed because of its political sensitivity. The National Transportation Act of 1967 began the process, but regulatory changes in the United States after 1980 and Ottawa's growing fiscal crisis in the 1990s eventually forced a thorough re-evaluation of government's role in this sector. By 2000, direct federal involvement in all modes of transportation—port management, the St Lawrence Seaway, Canadian National Railways, and Air Canada—had been severely reduced or eliminated.

## THE ROLE OF TECHNOLOGICAL CHANGE

Technological change in transportation during the twentieth century was continual and far-reaching in its geographical implications. Not only did new modes emerge, notably the automobile, truck, aircraft, and pipeline, but there was radical upgrading of rail and marine technologies and operating systems. In Canada, the movement of people, outside the public transit systems of urban areas and the commuter rail systems of Toronto and Montreal, is almost exclusively performed by private automobiles and passenger airlines. The latter have deployed a widening array of aircraft types to structure their networks and match the demand on each intercity link. VIA Rail (still a Crown corporation) provides a skeleton network of intercity passenger trains, primarily in the Windsor–Quebec City corridor. Nationally, intercity bus operations are gradually reducing their route networks.

Freight transportation involves essentially two markets: bulk commodity shipments, for which low ton/kilometre rates are the basic economic requirement, and shipments of all manner of fabricated goods, for which the 'quality' of shipment is paramount (whether measured in speed, security, or predictability of delivery). Among bulk commodities, pipelines are the principal infrastructure for interregional oil and gas movements from producing regions in western Canada. There are a few long-distance pipelines for petrochemical feedstocks, but proposals for pipelines to convey coal slurry east and west from Alberta have never proven viable.

For bulk commodity shipments within the Great Lakes and lower St Lawrence corridor, complementary waterborne movements of eastbound grain and westbound iron ore have been the basis of the viability of the shipping industry. The opening of the St Lawrence Seaway in 1959, which permitted the use of larger lake carriers, brought significant productivity gains to bulk transport on the Great Lakes. However, only marginal improvements to the transportation system have been possible since that time. The commercial attractiveness of the Seaway has been reduced since the late 1970s, when traffic reached its all-time peak, both by the changing geography of trade flows and the increased competitiveness of rival transportation systems. More efficient rail services have replaced shipping for some traffic and have made competing waterway routes (notably barges on the Mississippi River) accessible to prairie grain shippers. The vision of opening up the Great Lakes ports to the world's shipping fleet might have had some substance when the Seaway opened, but it was very quickly dashed by technological change. In 1959, the Seaway's locks could accommodate 60 per cent of the world's dry-bulk cargo vessels; in 1998 they could accommodate only 7 per cent (*Globe and Mail*, 12 Mar. 1998).

The economics of bulk shipments by rail have been transformed in North America since 1970 by the introduction of unit train operations, providing trainload movements of commodities directly from the shipping point (for instance, coal mine or inland grain terminal) to the destination (customer or export terminal). The greater pricing flexibility that carriers have gained from deregulation has been equally vital. The emergence of western Canada as a major coal exporter to Asia would not have been possible without these developments, because its global competitors (particularly Australia) all enjoy the economic advantage of shorter transits from coal mine to export terminal. Saskatchewan potash producers capitalized on lower unit train shipping costs to increase their share of the US fertilizer market. The use of unit train shipments to move grain from the Prairies to export terminals on the west coast and at Thunder Bay has been increasing since the mid-1990s, with the reduction of regulations limiting the abandonment of small rural elevators.

The movement of non-bulk freight has undergone profound changes since the 1960s. Technological improvements in trucking and the much greater commercial flexibility enjoyed by truckers in comparison to the heavily regulated railways were the supply-side developments that hastened the transfer of general cargo from rail to road. The demand-side factors have stemmed from the increased variety and higher unit value of manufactured goods, calling for shipments that are smaller, faster, and more reliable than traditional rail service offered. Reflecting this, the vast majority of factories constructed in recent decades are not connected to the rail network.

The transition from Fordist to flexible manufacturing systems has reinforced rather than created these trends, which have been most fully developed in the manufacturing heartland of central Canada. But the most profound transformation of general cargo movement has stemmed from the containerization of shipments, begun by the ocean carriers. By loading goods into standardized 'boxes' at the point of origin and transferring the container between transport modes as necessary en route to its destination, faster, more secure, and substantially cheaper transits can be offered to the shipper. Cargo handling at ocean ports was revolutionized by this intermodal system, and the eastern Canadian ports engaged in transatlantic trade were quick to seize on its advantages (Wallace, 1975). Gradually, the logic of using containers for the intermodal shipment of domestic, and not just international marine, cargoes was realized by North American railways, which had earlier moved in this direction with their 'piggyback' services for truck trailers. The long-haul economies that rail enjoys over road transport, together with the greater operational and commercial flexibility that intermodalism gives the rail carriers, allowed them to recapture some of the freight traffic that had previously been lost to long-distance trucking. In the mid-1990s, the added productivity to be gained by 'double-stacking' containers on rail freight cars prompted Canadian National (CN) to construct a new, larger tunnel under the St Clair River at Sarnia to provide easy access for such traffic from Halifax and Montreal to Chicago.

As in other economic sectors, technological change in the transportation industries has involved difficult adjustments in labour organization. Until the 1960s, uninterrupted railway and port operations were invariably deemed critical to the smooth functioning of the Canadian economy. These industries had developed labour relations reflecting their strategic and quasi-monopolistic role, characterized by strong unionization, restrictive labour practices, considerable labour militancy used to exploit bargaining power, and managements (often abetted by federal government action) willing to 'buy peace'. Technological change and deregulation both undermined the traditional status quo. Truckers (even when unionized) were able to exploit their lower fixed costs and greater geographical and service flexibility in competing for rail traffic.

Traditional longshore work was largely eliminated by containerization. The geography of resistance to these changes was itself influential in the evolution of the national transportation system. For instance, Vancouver lost container traffic to Seattle throughout the 1970s because of a labour contract that secured local longshore workers the right to 'destuff' (unload) most BC-bound containers in the dock area. This defeated most of the advantages of intermodalism and prompted many shippers to avoid Vancouver by routing their consignments through the US port, trucking containers to or from Canada. More recently, the development of short-line railways was delayed in the early 1990s in Ontario by legislation denying potential new rail operators some of the labour contract flexibility that formed the basis of their competitive viability vis-à-vis trucking. Commercially successful restructuring in the transportation industries has gradually been facilitated by the emergence of a more flexible, customer-focused, and less adversarial work environment than was often typical in the past.

### CHANGES IN TRANSPORTATION NETWORKS

Advances in technology and the lessening of government regulation both have worked to change the geography of Canadian transportation networks. This is most obvious in the shrinkage of the railway system. With the exception of the prairie branch-line network, which was substantially protected by legislation until the 1990s, low-density branch lines were continuously abandoned by the two major railways from the 1960s, but at a slower pace (dictated by regulatory constraints) than that justified by the loss of traffic to road transport. The 1987 National Transportation Act gave the railways greater (but far from complete) flexibility to withdraw services and encouraged the creation of independent short-line railways to take over routes that Canadian National and Canadian Pacific wished to abandon, but where lower-cost operators could provide a commercially viable service (Bloomfield, 1991). The eastern extremities of both the CP and CN transcontinental networks have been restructured in this manner, with CN selling the Truro-to-Sydney route and CP the Sherbrooke-to-Saint John route to short-line operators. Since the mid-1990s, short-line networks have appeared in Ontario, Quebec, and on the Prairies. The final elimination of the Crow's Nest rates and related regulation in 1995 triggered a major reshaping of the prairie rail network, involving both route abandonment and new short-line railway formation. The sale by the major railway companies of their regional feeder networks has enabled them to focus their investment on servicing freight flows concentrated into high-density corridors between major traffic nodes. This holds true both for bulk shipments such as grain and for domestic and overseas general cargo consolidated at 'inland load centres' (Slack, 1990).

The geography of commercial air transport has seen a similar trend towards traffic consolidation on routes serving major 'hub' airports, such as Toronto, Montreal, and Vancouver. These are linked by frequent, wide-body jet service provided by Air Canada (having incorporated its former competitor, Canadian Airlines, in 2000) and by some smaller, predominantly charter, airlines. The heaviest passenger traffic in 1997 was on the Montreal–Toronto and Toronto–Vancouver links (Table 11.2). Each hub airport has a 'spoke' network of feeder services to smaller centres in its region. These are

**Table 11.2    Principal Canadian Domestic Airline Routes, 1997**

| | | Top Domestic Markets, 1997 | | | |
|---|---|---|---|---|---|
| Rank | City Pair | Scheduled Passengers | Charter Passengers | Total Passengers | Charter Share % |
| 1 | Montreal–Toronto | 1,181,770 | 104,862 | 1,286,632 | 8.2 |
| 2 | Toronto–Vancouver | 829,650 | 222,148 | 1,051,798 | 21.1 |
| 3 | Ottawa–Toronto | 688,880 | 487 | 689.367 | 0.1 |
| 4 | Calgary–Vancouver | 519,960 | 91,816 | 611,776 | 15.0 |
| 5 | Calgary–Toronto | 495,020 | 78,583 | 573,603 | 13.7 |
| 6 | Toronto–Winnipeg | 346,670 | 181,173 | 527,843 | 34.3 |
| 7 | Edmonton–Vancouver | 312,330 | 68,819 | 381,149 | 18.1 |
| 8 | Calgary–Edmonton | 308,020 | 1,107 | 309,127 | 0.4 |
| 9 | Halifax–Toronto | 289,380 | 119,260 | 408,640 | 29.2 |
| 10 | Edmonton–Toronto | 281,700 | 43,181 | 324,881 | 13.3 |
| 11 | Montreal–Vancouver | 193,590 | 91,601 | 285,191 | 32.1 |
| 12 | Ottawa–Vancouver | 176,520 | 13,639 | 190,159 | 7.2 |
| 13 | Vancouver–Winnipeg | 174,070 | 160,817 | 334,887 | 48.0 |
| 14 | Calgary–Winnipeg | 157,440 | 125,749 | 283,189 | 44.4 |
| 15 | Prince George–Vancouver | 146,650 | 558 | 147,208 | 0.4 |
| 16 | Thunder Bay–Toronto | 138,290 | 1,975 | 140,265 | 1.4 |
| 17 | St John's–Toronto | 127,540 | 50,039 | 177,579 | 28.2 |
| 18 | Calgary–Montreal | 125,370 | 10,872 | 136,242 | 8.0 |
| 19 | Kelowna–Vancouver | 112,090 | — | 112,090 | — |
| 20 | Calgary–Ottawa | 104,880 | 368 | 105,248 | 0.3 |

NOTE: Ranking is based on scheduled origin/destination traffic, excluding charter origin/destination traffic. Figures do not include passengers carried by WestJet Airlines and Vistajet.

SOURCE: Transport Canada, *Transportation in Canada, 1998* (Ottawa, 1999: 279).

provided by subsidiary or independent carriers using smaller aircraft appropriate to the level of traffic. At the same time, steadily growing traffic levels overall and the introduction of smaller 'regional jet' aircraft have encouraged the reintroduction of some direct flights (bypassing hubs) between major cities.

Because of the relatively greater dependence on air service of communities in northern Canada, where surface transportation may be unavailable or seasonal, and because low traffic levels and environmental conditions impose high costs, the federal government has retained greater regulatory control over air service in this region. Hub-and-spoke operations characterize the northern network also, however, with hubs such as Iqaluit and Yellowknife connected by trunk routes to southern Canada. In contrast, regulatory control over Canada–US cross-border flights was steadily relaxed during the 1990s, leading to a much more complex network of international flights from Canadian cities. The role of corporate and industrial linkages is evident in the demand for routes such as Calgary–Houston (oil) and Ottawa–Boston (high-tech).

With the exception of the shared federal involvement in the construction and improvement of the Trans-Canada Highway and its related ferries on the east and west coasts, the southern Canadian road network is a provincial responsibility. The distribution of highway capacity tends to reflect overall patterns of population density, with major corridors between relatively proximate metropolitan areas (notably Windsor–Montreal and Calgary–Edmonton) and distance-decay from metropolitan areas elsewhere.

Topography has exerted a major influence on port development on both the east and west coasts, and rationalization of shipping services has reflected this, among other factors. Despite the growing volume of Canadian trade with the Pacific Rim, transportation corridors from the East are limited to those few giving access to the ports of the Lower Mainland of BC and to Prince Rupert. Bulk commodity exports are handled at the major export terminals of Roberts Bank, south of the Fraser estuary, and at Prince Rupert, which was expanded in the early 1980s to service the new coal traffic from mines in the Tumbler Ridge area. Container traffic at Vancouver is moved through terminals in the traditional port area on Burrard Inlet and through a newer facility, with more room for expansion, at Roberts Bank.

On the east coast and along the St Lawrence, container traffic is overwhelmingly concentrated at Montreal and Halifax. Corporate concentration among shipping lines has made CP Ships a significant transatlantic carrier, serving northwestern Europe from its base in Montreal. Although Montreal is not accessible to the very largest modern container ships, its success in attracting European traffic to and from central Canada and the US Midwest has made it the third-largest container port on the east coast of North America (after New York/New Jersey and Charleston, South Carolina). Halifax benefits from its large deep-water harbour and from its position on the great circle sea lanes across the North Atlantic, being one day sailing time closer to Europe than New York. It attracts calls from container shipping serving the US east coast–Europe route, as well as from Japanese and other container shipping linking eastern Canada with the Pacific. The latter traffic was originally concentrated at Saint John, New Brunswick, but this smaller port was handicapped by its inability to offer round-the-clock access to large vessels on account of its limited draught (reflecting the large tidal range of the Bay of Fundy). However, with the emergence of a new generation of 'post-Panamax' container vessels (those too large to traverse the Panama Canal), New York's attractiveness as the east coast port situated in North America's overwhelmingly dominant market area has reinforced its hub character, and the volume of container traffic moving through Halifax has ceased to grow significantly.

## MAJOR TRAFFIC FLOWS

The 12 leading commodities shipped by rail in 1997 are listed in Table 11.1. With the exception of the container movements of (almost exclusively) manufactured goods, all this traffic is generated by traditional staples industries—minerals, grain, and forest products. The majority of these shipments originate in western Canada: the principal exceptions are iron ore (most of which is hauled by the Quebec North Shore and

Labrador Railway and the nearby Cartier Railway), gypsum (moved a short distance to Hantsport, Nova Scotia), bauxite/alumina (another short haul, from La Grande Baie to Alcan plants in the Chicoutimi area), and most of the newsprint traffic, which travels south from mills scattered across the central Canadian Shield. To a large degree, all these commodities are 'captive' to rail transport in that there is no economically viable alternative for shipping them to market. But that does not mean that the railways can charge grossly inflated rates. The product invariably faces competition from alternative foreign supplies (e.g., Canadian coal versus Australian coal in the Japanese market, or Canadian versus domestic newsprint in the US), so to a large degree the shippers and the carriers have a shared interest in keeping transportation costs in line so that markets are not lost. Where there are real transportation alternatives, shippers have been quick to use them. For instance, one of the southernmost potash mines in Saskatchewan has long trucked its output to a North Dakota railhead, where it has benefited from cheaper rates on a US railroad than it was able to obtain in Canada.

The St Lawrence Seaway is essentially a bulk commodity artery also. The balance of downstream grain flows and upstream iron ore shipments has been disturbed since the 1970s by a number of changes. The pattern of Canada's international grain trade has shifted away from traditional markets in Europe. Expanding grain markets in Asia and rail freight rates that have increasingly favoured westbound over eastbound shipments off the Prairies have resulted in the Seaway's share of Canadian grain shipments falling from about 60 per cent to close to 30 per cent. Meanwhile, the US steel industry has undergone restructuring, leading to a loss of integrated (i.e., iron ore-based, rather than scrap-based) production capacity in the Great Lakes catchment area. Coal traffic has been more stable, reflecting the steady demand for cross-border shipments of Appalachian coal to fuel Ontario Hydro's large thermal generating stations (Nanticoke, Lambton, etc.) and the continuing importance of Canadian steelmakers at Hamilton and Nanticoke. These movements are principally confined to the lower Great Lakes (Erie and Ontario), including the Welland Canal, but they have been augmented since the late 1970s by shipments of lower-sulphur Alberta coal from Thunder Bay. The restrictions on vessel size imposed by the lock dimensions of the Welland Canal (and the Seaway as a whole) have influenced the siting of major industrial facilities. The attraction of Nanticoke to Stelco and Ontario Hydro was partly the fact that, being on Lake Erie, it can be served by larger and more economical vessels that are confined to operating upstream of the Welland Canal. Their greater cargo capacity is possible because of the larger dimensions of the US Poe Locks, linking Lake Superior and Lake Huron at Sault Ste Marie.

The general absence of large tonnages of bulk commodity traffic on the railway network of eastern Canada and the keen competition of trucking for general cargo in central Canada and for traffic to and from the Maritimes have prompted the major railways to reduce substantially their track mileage in this half of the country, concentrate flows on a few main lines, and leave feeder traffic to short-line railways. At the same time, growing volumes of trade between Canada and the US, encouraged by freer trade within North America, have prompted Canadian railways to expand their operations south of the border (Figure 11.1). Purchases by CP Rail of bankrupt railroads in the northeastern United States and Midwest have given it access to industrial centres and major ports throughout the US manufacturing belt. By the early 1990s, CP Rail was already generating over half its traffic revenue on shipments to, from, or entirely within the US. CN has become a fully North American railway with its purchase in 1998 of the former Illinois Central Railroad, linking Chicago and New Orleans. In 1999, it proposed merging with the Burlington Northern Railroad, one of the largest US operators, but the size and market power of this combination attracted the attention of US regulatory agencies, which refused to sanction it.

At the other end of the shipment-size spectrum, the restructuring of the economy in favour of just-in-time production systems, high-technology equipment, and a vast expansion of producer service industries has led to dramatic growth in the courier and air-freight market within North America and internationally. Some of this traffic is carried in the holds of scheduled passenger services between major cities, but next-day delivery service depends on hub airports where packages can be sorted and night-time flights are permitted (Morrow, 1993). The major US firms, such as Federal Express and United Parcel Service, have their corporate hubs in the Midwest, but Mirabel airport (Montreal) and Hamilton International, both free of night curfews, have emerged as secondary hubs for Canadian traffic (*Globe and Mail*, 31 July 1997).

## CONCLUSION

Technological change, regulatory change, and, increasingly, spatial change in the relative importance of north-south versus east-west traffic flows have all been active in reshaping the geography of transportation in Canada during the past 30 years. Railways and shipping lines, modes that are particularly tied to heavy sunk costs in specialized infrastructure, have found it more difficult to adjust rapidly to shifting traffic demands than have road and airline operators. Federal transport policies have equally had difficulties in keeping up with the rapidly changing economic environment of this sector. Continental free trade and an increasingly deregulated global airline industry have forced a review of policies that formerly treated Canada much more as a discrete national market. For example, Air Canada's takeover of Canadian Airlines in 2000 highlighted the benefits of creating a more internationally competitive national airline versus concerns about creating a near-monopoly in the domestic market. The next set of changes facing the transportation industry are likely to focus more on its environmental impacts, as research to develop alternatives to fossil fuel-based technology, at least in road passenger vehicle applications, gathers momentum.

## FURTHER READING

Slack, B. 1990. 'Intermodal transportation in North America and the development of inland load centers', *Professional Geographer* 42: 72–83.

Transport Canada. 2000. *Transportation in Canada, 1999*. Ottawa: Public Works and Government Services Canada.

# PART III

# REGIONS

# Atlantic Canada

## INTRODUCTION

'The task of transforming an economy which has, in effect, stalled is enormous' (ACOA, 1994: 1–7). The sluggish economic performance that has characterized the Atlantic provinces for many decades reflects deep-seated problems both within the region and in its relationship to the wider world. The regional economy remains heavily dependent on natural resources, in the form of fishing, forestry, agriculture, and tourism. Activity in all of these sectors is noticeably seasonal. Dependence on low-productivity, and hence low-wage, jobs in many branches of these and related industries has been compounded until recent years by levels of formal education in the regional labour force that have been well below the national average, leaving many people ill-equipped to take up skilled or professional jobs in expanding sectors of the economy. Most of the mechanisms by which the federal government has sought, since the 1960s, to reduce Atlantic Canada's economic disparity with the rest of the country have had the effect of perpetuating traditional employment patterns and prolonging an unhealthy dependence on externally devised remedies to the region's problems. Regional industrial incentives, job-creation schemes, and (un)employment insurance (EI, formerly UI) regulations have been used overwhelmingly to maintain the status quo rather than to encourage grassroots entrepreneurship and innovation. These policies are now increasingly recognized, not least within the region itself, to have been 'part of the problem' rather than 'the solution' to the genuine challenges of adaptation that Atlantic Canada faces. And there are currently some positive signs that the region is working effectively towards regaining some of the dynamism and prosperity that its economy of lumber, fishing, (wooden) shipbuilding, and overseas trade generated in the mid-nineteenth century.

Some of the obstacles to stronger economic performance arise out of the region's location and territorial fragmentation. It is distant from the most dynamic regional markets of North America and even more so from those on both sides of the Pacific Rim. Domestic heartland/hinterland relations became entrenched in the late nineteenth century, as Maritime businesses lost out to central Canadian bankers and manufacturers, whose dominance was aided by the expansion of the national railway network. The continuing westward movement of Canada's economic centre of gravity during the twentieth century was no help to Atlantic Canada. Moreover, the disadvantages of being a hinterland region have been exacerbated by political fragmentation, which reflects the geographical fragmentation (Cape Breton really was an island until the Canso Causeway was opened in 1955; PEI was not linked permanently to the mainland until the Confederation Bridge opened in 1997; and Newfoundland, of course, is an island in the North Atlantic). Not only has representation and advocacy for this region of 2.4 million inhabitants been divided between four provincial governments, but within each province quite deep-seated parochial cultures have frequently hindered or delayed productive collaboration. It does not help in today's economy that the Atlantic provinces are the least urbanized of southern Canada's regions. Halifax, the largest metropolitan area, has a population of only 332,000 (1996), which limits its capacity to attract some of the high-level producer service jobs at the heart of contemporary metropolitan growth.

Nevertheless, the 1990s may prove to have been a turning point for the region. The heavy dependence on federal transfers, which reached a peak of 40 per cent of regional GDP in the early 1980s, was reduced as Ottawa cut program spending to balance its budget. Tougher political stances in some quarters towards the region's culture of dependency have resulted in a search for better ways of increasing people's economic opportunities. These include a shift in support towards community economic development (CED), which is inherently more attuned to local opportunities and direction than the top-down delivery of more uniform, bureaucratic programs. The catastrophic collapse of the region's cod fishery has in many ways forced change, although the main federal relief program, The Atlantic Groundfish Strategy or TAGS, proved to be more of a conventional income-support measure than a strategic response to communities facing a radically different future. Many of the attitudinal transformations in Atlantic Canada were best captured by the priorities and style of the Frank McKenna administration in New Brunswick (1987–97), which reasserted the need to build prosperity on local resources (social as well as natural) and sought to promote more self-confidence and self-reliance among the people of the province. Whatever the merits of McKenna's strategies (see below), it is notable that since 1993 per capita GDP in New Brunswick has pulled ahead of that in Nova Scotia, reversing the traditional relationship.

It is not as if all of Atlantic Canada's characteristics were economic liabilities. The very absence of large cities, congested suburbs, and a frenzied business culture may be a growing asset. The opportunities for small-town living, ready access to coastal and rural amenities, and scope for using modern telecommunications technologies to overcome isolation have made the Maritime provinces (but not yet Newfoundland) attractive to migrants (including return migrants) from central Canada. Many people find a quality of life, if not a level of income, that is higher in the Atlantic region than in other parts of the country. Undoubtedly, too, the new-found additions to the region's resource base, notably the offshore oil and gas fields and the (prospective) development of the Voisey's Bay nickel deposit, will expand the volume and range of job opportunities available there. It is to be hoped so, for the Atlantic provinces, particularly Newfoundland, still contain too many communities marked by poverty and poor prospects, hard-pressed to offer career opportunities to their own young adults.

There is no doubt that the Atlantic provinces enjoy a standard of living closer to the Canadian average than it was approximately 50 years ago, when impoverished Newfoundland had newly entered Canada, or even 25 years ago, when federal 'regional policy' was getting into full swing (see Chapter 2). Equalization payments have enabled the level of public services in this have-not region to be raised, and they, more than the grants and subsidies of regional policy programs, appear to have delivered the most important long-term benefit. This is especially evident with respect to higher education. Coulombe (1998) estimates, for instance, that 70 per cent of the convergence in provincial per capita income levels across Canada since 1951 has been due to the improved level of education of people in the poorer provinces. Newfoundland has been the greatest beneficiary of this process. But without other positive changes in the Atlantic economy, notably job creation in knowledge-intensive industries, well-educated young people will continue to leave to find employment elsewhere.

## REGIONAL CHALLENGES

While economic indices point to Atlantic Canada's climb towards the national average, the region can be expected to continue to trail the rest of the country on most measures of economic performance. Its employment structure (Table 12.1) reveals its relative vulnerability. The sectors with representation above the national average are, on the one hand, natural resource-based (especially fishing and forestry), subject to pronounced seasonal and cyclical fluctuations in demand, and, on the other, public-sector services (government, education, and health), which have been particularly subject to attrition by governments anxious to reduce their indebtedness and tax loads. In turn, the high levels of primary-sector employment, especially in the fishery, reflect limited educational attainment and hence occupational mobility. High-technology manufacturing is relatively insignificant, and much of it has depended on federal defence spending, which declined notably in the 1990s. Service-sector employment is well below the national average in the dynamic business services group, but above average in low-productivity retailing. Outside of government, the regional economy has very few powerful local players. The principal exceptions are family-run enterprises, notably the New Brunswick-based Irving and McCain Foods groups, and the two fishery transnationals, High Liner Foods (Nova Scotia) and Fishery Products International (Newfoundland). Otherwise, the largest private-sector employer is the French tire-maker, Michelin, whose three Nova Scotia plants are not strongly integrated into the regional economy.

Among the contradictions of federal regional policy in the 1960s and 1970s was that it applied band-aids to 'economically bruised' areas, but also aimed to invest in places of greater growth potential. Neither objective was achieved satisfactorily. Millions of dollars of federal and provincial (Nova Scotia) funds were directed to maintain jobs in the chronically uncompetitive coal and steel industries of Cape Breton, both of which have shrunk to a fraction of their size in the 1960s and barely survive today. But the theoretical value of concentrating investment and support in a few favoured localities, where linkages and multiplier effects might begin to appear, was dissipated by identifying too many 'growth centre' communities that were each too small (including

**Table 12.1    Employment Structure: Atlantic Canada, 1996**

| Sector | Newfoundland | Nova Scotia | New Brunswick | PEI |
|---|---|---|---|---|
| Agriculture | 2,130 | 9,920 | 8,385 | 5,175 |
| Fishing | 9,375 | 9,685 | 5,965 | 4,075 |
| Logging | 3,300 | 5,185 | 7,550 | 450 |
| Mining | 4,645 | 3,885 | 4,095 | 150 |
| Manufacturing | 22,085 | 45,415 | 45,730 | 7,095 |
| *Food* | *11,025* | *13,215* | *14,240* | *4,285* |
| *Textiles & clothing* | *240* | *2,610* | *1,645* | *90* |
| *Wood* | *1,225* | *3,075* | *6,635* | *370* |
| *Paper* | *2,680* | *3,050* | *6,240* | *60* |
| *Metal* | *120* | *1,170* | *925* | *20* |
| *Machinery* | *155* | *740* | *935* | *170* |
| *Transportation equip.* | *1,795* | *4,850* | *3,215* | *385* |
| *Electrical* | *225* | *1,310* | *705* | *75* |
| Construction | 17,215 | 26,065 | 23,850 | 4,965 |
| Transportation | 10,215 | 16,245 | 17,060 | 3,335 |
| Communication | 7,300 | 12,965 | 12,940 | 1,400 |
| Wholesale | 8,100 | 19,560 | 13,765 | 2,545 |
| Retail | 31,765 | 57,205 | 44,745 | 8,035 |
| Finance | 4,250 | 11,900 | 8,800 | 1,220 |
| Real estate | 2,715 | 6,810 | 4,100 | 815 |
| Business | 7,320 | 18,420 | 14,030 | 1,880 |
| Government | 21,480 | 42,225 | 29,475 | 6,295 |
| Education | 20,715 | 32,020 | 26,150 | 4,235 |
| Health | 26,465 | 46,715 | 37,680 | 6,930 |
| Accommodation | 14,050 | 28,720 | 23,230 | 5,730 |
| Other service | 16,110 | 31,885 | 24,650 | 5,075 |
| Total | 246,065 | 438,970 | 364,100 | 70,820 |

SOURCE: Statistics Canada, Cat. no. 93F0027XDB96008.

Port Hawkesbury, Nova Scotia, and Stephenville, Newfoundland) (Figure 2.1). Throughout the 1970s and 1980s, federal industrial incentives were given to firms that promised job creation but in industries that frequently were ill-suited to the regional economy. The failed Bricklin auto plant in New Brunswick was a high-profile example. Whereas Halifax might seem to be the obvious focus for measures to strengthen the economic self-sufficiency of the region, particularly in higher-order services, interprovincial rivalry has usually worked against this. As production from the Atlantic offshore oil and gas fields builds up, Halifax and St John's are competing to attract the related employment involved in managing and servicing the energy supply industry.

Atlantic Canada's economy remains characterized, therefore, by small firms in small communities and by limited prospects for manufacturing employment of the low-wage, peripheral Fordism variety (see Chapter 4). In the 1990s, necessity and conviction combined to turn people's and governments' attention to facilitating innovation and economic growth in this environment. In New Brunswick in particular, policies to improve public-sector performance, for example, in education, were accompanied by strategic infrastructure investment, most notably in telecommunications. As the first telephone utility in Canada to install a fully digital, high-capacity network, the former NB Tel was able to market the province as a place where traffic-intensive telecommunication functions could be efficiently localized. By 1999, schools in Atlantic Canada were showing more intensive use of the Internet than those in the rest of the country (*Globe and Mail*, 13 Oct. 1999). Newfoundland, however, faced a much more difficult challenge in weaning the small and isolated coastal communities off a cod fishery that could no longer support them. Although the Hibernia megaproject provided many construction jobs and some skill transfer, it represented the last round of an essentially obsolete policy response to the problems of the province. By the late 1990s, the Atlantic region fishery as a whole was making record earnings on the basis of increased effort devoted to other species, especially shellfish. But fears are being voiced that the new fishery could be heading for depletion, just as happened to the cod fishery. In any case, as the geographical pattern of income from the two fisheries is not identical, there remain serious challenges of social and economic restructuring in many communities. Again, for Atlantic Canada as a whole, tourism is an important and growing source of earnings, proportionately greatest in Prince Edward Island, but the season is relatively short and earnings are typically low.

## NEWFOUNDLAND

Newfoundland, the poorest province in Canada, illustrates the dangers of a resource-dependent economy falling into a 'staples trap'. Centuries of reliance on the fishery and very limited alternative sources of livelihood fostered habits and attitudes among many of its people that have made adjustment to change extremely difficult. The government's attempt to consolidate settlement from remote, scattered outports in the 1960s to better provide education and social services aroused deep resentment and was not pursued further. Starting in the mid-1950s, federal unemployment insurance regulations made it progressively easier for families to survive on the basis of seasonal jobs in fishing or fish-processing. This allowed them to avoid the social and economic costs of uprooting themselves in search of better job prospects (although single males of working age left the province in large numbers), but it permitted a culture that found little value in formal education to flourish. Between 1961 and 1980, the number of registered inshore fishermen in Newfoundland rose from 13,736 to 33,640. Federal support for an even larger fishery followed Canada's declaration of the extension of its territorial waters to the 200-mile limit in 1977. These policies reinforced the apparent viability of traditional livelihoods. The shock of the cod moratorium declared in 1992, resulting in regional unemployment rates of up to 35 per cent, was therefore all the greater and the basis for successful economic diversification all the weaker. Between 1991 and 1996, the decline in food-processing employment (dominated by female workers in fish plants) was much steeper, at 53 per cent, than the decline (17 per cent) in employment (mainly male) in fishing and trapping (Figure 12.1).

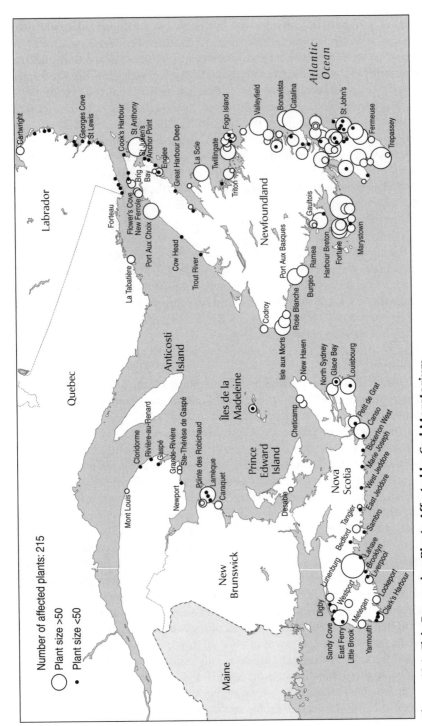

**Figure 12.1 Fish-Processing Plants Affected by Cod Moratorium**

SOURCE: Fisheries and Oceans Canada (1993: 29).

Geographically, Newfoundland consists of a set of nested peripheries. The province is peripheral, spatially and economically, to the rest of Canada. Labrador is peripheral in the same respects to the island core of the province (see Chapter 15). On the island, the Avalon Peninsula, with the one large city, St John's, is the core region that controls and services a poorly connected set of small, mainly coastal, communities. In the early years of transatlantic flight, Newfoundland's location within North America was strategic as a refuelling stop. But unlike its equivalent in Shannon, Ireland, Gander's international airport never levered that function into the basis for industrial development. Corporately, Newfoundland has been an outpost of foreign capital (in the pulp and paper and mining sectors) with very little local control over decision-making, and where local companies have grown to be significant transnationals (Fishery Products International and CHC Helicopter Corporation), their prosperity is increasingly based on activity outside the province.

In the 1960s and 1970s, the provincial government's desperate search for economic growth and diversification led it into commitments that demonstrated its lack of bargaining power. In particular, development of the large Churchill Falls hydroelectric scheme went ahead on terms that were overwhelmingly favourable to Hydro-Québec. Attempts to promote industrialization produced many ill-advised (if also, in some instances, unlucky) projects. The Come-by-Chance oil refinery, for instance, was planned in the late 1960s, when the prospects for a deep-water refinery to supply petroleum products to the import-dependent New England market looked bright. But the global energy crisis that soon followed closed off this option, and the plant stood idle (and rusting) for a number of years before being reopened.

This sorry history of shattered hopes of economic prosperity has shaped the provincial government's approach to more recent opportunities. It fought with some limited success in the 1980s to maximize its potential revenues from the development of the offshore oil and gas resources, ownership of which rests with Ottawa. In the late 1990s it battled the minerals transnational Inco to a temporary stalemate over how the rich nickel deposits discovered at Voisey's Bay, Labrador, are to be exploited. Not wanting to repeat the pattern of Newfoundland's resources being sold cheaply to benefit more industrialized regions elsewhere, the government insisted that the nickel ores be processed within the province, at a proposed smelter at Argentia. But Inco's insistence that it is currently uneconomical to do so and that mining will not begin unless the ores can be shipped, at least initially, to its existing smelters has delayed the development of the entire project. Neither energy nor minerals-related developments, however, are likely to become really large employers in the province.

Newfoundland is the only province where, in 1996, the majority of the population was still classified as 'rural'. Corner Brook, the regional service centre of the west coast, is the only urban centre outside of St John's with a population greater than 10,000. Its industrial base is the pulp and paper mill, which has hung on through some difficult times in recent years (Norcliffe and Bates, 1997). Undoubtedly, St John's and communities within its commutershed around Conception Bay offer the best prospects for the growing knowledge-based economy in the province. University and

government laboratories, including the Centre for Cold Ocean Research, are significant resources for innovation by local firms that marry the province's traditional
maritime experience to modern technologies. But they, and business services firms,
will need to keep growing if the 'brain drain' of modern Newfoundland's well-
educated young people is to be reversed.

## NOVA SCOTIA

The Sydney region of Cape Breton Island has been Canada's single, albeit small,
example of a nineteenth-century industrial coalfield, more typical of Britain or
Pennsylvania. It, too, developed 'staples trap' social and economic characteristics,
accentuated by distant foreign ownership prior to 1968, when the federal and Nova
Scotia governments took control. (It also acquired a dubious environmental legacy
not uncommon in such situations, the toxic tar ponds resulting from years of dump-
ing by the coke ovens.) Just as UI (now EI) payments postponed a necessary reduction in Atlantic Canada's fishery employment, government subsidies delayed, at great
expense and no long-term benefit, rationalization of the Cape Breton coal and steel
operations. Despite public spending of $3 billion since 1967, by 2000 the Sydney Steel
Co. had been reduced to a single mini-mill employing fewer than 500 workers (one-
eighth of the labour force in 1965). After many unsuccessful attempts to find a buyer,
the provincial government finally closed the mill in 2001. And despite $1.6 billion
spent subsidizing the coal industry, by mid-2000 only one mine remained in production (following the accelerated closure of another due to rock falls). Its future is in
doubt with the loss of a captive local market resulting from privatization of the Nova
Scotia Power Corporation, which freed the utility to purchase more competitively
priced fuels. The region's economically and technologically uncompetitive steel
industry attracted almost no linked manufacturing after World War II, and the railcar works at Trenton, on the mainland, also swallowed subsidies while shedding jobs.
It took until the 1990s for federal regional development agencies and the Nova Scotia
government finally to acknowledge that the economic future of Cape Breton will
depend on small enterprises in non-traditional sectors more suited to the region's
cultural and natural environment.

Against this background of decades of policy fixation on keeping a dying industrial
base alive, understandable attention is now being given to what are still small harbin-
gers of the region's future. The old courthouse in downtown Sydney has been reno-
vated as an incubator centre for software development firms, including some that
harness the musical and artistic creativity for which Cape Breton is famed. The
University College of Cape Breton provides research and training support to 'new
economy' enterprises. It is estimated that there are already more high-technology
workers on the island than there are steelworkers (*Globe and Mail*, 18 Jan. 2000).
Elsewhere on Cape Breton, loss of traditional jobs in the fishery has been met with
enterprising community initiatives. One widely acclaimed example of CED is Isle
Madame, an Acadian settlement of about 4,000 people. A variety of businesses,
including aquaculture, a new shrimp fishery, and a small telephone call-centre, have

taken root and, notably, given rise to spinoff activities in related sectors (*Globe and Mail*, 18 Jan. 1999).

Halifax is the largest metropolitan area in the Atlantic region, and this is reflected in the size and scope of its service sector. Its traditional maritime roles as the main base of the Canadian Navy and Canada's major east coast port provide less employment than formerly, and its many public-sector institutions in the government (federal and provincial), health, and education sectors shed jobs in the 1990s; but employment in business services, both high order and lower order (telephone call-centres), is growing. The city's small but varied manufacturing sector owes much to regional policy inducements in the 1960s and 1970s, and plants tend not to have strong local linkages. For many years, Volvo cars were assembled for the North American market from knock-down parts imported from Sweden, but this operation closed in 1999. Aerospace and electronic equipment are among the advanced-technology sectors represented in the city.

Apart from Sydney, no urban centre in Nova Scotia is much more than one-tenth the size of Halifax. But good highway links along the Annapolis Valley to Yarmouth and to Truro and the northeastern part of the province make the high-order functions of Halifax relatively accessible to much of the scattered rural and small town population. The South Shore was hit by the cod fishery moratorium but has recovered some of its prosperity with a switch to other species. High Liner Foods, the largest seafood processor in the province, has contracted operations while retaining its base in Lunenburg, but most of the fish handled there is imported. Agriculture in the Annapolis Valley supports a regional concentration of food-processing plants, but in recent years the value of the local apple crop has been surpassed by that of blueberries grown in the less fertile northeastern parts of the province. The forest sector has been expanding, benefiting from the absence of constraints on exporting lumber to the US. The tourist and related industries (such as Pugwash-based Seagull pewter, which employs 300) are gradually expanding, but extending the season remains a challenge. Gradually, the economic base of many small communities in environmentally appealing locations is changing as people, both local and migrants from central Canada, find opportunities to pursue careers in knowledge-based occupations.

## NEW BRUNSWICK AND PRINCE EDWARD ISLAND

New Brunswick made considerable progress in transforming its economy during the 1990s, even if not quite as fully as some of its promotional publicity would suggest. The most distinctive new industry to emerge is telephone call-centres, in which the province has attracted facilities for a large number of national firms (including United Parcel Service, Purolator, CP Hotels, and Royal Bank). Its success in doing so reflects a number of complementary factors, including the province's early investment in digital telecommunications infrastructure and its bilingual workforce. Moncton, the capital of the province's Acadian population, has been particularly successful, and by 2000 had 5,000 people employed in 40 call-centres. Fredericton, Bathurst, and Saint John have attracted a number of similar operations. The provincial government sought to establish a 'favourable' business climate for this new economic sector, which included the controversial reduction of workers' compensation levies in this industry, as well as its promotion of the province's lower wage levels and cost of living as compared to central Canada.

Another modern addition to the provincial economy has been the aquaculture industry. The Fundy shore, in particular, has developed Atlantic Canada's largest concentration of salmon farms, which by the mid-1990s were employing around 1,000 people at 66 grow-out sites (where fish are reared in sheltered coastal waters) and generating at least 10 per cent of the landed value of the entire Atlantic provinces fish catch. The federal fisheries research station at St Andrews and a few large firms assisted in developing an integrated regional complex of hatcheries, feed plants, etc. A serious virus outbreak in 1997, which required the killing of affected stock, suggested that the industry had developed too intensively and resulted in a 23 per cent reduction in the salmon harvest in 1998. But with careful management the industry offers a more sustainable source of employment than the traditional fisheries of the province.

New Brunswick's manufacturing sector faces uneven prospects. For instance, the Saint John Shipyard was engaged in fulfilling a $6 billion defence contract during the 1982–96 period as part of the Canadian Navy frigate construction program. At its peak, this project employed 3,500 and was a vehicle for upgrading the skills, technology, and managerial experience of those involved. But following the completion of that contract, and in the absence of a federal loan guarantee policy that allows Canadian shipbuilders (including yards elsewhere in Atlantic Canada) to be more competitive internationally, the shipyard has had a dearth of orders and employment had dropped to 450 by the end of 1999. Saint John's long-established food-processing industries have suffered from the decline of the port as a gateway to Canada and from corporate rationalization following mergers (leading to the closure of the sugar refinery). The large oil refinery at nearby Lorneville exports half of its output to the northeastern United States.

In terms of employment, the forest products industry in New Brunswick is only marginally less significant to the provincial economy than it is in British Columbia. Both the lumber and the pulp and paper sectors have benefited from new investment, although the latter experienced job losses and a number of temporary mill closures during the 1990s. Employment in the wood industries has been slowly rising, as producers have shared in the more buoyant markets enjoyed by eastern Canadian firms in recent years, as they are exempt from the cross-border lumber trade restrictions applied in western Canada (see Chapter 9). The principal agricultural specialization of both New Brunswick and Prince Edward Island is potatoes, which have formed the basis of a major processing industry in the upper Saint John Valley (home of the transnational McCain Foods enterprise) and a more diversified industry, including seed, table, and processing potatoes, in PEI. Although the power of the McCain and Irving family business empires, especially the latter, has often been portrayed as detrimental to the economic development of New Brunswick, they have exploited economies of scale and scope to create internationally competitive industries in a peripheral region that would scarcely have attracted comparable enterprise from firms lacking local roots.

Although New Brunswick and Prince Edward Island shared in the Canada-wide reduction in government services employment during the 1990s, a number of communities actually benefited from the decentralization of federal administrative functions. Jobs were transferred from Ottawa–Hull to Charlottetown (Veterans Affairs) and Bathurst, New Brunswick (Health and Welfare), and, following the closure of its air base, Summerside, PEI, was chosen as the location of the Goods and Services Tax (GST) national data-processing centre. In both provinces, the share of business services employment is well below the national average. Tourism, however, contributes proportionately more to the provincial economy of PEI than to any other in Canada. The opening of the Confederation Bridge in 1997 led to a 60 per cent increase in the number of visitors over the previous year, giving urgency to many of the debates on the Island about the scale and type of tourist attractions that should be developed. Although a 1993 survey found only 2 per cent of visitors arriving from outside North America, the popularity of L.M. Montgomery's *Anne of Green Gables* among Japanese tourists has emerged as a distinctive component of the industry.

Despite continuing inadequacies in the regional highway system, including stretches of the Trans-Canada Highway, Moncton has been consolidating its nodal role as the major distribution centre for the Maritime provinces. Completion of the Confederation Bridge to PEI has reinforced this. The decline of Saint John as a general cargo port and CP Rail's subsequent sale of its route through Maine to a regional short-line operator reflect that city's loss of a national transportation function. Fredericton's lack of traditional industrial sectors and the predominance of service-sector employ-ment have made its adjustment to a changing economy easier, particularly as some of the noted research units of the University of New Brunswick, such as forestry and survey engineering, are acting as incubators for high-technology firm formation.

## CONCLUSION

The economic difficulties Atlantic Canada has experienced, in various forms, for almost a century have multiple causes. Its location within Canada and the currents of world trade have meant that the region is no longer as strategic as it once was, given the west-ward shift of population and markets in North America and the rise of the Pacific Rim economy. Its historical resource base, the fishery, has been mismanaged and overex-ploited, far more as a result of policies and decisions made outside of the region than within it. Its terrestrial resources have always been relatively limited. With poor economic prospects at home, many of its younger and more enterprising inhabitants have for decades migrated to more prosperous regions of the country. Parochial atti-tudes at the local and provincial levels have long handicapped efforts to promote 'bottom-up' development, and federally promoted 'top-down' initiatives have too often been ill-suited to the region's real needs and resources (see Chapter 2). The limited and scattered network of larger urban centres has hindered attempts to stimulate economic growth in an increasingly metropolitan-focused world economy.

But, as noted above, the 1990s brought promising signs that many of these long-standing problems are being looked at in a new light and with a new enthusiasm for constructive change. The region's location is less peripheral, as freer cross-border trade allows traditional ties to New England to be renewed. Greater co-operation among governments in Atlantic Canada is reducing the fragmentation of its markets. A more imaginative assessment of the real comparative economic strengths of the region's environmental and cultural resources is channelling investment into predominantly small businesses that capitalize on these resources. Underpinning all these developments is a widely shared recognition that in many ways an unhealthy dependency culture had developed in the region, abetted by well-intentioned mechanisms to address regional and household income disparity on the part of the federal government. Ottawa's support of the region's economy is still needed and welcomed, but to a much greater extent than a generation ago the citizens and institutions of Atlantic Canada are successfully taking charge of their own economic development.

## FURTHER READING

Savoie, D.J. 1999. 'Atlantic Canada: Always on the outside looking in', in F.W. Boal and S.A. Royle, eds, *North America: A Geographical Mosaic*. London: Arnold, 249–55.

Whynn, G. 1998. 'Places at the Margin: The Atlantic Provinces', in L.D. McCann and A. Gunn, eds, *Heartland and Hinterland: A Geography of Canada*, 3rd edn. Toronto: Prentice-Hall Canada, 169–26.

# Central Canada

## INTRODUCTION

Ontario and Quebec, the two provinces forming central Canada, together dominate the national economy by almost every measure. They contain 62 per cent of the Canadian population and produce 63 per cent of GDP (Figure 13.1). Only with respect to fossil-fuel extraction do they fall significantly short of leading the nation. The political power that stems from this demographic and economic dominance, as well as the localization of corporate control that reflects it, has been a source of discontent in other parts of Canada for over a century, feeding various expressions of alienation in the West and complaints of neglect in the East. Hinterland regions have long tended to view federal economic policy as being essentially shaped by central Canadian interests and, in the postwar period, especially by those of the Toronto-based financial and corporate élites. Tariff policy was in the past viewed, particularly in the West, as protecting Ontario manufacturers at the expense of the country's primary producers. They had to pay higher prices for Canadian goods, such as machinery, when imports from the United States would have been cheaper, while their earnings were exposed to the fluctuations of world commodity prices.

Yet Ontario and Quebec are both such large provinces that each displays marked centre/periphery patterns of regionalization. Physiographically, the majority of the land area of each province is occupied by the Canadian Shield and is covered by the boreal forest. The urban-industrial core regions of each province are relatively small southern appendages to this extensive hinterland, yet the metropolitan economies of the St Lawrence Valley and the southern Great Lakes today produce the bulk of central Canada's output. These provincial core regions are the principal focus of this chapter, whereas the northern peripheries are subsumed within the North (Chapter 15). But because of the highly influential role of the provincial governments of Canada's two largest provinces in shaping economic opportunities, some of the discussion relates to central Canada as the entire region defined within the provincial boundaries of Ontario and Quebec.

If, seen from the Atlantic region or from the West, central Canada is uniformly presented as the core of the national economy and the seat of political power, it is a region that nevertheless is markedly fractured by the Ontario–Quebec border. The boundary is not sharply delineated in the landscape or in spatial patterns of economic activity, but it is expressed primarily in terms of institutional differences. Quebec, the

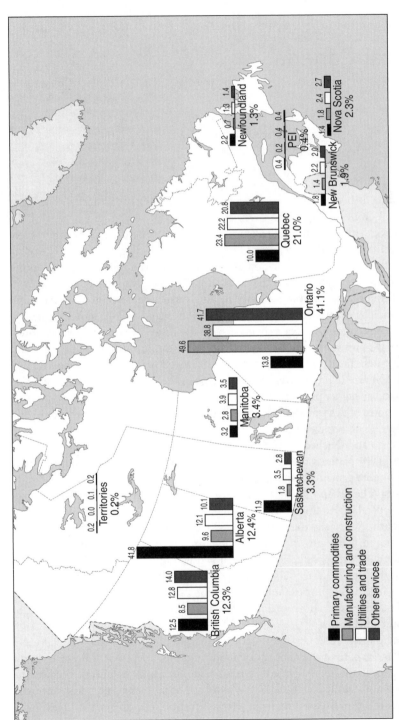

**Figure 13.1  Size and Structure of Provincial Economies, 1998.**
**Provincial economies as a percentage of the Canadian economy (based on value–added).**

*SOURCE:* Transport Canada (2000: 40).

primary political home of North America's francophone population, with its own code of civil law and its distinctive culture (no less evident in the sphere of business), differs in very many ways from Ontario, the bastion and beneficiary of the heritage of 'English Canada', not least in the political and economic advantages that have flowed from that.

## CONTRASTS IN THE CORE

With a provincial economy that is the largest, most diversified, and historically most prosperous, Ontario consolidated its reputation in the second half of the twentieth century as *the* prosperous core of Canada. In the years following World War II, growing federal government spending on goods and services tended to be disproportionately secured by Ontario suppliers. The benefits of the Auto Pact have been overwhelmingly concentrated in the province (see Chapter 7). Viewed the other way, however, Ontario's postwar prosperity largely underwrote the great expansion of federal spending that helped to reduce regional disparities and created Canada's now-fraying social safety net. Whatever the rights and wrongs of the province's powerful role in Canadian economic history, the early 2000s have shown once more that Ontario remains the principal engine of the national economy. Ontario contributed 41.5 per cent of Canada's GDP in 1998, almost double Quebec's share and more than the combined total of all the remaining regions of the country (Statistics Canada, 2000a). Its physical endowments provide the basis for the most productive agriculture in Canada and for a forest- and mineral-based economy that is substantial in size and scope. The province contains 45 per cent of Canadian manufacturing employment and produces over 75 per cent of national manufactured exports. The Toronto region encompasses a depth and diversity of service-sector skills that far surpass those of any other part of the country. Although the early 1990s found Ontario in a much less affluent and confident position than had been the norm, as the branch-plant economy that had underlain much of its postwar growth contracted and was significantly restructured (see Chapters 4 and 5), by the late 1990s it was again experiencing strong economic growth. This was primarily driven by growing demand within the US economy, with which the Ontario economy has become increasingly integrated (Courchene and Telmer, 1998), aided by the weakness of the Canadian dollar. Currently, this dependence is both the province's greatest economic asset and its potential weakness (Gertler, 1999).

Quebec's distinctiveness is not confined to the cultural sphere. As is true of the provinces of anglophone Canada, its political economy reflects a particular social and historical context. Both before and after the Quiet Revolution of the 1960s, Quebec's economy has differed in important respects from that of the rest of Canada, and most notably from that of Ontario. The predominantly rural society of New France adjusted to the British conquest of 1760 by shaping its social life through engagement in politics, the law, and the Church, but leaving leadership in business to British or American interests. Demographic pressure on the limited agricultural resources of the St Lawrence Valley prompted a wave of out-migration to the industrializing towns of New England in the period after 1850 (Waddell, 1987). Poorer agricultural resources and productivity than in Ontario were reflected in the limited development of towns and industries in Quebec outside of Montreal and Quebec City, where business enterprises run by the English-speaking élite grew to dominance (McCallum, 1980). In particular, Montreal's emergence as the industrial metropolis of Canada was not associated with those functional linkages to other towns in the province that characterized Toronto's relations with southwestern Ontario. New industries that developed in Quebec in the early twentieth century around the hydroelectric staple, notably in the paper, metal, and chemical sectors, developed at sites distant from Montreal, such as Shawinigan, and in the hinterland regions of Lac St Jean and Abitibi, where they attracted few manufacturing plants involved in further fabrication (Dales, 1957).

The transformation of Québécois society since the early 1960s has involved the explicit identification of the provincial government apparatus (the 'state') as an agent for achieving a new social and economic order. In this respect, Quebec has followed a European, and especially French, model of development, rather than the *laissez-faire*, private-sector model most clearly associated with the United States and most of anglophone Canada. Public-sector institutions, such as Hydro-Québec and the Caisse de dépôt et placement (public pension fund agency), and planning initiatives involving government support to particular industry 'clusters' (Gagné and Lefèvre, 1993) have created a very different business culture from that prevailing in the rest of Canada. These traits are part of the provincial economic milieu irrespective of whether they are harnessed to the specific project of achieving Quebec sovereignty. Together with related provincial government priorities, such as those determining language laws and entitlements to education in English, they have created a political environment in which economic growth appears to have been retarded. This applies most clearly to the fate of Montreal, whose decline, especially in comparison to Toronto, has become quite clear (Higgins, 1986). But the changing geography of the international and continental economy has negatively impacted Quebec independent of domestic conditions.

## RECENT ECONOMIC PERFORMANCE OF CENTRAL CANADA

Central Canada appears to offer a clear example of a post-industrial, service-based economy. By 1996, employment in the primary sector had dropped to just over 3 per cent and that in manufacturing to below 17 per cent, leaving four people out of five employed in the service sector. Structurally, the provincial economies of Quebec and Ontario appear almost identical—the share of provincial employment in each major sector (treating the manufacturing sector as a single aggregate for the moment) differs by less than one percentage point, with the significant exception of business services (Table 13.1). Some provinces, including British Columbia and Nova Scotia, have an even greater proportion of their jobs in services, but not as large a share in the expanding and well-paid business services sector. Ontario accounts for 44 per cent of all Canadian jobs in this sector, and Quebec for almost 23 per cent, so that central Canada holds two-thirds of the national total.

At the same time, Ontario and Quebec are still Canada's most industrialized provinces, and their manufacturers have been particularly affected by the growing

**Table 13.1    Employment Structure: Quebec and Ontario, 1991 and 1996**

| Sector | Quebec | | | Ontario | | |
|---|---|---|---|---|---|---|
| | 1991 | 1996 | %* | 1991 | 1996 | %* |
| Agriculture | 84,755 | 77,655 | 2.2 | 139,880 | 131,060 | 2.3 |
| Fishing | 4,185 | 3,895 | 0.1 | 1,965 | 1,915 | — |
| Logging | 25,405 | 24,560 | 0.7 | 13,965 | 11,410 | 0.2 |
| Mining | 23,490 | 19,090 | 0.5 | 34,360 | 26,050 | 0.5 |
| Manufacturing | 609,910 | 582,750 | 16.5 | 942,995 | 922,570 | 16.5 |
| Food | 61,130 | 56,880 | 1.6 | 73,990 | 76,320 | 1.4 |
| Textiles & clothing | 105,435 | 93,500 | 2.6 | 49,440 | 48,295 | 0.9 |
| Wood | 36,930 | 44,340 | 1.3 | 25,330 | 30,235 | 0.5 |
| Paper | 43,955 | 37,010 | 1.0 | 41,375 | 38,145 | 0.7 |
| Metal | 31,930 | 28,760 | 0.8 | 65,805 | 47,770 | 0.9 |
| Machinery | 18,740 | 18,730 | 0.5 | 41,030 | 42,235 | 0.8 |
| Transportation equip. | 45,580 | 46,030 | 1.3 | 174,275 | 176,485 | 3.2 |
| Electrical | 39,140 | 37,355 | 1.1 | 80,895 | 79,275 | 1.4 |
| Construction | 208,100 | 161,640 | 4.6 | 358,890 | 290,430 | 5.2 |
| Transportation | 136,650 | 137,035 | 3.9 | 187,830 | 198,555 | 3.6 |
| Communication | 115,750 | 105,775 | 3.0 | 188,630 | 173,040 | 3.1 |
| Wholesale | 148,130 | 170,010 | 4.8 | 233,910 | 278,220 | 5.0 |
| Retail | 453,125 | 434,035 | 12.3 | 700,920 | 662,815 | 11.9 |
| Finance | 150,395 | 128,430 | 3.6 | 253,140 | 228,880 | 4.1 |
| Real estate | 41,205 | 48,370 | 1.4 | 100,090 | 111,895 | 2.0 |
| Business | 182,290 | 210,830 | 6.0 | 367,200 | 411,070 | 7.4 |
| Government | 255,025 | 215,555 | 6.1 | 411,455 | 304,640 | 5.5 |
| Education | 233,470 | 241,035 | 6.8 | 365,230 | 369,325 | 6.6 |
| Health | 329,205 | 342,315 | 9.7 | 457,115 | 513,615 | 9.2 |
| Accommodation | 215,010 | 221,425 | 6.3 | 322,955 | 350,945 | 6.3 |
| Other service | 224,695 | 253,640 | 7.2 | 355,310 | 414,980 | 7.4 |
| Total | 3,537,640 | 3,536,205 | 100 | 5,511,240 | 5,586,975 | 100 |

*Percentage of provincial total for 1996.
SOURCE: Statistics Canada, Cat. no. 93F0027XDB96008

continentalism of North American production systems since the late 1980s. Nevertheless, the industrial composition of the respective provincial manufacturing sectors points to a major difference between the two heartland provinces. The textile and clothing industries account proportionately for almost three times the jobs in Quebec that they do in Ontario. Conversely, employment in transport equipment manufacturing is two and a half times more prominent in Ontario than in Quebec. The productivity and wage gap between these two sectors, with their very different skill requirements, indicates some of the relative weaknesses of Quebec's economy; although within the transportation equipment sector Quebec's strength in aerospace involves a more highly skilled workforce than Ontario's concentration in automotive products.

The recession of 1989–93 hit the central Canadian manufacturing sector extremely hard, but Ontario felt the brunt of the decline. Census data show that between 1986 and 1996 Quebec lost 5 per cent of its manufacturing workforce, but Ontario lost almost 14 per cent. The corporate restructuring that followed the introduction of the Canada–US Free Trade Agreement magnified the impact of the recession among the US branch plants concentrated in Ontario. In the 1989–93 period, Toronto alone lost 70,000 manufacturing jobs, or about 20 per cent of its employment in this sector, but there were also widespread plant closures in other cities and small towns in southern Ontario (Leach and Winson, 1999). Montreal lost a similar percentage of manufacturing employment, but the number of jobs in particular industries such as metal products, furniture, and textiles plummeted by 40 per cent.

Decline in manufacturing employment accentuated the profile of central Canada as a service-based economy. Overall, Ontario lost over 125,000 manufacturing jobs (12 per cent) between 1986 and 1991, but it gained almost 110,000 (41 per cent) in business services, 90,000 (24 per cent) in health and social services, 75,000 (23 per cent) in government services, and almost 65,000 (21 per cent) in the education sector. Quebec's service-sector employment growth in the 1986–91 period was not quite as strong as Ontario's (business services up 35 per cent, health and social services up 19 per cent, government services up 12 per cent, and education up 8 per cent), although its manufacturing job losses were considerably less marked (3,400, or less than 1 per cent).

By 1996, despite the beginnings of an economic upturn, manufacturing employment in Ontario had dropped a further 20,000 (2 per cent) from the 1991 total (Table 13.2). But by the mid-1990s, substantial downsizing of government services at all levels was being reflected in job losses in that sector (107,000, or 26 per cent), contributing substantially to the mere 1 per cent growth in aggregate provincial employment during the 1991–96 period. Net provincial employment change in Quebec in the first half of the 1990s was even lower (essentially nil). The decline in manufacturing employment increased, with a loss of 27,000 jobs (less than 5 per cent), and government services lost 40,000 jobs (15 per cent) On the other hand, business service employment in Quebec expanded by 30,000 (at a faster rate than in Ontario).

The nature and origin of the divergence between the industrial profile of Ontario and Quebec have long been of interest (Gilmour and Murricane, 1973). Factors such as their differential comparative advantage with respect to hydro-power potential, access to cheap coal and steel, agricultural productivity, and the orientation of their business cultures have been cited. The concentration of low-wage industries in Quebec partly reflects the immobility of francophones with limited education. This concentration has been sustained by federal policies to protect jobs, notably in clothing and textiles, from competition from low-wage developing countries, and to support food-processing employment in the province. In recent decades, as the service sector has grown in importance, Toronto's leadership in financial affairs and corporate decision-making has attracted a scale and range of producer service employment greatly superior to that of Montreal, despite the depth of business management education now established in Quebec.

The relative decline of Montreal since the 1960s has many complex roots. Population and economic growth in Ontario and western Canada has outpaced that in Quebec and the Atlantic region. The influx of US-owned manufacturing plants into Canada in the 1950s and 1960s, especially but not only in the auto sector, disproportionately benefited Toronto and southern Ontario rather than Montreal (Ray, 1971). Despite federal policies that sought to strengthen Montreal's role as an international air traffic gateway (culminating in the construction of Mirabel airport), market forces increasingly favoured Toronto as central Canada's principal international node. The Quiet Revolution began the process of the departure of anglophone corporate offices to Ontario, a flow greatly increased following the Parti Québécois election victory in 1976. It also brought a shift in power within Quebec from the private business sector, based in Montreal, to the provincial public sector, based in Quebec City, although Hydro-Québec, which played a pivotal role in the province's economic development in the 1960s and 1970s, is based in Montreal. (Its headquarters building houses the Quebec Premier's Montreal office.) As provincial politics have become increasingly shaped by the ambitions of a francophone Québécois nationalism, electorally strongest in rural and hinterland Quebec, many have detected a lack of sympathy by the provincial government for the challenges of economic restructuring faced by Montreal. Its cosmopolitan society, with large anglophone and immigrant allophone minorities, is unique among the cities of Quebec. But more so than Toronto, Montreal faces many of the problems of economic adjustment experienced by comparable nineteenth-century industrial cities in the US manufacturing belt. That said, the late 1990s saw a considerable revival in the Montreal economy (see Chapter 5).

With the exceptions of its resource-processing industries, notably pulp and paper and metals, and its auto sector structured by the Canada–US Auto Pact, Ontario's manufacturers have traditionally found their markets within the province and the rest of Canada. But as noted in Chapter 2, the province's sustained economic growth through the latter half of the 1990s emphasized the extent to which its economy has become functionally part of a midwestern North American economy. There is still debate around the issue of whether this evolution is at the expense of Ontario's east-west links within Canada and whether it will prove a benefit or a handicap to the province in the long run. Using data up to 1996, Gertler (1999) noted a polarization between Ontario's fast-growing export-oriented sectors and its domestic-oriented producers, who experienced an almost flat level of demand. On the other hand, Helliwell (1999) pointed to findings that, except in the specific case of the automobile and auto parts trade between Ontario, Quebec, and Michigan, interprovincial trade within Canada is still considerably stronger than comparable north-south trade. The export/domestic polarization Gertler noted is consistent with the stagnation of average Canadian living standards through much of the 1990s. Whether the revival of domestic purchasing power evident by the early 2000s has translated into a stimulus to Ontario manufacturers (and to a lesser extent to those in Quebec) remains to be seen.

## REGIONAL ECONOMIC STRUCTURE

The two provinces constituting central Canada have strongly developed core-periphery structures, and while there is substantial interprovincial interaction within the Windsor–Quebec corridor, the two provincial hinterlands are relatively discrete, each primarily linked to its respective provincial core. Within Ontario, the principal regional division is between the southern core and the northern Ontario periphery. 'Northern' can carry varying definitions (see Chapter 15), but it is essentially the Ontario of the Canadian Shield, although that large region is internally differentiated. So, too, is the economic core itself. The Toronto-centred region, the functional boundaries of which have been constantly expanding since the 1950s, is Canada's largest, richest, and most diversified metropolis. It merges, to the southwest, with an arc of important secondary urban centres, stretching from St Catharines, through Hamilton and Kitchener–Waterloo, to London, which is home to a diversified manufacturing and service-based economy. Beyond this sprawling agglomeration, the axes of Highways 401 and 400 provide easy access to more distant urban clusters, including Windsor, the towns around Georgian Bay, and the more sparsely distributed urban centres along the northern shore of Lake Ontario, extending to the Quebec border.

Although Ottawa is the core of the Ottawa–Hull metropolitan area and itself the second-largest metropolitan area in Ontario, the city was for a long time, and by many measures (including highway accessibility), more strongly linked to Montreal than to Toronto. If authorities in Montreal have felt in recent years that their difficulties have been neglected, or worse, by the government and bureaucrats in Quebec City, their civic and business counterparts in Ottawa have long had the same sense of frustration with perceived neglect by Queen's Park (the Toronto home of the Ontario government).

But the hinterland communities of northern Ontario have more substantive cause to feel that their needs are frequently overlooked by a distant government (Weller, 1977). Granted, Sudbury and Thunder Bay have both been transformed over the years from narrowly specialized urban centres based on locationally specific functions (mining and transshipment, respectively) to become the regional capitals for northeastern and northwestern Ontario. Elsewhere in the Canadian Shield area of Ontario, however, as in its continuation in Quebec, isolated single-industry resource towns are the predominant form of settlement.

The Quebec economy has an equally pronounced core-periphery spatial structure. The dominance of Montreal reflects its strategic location at what was, until the opening of the St Lawrence Seaway in 1959, the head of ocean navigation and the focus of valley corridors linking the city to New York, the Great Lakes, and, via the Ottawa Valley, the Canadian West. It developed as an archetypal gateway city (Burghardt, 1971), with major transportation and wholesaling functions that paved the way for a diversified manufacturing sector to emerge. Until the 1950s it was Canada's largest city, financial hub, and foremost industrial centre. This stature was attained, however, primarily on the basis of its role in national and international networks of production and trade, rather than on economic activity generated within its immediate regional setting. Rural Quebec, even on the Montreal plain, did not generate the agricultural prosperity of much of southern Ontario that stimulated the growth of manufacturing towns. These interprovincial contrasts in economic development have been ascribed to Ontario's more environmentally favoured agriculture, its closer proximity to US markets, and a cultural orientation more conducive to business innovation than that of rural Quebec (McCallum, 1980). Quebec City developed primarily as an administrative centre, with some resource-processing industries associated with its hinterland; Sherbrooke saw its early growth as a regional central place and industrial centre stall by the 1920s; and the industrial centres of the Mauricie (Trois-Rivières, Shawinigan) and Lac St Jean (Chicoutimi–Jonquière) conurbations, though larger than more remote single-industry towns, developed with a similarly narrow economic base.

## QUEBEC SUBREGIONS

It bears noting that only in Quebec, of Canada's large provinces, can sub-provincial regional economic analysis be readily undertaken from published sources (www.micst.gouv.qc.ca/PME-REG). This has not always been the case, and it points to the greater commitment to regionalized planning in that province than in anglophone Canada. Variations in per capita income (Figure 13.2) and economic structure (Figure 13.3) among the administrative regions of Quebec demonstrate clearly the province's core-periphery structure. The five richest regions, with average 1996 incomes above the provincial average, are entirely or very largely metropolitan, focused on Montreal, Quebec City, and Hull. The two poorest regions, with approximately 80 per cent of the provincial average income, are found along the south shore of the lower St Lawrence. The second-poorest group, with incomes between 85 and 90 per cent of the provincial average, form a ring around the Quebec City region, in the middle St Lawrence Valley. The remaining group, where incomes are between 94 and 98 per cent of the provincial average, consists of the regions northwest of Montreal and on the lower North Shore, where single-industry resource-based communities are typical. The distinction between the last two groups appears to suggest that, in general, the presence of a larger agricultural population tends to lower regional average incomes.

Figure 13.3 provides an indication of regional economic structure, with a detailed (though less recent) sectoral breakdown of employment. The share of primary-sector employment (forestry and mining) is three times greater than the provincial average in the remote regions of Abitibi, the North Shore, the lower St Lawrence, and Gaspésie. The role of resource-based manufacturing (pulp and paper and electro-metallurgy) approaches or exceeds twice the provincial average in Saguenay, the North Shore, Mauricie, and Abitibi. The relative importance of a diversified manufacturing sector in Mauricie-Bois Francs and l'Estrie is noteworthy, and it is an even greater feature (although this is obscured by the region's grouping with Quebec City in Figure 13.3) of Chaudière-Appalaches, which includes the region commonly known as the Beauce. In 1996, these three economic regions were quite clearly the most specialized in manufacturing in Quebec, with a 30–40 per cent greater share of employment in this sector than the provincial average of 18 per cent (note that the provincial data give a slightly

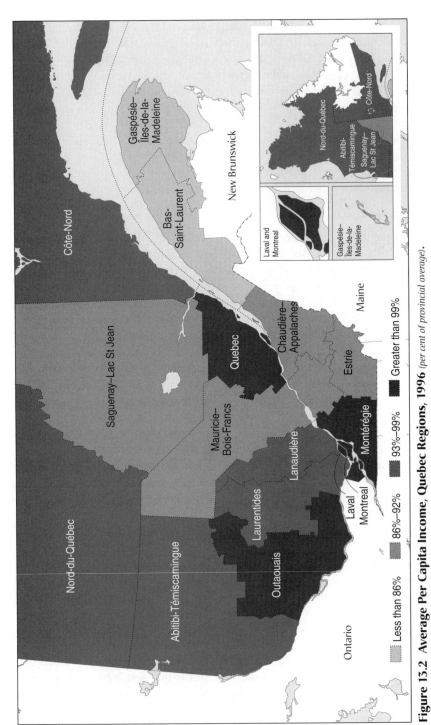

**Figure 13.2  Average Per Capita Income, Quebec Regions, 1996** *(per cent of provincial average)*.

*Source:* Government of Quebec Web site: <www.micst.gov.qc.ca/PME-REG>.

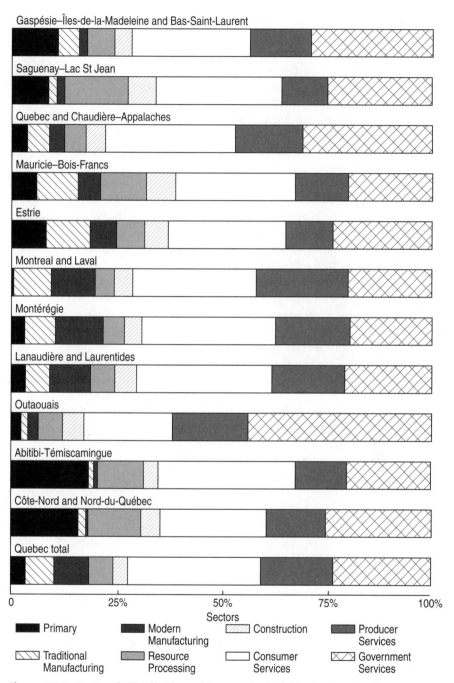

**Figure 13.3  Sectoral Distribution of Economic Activity, Quebec Regions, 1989**

SOURCE: Québec OPDQ (1991: 114).

higher employment share to manufacturing than do the census data in Table 13.1). The extreme dependence of the Outaouais on government-sector employment in Ottawa–Hull is notable (more marked, at 22 per cent, than in the Quebec City region, at 13 per cent, in 1996), given the issues that would arise for federal public servants resident in Quebec if provincial sovereignty were to materialize.

The Montreal economy is critical to Quebec's economic health, but its restructuring has not been a smooth experience (Germain and Rose, 2000). Job loss has been heavy in traditional sectors such as clothing, food, and tobacco, and in railway and port-related activities, largely concentrated in the inner city. At the same time, the city has seen a steady influx of immigrants, many of whom have sought work, at least initially, in low-wage manufacturing sectors. Growth in the aerospace and pharmaceutical sectors has employed workers (including a share of the immigrant stream) with very different skills, and it has taken place in the outer suburbs, thereby contributing to socio-economic polarization across the metropolitan area. A series of expensive urban megaprojects, notably construction associated with the 1967 World Fair (Expo) and the 1976 Olympic Games, and extensive transportation investment (subway and expressway construction) burdened the city with debt at a time when its economic base was contracting. The loss of corporate head offices and of anglophone professionals between the 1970s and 1990s aggravated the economic decline.

Increasingly, Montreal's service sector is geared towards the provincial and regional market rather than the national one. It maintains much of its international role, however, exemplified by the headquarters of the International Air Transport Association. The extremely fragmented structure of local government in the Montreal region has allowed inner-city/suburban conflicts of interest and priorities to remain largely unresolved, especially given the disinclination of the provincial government to intervene. The outer (off-island) suburbs are solidly francophone middle-class communities, electorally supportive of the Parti Québécois, and they resist any move towards metropolitan regional government that would unite them with the cosmopolitan metropolitan core. Even the 20-plus socially and linguistically more heterogeneous jurisdictions on the Island of Montreal have resisted the call for 'One Island, One City', but this amalgamation was finally imposed by the provincial government in 2001. As noted in Chapter 5, the Montreal metropolitan economy was showing signs of renewed vigour at the start of the 2000s. The provincial government has sought to bolster the city's attraction as a 'new economy' business centre with tax incentives for firms establishing their operations in an e-commerce centre downtown (Globe and Mail, 12 May 2000).

Outside Montreal, resource-based industries continue to be a major component of Quebec's industrial structure. Prior to the 1960s, the hydroelectric potential of rivers draining off the Shield into the St Lawrence was developed by a number of private utilities that favoured bulk sales to heavy power users in the metals, chemicals, and pulp and paper sectors (Dales, 1957). This strategy of development became a key to the growth of the provincial economy once the utilities were nationalized to form

Hydro-Québec as part of the Quiet Revolution. By harnessing increasingly large and remote river systems, culminating in the James Bay scheme, the utility has generated large quantities of power to support energy-intensive industrialization and export sales to the United States. It has also nurtured internationally competitive Quebec-based firms in project construction and electrical engineering (e.g., SNC-Lavalin). Alcan, which has maintained its own water rights in the Lac St Jean region, has enjoyed very low and stable energy prices, encouraging it to modernize and expand its aluminum smelting complex, with new smelters being built at Laterrière and Alma. Other smelters, owned by foreign transnationals, were attracted to sites on the St Lawrence in the 1980s with the aid of provincially subsidized power contracts. Aluminum and magnesium refineries have boosted Quebec's role as a globally significant locale for electro-metallurgy.

The limited hydro power potential of the south bank tributaries of the St Lawrence prompted the early utilities developing them to structure power rates that, until nationalization, were most favourable to small businesses and industries. This, and the more populated and productive agricultural region south of the river, helped to localize a variety of manufacturing industries in the towns of the region. In the Beauce, in particular, a regional culture that has fostered business development in manufacturing has seen the creation of firms specializing in food-processing, construction engineering, vehicle fabrication, and clothing. For example, the largest manufacturer of jeans in Canada has 13 plants in the towns and villages of the area, employing over 1,400 workers (*Globe and Mail*, 14 Oct. 1997). The development of Sherbrooke and Magog as centres of textile manufacturing started early, when the opening of the railway between Montreal and Portland, Maine, in 1853 made them accessible to markets and to imported cotton. The attraction of engineering industries to the Granby/Bromont region in the 1970s and 1980s followed completion of the autoroute from Montreal and was aided by federal and provincial regional development incentives. But the high-technology plants attracted to the industrial park at Bromont, including those of IBM, General Electric, and Mitel and also, for a period in the late 1980s, the Hyundai auto assembly plant (since closed), have not generated local industrial linkages.

Those activities more integrated into the regional economy south of the St Lawrence include the widely distributed food sector, of which Agropur, a large and successful dairy co-operative based in Granby, and Lassonde, a major processor of apples, based in Rougemont, are illustrative. The resource-based industries of the southeastern parts of the province have never matched the scale of those on the Shield. The mining sector is in decline, as asbestos production at Asbestos and Thetford Mines has dropped to match greatly reduced demand, a result of legislation in European and North American markets banning or severely restricting its use on health grounds. The tailings at Asbestos, however, have become the basis for a new magnesium smelter. The forest sector consists primarily of small private woodlots feeding a number of small-to-medium mills. But following the signing of the FTA, Domtar built a large fine-paper mill at Windsor, Quebec, near Sherbrooke, that is competitive with US producers. Labour-intensive manufacturing in the clothing, leather, and electrical goods sectors characterizes towns such as Drummondville and Cowansville. The initial Bombardier snowmobile plant at Valcourt has created some local industrial linkages. Sherbrooke has experienced decline in many of its traditional manufacturing sectors (textiles, clothing, and food-processing) but has increased employment in various branches of engineering. As a major regional centre for the southeastern part of the province, it has benefited from the expansion of service-sector employment.

The Abitibi economy is principally dependent on the forest products sector and on mining. The strong price of gold during much of the 1980s revived the region's generally high-cost producers and saw some new mines open, but lower prices in the 1990s saw the industry contract. The Noranda copper smelter has required considerable upgrading to meet modern environmental standards, but production has been maintained by a number of corporate takeovers that have secured it access to adequate ore supplies. Corporate consolidation and greater vertical integration in the forest industry have improved the earnings and export performance of the region's lumber producers, although they have been negatively affected by the Canada–US softwood lumber dispute.

The economy of Gaspésie is similarly resource-dependent. The Murdochville copper smelter has so far survived, despite the exhaustion of local ores and their replacement by imports from Chile. Fishing has suffered from the decline of stocks, exacerbated by government-supported investment in modern vessels with enhanced equipment. Tourism has grown in importance but enjoys only a brief season. The economy of the North Shore has been built primarily around the iron ore industry, which comprises the port cities of Port Cartier and Sept Îles and inland mining communities, of which Labrador City, Newfoundland, is the largest. Higher production costs and stronger international competition adversely impacted the mining sector in the 1980s and 1990s and resulted in the closure of the Sept Îles iron pellet plant, but this is expected to reopen in 2002. The opening of an aluminum smelter in the early 1990s helped to reduce the city's high unemployment rate.

The recreational demands of a provincial population concentrated in a few major cities have been increasingly dispersed over surrounding environmentally attractive regions made more accessible by highway construction. The Laurentians northwest of Montreal first developed as a zone for cottages and winter sport sites in the railway era. More recently, expanded and upgraded facilities owned and effectively marketed by transnational firms such as Intrawest (which invested $52 million at Mont Tremblant in the early 1990s) have increased the volume and seasonal range of recreational visits. The former railway to Mont Laurier has been converted into a trail for walkers and cyclists (and cross-country skiers and snowmobilers in winter). Less spectacular developments have nevertheless improved the all-season appeal of the Mont Orford/Lac Memphremagog region and other centres in the Eastern Townships (l'Estrie) and in the hinterland of Quebec City.

## ONTARIO SUBREGIONS

The 'Golden Horseshoe', stretching along the shore of Lake Ontario from St Catharines, through Toronto, to Oshawa, is a region so central to the Canadian economy—or at least that part of it not grounded in the traditional staples sectors—that much of its economic activity has been recorded in earlier chapters. If reaching a level of employment that was approximately the same in 1996 as in 1991 was a considerable achievement for the hinterland metropolitan areas of Ontario, in the Golden Horseshoe it was a measure of the depth of the recession of the early 1990s. (Toronto's experience was detailed in Chapter 5 and the nature of economic restructuring in southern Ontario is further analysed in the following section.) Hamilton lost 30 per cent (6,800) of the jobs in its dominant steel industry, but this accounted for the bulk of the employment loss in the city's manufacturing sector, and some industries (food, transportation equipment) saw considerable expansion. Business services growth was notably faster (at 17 per cent) than in the other cities in this region, apart from Toronto. St Catharines also witnessed employment shrinkage in its (much smaller) primary metals sector, and more seriously in transportation equipment (2,600 jobs, an 18 per cent loss), but otherwise there was not much change in individual sectors, apart from losses in government services. Oshawa gained employment (just over 5 per cent) overall between 1991 and 1996, despite shrinkage (2,300 jobs, or 14 per cent) in its dominant auto sector. Kitchener–Waterloo (functionally, if not formally, part of the Golden Horseshoe) also increased its aggregate employment during this period. What is perhaps most noticeable is that most of its 'old economy' manufacturing sectors (clothing, furniture, leather goods, textiles) retained their level of employment, despite the losses noted below. Expansion in a range of metal fabrication and engineering industries (including a 57 per cent increase, to 4,750, in the machinery sector) helped to make Kitchener–Waterloo the only metropolitan area in Ontario, apart from Windsor, to increase its manufacturing employment in the first half of the 1990s. Meanwhile, employment within the insurance industry localized in this area dropped 25 per cent (see Chapter 6).

Apart from the Ottawa metropolitan area, eastern Ontario is the least developed region of the southern core of the province. The extension of the Canadian Shield to the St Lawrence River east of Kingston limits the amount of productive agricultural land, and dairying dominates the farm economy. Corporate consolidation and economies of scale in the food-processing sector have eliminated many small plants since the 1970s, but cheese remains a regional specialty, and Smiths Falls is the home of Hershey Canada (chocolate products). The size and diversity of the manufacturing sector overall has been limited by what Ray (1965) identified as the 'economic shadow' that renders eastern Ontario a less attractive location for most US branch plants than Toronto and the southwest. The region contains a disproportionate share (over one-quarter) of provincial employment in the textile and leather industries, both of which feel strong foreign competition. Towns close to the Quebec border, notably Cornwall and Hawkesbury, have benefited to some extent from the political uncertainty about that province's future in Canada, which has resulted in the expansion or relocation of some firms on the Ontario side. Ottawa is the regional service centre, and Kingston has a long tradition in manufacturing and government services, as well as being home to Queen's University and its teaching hospitals.

In contrast to eastern Ontario, the southwest contains Canada's richest farmland and has benefited from its location adjacent to the centre of the US auto industry in Michigan. Employment in Windsor is dominated by the auto assembly and vehicle parts sectors (considerably more so than in Oshawa), which comprise over 60 per cent of its manufacturing jobs. A Ford van plant in St Thomas provides more auto-sector jobs in this region. Other establishments located in Windsor, notably the Hiram Walker distillery and Ontario's first casino (see Chapter 2), also reflect the border's influence. The Sarnia area retains a specialization in petrochemical products initially associated with local oil extraction (see Chapter 10). London displays all the characteristics of a regional central place, but it also has large manufacturing plants (transport equipment, food-processing, industrial materials) and is a major centre of the insurance industry. Food-processing is important in many of the smaller towns of the region (e.g., Leamington). Huron, Bruce, and Gray counties support a less prosperous agriculture and are more remote from the major transportation axes radiating from Toronto. Owen Sound has a number of manufacturing plants, but the service sector, including a growing recreational and retirement-related component, is the basis of the economy in these counties.

The economic development of northeastern Ontario was shaped in the early years of the twentieth century by the provincially promoted Temiskaming and Northern Ontario Railway (Robinson, 1969; Tucker, 1978), which opened up an unexpected wealth of minerals (silver and gold, at Cobalt, Kirkland Lake, and Timmins), as well as forest and agricultural resources. The rich copper/zinc Kidd Creek mine, developed in the late 1960s, justified construction of a smelter at Timmins. The region's forests continue to support a widespread and competitive lumber industry, although some of its old-growth stands (notably in Temagami) have attracted sustained anti-logging campaigns similar to those in British Columbia. Further north, power plants on rivers draining into Hudson Bay support industrial demand in the Sudbury region and feed markets further south. Despite losing half its employment in primary metal production and 8 per cent of its mining workforce between 1991 and 1996, Sudbury scarcely dropped in aggregate employment over that period. This demonstrated considerably more resilience in the local economy than was typical of recessions in the 1970s and 1980s, when the share of jobs in the minerals sector was considerably greater (see Chapter 9).

Northwestern and far northern Ontario are in every sense the most peripheral parts of the province. Thunder Bay is 1,400 km from Toronto and the road network north of the Trans-Canada Highway is rudimentary to non-existent. Indeed, the tract of Shield north of Lake Superior is Canada's empty heart, historically the biggest obstacle to creating a country and national economy integrated from sea to sea (Wallace, 1998). Lumber and gold were the commodities that attracted settlement in the early twentieth century and both remain important, the former regionalized between Kenora and Sioux Lookout and around Thunder Bay, the latter now concentrated at

Hemlo, as higher-cost mines in the Red Lake area go out of production. Thunder Bay retains its distinctive role as a transshipment point for prairie grain, although that traffic has declined with the reorientation of Canada's grain export trade towards the west coast. Service-sector employment reflects its role as the regional capital; and, like Sudbury, Thunder Bay scarcely showed a net loss of jobs between 1991 and 1996. Manufacturing is primarily resource-based (pulp and paper and timber), but a large transportation equipment plant, now operated by Bombardier, is a legacy of industrial expansion during World War II.

## CHALLENGES OF ECONOMIC RESTRUCTURING

As the region containing Canada's highest ranking 'world city' and the greatest concentration of national manufacturing capacity, southern Ontario has experienced a wide range of the forces of change associated with economic globalization and the specifically North American dynamics of continental free trade. A regional manufacturing sector characterized by miniature replica branch plants until the 1970s has had to face the pressures of the Fordist to post-Fordist transition, the dynamics of cross-border corporate rationalization, and the demands that technological innovation makes on a regional industrial system that is in some important respects poorly equipped to deal with them (see Chapter 4 and Gertler, 1999). Nor are the pressures of change confined to the manufacturing sector. Continental-scale deregulation and technical change, for instance, have aggravated the severe financial problems that Ontario Hydro (long regarded as a pillar of the province's industrial infrastructure) ran into as a result of its overinvestment in increasingly problematic nuclear generating capacity. Similar forces reach beyond the goods-producing sector into many branches of the service industries. And whereas southern Ontario's metropolitan areas are among the best-equipped centres in Canada to benefit from the growth of business services and the knowledge economy, they are also the centres most exposed to pressures coming from competing metropolitan regions, globally and particularly in the United States.

Although distinctive, the restructuring experience of the Ottawa region since the 1980s well illustrates some of the global/national/local restructuring issues that arise in contemporary Ontario. The dramatically expanded role of the national state in the era of postwar Fordism lay behind the huge growth of the federal public service in Ottawa. By the 1970s, the city's dominant employer had come to be associated with relatively good earnings and almost guaranteed job security, feeding the widespread image of Ottawa as a 'fat cat', single-industry town, out of touch with the economic realities in most other parts of the country. Responding to the cultural and political fallout of growing Quebec separatism, the federal government instituted official bilingualism and took the symbolic decision to situate a substantial number of government offices across the river in Hull, extending the benefits of federal employment more fully into the National Capital Region's francophone community. Although Ottawa subsequently lost some civil service jobs over the years, primarily through relocation to hinterland regions (see Chapter 2), the federal government's 1995 decision to shed 15,000 local employees over three years threatened a major economic upheaval.

At the same time, however, the Ottawa region's high-technology sector, which had been expanding slowly during the 1970s (Steed and DeGenova, 1983) and had met with some reversals in the early 1980s, began to display the accelerating growth that continued for some years (see Chapter 7). One result of that expansion was that high-tech firms increasingly identified a persistent shortage of qualified staff. Yet just as in smaller centres, in Ottawa, too, redundant workers in one sector have not been painlessly absorbed into another. The labour market issues have reflected the very different workplace cultures and geographies of the public service and high-tech sectors. As a generalized distinction, one can identify the federal public service as an institutionally conservative and bureaucratic workplace regime, relatively unexposed to market pressures, highly unionized, visibly committed to the implementation of a variety of employment equity provisions, and concentrated in the downtown core of Ottawa–Hull. The high-tech sector, on the other hand, is characterized by innovativeness and flexibility in dynamic and highly competitive markets, with non-unionized workers in relatively open, non-hierarchical management structures associated with a workplace culture that is gendered (which is not to say that women are not employed) and anglophone, and not particularly proactive in its employment equity policies. It is also concentrated in the western parts of the Ottawa metropolitan area, with relatively few establishments in the east or across the Ottawa River in Quebec. At the macro level the impact of federal downsizing on the Ottawa's economy was significantly mitigated by the continued expansion of the high-tech sector, but there were significant micro-level disjunctures. These included attitudinal barriers to intersectoral transferability among both labour and management, differences in the household impact of the contrasting workplace cultures, and differences in the social geography of those gaining and losing employment (Wallace, 1999b). As competition within the metropolitan labour market for professionals in the high-tech sector has become more intense, private-sector salaries (and often stock options) have increasingly left behind federal public-sector salaries, which were frozen for much of the 1990s. But while the public sector has thus experienced somewhat of a 'brain drain' to high-tech and business service firms in the private sector, Ottawa's high-technology firms have themselves lost talented workers to centres of the US high-technology industry, such as California's Silicon Valley and Boston; so far they have been able to offset these losses with the recruitment of immigrant professionals.

Different restructuring issues are highlighted in the experience of many manufacturing firms in south-central Ontario. When the Canada–US Free Trade Agreement created a new continental-scale business environment, the age, relatively small size, and sometimes low utilization levels (especially in the food processing-sector) of many US branch plants in Ontario made them prime candidates for closure, as their parent firms responded to opportunities for production rationalization. Communities of all descriptions were affected, including Scarborough, a Toronto industrial suburb; diversified industrial cities in southwestern Ontario, such as Kitchener, which lost 6,000 manufacturing jobs between 1990 and 1993 in industries including tires, shoes, and brewing and distilling; and smaller, less diversified industrial cities in eastern Ontario, such as Cornwall, which lost 2,600 jobs, mainly in textiles and related sectors (Rutherford, 1995; *Globe and Mail*, 9 Jan. 1993). But among firms and plants that survived that initial shake-out, whether Canadian or foreign-owned, the search for higher productivity and competitiveness has involved a significant increase in capital spending on high-technology machinery and changes in the labour process ('leaner and meaner' production). As noted in Chapter 4, however, a firm's success in implementing these responses is strongly influenced by the culture, both in the workplace and in regional labour markets, that frames their application (Gertler, 1999).

Increasingly, successful firms prove to be those that work collaboratively with suppliers in pursuing innovation and efficiencies within the production chain, and also that involve workers in continuous training, not least to optimize the performance of new machines. Although there are clear indications that such practices are spreading in Ontario, there are still considerable obstacles. In the absence of effective apprenticeship or training schemes at the provincial level, much depends on individual management priorities. From the perspective of the worker, job seekers may be hindered by a lack or mismatch of specific skills; but the changed nature of the job market, in which attitudinal and broadly social skill attributes are increasingly important to employers, plays a significant role that is geographically sensitive to community characteristics (Rutherford, 1995). Overall, the culture of workplace flexibility in many growth-sector firms tends to increase the locational appeal of smaller centres without a history of labour organization (for example, Alliston, which attracted Honda's auto plant) over locations that have seen the decline of formerly unionized industries that employed workers with limited educational qualifications.

In most of Ontario north of the Windsor–Quebec corridor (Yeates, 1991), the challenge of responding to a changing economic environment is very similar to that faced in other resource-based hinterlands. Particularly under the NDP government that was in power during the recession of the early 1990s, a number of initiatives were undertaken to assist failing firms in single-industry communities to restructure their operations. All involved partnerships between the public and private sectors and the relevant workforce. They also involved redundancies and the introduction of more flexible work practices (see Chapter 9). At Algoma Steel in Sault Ste Marie, for instance, the workforce was cut from 6,900 in 1992 to 5,300 in 1995 and a much improved climate of labour relations was introduced. The downsizing of the Atomic Energy of Canada research laboratories at Chalk River in 1996, on the other hand, was not a situation where employee buyouts were a meaningful response, and the result was a net loss of professionals and their incomes from the hinterland community.

In general, the prospects for economic growth in Ontario's hinterland are seen to lie primarily with small- to medium-sized businesses building on local expertise and resources (a prescription similar to that now accepted in Atlantic Canada, as noted in Chapter 12). Absentee ownership has often been associated with a lack of investment and unimaginative marketing, handicaps that can be overcome with the commitment of local entrepreneurship. The resurrection of the Pembroke-based Eddy Match Company demonstrates the positive spinoffs that help to build the capacity for regional diversification. A tool-making subsidiary supplies other local firms (producing office furniture and aerospace castings) that have adopted flexible, advanced technologies (*Globe and Mail*, 8 July 1996). Another example is North Bay's fur auction, which in the 1980s had been a major outlet for Ontario trappers. It was rescued from receivership by a slimmed-down agency half-owned by the Union of Ontario Indians. A joint venture between a local Indian band and a leading Italian furrier developed the current international fur auction and fur-dressing operation (*Ottawa Citizen*, 1 Mar. 1992; www.furharvesters.com).

## CONCLUSION

Central Canada's dominance of the national economy remains firm, despite the very real economic growth and diversification of the West, which is reviewed in the next chapter. The metropolitan economies and the industries of the Windsor–Quebec City corridor contain most of Canada's sources of innovation and the financial infrastructures to commercialize their products in the worldwide marketplace for knowledge-based goods and services. There are inherited weaknesses from past regimes of economic development—notably the dependent Fordism of the postwar branch-plant economy and the linguistically reinforced class structure of industry in Quebec prior to the 1970s—but much has been accomplished in the past generation to create the conditions for the region's competitiveness in continental and global markets.

Particularly interesting are the very different political and cultural matrices within which the Ontario and Quebec components of this region are pursuing their economic development strategies. At the start of the 2000s, the governments of both provinces had visions of themselves as 'regional states', Ontario within a Midwest North American economy (see Chapter 2), Quebec as a 'nation' within a loose continental governance structure (NAFTA). Yet they had contrasting views on how far the state should be actively involved in managing the economy and very different views as to how their jurisdictions should relate to the federal Canadian state. One rarely finds two such different models of economic development strategy being played out in such an otherwise integrated region.

## FURTHER READING

Germain, A., and D. Rose. 2000. *Montréal: The Quest for a Metropolis*. Chichester: John Wiley.

Gertler, M.S. 1999. 'Negotiated path or "business as usual"? Ontario's transition to a continental production regime', *Space and Policy* 3: 171–97.

———. 2001. 'Central Canada and the global economy: politics and possibilities', *Canadian Geographer* 45: 31–5.

Gilmour, J., and K. Murricane. 1973. 'Structural divergence in Canada's manufacturing belt', *Canadian Geographer* 17: 1–18.

Saarinen, O. 1992. 'Creating a sustainable community: the Sudbury case study', in M. Bray and A. Thomson, eds, *At the End of the Shift: Mines and Single-Industry Towns in Northern Ontario*. Toronto: Dundurn Press, 165–86.

# Western Canada

## INTRODUCTION

The provinces west of Ontario have conventionally been grouped into the three Prairie provinces, as one region, and British Columbia, as the other. However, for a variety of reasons this is an increasingly unsatisfactory arrangement. By many measures, particularly economic ones, the Saskatchewan/Alberta border might be a more meaningful boundary to subdivide the West. The economy of western Canada used to be dominated by renewable resource-based industries (wheat, cattle, forest products) whose distribution was largely determined by physiography. The boundary between the cropland and rangelands of the prairies and the forested terrain of the western Cordillera approximately corresponds, at least in the south, to the Alberta/BC border. In a comparable way, the southern edge of the Canadian Shield in Manitoba and Saskatchewan marks the transition from the agricultural economy of the south to the even more sparsely populated forested hinterland to the north (see Chapter 15).

Since the early 1970s, however, new economic forces have come into play. The oil and gas industry, overwhelmingly concentrated in Alberta, has become a vastly greater source of wealth than it was during its first two decades of production (see Chapter 10), attracting population and supporting economic diversification in that province. In contrast, the prairie farming economy still dominates southern Saskatchewan and southwestern Manitoba, and mining is the major sector in the northern parts of the two provinces. These sectors have been decidedly less prosperous than the energy sector in recent years. Moreover, British Columbia has been the principal beneficiary of the expansion of Pacific Rim trade (involving increased overseas demand for western Canadian resources and tourist attractions), an influx of affluent immigrants (particularly from Hong Kong in the 1990s), and the continuing arrival of migrants from eastern Canada. These influences have enabled the provincial economy to diversify (although the role of the forest sector remains very large), and for a number of years, until the Asian financial crisis of the late 1990s, its economic growth outperformed that of the rest of the country. It is now as appropriate, therefore, to talk of western Canada in terms of two economic zones—one richer, more dynamic, and primarily Pacific-oriented; the other less rich, with fewer growth sectors, and primarily North America-oriented—as it is to focus on the political boundary between the Prairies and BC. The sub-regional boundaries are certainly not clear-cut, and the functionally defined zones they delimit overlap in places, but it is important to recognize the realities that they point to. Initially, however, this chapter is framed by the traditional regional subdivision.

## THE CHARACTER OF THE PRAIRIE ECONOMY

European settlement of the Prairies dates essentially from the arrival of the railways that linked them to the East, first through the United States and then, by 1883, across the Ontario Shield. Winnipeg developed as a classic gateway city, from which the railway and grain-handling infrastructure spread westward in a fan-shaped pattern, funnelling trade through the city (Figure 14.1). With the growth of the regional farm population, Regina, Calgary, Saskatoon, and Edmonton emerged as central places, eroding some of Winnipeg's control over its hinterland. The only significant diversifications of the predominantly grain-based economy that had emerged by the 1930s included ranching in the Alberta foothills, some irrigated agriculture in the dry Palliser Triangle of southern Alberta and Saskatchewan, a few pulp and paper and mining operations in the Shield of southeastern Manitoba, and localized oil and gas exploitation in southern Alberta. The drought and global economic crisis of the Depression years devastated the economy of the Prairie provinces and emphasized the region's vulnerability to forces outside the control of its inhabitants. The federal government initiated a limited program of regional assistance through the Prairie Farm Rehabilitation Administration in 1935, but the lesson that communal self-help was the only reliable strategy of survival found political expression in the emergence of Social Credit (forerunner of the modern Canadian Alliance Party) in Alberta and the Co-operative Commonwealth Federation (forerunner of the modern New Democratic Party) in Saskatchewan. Between 1931 and 1951, Saskatchewan lost almost 10 per cent of its population and the total population for the Prairie provinces stagnated (Barr and Lehr, 1987). Had Alberta's oil industry not finally developed on a significant scale after 1947, it has been suggested that that province would have lost population also.

Canada's postwar period of rapid growth brought renewed prosperity to the Prairie provinces, but not an escape from the boom-and-bust cycles typical of resource-based economies. Diversification away from primary products has therefore been a goal of provincial governments over the past 50 years, but progress has been slow (Economic Council of Canada, 1984) (Table 14.1). The challenge facing the three provinces has been, in fact, quite different. Manitoba has always had the most diversified provincial economy in western Canada, reflecting the importance of Winnipeg as a trading and manufacturing centre, as well as the role of mining (at Flin Flon and Thompson) and forest products (at Pine Falls and The Pas) in diversifying the resource-based sector. Even Manitoba's farming is more diversified than that of Saskatchewan and Alberta. Dairy, hog, and field crop specialties are significant additions to the grain sector. Saskatchewan's challenge to reduce its wheat dependence has been the greatest, but the province has benefited from the development of some of the world's richest potash and uranium mines, as well as from the

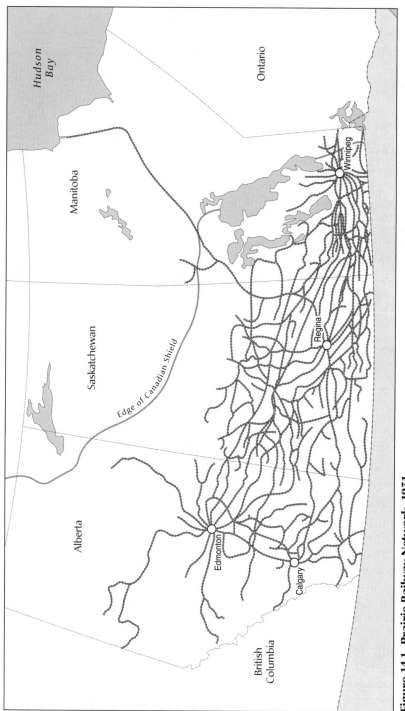

**Figure 14.1  Prairie Railway Network, 1931**

*SOURCE:* Warkentin (1968: Figure 12-4).

## Table 14.1    Employment Structure: Prairie Provinces, 1996

| Sectors | Manitoba | Saskatchewan | Alberta |
|---|---|---|---|
| Agriculture | 39,660 | 77,765 | 88,815 |
| Fishing | 1,010 | 220 | 370 |
| Logging | 1,940 | 2,575 | 5,760 |
| Mining | 4,515 | 12,035 | 75,200 |
| Manufacturing | 62,575 | 31,240 | 121,365 |
| *Food* | *8,605* | *4,945* | *16,285* |
| *Textiles & clothing* | *6,380* | *895* | *3,845* |
| *Wood* | *4,605* | *2,060* | *10,695* |
| *Paper* | *1,745* | *1,555* | *4,620* |
| *Metal* | *2,755* | *1,440* | *3,320* |
| *Machinery* | *4,000* | *4,300* | *8,755* |
| *Transportation equip.* | *8,060* | *1,605* | *4,880* |
| *Electrical* | *2,320* | *1,475* | *6,065* |
| Construction | 27,310 | 24,465 | 100,675 |
| Transportation | 30,485 | 21,480 | 72,145 |
| Communication | 19,750 | 15,215 | 43,320 |
| Wholesale | 27,395 | 23,060 | 76,110 |
| Retail | 63,995 | 56,985 | 178,130 |
| Finance | 18,000 | 15,215 | 40,070 |
| Real estate | 9,105 | 7,510 | 28,015 |
| Business | 24,385 | 16,885 | 101,795 |
| Government | 39,725 | 30,740 | 75,410 |
| Education | 42,470 | 36,815 | 97,535 |
| Health | 65,015 | 53,270 | 132,610 |
| Accommodation | 37,995 | 34,065 | 107,975 |
| Other service | 38,545 | 33,880 | 116,040 |
| Total | 567,825 | 503,500 | 1,486,980 |

SOURCE: Statistics Canada, Cat. no. 93F002XDB96008.

research that made canola a significant oilseed crop. Technological change that has greatly expanded the range of uses for aspen and other hardwoods of the parkland belt lies behind the expansion of the forest products industry in northern Saskatchewan and Alberta. The principal aim of the Alberta government, however, has been to develop forward and backward linkages from the province's oil and gas sector by encouraging the emergence of a petrochemical and related products industry and, equally, the development of expertise in the oil-field supply and geophysical analysis sectors. Attempts in the 1980s to use oil revenues to jump-start diversification into high-technology industries (telecommunications, toxic waste processing, etc.) did not prove successful, but by 2000 the province was developing a solid base of varied manufacturing. Research-intensive services and manufacturing are steadily expanding in size, particularly in Calgary (wireless communications) and Edmonton (biomedicine).

## THE CHARACTER OF THE BRITISH COLUMBIA ECONOMY

More than any other province, British Columbia was transformed in the closing decades of the twentieth century by the rapid economic growth of the Asia-Pacific region. Vancouver, a city that started life as the remote terminus of a transcontinental railway reaching out from the heartland of British North America, has become a true gateway city, articulating the flows of people, goods, and wealth linking Canada and the countries of East and Southeast Asia (Hutton, 1998). The speed and extent of change in the province since the 1960s are reflected in its population growth and in the diversification of the economy away from reliance on the forest staple. However, the geographical distribution of change has been uneven. The forestry, pulp and paper, and wood products industries remain the major employers and sources of income throughout most of British Columbia's hinterland regions. Apart from the forest-based sectors, moreover, manufacturing in BC has traditionally been inhibited by the small regional market and by a freight rate structure that allowed tariff-protected industries in central Canada to dominate that market. In recent decades, trade liberalization has allowed manufactures from across the Pacific (Japan, the Asian newly industrialized countries, and now also China) and from the western US to become increasingly competitive, thereby continuing to limit provincial diversification in this sector. Rather, the metropolitan-focused service sector in BC has seen the emergence of most new economic activity. As a result, the core (Vancouver)/ periphery (rest of BC) spatial structure of the provincial economy has been reinforced in the post-industrial era (Bradbury, 1987).

As already noted, the provincial boundary between BC and Alberta is not always functionally meaningful. The Peace River district, east of the Cordillera, is an extension of the prairie agricultural economy and of the gas fields of the Alberta foothills. There, and in the coal-mining communities of the Kootenays, the sense of remoteness from Victoria and the significant tax differential across the nearby Alberta border (where income tax rates are lower and there is no provincial retail sales tax) generate frustration leading to occasional calls for secession from BC. Banff and Jasper, in Alberta, are, like Whistler, BC, outlying nodes of the international tourist and recreational circuits that radiate from Vancouver (see Chapter 6). The bulk commodities that constitute the baseload of traffic at marine terminals in the Lower Mainland and Prince Rupert are as much of prairie origin (wheat, potash, sulphur) as they are from BC (coal and forest products).

Despite some shared experiences of economic stimulus since the 1970s, significant differences remain between Canada's two westernmost provinces. This became particularly apparent after 1997, when the Asian financial crisis had a much more severe impact on British Columbia's export sectors than on those of Alberta (*Globe and Mail*, 22 Nov. 1999). Politically, BC, where the unionized labour movement has always been strong, contrasts with the vigorously free-enterprise culture of Alberta, although at the federal level the populist Canadian Alliance gives expression to sentiments that are pervasive in the non-metropolitan areas of both provinces. Culturally, Alberta's broad, but mainly European, ethnic diversity contrasts with a BC society that has until recently been primarily of British origin and has now gained a large population of Asian ethnicity, concentrated in metropolitan Vancouver. Immigration from central and eastern Canada has contributed to the recent growth of both BC and Alberta, but whereas flows into (and, in the 1980s, out of) the latter have tended to be tied directly to job opportunities, BC has experienced a steady influx of retirees and 'lifestyle migrants'.

British Columbia is a region where the contemporary challenges of maintaining economic growth and environmental sustainability are particularly sharply focused. The west coast has emerged as a distinctive cultural region ('Cascadia' or 'Ecotopia'), the Canadian extension of 'the northern Californian lifestyle', in which an affluent, cosmopolitan population combines commitment to environmental values with the active pursuit of pleasure in attractive natural surroundings (Wallace and Shields, 1997). As a result, the coastal rain forest in particular has acquired a much wider set of meanings than merely a prime source of lumber. The competing claims of environmental preservation, commercial forestry, and non-consumptive recreational uses of the forest have greatly altered the ground rules for determining public land-management policy since the 1970s. They have also achieved more than provincial, or even national, salience, for the passions and arguments aroused by the protagonists have been globalized through the international ENGO (environmental non-governmental organization) community to match the geographical scale of the forest industry's trading linkages (Hayter and Soyez, 1996). At times, the contest has appeared to be framed in BC in terms of the aesthetic and cultural values of the metropolis versus the livelihood interests of resource-based communities in the periphery. But there are contradictions, too, in the emergence on the west coast of 'clear-cut condos' (*Globe and Mail*, 8 Aug. 1992) to house those who have come ostensibly to enjoy its beauty, and also in the smog-inducing sprawl of Vancouver's commutershed. Moreover, the delayed recognition of the legitimacy of long-ignored Aboriginal land claims within the province has added a further element of conflicting cultural and political priorities that impact the course of economic development.

## ECONOMIC RESTRUCTURING IN WESTERN CANADA

Grain farmers on the Canadian Prairies have experienced substantial fluctuations in their incomes and prospects over the past 30 years. Through the 1970s and 1980s, negative impacts were considerably (though never adequately, in farmers' eyes) mitigated by government action. Booming wheat sales in the early 1970s revealed bottlenecks in the grain transportation system, which prompted investment in new hopper cars, export terminals (notably at Prince Rupert, BC), and increased track capacity on rail routes to the west coast. Depressed sales and incomes in the early 1980s, as a result of high interest rates and competition from subsidized exports from Europe and the United States (see Chapter 8), encouraged many farmers to diversify, where possible, into more lucrative crops, notably canola (Figure 14.2). However, the early 1990s brought the combined forces of tightening federal budgets and the new trading regime of the FTA into play.

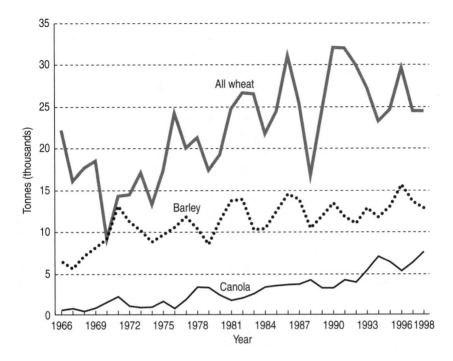

**Figure 14.2  Wheat, Barley, Canola Production, 1966–1998**

*SOURCE*: Statistics Canada, (1999b: 114)

On the one hand, the long-standing federal subsidies to overseas grain exports, notably the statutory Crow's Nest railway rates, were eliminated and branch-line subsidies were phased out. This hastened the demise of the network of rural grain elevators and the concentration of grain shipments through large-capacity inland terminals. On the other hand, the higher returns available from selling feed grain into the US market turned many farmers' attention to that opportunity. The traditional prairie landscape of branch lines and rural elevators every 12 kilometres or so—the backbone of the region's initial central place system—has undergone rapid decline. By mid-1999 there were 1,011 primary elevators remaining in western Canada (Manitoba: 211; Saskatchewan: 541; Alberta: 252; BC: 7), down from 1,967 in 1984. By the same date, 28 high-capacity elevators (over 20,000 tons) had been brought into service (Canadian Grain Commission, 2000). Often, with the closure of the country elevator goes a substantial part of the local community's tax base.

Development of a food-processing industry on the Prairies on a scale to match that of the agricultural economy has long been hindered. The subsidization of wheat exports, which increased farmers' returns from that crop, transport subsidies on feed-grain shipments to central Canada, which encouraged livestock rearing and processing there, and railway general freight rates that favoured shipping unprocessed over processed products from the Prairies to major North American markets all worked to discourage food manufacturing in the region. Now that the subsidies have been eliminated and the domestic transport system is more competitive, new spatial patterns of comparative advantage are emerging. In particular, the meat-packing industry has declined significantly in Ontario and expanded in Alberta and Manitoba, where feed costs are lower, and new, rural, non-union packing plants have replaced aging facilities and unionized workforces in metropolitan centres further east (see Chapter 8). The Cargill beef plant at High River, Alberta, and the hog operation at Neepawa, Manitoba exemplify this trend. Expanded capacity at oilseed crushing plants in Alberta and Saskatchewan, related to increased sales into the United States since 1989, is another sign of change in the prairie economy. By 1996, the food-processing industry's share of employment in Manitoba had reached the national average (1.5 per cent), but it remained below that average in Saskatchewan and Alberta.

Throughout the twentieth century, average incomes in British Columbia have been among the highest in the country. They have shown some of the cyclical behaviour typical of resource-dependent economies, but their prevailing strength has been attributed to the wealth of the province's resource base, especially its forests, and to the ability of organized labour to capture a significant share of the rents that the forest resource has generated. The gradual convergence of provincial average income towards the national average has certainly reflected federal policies of reducing regional disparity within Canada, but it has also marked the steadily declining share of employment in British Columbia generated by the resource-based sectors. Moreover, even before the impact of the Asian economic crisis in the late 1990s there were signs that BC's high-wage economy was harming its economic prospects. In 1997, the provincial average hourly wage was 8.7 per cent above the Canada-wide average: only Ontario, at 4.6 per cent, also had earnings that exceeded the national average, and it has a very different employment profile (*Globe and Mail*, 14 Dec. 1998). Yet compared specifically to Alberta, productivity growth in the BC economy in the second half of the 1990s was poor, and the anecdotal evidence of firms choosing Alberta over BC to locate new or expanded production suggests that the differential (together with Alberta's lower taxes) was significant (Figure 14.3).

In fact, the forest industries have been struggling since the recession of the early 1980s, which hit British Columbia particularly hard. Adjustment to a much more competitive international environment, involving rival sources of production in the United States and around the Pacific, has forced the BC forest sector to radically restructure its operations (Hayter, 2000). This has involved job losses to increased mechanization, both in the woods and in the mills, but also the creation of a more flexible workforce less able to maintain its historic share of resource revenues (Grass and Hayter, 1989). Simultaneously with having to cope with changed market prospects, however, the forest industries began to face fundamental changes in wood supply. Until the 1990s, forest policy in British Columbia had been geared, in effect, to the removal of old-growth forests (primarily on

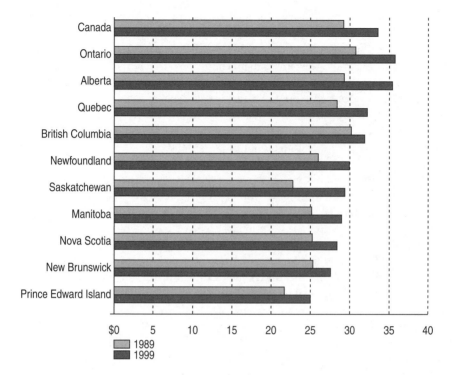

**Figure 14.3 Provincial Labour Productivity, 1989 and 1999**

Note: Measured as GDP, 1992 dollars, per hour worked.
SOURCE: *Globe and Mail* 20 Nov. 2000, B9

the coast) and their replacement by 'managed' secondary forests. Experts have long recognized that this implies that in the long run the sustainable timber harvest will be below the cutting levels of the 1970s and 1980s. The transition from the old harvesting regime to a sustainable one—the 'fall-down'—has now become necessary, its arrival hastened by changing public attitudes. Province-wide, the fall-down implies a reduction of wood harvesting of 6 per cent, but in some forest management areas, notably on Vancouver Island, it may involve reductions of up to 20 per cent. This scale of shrinkage in available timber resources significantly exceeds in most places the added reduction associated with the introduction of much stronger measures to protect old-growth forest by the extension of wilderness set-asides (Hoberg, 1996).

Not only is the resource base of the forest industries shrinking, but the cost of lumber is rising. The provincial Forest Renewal Plan, introduced in 1994, doubled stumpage rates (the royalties paid to the provincial government as landowner), with the intent of both promoting more effective reforestation and blunting the cross-border trade harassment of the US lumber lobby. It also established a much more stringent Forest Practices Code, governing the conduct of logging operations, largely in response to the growing weight of ENGO criticism of the environmental destructiveness of many woodland operations. As a result of this legislation, the cost of logs in BC jumped 75 per cent between 1992 and 1996 (*Globe and Mail*, 7 April 1997). But at the same time, the provincial government committed itself to increasing forest-based employment—to replace jobs lost by the creation of new wilderness areas and by encouraging more intensive forest management and higher value-added processing of timber. It subsequently proposed reducing the costs it imposes on the forest industry in return for a commitment by firms to create 21,000 new jobs over five years. However, the impact of the Asian economic crisis at the end of the decade undermined such efforts. Particularly among coastal mills there has been a noticeable increase in exports of customized building products to the Japanese construction sector, but the computerized wood-handling technologies involved are not labour-intensive (Edgington and Hayter, 1997).

Like the forest industries, the BC mining sector, particularly the coal mines dependent on Japanese purchases, has had to increase labour productivity to remain competitive. Steady reductions in the contract price of coal have forced a reduction and restructuring of the labour force and hastened the closure of some mines (see Chapter 9). Profitability at the province's base-metal mines (especially copper, which is not smelted in the province) has always fluctuated with world metal prices, which kept falling in the late 1990s, leading to temporary mine closures. With unemployment rising in the resource industries, the provincial government has faced steady demands from the electorate of the BC Interior to respond to the plight of their communities. It has replied since the mid-1980s with a 'critical industries' or 'job protection' commissioner, charged with brokering the continuation of threatened major employers in the provincial hinterland. The problem is that, as in Cape Breton (see Chapter 12), financial resources have been spent trying to maintain an employment structure that cannot avoid disruptive change, and this has been done at the cost of initiatives that might ease the transition to an economy with better prospects of long-term sustainability.

## REGIONAL ECONOMY OF THE WESTERN PROVINCES

### Manitoba

With 60 per cent of the provincial population and 62 per cent of employment, Winnipeg dominates the Manitoba economy (Welsted et al., 1996). Despite the diversity of its industrial base, which includes food-processing, clothing, and transportation equipment, and business services associated with the grain trade and insurance, the city's recent growth has been weak compared to metropolitan areas of comparable size elsewhere in Canada. Like Montreal, it has lost a measure of its national role and has become more of a regional capital. There was relatively little change in the city's employment profile between 1991 and 1996: a loss of close to 6,000 government service jobs was partly offset by an increase of 3,600 in business services. Manitoba's most prosperous agricultural regions lie to the south and west of the city, supporting small towns with specialized manufacturing as well as central place functions, a mix that in recent years has produced some of the lowest unemployment levels in the country

(*Globe and Mail*, 12 July 2000). Much of the manufacturing involves branch plants, some of which have grown significantly (e.g., the McCain Foods potato-processing plant at Portage la Prairie is the firm's largest), while others have been eliminated through corporate rationalization, especially since the late 1980s and the signing of the FTA (e.g., what was the only Canadian Tupperware plant, at Morden). Restructuring of federal agencies in the 1990s also led to employment reductions in Portage la Prairie and Gimli (both defence-related) and threats of the closure of the Whiteshell atomic energy research laboratories at Pinawa.

The economy of that part of Manitoba encompassed by the Canadian Shield depends on the mineral, forest, and hydro sectors. Development of the Nelson River has involved a series of major construction projects and provided the provincial utility with an exportable surplus of power, which is transmitted to the United States. Various attempts to attract aluminum smelters or other heavy users of cheap electricity have foundered on the relative inaccessibility of Manitoba to offshore markets and sources of raw materials. The largest forest sector operation, a pulp mill at The Pas, started life as a major regional development project in the 1970s that became mired in cost overruns and unfulfilled commitments. The provincial government eventually rescued the insolvent plant before selling it back to the private sector. Inco's nickel mine at Thompson continues to be a relatively low-cost producer, but some of Manitoba's other mineral properties developed since the 1950s have ceased to be viable. The provincial and federal governments both have assisted the Flin Flon copper smelter in reducing its $SO_2$ emissions. The development of a private-sector space station for launching commercial satellites has been proposed near Churchill. The port of Churchill on the west coast of Hudson Bay, which has only a three-month shipping season, has in recent years frequently been threatened with closure. The orientation of grain sales towards Pacific Rim rather than North Atlantic markets and the drive for economies of scale in grain handling saw its exports shrink drastically by the late 1980s. However, privatization of the port and the connecting rail line from the south in 1997 has brought cost savings and also more enterprise in marketing the port's advantages for prairie region trade with Europe and Russia.

### Saskatchewan

Of the three Prairie provinces, Saskatchewan is the most dependent on the grain economy. Unintentionally, no doubt, diversification of agricultural output has been discouraged by federal policies put in place to protect grain farmers' incomes (some long-standing, such as the Crow's Nest freight rates, others more recent, such as the Gross Revenue Insurance Plan of the 1980s). The province's farms are also, simply, the furthest away from major markets or export terminals and so the least well placed to diversify away from extensive grain farming. Hence, while the area planted to canola and to a variety of other crops has increased in recent years, wheat remains the principal crop in each of the province's agricultural census divisions (Statistics Canada, 1994). Economic pressures and technological advances have brought about a steady decrease in farm numbers and an increase in farm size.

Despite being augmented by rural depopulation, Regina and Saskatoon have increased in size only slowly. Meanwhile, there have been many years in recent decades when the province as a whole has lost population through out-migration. Latterly, it has failed to sustain the psychologically significant total of one million inhabitants (the 1996 population was 990,237). Of 141 towns and villages that were classified as viable in 1961, only 62 remained in 1991 (*Globe and Mail*, 5 Jan. 1994). Consolidation of schools followed the massive expansion of paved highways in the 1950s and 1960s; the number of rural grain elevator points has been steadily shrinking for many years, despite federal protection of the railway branch-line network; the agricultural recession of the early 1980s saw many auto and farm equipment dealerships close; and in the 1990s, provincial government cutbacks have triggered widespread rural hospital closures or amalgamation (Stabler and Olferi, 1993).

Discovery of rich uranium deposits in the far north of the province since the early 1970s has been associated with 'fly-in' mining at remote sites, such as Key Lake and Wollaston Lake, rather than the construction of new single-industry towns (Shrimpton and Storey, 1992). Workers commute by air for two-week shifts from centres such as Prince Albert, where wider social and employment opportunities exist for their families. Setting the employment and revenue benefits of uranium mining against the concerns of some groups about its environmental, health, and social impacts has at times caused tension within the provincial government. The future of the industry is very much tied to the long-term prospects of the global market for nuclear power generation, which by the early 2000s could not be taken for granted. However, the Saskatchewan uranium producers enjoy some of the lowest production costs in the world, so their prospects are reasonably bright. The province's potash industry is equally competitive globally. It was established in the 1960s in the southern half of the province, and for a period starting in 1976 some of the major producers were taken into public ownership. The industry is subject to fluctuating revenues that reflect trends in world agricultural markets, but it can expect to see demand from Asia-Pacific markets continue to rise. Since its privatization in 1990, the Potash Corporation of Saskatchewan (headquartered in Saskatoon) has become one of the world's largest and most diversified fertilizer transnationals.

Diversification within the metropolitan economies of Regina and Saskatoon has slowly increased. The Regina-based steel producer, Ipsco, has prospered with the growth of the western Canadian energy and pipeline industries. The city has attracted business service activity, including the relocation of back-office work in the insurance sector from Toronto and a Sears telephone call-centre, but its total employment and sectoral profile saw almost no change between 1991 and 1996. Saskatoon has developed an increasingly mature high-technology complex that, while small compared to that of Ottawa, has similarly been nurtured by the presence of National Research Council laboratories (notably in plant biotechnology) and the attraction of important activity by large firms, such as IBM (computer services) and Nortel (fibre optics), together with research spinoffs from the University of Saskatchewan. Employment in manufacturing increased over 20 per cent (to 10,700) between 1991 and 1996, with the greatest increases in the machinery and electronics sectors.

## Alberta

Alberta stands apart from the other two Prairie provinces in terms of its prosperity and growth in recent decades. Its economy is still vulnerable to the instabilities associated with resource dependence (Mansell and Percy, 1990), but by the end of the 1990s there were signs that the province has finally achieved a level of economic diversification that will insulate it from the worst of future downturns in the energy sector. Energy markets have been relatively stable since the mid-1980s, in marked contrast to their turbulence during the 1973–85 period. Conventional oil production in the province is in decline, but there is confidence in the long-term outlook for oil-sands extraction, and the natural gas industry has good prospects, given rising demand from the United States. As in other fossil fuel-producing regions around the world, the Alberta government has tended to be critical of proposed measures (including 'green taxes') that might curtail energy industry operations in the province for the sake of global climate change mitigation, but many components of the energy sector are involved in research to reduce its inescapable environmental impacts.

Since the first oil-sands plant was opened near Fort McMurray in 1967, there has been a continuous process of technological learning that has brought production costs of synthetic oil down to levels that are easily viable even in relatively weak markets. With the continuing depletion of conventional crude oil reserves in North America as a whole, the buildup of synthetic oil production capacity is gathering pace. In the late 1990s, expansions and new projects were announced that will more than double production capacity by 2005, assuring northern Alberta of a period of major new investment and job creation. In this context, it is interesting to note that one-third of the residents of Fort McMurray (population 40,000) are natives of Newfoundland, who moved west for the sake of steady employment (*Globe and Mail*, 23 Feb. 1998).

Other resource-based sectors are also expanding. The North American beef market is characteristically cyclical but, as noted above, Alberta has recently attracted a greater share of the meat-processing industry, which gives greater economic stability. The province is less exposed to the vagaries of the grain sector than is Saskatchewan, but the drylands are subject to climatic variability. Alberta has almost 65 per cent of western Canada's irrigated land, concentrated in a belt north and south of Lethbridge, but there has been criticism that too much of it is in forage and grain, rather than higher-yielding specialty crops. The forest-based industry in the north has not fully lived up to the claims made for it when the region's resources were initially developed in the early 1980s, but its prospects are reasonably good (see Chapter 9).

At the peak of the late 1970s boom, the provincial government, recognizing that oil wealth would not last for ever, put aside revenue to create the Alberta Heritage Savings Trust Fund. The intention was to build up sources of capital that would be used to encourage diversification of the provincial economy and so ensure its long-term prosperity. The high-profile failures of some early projects have not prevented steady gains in Alberta's capacity to attract and nurture a variety of new ventures. Overall, Alberta's manufacturing sector became the third largest in the country (measured by value of shipments) for the first time ever in 1998, displacing British Columbia. This certainly owed something to the serious problems facing the BC forest sector, but it equally marked the steady development of Alberta's economic diversification.

Calgary's growth and economic diversification have been driven by forces both internal and external to the province. Building on its strengths as the business capital of the Canadian energy sector, it has attracted a widening range of corporate head-quarters from other cities and is now clearly Canada's second most important centre of corporate control. Some firms have moved from central Canada as part of the ongoing westward shift of the nation's centre of gravity (see Chapter 2). The reloca-tion of Canadian Pacific Ltd from Montreal, for instance, was encouraged by the increasing western orientation of some of the conglomerate's major business sectors (including railways and energy). Other firms in recent years have moved from the west, usually identifying Alberta's better business climate and lower tax regime than those of British Columbia as part of their rationale. Employment in the city rose by 7 per cent overall (to 473,000) between 1991 and 1996, but the business services sector expanded by 28 per cent (to 51,800) and manufacturing by 20 per cent (to 44,000). The gains were widely spread across industry groups. Calgary's development as a centre for wireless communications research (led by Nortel and Telus) builds on the oil and gas sector's long-standing reliance on wireless technologies (*Globe and Mail*, 24 Aug. 2000).

Although still slightly larger than Calgary, the Edmonton metropolitan area has not enjoyed the same economic dynamism in recent years, and its total employment in 1996 was the same as in 1991. It has suffered from some handicaps that Calgary has not, including greater municipal fragmentation, a (fading) reputation for being less welcoming to private business, and a less conveniently located and less nodal interna-tional airport. The Alberta government's decision to cut government spending sharply in the early 1990s resulted in a 30 per cent loss of employment (12,400 jobs) in that sector in the city between 1991 and 1996. The 5,800 jobs Edmonton added in the busi-ness services sector during that period was only just over half the total added in Calgary. The West Edmonton Mall, the largest shopping centre in North America, has widened the city's appeal as a retailing and tourist centre, but proportional to the city's size wholesaling is more significant, reflecting its gateway functions with respect to Yukon and the western Arctic (Coffey, 1994). Public-sector institutions have played an important role in the emergence of knowledge-intensive activity in the city. The Alberta Research Council, established in the 1930s, and the more recent stimulus to research (including that at the University of Alberta) provided by the Alberta Heritage Fund have assisted Edmonton in becoming a major centre for medical research and related biotechnology enterprises. They also contributed to the attraction of corporate research laboratories in advanced industrial materials (Wallace, 1996). Elsewhere in the province, the economies of medium-sized cities are growing, notably in Red Deer, with an expanding petrochemical complex, and in Lethbridge, with an increasingly diversified mix of industries.

## British Columbia

The Vancouver metropolitan area alone generates just over half the total employment of British Columbia. Almost 80 per cent of its jobs are in services, with disproportionate strength in the dynamic business-oriented sectors. Between 1991 and 1996 the city's labour force grew by just under 11 per cent (to 993,000). Manufacturing employment was essentially static (at 99,000), with no major shifts within subsectors, although machinery and electrical and electronic products, which in 1996 together employed 12,000, showed increases of 19 and 15 per cent, respectively. An increase of 25 per cent (17,500) in business services employment (to 87,500) made that sector the fastest growing of the major service categories, although it was augmented by, for instance, a 48 per cent increase in amusement and recreational services employment (to 25,400), part of which captured Vancouver's emergence as a favoured film-making location by Hollywood studios (*Globe and Mail*, 29 Jan. 1997). The Vancouver CMA is by far the largest centre of high-technology industry in the province, with firms developing specializations in photonics (telecommunications and medical applications) and in alternative energy technologies (notably Ballard fuel cells).

The rest of the province can usefully be divided into the Victoria metropolitan area and the primarily resource-dependent hinterland, or 'the Interior' (Davis, 1993). Victoria's economy is even more heavily dependent on services (85 per cent) than is Vancouver's, but the emphasis is on public-sector activities (government, health, and education) and on traditional consumer-oriented services. Between 1991 and 1996, aggregate employment increased by just under 7 per cent (to 161,000), with business services expanding over twice as fast (by 15 per cent to 10,500). Government service employment held steady overall, but within this, provincial government employment rose by 28 per cent (to 12,600). The Interior stands out by virtue of its disproportionate reliance on primary-sector jobs (in forestry, agriculture, and mining) and on resource-based manufacturing. The spatial structure of the Interior is strongly shaped by topography. Kamloops (population 85,000) and Prince George (population 75,000) have developed as strategically located regional service centres, while the productive agricultural land of the Okanagan Valley has been the foundation of a string of towns from Penticton to Vernon, with Kelowna the largest (population 137,000). Nanaimo (population 86,000), the Vancouver Island ferry terminal closest to Vancouver, is the service centre for the Island's northern hinterland, and the much smaller Dawson Creek (population 11,000) provides similar functions for the Peace River district. Beyond these urban centres, the settlement pattern of non-metropolitan British Columbia is dominated by widely scattered small or medium-sized resource-based communities.

Aggregate employment data for British Columbia between 1986 and 1996 (Table 14.2) reveal some of the major changes in its economic structure that took place during that period. Even allowing that the early 1980s recession had hit BC very hard, the provincial labour force grew rapidly (32 per cent during the decade), being strongly driven by population growth. This is reflected in increases of 57 per cent in health and social service employment and 53 per cent in education employment. Against this underlying dynamic, the mild declines in logging and forestry services and in wood industries manufacturing

Table 14.2    Employment Structure: British Columbia, 1986 and 1996

| Sector | 1986 | 1996 | %* |
|---|---|---|---|
| Agriculture | 39,555 | 44,865 | 2.3 |
| Fishing | 8,705 | 8,850 | 0.5 |
| Logging | 40,815 | 39,390 | 2.0 |
| Mining | 19,355 | 15,935 | 0.8 |
| Manufacturing | 178,825 | 198,230 | 10.1 |
| *Food* | *19,815* | *21,675* | *1.1* |
| *Textile* | *6,610* | *9,270* | *0.5* |
| *Wood* | *49,075* | *48,375* | *2.5* |
| *Paper* | *18,680* | *19,935* | *1.0* |
| *Metal* | *7,090* | *5,580* | *0.3* |
| *Machinery* | *5,435* | *6,880* | *0.4* |
| *Transportation* | *9,595* | *9,705* | *0.5* |
| *Electrical* | *6,760* | *8,770* | *0.4* |
| Construction | 89,885 | 142,160 | 7.3 |
| Transportation | 82,510 | 89,270 | 4.6 |
| Communication | 45,415 | 53,030 | 2.7 |
| Wholesale | 63,430 | 91,915 | 4.7 |
| Retail | 186,845 | 238,420 | 12.2 |
| Finance | 49,855 | 64,555 | 3.3 |
| Real estate | 31,845 | 45,415 | 2.3 |
| Business | 70,990 | 129,105 | 6.6 |
| Government | 98,820 | 111,425 | 5.7 |
| Education | 85,545 | 130,980 | 6.7 |
| Health | 114,705 | 180,245 | 9.2 |
| Accommodation | 118,650 | 160,830 | 8.2 |
| Other service | 110,220 | 159,880 | 8.2 |
| Total | 1,484,180 | 1,960,665 | 100 |

*Percentage of provincial total for 1996.
SOURCE: Statistics Canada, Cat. no. 93F0027XDB96008.

employment represented a significant relative drop in the contribution of the provincial forest-based sector. Growth in aggregate manufacturing employment slowed in the 1991–6 period, but this was a much stronger performance than in central Canada, reflecting the important differences between the two parts of the country in the markets and structure of the manufacturing sector. Business services employment increased by 82 per cent from 1986 to 1996. Government service jobs grew by 15 per cent over the 1986–91 period, but then fell back slightly by 1996. BC provincial government employment, however, grew steadily throughout the decade. By the end of the 1990s, strong growth in the still relatively small high-technology sector was offsetting, to some extent, continuing problems in the provincial resource-based industries. It was estimated that high-technology industries were employing 52,000 people in 1999, a larger total than for BC's wood products industry. But there are both skill and spatial mismatches in the labour force attributes of expanding and contracting sectors in the province.

The geography of resource extraction has moulded regional differentiation within the provincial hinterland. The suitability of the protected waters of Georgia Strait to serve as a shipping corridor for log booms and barges allowed the coastal forest industry to localize sawmills in Vancouver and the Fraser estuary while extending logging steadily northwards. The Fraser estuary continues to have the greatest single concentration of mills, but other complexes have developed on Vancouver Island at Nanaimo, Crofton, Campbell River, and Port Alberni. The forest industry in the Interior grew appreciably during the postwar boom (1948–72), on the basis of evolving technology that could utilize the smaller trees and the northward extension of the British Columbia Railway network, which gave more parts of the province access to the expanding US market. Prince George, Quesnel, and Williams Lake, in the upper Fraser Valley, emerged as the largest processing centres.

The now-threatened wild salmon fishery supports a large number of small, isolated coastal communities, where salmon aquaculture has considerably increased its share of fish production. The majority of processing plants (canneries) are in larger centres such as Vancouver and Prince Rupert. Most minerals-sector employment has been concentrated in the southern Interior, notably by Cominco's lead/zinc smelter at Trail; base metal mining at Highland Valley (copper) and Kimberley (lead/zinc, now exhausted); and coal-mining in the Sparwood-Fernie region. A number of mining communities further north (McLeese Lake, Granisle) came into existence during the 1960s, but their fortunes have fluctuated markedly with the cycles in metal markets. Tumbler Ridge, built as a new town in the early 1980s to service the northeast coalfield megaproject, lost its *raison d'être* only 20 years later, when the checkered economic fortunes of that development finally gave out.

Diversification of the non-metropolitan economy of British Columbia will partly depend on a more varied exploitation of the natural environment than has been traditionally encouraged. There is a growing market for the non-consumptive enjoyment of the scenery, wilderness, and wildlife of the province, particularly in remote northern and coastal areas. Ecotourism is already taking root in Clayoquot Sound (where logging has been curtailed) and in the Tatshenshini-Alesk Wilderness Park (where development of a proposed large copper mine was disallowed). Visitor numbers are small and the season is relatively brief, but locally retained earnings are quite significant. There is also the prospect of more diversified economic activity, including eco- or cultural tourism, developing in many parts of the province if substantive progress can be made towards giving Aboriginal communities a secure and expanded role in resource management decisions.

Population growth and various forms of successful entrepreneurship are consolidating economic diversification in the Okanagan–Kamloops region. Kelowna boasts a climate and a lifestyle (and much cheaper housing than Vancouver) that has attracted more than just retired seniors (together with the financial service professionals who handle their investments). It has the greatest proportion of self-employed business people in the province, is the headquarters of an expanding mining firm, and has added major cultural and health-sector facilities to its central place functions. Its accessibility from the east was enhanced in 1996 by the start-up of short-lived

Greyhound Air, involving a locally based operator, but its airport has continued to attract regular discount carriers. The regional orchard-based agricultural and food-processing economy survives, and the local wine industry, like that of Ontario, has successfully re-created itself as an internationally competitive producer. The dominant manufacturing employer, Western Star Trucks, has diversified from its original special-ist niche of forest-industry vehicles to include light military trucks, and benefits from its modest size, which provides a flexible competitive advantage in entering other niche markets. Its remoteness from major component suppliers is offset by wage rates that are lower than in central Canada, combined with high levels of craft competence in the local labour force (*Globe and Mail*, 20 Sept. 1994).

While many communities in the southern Interior of British Columbia, such as Nelson, have experienced major economic upheaval resulting from the restructuring of traditional resource-based employment, they have generally had greater capacity for adjustment and diversification than communities in the north of the province (Mackenzie, 1987; Copeland, 1999). The two-thirds of BC that lies north of 53° N (or Williams Lake) contains only just over 300,000 people, of whom one-quarter live in the regional capital, Prince George. The intra-regional transportation network is rudi-mentary, and the northwest in particular, where 35 per cent of the population is Aboriginal, is remote and inaccessible. Logging costs are correspondingly high, making the expansion of commercial forestry improbable, despite some optimistic estimates of the potential harvest. Prince Rupert has never fulfilled the early hopes that it would become a major Canadian marine terminal for Pacific Ocean trade: even the traffic associated with the northeast coal project of the early 1980s proved to be well below initial expectations. Sustainable economic development and population reten-tion in the north requires imaginative new approaches that build up the local capac-ity for entrepreneurship and management. The University of Northern British Columbia in Prince George, opened in 1994, has made contributing to this challenge one of its institutional goals (Weller, 1994).

## CONCLUSION

By virtue both of population increase and growth of economic output, the West (particularly Alberta and British Columbia) continues to increase its relative weight within Canada. However, this has not been reflected in the arena of federal institutions (despite Albertan proposals for Senate reform) or policy-making authority, which accounts for the contemporary appeal in the West of a political party (Canadian Alliance) that carries a regional voice to Ottawa (see Chapter 2). But the substantial accumulating wealth of Alberta is giving its government increasing capacity to define policies and create incentives that appeal to business and research professionals, and thus to promote the province's economic development irrespective of federal initia-tives. Although the pace of exploitation of the Athabasca tar sands will be constrained by the availability of skilled labour and financing, and possibly moderated by interna-tional action to limit global warming, the size of the resource base and the level of North American demand promise to maintain Alberta's petroleum royalty income.

In contrast, Saskatchewan and Manitoba face continuing challenges associated with the dislocations in world agricultural markets (see Chapter 8). The grain economy is exposed to international pressures against which Ottawa has limited powers to cushion them, even if that is a federal priority (which western farmers often doubt). Like Atlantic Canada, the agricultural ecumene of these provinces lacks a dense network of larger urban centres, which focuses attention on the capacity of the metropolitan economies of Winnipeg, Saskatoon, and Regina to foster growth in knowledge-intensive services.

British Columbia faces the most complex challenges of all four western provinces: in adjusting to a transformation in how its forest resource is culturally valued and economically best used; in reaching a just settlement of overdue Aboriginal land claims; in how to moderate the sharp spatial polarization of economic opportunities between the Vancouver-centred core and the resource-based periphery; and in encouraging Vancouver's growth as a Pacific Rim gateway without damaging its attractive metropolitan quality of life.

## Further Reading

Davis, H.C. 1993. 'Is the Metropolitan Vancouver economy uncoupling from the rest of the province'?, *BC Studies* no. 98: 3–19.

Hoberg, G. 1996. 'The politics of sustainability: forest policy in British Columbia', in R.K. Carty, ed., *Politics, Policy, and Government in British Columbia*. Vancouver: University of British Columbia Press, 272–89.

Welsted, J., J. Everitt, and C. Stadel. 1996. *The Geography of Manitoba: Its Land and Its People*. Winnipeg: University of Manitoba Press.

Wynn, G., and T. Oke, eds. 1992. *Vancouver and Its Region*. Vancouver: University of British Columbia Press.

# Northern and Aboriginal Canada

## INTRODUCTION

Canada's North is not exclusively populated by Aboriginal peoples, nor is the geography of Aboriginal society exclusively northern (Peters, 2000). Nevertheless, both the region and the peoples occupy the margins of the urban-industrial and rural-agricultural economy of southern Canada. Although the proportion of Canada's Aboriginal population living in urban areas has grown rapidly (from under 10 per cent in 1951 to over 50 per cent in 1996), the presence of Aboriginal people is proportionately strongest in those parts of the country beyond the agricultural ecumene, where the overall density of population is extremely low. Since the early 1970s, relations between Aboriginal and non-Aboriginal Canadians have slowly but profoundly changed, and in the process established geographical concepts have been thrown into question. One of them is 'the North' itself; another is what constitutes 'economic development' for the people living within the region (Bone, 1992).

Politically, the North was long defined as comprising Yukon and the Northwest Territories (NWT). Since 1999, that geography has evolved through the creation of Nunavut out of the eastern and central parts of the former NWT, leaving the western part to keep the territorial name (Figure 15.1). The essence of the political definition of the North is that it is that part of territorial Canada beyond provincial boundaries, and hence beyond the constitutional federal-provincial division of powers. This means that the territorial legislatures have a more limited range of powers and responsibilities than have the provincial governments—essentially those the federal government has chosen, over time, to delegate to them. Crucially, except in Nunavut, which was created with a larger degree of self-government, reflecting its origin in a settlement of Inuit land claims, the territories do not have jurisdiction over their mineral resources. As a result, in a region almost devoid of the renewable agricultural and forest resources of southern Canada, the level of government closest to most of its inhabitants has no guaranteed access to revenues from whatever non-renewable resources might prove viable for development (Difrancesco, 2000). Economically, then, as well as in other respects, the North remains a dependency of Ottawa.

The same handicapping dependency characterizes the status of those Aboriginal peoples occupying Indian reserves in southern (provincial) Canada. Having been dispossessed of their original territories and assigned an official status linked to their occupancy of the limited and scattered land base of the reserves, members of

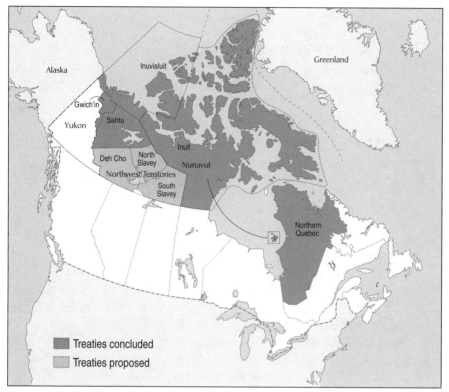

**Figure 15.1 Modern Treaties and Political Units in the Canadian North**

*SOURCE*: Based on Saku and Bone (2000: 262).

Canada's First Nations, except in a few recent cases of land settlements in BC have been denied meaningful self-government. Their lack of control over reserve land, which has hindered them from effectively harnessing the institutional structures of the Canadian economy (in which, for instance, individual title to land has been the traditional form of collateral for commercial bank loans), has been a serious impediment to economic diversification and development, far outweighing the benefits of the reserves' tax-free status.

The politically significant sixtieth parallel is in most other respects, however, a meaningless boundary. Biophysical, social, and economic characteristics of 'northernness' are much more extensive. Conditions that help to set apart Canada's northern hinterland regions, such as the extent of discontinuous permafrost, or remoteness from the developed transportation infrastructures of the south, extend, with declining intensity, well into the 'provincial norths' that exist in all but the Maritime provinces. These provincial hinterlands, remote from their respective legislatures and the urbanized populations whose interests dominate them, share most of the

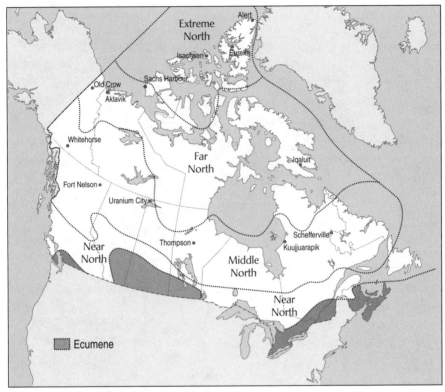

**Figure 15.2 Hamelin's 'Nordicity' Index**

SOURCE: Bone (1992: 10).

constrained economic opportunities and relative political powerlessness of the territorial North (Weller, 1977). Hamelin's (1979) mapping of 'nordicity' shows clearly how
much of Canada is distinctively northern (Figure 15.2). The variables used to calculate this index include measures of climatic severity, vegetation cover, population
density and accessibility by transportation modes from the south, which suggest that
the concept is framed primarily through the eyes of southerners. Recently, Statistics
Canada has created a standard delineation of the North for statistical purposes, which
includes many of the same variables together with a cost-of-living index (McNiven
and Puderer, 2000).

In southern Canadian mythology, this 'different' northern place has traditionally
been portrayed as a 'frontier'—of the human spirit ('the true North strong and free')
as much as of resource development (Shields, 1992). But to its indigenous inhabitants it always was, and remains, a 'homeland' (Berger, 1977). Only in the past 30
years have the aspirations and priorities of the Aboriginal residents begun to achieve
substantive expression. Their emergence from the 'internal colonialism' of federal

policies that originated in, and long reflected, a nineteenth-century racist paternalism is still a work in (slow) progress. However, the achievement in some parts of northern and Aboriginal Canada of significant degrees of self-government or co-management of resources has begun to erode long-entrenched obstacles to Aboriginal entrepreneurship and economic diversification. In fact, more progress has been made in the territorial North, where the Aboriginal population is a local majority in most places and where the federal government alone controls most of the policy variables, than in the south. In southern Canada, Aboriginal claims to land or to involvement in decision-making about resource use regularly conflict with competing claims by non-Aboriginals, whether as individuals or as provincial governments, and come up against the consequences of the inherited institutional apartheid of the Indian reserves.

The emerging expressions of Aboriginal aspirations for social and economic development have challenged conventional southern definitions of 'northern development'. The latter have been framed by the needs of the industrial economy of southern Canada (and of other core regions around the globe) and have typically been embodied in extractive and impermanent activities controlled by, and employing almost exclusively, non-Aboriginals. During the twentieth century, the principal activities of this nature were mining, hydrocarbon exploration, the operation of defence installations, and, south of the tree line, commercial forestry. In contrast, Aboriginal peoples are anxious to create a modern economy that reflects their cultural values, one shaped by communal institutions and a holistic ethic of society/environment relations and that is as compatible as possible with living permanently and sustainably 'on' and 'from' the land. The 'homeland' economy ideally combines traditional subsistence activities (hunting, trapping, fishing); land-based income-generation (the fur trade, outfitting, tourism); waged employment in extractive industries managed to accommodate local priorities; handicrafts and other small businesses; and Native involvement in all forms of service occupations. Realizing these aspirations still has a long way to go, however. Aboriginal peoples remain, on average, significantly poorer and less equipped (in terms of formal training, etc.) to participate in the market economy than other Canadians. Yet their youthful demography makes improved economic opportunities urgent.

The circumstances facing Nunavut illustrate many of these issues. The new territory, formally established on 1 April 1999, represents the settlement of a comprehensive land claim on the part of the Inuit of the eastern and central Arctic. As 85 per cent of the population is Inuit, and as Ottawa has devolved a substantial degree of ownership and control of resources to its government, the creation of Nunavut provides the Inuit with effective mechanisms for directing development according to their own priorities. But the scale of what needs to be achieved defies confidence about the outcome. The territory occupies one-quarter of the Canadian land mass but contains only 25,000 people. Almost half the Inuit population is under 20 years of age, and the birth rate in 1996 was almost 2.5 times the Canadian average. Education levels are improving, but health and social conditions remain significantly poorer than the national average and are, as much as anything else, consequences of the lack of opportunities for gainful activity. In 1996, one-third of the population depended on welfare. Public-sector jobs (administration, health, education, housing) are the core of the territory's regular employment. At the time that Nunavut was carved out of the former NWT, it was estimated that its administrative costs (paid by Ottawa) were around $600 million per year, only 10 per cent of which is generated from within the region itself. In terms of per capita income, Nunavut is Canada's poorest jurisdiction—poorer than the current NWT and 30 per cent poorer than the poorest province, Newfoundland (*Globe and Mail*, 5 June 1998).

The negotiation of modern Native land claim settlements was ushered in by the era of resource industry megaprojects that marked the 1970s. The precedent-setting James Bay and Northern Quebec Agreement with the Cree (1975) was conceded belatedly by the federal and Quebec governments in response to the impacts of hydroelectric development, which the Natives had had no part in shaping (Salisbury, 1986). The Agreement has had mixed results, economically and socially; but subsequent land claims settlements in Yukon (1991) and northern British Columbia (1996) have been generally positive for the parties involved. These modern-day 'treaties' between the Crown (Ottawa, and the provincial government where relevant) and indigenous peoples establish Aboriginal rights of resource and environmental management and provide financial resources that enable Aboriginal entrepreneurship to become established. At one level, then, the position of northern and Aboriginal Canadians in national life and their participation in the economy have been irreversibly strengthened (Saku and Bone, 2000). But numerous unresolved issues temper this assessment. Native land claims in British Columbia, where (with minor exceptions on Vancouver Island) no treaties were signed with the Aboriginal peoples at the time of initial European settlement, are meeting with much stronger opposition (or institutional inertia) than those in sparsely populated subarctic regions where established property rights are not felt to be threatened. And in the absence of federal-provincial agreement to transform the status of Indian reserves and remove the obstacles to effective self-governance of their peoples, the poverty and social pathology that still characterize too many reserves and remote northern communities will not easily be eradicated.

## THE NORTHERN ECONOMY

The frontier character of the North is reflected in a high-cost and narrowly based market economy. Long distances from manufacturing centres, limited overland transportation networks, water transport confined to a restricted ice-free season, the expensiveness of air transportation, and the costs and unpredictability associated with extreme weather conditions combine to inflate the cost of living and of doing business. Equally, remoteness and climatic constraints impose costs on the exploitation of natural resources that severely limit the number of economically viable projects.

Throughout the twentieth century, mining was the principal focus of industrial development and private-sector wage employment in the North. Uranium (initially at Uranium City, but now confined to modern, richer, and more accessible mines in northern Saskatchewan), gold (starting with the Yukon gold rush, but now mined at very few remote northern sites), and, within the past few years, diamonds (northeast of Yellowknife) are minerals whose value/weight ratio has permitted the development of remote mines heavily dependent on winter roads over frozen terrain and on air transport. The commercial mining of base metals has been confined to relatively rich deposits accessible by sea (currently, zinc at Nanisivik, Baffin Island and Polaris, Little Cornwallis Island, and the Raglan nickel mine near Déception, Quebec) or by northern extensions from the railway network of southern Canada (a means of gaining access that ceased to be economically viable by the mid-1970s) (Wallace, 1977). Revenue resulting from mining activity has been critical to the public finances of Yukon. Its marked instability since the early 1980s, related particularly to the fluctuating fortunes of the Faro lead-zinc mine, which has closed on a number of occasions, emphasizes the vulnerability of narrowly based frontier economies.

Exploration for hydrocarbons in the Mackenzie Delta and Beaufort Sea was heavily subsidized by Ottawa in the early 1980s as part of the National Energy Program (Figure 10.4), but the cost, technological challenges, and social and environmental impacts of exploiting the reserves that were found at that time inhibited their immediate development. With a tightening North American market for natural gas at the opening of the twenty-first century, proposals for a pipeline up the Mackenzie Valley have been revived. In addition, a gas pipeline following the route of the Alaska Highway has been proposed to tap gas from the Alaska North Slope and the Mackenzie Delta (*Globe and Mail*, 3 Mar. 2001). Each route has its advantages, and it is possible that both pipelines may eventually be constructed; but there are significant political uncertainties (reflecting domestic US issues as well as Canada–US relations) in addition to the economic ones. At this stage, moreover, as opposed to the situation that prevailed in the early 1970s, such developments will proceed only with the involvement of the Aboriginal peoples whose land is affected and with their sharing in the economic benefits.

The 'homeland' economy of the North is, or was, based principally on subsistence hunter-gatherer activity with some market-oriented elements (Usher, 1998). Hunting or trapping for 'country food' is still extremely important, both as an element of cultural continuity and as a significant contribution to nutrition and household budgets, given the cost of foodstuffs imported from the south. The degree to which traditional lifestyles have survived the disruptive impact of non-Aboriginal society varies considerably among communities, but the economic and social stresses have generally been enormous. Major dislocations have been associated with such factors as the early fur trade and whaling, the increasingly pervasive penetration since the 1950s of southern Canadian culture, institutions, and commodities, and the more recent impact of foreign ENGOs, whose opposition to the seal hunt in the eastern Arctic had ruinous consequences in the 1980s. Whether in the Arctic or on Indian reserves further south, the cumulative impact of a wide range of external and internal pressures has forced a fundamental reassessment of what development implies in northern Canada. Traditional economies have been undermined by the consequences of demographic expansion in regions of limited resources, by the minimal incorporation until very recently of Aboriginal people into waged employment by southern-based firms or governments, and by the perverse consequences of residential schools and 'welfare dependency' (however well-intended the incorporation of Native peoples into the southern welfare state may have been in some quarters).

The extractive economy is not something to which most Aboriginal peoples are opposed in principle, and it continues to be important. The development of the diamond resources discovered in the NWT in the 1990s was approved by those whose lands were involved, once environmental concerns had been met and a commitment to locate cutting and polishing facilities in the territory was negotiated. The Syncrude tar sands plant at Fort McMurray, Alberta, is the largest industrial operation in northern Canada and one where the involvement of Aboriginal personnel has been successfully encouraged. Their share of employment in remote mines, from northern Ontario to the High Arctic, has also increased. The growing involvement of Aboriginal peoples in land and forest co-management is leading to the greater integration of traditional knowledge into resource exploitation decisions, with a focus on the sustainability of wildlife and forest resources in the provincial norths (Berkes and Fast, 1996).

Perhaps the most important transformation of the northern economy in recent years, however, has flowed from the great expansion of managerial control by the region's residents, involving especially its Aboriginal inhabitants. In both the public and private sectors, key businesses have been taken over by those immediately involved in their operations. In 1987 the Hudson's Bay Company sold its network of northern stores to a group of investors, including 415 (16 per cent) of its northern employees. The successor company, North West Co., based in Winnipeg, operates in 156 communities and is the largest private-sector employer of Aboriginal people in the country (1,700 out of a total of 3,700 employees). Many new stores are joint ventures between the company and local Indian bands (*Globe and Mail*, 1 Feb. 1994). Northern transportation systems are now largely in Aboriginal hands, including truck and barge operations in the Mackenzie Valley and Delta, privatized by the federal government, and the major air carrier in the eastern Arctic, First Air, controlled by the Inuit-owned Makivik Corporation.

The financial component of comprehensive land-claim settlements has provided the recipient groups of Aboriginal peoples with capital, largely regarded as a heritage fund, that has been invested both locally and further afield (Bone, 1992; Saku and Bone, 2000). By the mid-1990s, for instance, the Natives of the Mackenzie Delta region had established the Inuvialuit Development Corporation (IDC). Its 20 subsidiaries included: the Calgary-based Inuvialuit Petroleum Corp.; Umayot Corp., which markets musk-ox products (meat and wool) from Sachs Harbour on Banks Island; one of Canada's largest manufacturers of modular homes (for which there is a steady demand in the North), based in the Okanagan Valley; and specialized engineering plants in Edmonton and Calgary supplying the oil and gas and chemical industries. The IDC was also at one time a majority owner of an investment company, registered in the tax-sheltered Cayman Islands and investing in Asia from a Hong Kong base (*Financial Post Magazine*, Mar. 1993; *Globe and Mail*, 4 July 1994). In cases where Indian bands have negotiated 'specific' land-claim settlements (to remedy particular unmet obligations on

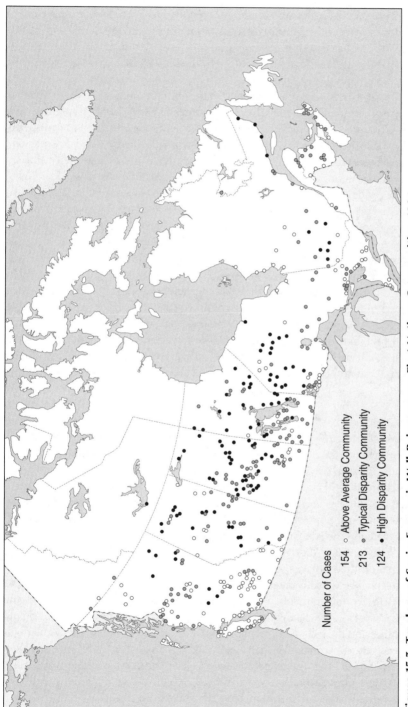

**Figure 15.3  Typology of Socio-Economic Well-Being among First Nations Communities, 1996**

*SOURCE:* Armstrong (1999: 5).

the part of the federal government), they are required to invest any cash payment in land, and some have entered the urban real estate market to create business and income opportunities. Saskatchewan has 17 such new urban reserves, including the McKnight Commercial Centre in Saskatoon, developed by the Muskeg Lake Cree Nation on 14 ha of run-down city property (Tallow, 2001).

Most Indian bands have not been beneficiaries of modern land-claim settlements and they vary considerably in their financial resources. Relative location and the extent of natural resource endowments significantly determine the potential for prosperity (Figure 15.3). Socio-economic variables suggest that bands can draw on more than one model to achieve economic success: some of those with 'above average' well-being are relatively 'modernized', whereas others are more 'traditional' (Armstrong, 1999). In the Vancouver region, one band has developed and leased townhouses, while another runs the third-largest shipyard in the province. A number of Alberta bands have lucrative oil and gas resources on their territory. But elsewhere, the inalienable tenure of reserve land, which negates its use as collateral, is a serious barrier to First Nations' economic development. Efforts to provide venture capital for small Aboriginal-owned businesses include the formation of 'borrower circles', and the Canadian chartered banks are slowly increasing their support for Aboriginal entrepreneurship. But until reserves are granted much fuller powers of self-government than they have been conceded to date, the Native economy will remain in a straitjacket. Where it is geographically facilitated (by proximity to metropolitan markets or to permeable international borders), as it is especially in the Montreal region, the underground economy (smuggling, etc.) and contested enterprises (such as casinos) will continue to offer appealing income opportunities in the absence of more constructive alternatives.

## CONCLUSION

Canada has frequently been ranked in first place since the United Nations Development Program began publishing its Human Development Index (HDI) in the early 1990s. Undoubtedly, the underlying statistics (measuring life expectancy, educational attainment, and average income) fairly record the country's standing relative to other nations. But if one were to calculate the HDI separately for Canada's Aboriginal and non-Aboriginal populations, the results would not be so flattering. An Aboriginal HDI calculated in the late 1990s placed that population approximately halfway down the UN ranking. The Aboriginal income variable is the one that has shown least improvement in recent years (Globe and Mail, 15 Oct. 1998). Unemployment among Aboriginal peoples remains much higher than among non-Aboriginal Canadians, and the problem is more difficult to solve because of the higher growth rate of the Aboriginal working-age population. This demographic characteristic of Aboriginal communities and the lack of economic opportunities keep unemployment rates high on reserves and contribute to urban Aboriginal unemployment rates that are often three times higher than the overall average (Globe and Mail, 24 June 1999). High unemployment rates also reflect social pathologies (such as children born with fetal alcohol syndrome) that are themselves rooted in cultural dislocation.

The hinterland economy of Canada's northern residents, among whom Aboriginal peoples are a major and frequently majority group, depends on development that is environmentally and socially sustainable. As Justice Thomas Berger (1977) identified in his report on the 1970s Mackenzie Valley pipeline proposal, the possibility of development that meets these criteria rests on the prior settlement of Native land claims and the institutional accommodation of Aboriginal self-governance. Significant progress has been made on these issues in the North since the Berger Inquiry, and northern entrepreneurship is gradually developing in its wake. The ground rules for appropriate non-renewable resource development, including future energy megaprojects, are also in place. But progress in finding a just and workable framework for bringing those Aboriginal peoples whose identity and rights have historically been tied to Indian reserves into the mainstream of the modern Canadian economy has been much less evident. It is a major political challenge that will not go away.

## FURTHER READING

Difrancesco, R.J. 2000. 'A Diamond in the rough?: an examination of the issues surrounding the development of the Northwest Territories', *Canadian Geographer* 44: 114–34.

Saku, J.A., and R.M. Bone. 2000. 'Looking for solutions in the Canadian North: modern treaties as a new strategy', *Canadian Geographer* 44: 259–70.

Usher, P. 1998. 'The North: one land, two ways of life', in L.D. McCann and A. Gunn, eds, *Heartland and Hinterland: A Geography of Canada*, 3 edn. Toronto: Prentice-Hall Canada, 357–94.

# Conclusion: Continuity and Change

## INTRODUCTION

Looking back approximately 40 years from 2000 provides a basis for taking stock of the economic geography of Canada. To what degree has it changed during that period and to what degree do seemingly irreversible spatial patterns persist? By 1960, the exploitation of Alberta's oil and gas reserves was well underway; the British Columbia Railway (then still called that paradox of colonial naming, the Pacific Great Eastern) was opening up the forests of the province's interior; the St Lawrence Seaway was newly in business as the intended highway for the traffic of industrial North America, and with it the Quebec/Labrador iron ore fields; and Prime Minister Diefenbaker was enunciating his vision of development in Canada's empty North as the key to the country's maturing as a 'northern nation'. As it had been for over a century already, Canada's physical geography, and the resources it encompassed, seemed for many to be its economic destiny—and a bright one at that! One of the leading geographers of the day took environmental determinism even further, predicting that in Alberta, where coal (and the industries it would support) was most plentiful, the highest population densities in the country would develop (Taylor, 1961).

## CANADA TODAY

Today, physical determinism is discredited by geographers, especially as a measure of economic potential. Staples theory is still recognized as an insightful analysis of the very geographically expressive course of Canadian economic history, but resource staples no longer dominate national employment and output. And yet . . . In 2000, Newfoundland labours under a prolonged crisis in the cod fishery even as it looks to offshore hydrocarbons and a revived mining industry to stimulate its economy. The British Columbia government grapples with what sustainable forestry means in a region that still has pristine stands but is keen to generate more employment from its trees. Alberta sees major expansions (with more certainly to come) in its oil-sands plants. The agricultural economy of the Prairies is actively being restructured by forces of deregulation and globalization in the grain trade. The development of hydroelectricity for export is still there in the background as an item on the economic development agenda of Quebec. Nor can Ontario, recently identified as the third most pollution-intensive jurisdiction in North America, pretend to ignore the role of the biophysical environment in the maintenance of Canadian prosperity.

Partly because of the strong presence of the natural environment in shaping Canada's ecumene, there remains much basic continuity in the regional structure of the economy. Despite the beneficial impact of equalization payments and other mechanisms of income transfer, Ontario remains the richest region, Alberta and BC are not far behind, Atlantic Canada is the poorest (apart from the territories), and Quebec, Manitoba, and Saskatchewan rank in the middle. There have been changes at the top of the metropolitan hierarchy, but no dramatic shifts in the upper ranges of the national urban rank-size distribution. Manufacturing is still overwhelmingly concentrated in southern Ontario and Quebec. Compared, then, to the United States, where the past 40 years have seen some dramatic swings in the geography of regional prosperity, developments in Canada have been pretty tame.

But if you have lived only half that time in Montreal, or Calgary, or Vancouver, or in smaller communities within an hour's driving time of these centres, changes have been anything but tame. Nor, in scale, have they been in the greater Toronto region, where population and economic growth rates, which were already rapid in the early 1960s, have dipped but never really abated. Forty years ago Montreal was still the manufacturing capital of Canada: few then would have predicted Calgary's emergence as the second-largest concentration of corporate head offices in the country, or that Ottawa would have a high-tech sector employing approximately the same number of people as its federal public service. As has been noted at various points in the text, Canada, like other advanced economies, has become increasingly a nation of metropolitan-centred regions. Its hinterland resource-based economies are more important to Canada than to comparable states, but the knowledge-based economies of its major urban areas are increasingly what constitute the basis of the nation's wealth at the start of the twenty-first century.

## THE IMPACT OF GLOBALIZATION

Globalization cannot help but bring change to the world's second-largest piece of national territory, a nation that faces three oceans and whose economy has always been more open and vulnerable than most to the currents of foreign trade. The emergence of a multi-polar world trading system, in which the Pacific has grown to rival the Atlantic Ocean as a highway of commerce, has played a major part in moving Canada's economic centre of gravity westward. Yet for Canadians who live next door to the 'the elephant' (as Prime Minister Trudeau described the geopolitics of Canada–US relations), the United States has lost none of its economic importance—indeed, the ties of trade have been strengthened. Nor has the US lost its power to impact, for good or ill, the conduct of domestic Canadian affairs. Whether through the channels of cross-border intra-corporate trade, the spillover effects of US deregulation (as in the transportation and energy sectors), or the exercise of US political-economic 'muscle' (as in the softwood lumber disputes, west coast salmon quotas, and 'split runs' in the Canadian magazine industry), the Canadian economy is bound to that of its neighbour. Indeed, under free trade, north-south axes of economic linkage have grown considerably in importance, at the expense of many of the east-west linkages that have been part of Canada's *raison d'être* for over a century. It is not just 'the Quebec question' that threatens to balkanize the federation.

Globalization also increases the difference between Canada's GDP (gross domestic product) and its GNP (gross national product). As the Canadian economy is becoming ever more open to foreign investment and trade, so is the world (faster in some parts than others, certainly) becoming more open to Canadian companies. The economic geography of Canada, which maps GDP, is becoming increasingly distinct from the geography of Canadian economic activity, which maps GNP. Some Canadian firms and financial institutions have a long history of overseas business (e.g., the Royal Bank in the Caribbean, Brascan in Brazil), but the scale and scope of Canadian foreign investment and non-traditional exports (such as professional services) are growing very fast. Nova (based in Calgary) has built a gas pipeline across the southern Andes; Trizec (based in Toronto) manages shopping-centre developments in Hungary; Quebecor (based in Montreal) bought the second-largest commercial printer in Chile; and Drewlo Homes (of London, Ontario) has built an executive subdivision for expatriates in Shanghai (examples drawn from news items in the *Globe and Mail Report on Business* in the late 1990s). Revenues, purchases, and employment flow into the domestic Canadian economy from all such activity, just as they have long flowed out of it (and still do), particularly to the United States.

## CONCLUSION

As this book has demonstrated, however, Canada is no mere appendage of its larger southern neighbour, nor is its economic geography simply a postscript to that of the United States. Nearly 40 years ago, Camu, Weeks, and Sametz (1964) provided a detailed analysis of the geography of Canada's economy when it was in the middle of the long postwar boom. This briefer contemporary survey has attempted to trace the major geographical dimensions of the changes that since then have created a Canada that is in many respects quite different, but is identifiably the same country.

The twenty-first century may not belong to Canada, as the twentieth was confidently claimed to in its early years, but the new century will certainly see the ongoing transformation of this fascinating land as the currents of globalization and the evolution of Canadian responses to them take shape. The economic geography of Canada remains a work in progress.

## FURTHER READING

Barnes, T.J., et al. 2000. 'Canadian economic geography at the millennium', *Canadian Geographer* 44: 4–24.

# Glossary

**AGRICULTURAL ECUMENE**   The total extent of occupied farmland.

**APPROPRIATIONISM**   The gradual replacement, by substitutes purchased from large industrial firms or specialized agents, of goods and activities traditionally provided or carried out by the farmer.

**BACK OFFICE**   Corporate office devoted to the transaction of routine business (such as processing insurance claims) by predominantly non-managerial employees, not requiring a downtown location.

**CIRCULAR AND CUMULATIVE CAUSATION**   Processes of economic development that are mutually reinforcing and build on themselves over time; frequently associated with growing geographical polarization between well-situated (core) and disadvantaged (hinterland) areas.

**CORE REGION**   A region that is *functionally* dominant (it may or may not be geographically central) within a larger territory. It has a diversified and prosperous economy and is a centre of political power and cultural dominance. Frequently contrasted with 'the periphery'.

**ECUMENE**   The total extent of permanently inhabited territory.

**EQUALIZATION PAYMENTS**   Payments by the government of Canada to poorer provinces to enable them to fund government services (including health care and education) at the national average level per capita.

**FALL-DOWN**   The transition from a regime of harvesting old-growth forest to one of harvesting second-growth forest. It involves a reduction in the available wood fibre.

**FLEXIBLE PRODUCTION**   The characteristic post-Fordist (see below) form of industrial production that has emerged with the widespread diffusion of computers. 'Smart' machines undercut many rigidities of Fordist production, allowing a wider variety of goods to be manufactured efficiently and at short notice. Firms have adjusted their labour force to match, favouring multi-skilled workers, cutting permanent staff, and increasing temporary (contract) employees.

**FORDISM (FORDIST PRODUCTION)**   The distinctive form of industrial production, and the broader set of societal practices that accompanied it, associated with the dominance of systems of mass production pioneered by Henry Ford in the automobile industry. In the workplace, it involves mechanized production of standardized goods by a large workforce, with each person having narrowly specialized skills. Strong labour unions ensure that workers are well paid and thus able to be consumers of the output of the industrial system. The state regulates the national economy to sustain prosperity and a large degree of social harmony.

**GLOBALIZATION**   A poorly defined but popular term that focuses on distinctive aspects, especially economic and cultural, of change in the contemporary world. It captures the growing integration of local- and global-scale processes, the power of transnational actors (firms and social movements), and the role of technology in 'shrinking' time and space.

**KONDRATIEFF WAVES**   Long-term cycles, of approximately 50 years, in the performance of industrialized capitalist economies. Thought to be related to the diffusion of new technologies, bringing periods of rapid growth but also demanding institutional change, which is more difficult to achieve. Named after an early twentieth-century Russian economist.

**LOCATION QUOTIENT**   An index of geographical concentration, often comparing the proportionate size of an industry at the regional or metropolitan level with its proportionate size at the national level. An index of 1.0 (or 100) corresponds to the national average; a value of more than 1.0 (100) indicates geographical specialization in that activity.

**MARSHALLIAN INDUSTRIAL DISTRICT**   A region of concentrated industrial activity characterized by dense networks of interdependence between many specialized small and medium-sized firms. Named after the early twentieth-century British economist, Alfred Marshall.

**POST-FORDISM**   The distinctive form of industrial production, and broader set of societal practices accompanying it, that has become dominant since the 1980s. It reflects the emergence of global rather than national markets, reduced state intervention in the economy, a decline in social welfare provision, and a loss of trade union power (leaving workers more exposed to negative aspects of flexible production systems).

**PRODUCER SERVICES**   Service industries selling primarily to other businesses and public-sector clients.

**REGULATION THEORY**   A conceptual framework that identifies a significant role for the state in the social and economic management of capitalist societies, notably in balancing the demands of firms and citizens (consumers) through 'modes' of regulation embodied in institutions and social practices that promote steady economic expansion.

**SATELLITE ACCOUNTS**   An accounting framework for statistics that records activity not documented by the conventional systems of national economic accounting used to calculate gross national (or domestic) product. Canadian examples include satellite tourism accounts, bringing together measures of activity in the many component parts of the tourism sector, and satellite environmental accounts, which record changes in natural resource stocks (such as forests) and interactions within the biosphere (such as pollution) as well as related economic transactions in resource-based industries.

**STAPLES (STAPLE INDUSTRIES)**   Natural resource products, raw or semi-processed, that are exploited primarily for export to foreign markets (which determine the level of demand and hence price).

**STAPLES TRAP**   The fate of a regional economy that, as a result of exclusive dependence on a staple industry, experiences extreme difficulty in adjusting to the demise of that industry (through exhaustion of the resource or loss of competitiveness).

**STUMPAGE**   Fees paid by forest companies to provincial governments for the right to harvest trees from Crown land.

**SUBSTITUTIONISM**   The gradual replacement of unprocessed or traditionally processed agricultural produce by food products derived from industrially manufactured ingredients.

**SUPPLY MANAGEMENT**   Government regulation of production and marketing in specific agricultural sectors (e.g., dairying) that limits imports so as to provide domestic producers with a steady, guaranteed market.

**TRUNCATED BRANCH PLANT (TRUNCATION)**   A subsidiary of a foreign corporation that lacks high-level managerial and research and development (R&D) functions in the host country (i.e., Canada).

**UNIT TRAIN**  A train carrying a single commodity transported in specialized freight cars that runs directly from a single point of origin to a single destination (e.g., from a coal mine to an export terminal).

# References

Anderson, M. 1995. 'The role of collaborative integration in industrial organization: Observations from the Canadian aerospace industry', *Economic Geography* 71: 55–78.

——— and J. Holmes. 1995. 'High-skill, low-wage manufacturing in North America: A case study from the automotive parts industry', *Regional Studies* 29: 655–71.

Anderson, W.P. 1987. 'The changing competitive position of the Hamilton steel industry', in M.J. Dear, J.J. Drake, and L.G. Reeds, eds, *Steel City: Hamilton and Region*. Toronto: University of Toronto Press, 202–21.

Andreae, C. 1997. *Lines of Country: An Atlas of Railway and Waterway History in Canada*. Erin, Ont.: Boston Mills Press.

Armstrong, R.P. 1999. 'Geographical patterns of socio-economic well-being of First Nations communities', *Rural and Small Town Canada Bulletin* 1, 8. Statistics Canada Cat. no. 21-006-XIE.

Atlantic Canada Opportunities Agency (ACOA). 1994. *Atlantic Canada: Facing the Challenge of Change—A Study of the Atlantic Economy*. ACOA.

Baldwin, J., and P. Hanel. 2000. 'Multinationals and the Canadian innovation process', *Working Paper 151*. Statistics Canada, Micro-Economic Analysis Division, 11F0019MPE No. 151.

Barnes, T. J. 1999. 'Industrial geography, institutional economics and Innis', in T.J. Barnes and M.S. Gertler, eds, *The New Industrial Geography: Regions, Regulation and Institutions*. London: Routledge, 1–20.

——— and R. Hayter. 1992. '"The little town that did": Flexible accumulation and community response in Chemainus, British Columbia', *Regional Studies* 26: 647–63.

———, ———, and E. Grass. 1990. 'Corporate restructuring and employment change: A case study of MacMillan Bloedel', in M. de Smidt and E. Wever, eds, *The Corporate Firm in a Changing World Economy*. London: Routledge, 145–65.

Barr, B.M., and J.C. Lehr. 1987. 'The western interior: The transformation of a hinterland region', in McCann (1987: 287–349).

Bathelt, H. 1991. 'Employment changes and input-output linkages in key technology industries: A comparative analysis', *Regional Studies* 25: 31–43.

——— and A. Hecht. 1990. 'Key technology industries in the Waterloo region: Canada's Technology Triangle (CTT)', *Canadian Geographer* 34: 225–34.

Beauchesne, Audric, and Christopher Bryant. 1999. 'Agriculture and innovation in the urban fringe: The case of organic farming in Quebec, Canada', *Tijdschrift voor Economische en Sociale Geografie* 90: 320–8.

Berger, T.R. 1977. *Northern Frontier, Northern Homeland: The Report of the Mackenzie Valley Pipeline Inquiry*, vol. 1. Ottawa: Minister of Supply and Services Canada.

Berkes, F., and H. Fast. 1996. 'Aboriginal peoples: The basis for policy-making toward sustainable development', in A. Dale and J.B. Robinson, eds, *Achieving Sustainable Development*. Vancouver: University of British Columbia Press, 204–63.

Berton, Pierre. 1970. *The National Dream*. Toronto: McClelland & Stewart.

Bloomfield, G.T. 1991. 'The railway life cycle in southwestern Ontario: The contraction phase, 1923–1990', *The Operational Geographer* 9, 2: 2–9.

Bollman, R.D., and B. Biggs. 1995. 'Rural demography: Key structural features', presentation notes for Canadian Society of Extension. Ottawa: Statistics Canada, 11 July.

Bone, R.M. 1992. *The Geography of the Canadian North*. Toronto: Oxford University Press.

Bourne, L.S. 1989. 'Are new urban forms emerging? Empirical tests for Canadian urban areas', *Canadian Geographer* 33: 312–28.

———. 1995. 'Urban growth and population redistribution in North America: A diverse and unequal landscape', *Major Report* 32, Centre for Urban and Community Studies, University of Toronto.

———. 2000. 'Urban Canada in Transition to the Twenty-First Century: Trends, Issues, and Visions', in Bunting and Filion (2000: 26–51).

——— and A.E. Olvet. 1995. 'New urban and regional geographies in Canada: 1986–91 and beyond', *Major Report* 33, Centre for Urban and Community Studies, University of Toronto.

Bowler, I.R. 1994. 'The institutional regulation of uneven development: The case of poultry production in the province of Ontario', *Transactions of the Institute of British Geographers* (new series) 19: 346–58.

Bradbury, J. 1987. 'British Columbia: Metropolis and hinterland in microcosm', in McCann (1987: 400–40).

——— and I. St-Martin. 1983. 'Winding down in a Québec mining town: a case study of Schefferville', *Canadian Geographer* 27: 128–44.

Britton, J.N.H. 1976. 'The influence of corporate organization and ownership on the linkages of industrial plants: A Canadian enquiry', *Economic Geography* 52: 127–41.

———. 1987. 'High technology industry in Canada: Locational and policy issues of the technology gap', in M.J. Breheny and R. McQuaid, eds, *The Development of High Technology Industries: An International Survey*. London: Croom Helm, 143–91.

———. 1993. 'A regional industrial perspective on Canada under Free Trade', *International Journal of Urban and Regional Research* 10: 559–77.

———, ed. 1996a. *Canada and the Global Economy: The Geography of Structural and Technological Change*. Montreal and Kingston: McGill-Queen's University Press.

———. 1996b. 'High-tech Canada', in Britton (1996a: 255–72).

———. 1999. 'Does nationality still matter? The new competition and the foreign ownership question revisited', in T.J. Barnes and M.S. Gertler, eds, *The New Industrial Geography: Regions, Regulation and Institutions*. London: Routledge, 238–64.

——— and J.M. Gilmour. 1978. *The Weakest Link: A Technological Perspective on Canadian Industrial Underdevelopment*. Background Study 43. Ottawa: Science Council of Canada.

Bryant, C.R., and T.R.R. Johnston. 1992. *Agriculture in the City's Countryside*. Toronto: University of Toronto Press.

Bunting, T., and P. Filion, eds. 1991. *Canadian Cities in Transition*. Toronto: Oxford University Press.

——— and ———, eds. 2000. *Canadian Cities in Transition: The Twenty-First Century*. Toronto: Oxford University Press.

Burgess, B. 2000. 'Foreign direct investment: Facts and perceptions about Canada', *Canadian Geographer* 44: 98–113.

Burghardt, A.F. 1971. 'A hypothesis about gateway cities', *Annals, Association of American Geographers* 61: 269–85.

Camu, P., E.P. Weeks, and Z.W. Sametz. 1964. *Economic Geography of Canada: Foundations, Growth, Trends*. Toronto: Macmillan of Canada.

Canada. 1984. *Soil at Risk*. Report by Senate Standing Committee on Agriculture, Fisheries, and Forestry. Ottawa: Senate of Canada.

———. 1991. *The State of Canada's Environment*. Ottawa: Supply and Services Canada.

Canada, EMR. 1989. *Ownership Structure and Control of the Canadian Nonfuel Minerals and Coal Sectors (as of December 31, 1988)*. Ottawa: Energy, Mines and Resources Canada.

Canadian Council of Resource and Environment Ministers (CCREM). 1987. *Report*, National Task Force on Environment and Economy. Ottawa: CCREM.

*Canadian Geographic*/Geomatics Canada. 1996. 'Natural Hazards', *National Atlas of Canada*, MCR 1403.

Canadian Grain Commission. 2000. www.cgc.ca/FAQ/elevdecr-e.htm (accessed 16 Aug. 2000).

Cannon, J.B. 1989. 'Directions in Canadian regional policy', *Canadian Geographer* 33: 230–9.

———. 1996. Restructuring in mature manufacturing industries: The case of Canadian clothing', in Britton (1996a: 215–29).

Castells, M. 1996. *The Information Age: Economy, Society and Culture*, vol. 1, *The Rise of the Network Society*. Malden, Mass.: Blackwell.

———. 1997. *The Information Age: Economy, Society and Culture*, vol. 2, *The Power of Identity*. Malden, Mass.: Blackwell.

———. 1998. *The Information Age: Economy, Society and Culture*, vol. 3, *End of Millennium*. Malden, Mass.: Blackwell.

——— and P. Hall. 1994. *Technopoles of the World: The Making of 21st Century Industrial Complexes*. London: Routledge.

Chapman, K. 1991. *The International Petrochemical Industry*. Oxford: Clarendon Press.

Chiotti, Q. 1992. 'Sectoral adjustments in agriculture: Dairy and beef livestock industries in Canada', in I. Bowler, C. Bryant, and M.D. Nellis, eds, *Contemporary Rural Systems in Transition*, vol. 1, *Agriculture and Environment*. Wallingford, UK: CAB International, 43–57.

Christaller, W. 1966. *Central Places in Southern Germany*, trans. W. Baskin, Englewood Cliffs, NJ: Prentice-Hall.

Clapp, R.A. 1998. 'The resource cycle in forestry and fishing', *Canadian Geographer* 42: 129–44.

Clark, G.L. 1986. 'The crisis of the midwest auto industry', in A.J. Scott and M. Storper, eds, *Production, Work, Territory: The Geographical Anatomy of Industrial Capitalism*. Boston: Allen and Unwin, 127–48.

Coffey, W.J. 1994. *The Evolution of Canada's Metropolitan Economies*. Montreal: Institute for Research on Public Policy.

———. 1996. 'The role and location of service activities in the Canadian space economy', in Britton (1996a: 335–51).

———. 2000. 'Canadian cities and shifting fortunes of economic development', in Bunting and Filion (2000: 121–50).

——— and R. Drolet. 1994. 'La décentralisation des services supérieurs dans la région métropolitaine de Montréal, 1981–1989', *Canadian Geographer* 38: 215–29.

——— and M. Polese, eds. 1987. *Still Living Together: Recent Trends and Future Directions in Canadian Regional Development*. Montreal: Institute for Research on Public Policy.

Collins, L. 1998. 'Environmentalism and restructuring of the global pulp and paper industry', *Tijdschrift voor Economische en Sociale Geografie* 89: 401–15.

Copeland, G. 1999. *Acts of Balance: Profits, People and Place*. Gabriola Island, BC: New Society.

Coulombe, S. 1998. 'Economic growth and provincial disparity: A new view of an old Canadian problem', *Commentary* No. 122. Toronto: C.D. Howe Institute.

———. 1995. 'Glocalization: The regional/international interface', *Canadian Journal of Regional Science* 18: 1–20.

Courchene, T.J. 1980. 'Energy and equalization', in Ontario Economic Council, *Energy Policies for the 1980's: An Economic Analysis*, vol. 1. Toronto: Ontario Economic Council, 103–31.

———, with C.R. Telmer. 1998. *From Heartland to North American Regional State: The Social, Fiscal and Federal Evolution of Ontario*. Toronto: Centre for Public Management, University of Toronto.

Dales, J.H. 1957. *Hydroelectricity and Industrial Development: Quebec 1891–1940*. Cambridge, Mass.: Harvard University Press.

Darling, H.J. 1980. *The Politics of Freight Rates: The Railway Freight Rate Issue in Canada*. Toronto: McClelland & Stewart.

Davis, H.C. 1993. 'Is the Metropolitan Vancouver economy uncoupling from the rest of the province?', *BC Studies* no. 98: 3–19.

De Benedetti, G.J., and R.H. Lamarche. 1994. *Shock Waves: The Maritime Urban System in the New Economy*. Moncton: Canadian Institute for Research on Regional Development.

Difrancesco, R.J. 2000. 'A diamond in the rough?: An examination of the issues surrounding the development of the Northwest Territories', *Canadian Geographer* 44: 114–34.

Drache, D., and M.S. Gertler. 1991. 'The world economy and the nation-state: The new international order', in Drache and Gertler, eds, *The New Era of Global Competition*. Montreal and Kingston: McGill-Queen's University Press, 3–25.

Economic Council of Canada. 1984. *Western Transition*. Ottawa: Supply and Services Canada.

———. 1991. *Employment in the Service Economy*. Ottawa: Supply and Services Canada.

Edgington, D. 1998. 'Japanese tourism in western Canada', paper presented at the annual meeting of the Canadian Association of Geographers, Ottawa.

——— and R. Hayter. 1997. 'International trade, production chains and corporate strategies: Japan's timber trade with British Columbia', *Regional Studies* 31: 151–66.

Elias, P.D. 1995. *Northern Aboriginal Communities: Economies and Development*. North York, Ont.: Captus Press.

Ellis, L. 1993. 'Sea of cranberries', *Canadian Geographic* (Sept.-Oct.): 46–51.

Environment Canada. 1991. *Understanding Atmospheric Change: A Survey of the Background Science and Implications of Climate Change and Ozone Depletion*. SOE Report 91-2. Ottawa: Supply and Services Canada.

Fisheries and Oceans Canada. 1993. *Charting a New Course: Towards the Fishery of the Future*. Report of the Task Force on Incomes and Adjustment in the Atlantic Fishery. Ottawa: Supply and Services Canada.

Forward, C.N. 1990. 'Variations in employment and non-employment income in Canadian cities as indicators of economic base differences', *Canadian Geographer* 34: 120–32.

Fuller, A.M. 1994. 'Sustainable rural communities in the arena society', in T.R. Bryden, ed., *Towards Sustainable Rural Communities*. Guelph, Ont.: University School of Rural Planning and Development.

Furtan, W.H., and R.S. Gray. 1991. 'The constitutional debate: some issues for agriculture', *Canadian Public Policy* 17: 445–55.

Gad, G. 1991. 'Office Location', in Bunting and Filion (1991: 432–59).

Gagné, P., and M. Lefèvre. 1993. *L'Atlas industriel du Québec*. Montréal: Publi-Relais.

Gagnon, S. 1999. '"We're Swimming Upstream" . . . Into the Mainstream? An Overview of the Social, Economic, and Institutional Aspects of Organic Farming in Nova Scotia', MA thesis, Carleton University.

Garreau, J. 1991. *Edge Cities: Life on the New Frontier*. New York: Doubleday.

Gentilcore, R.L. 1993. *Historical Atlas of Canada: Vol. II, The Land Transformed 1800–1891*. Toronto: University of Toronto Press.

Germain, A., and D. Rose. 2000. *Montréal: The Quest for a Metropolis*. Chichester, UK: John Wiley.

Gertler, M.S. 1993. 'Implementing advanced manufacturing technologies in mature industrial regions: Towards a social model of technology production', *Regional Studies* 27: 665–80.

———. 1995a. 'Groping towards reflexivity: Responding to industrial change in Ontario', in P. Cooke, ed., *The Rise of the Rustbelt*. New York: St Martin's Press, 103–24.

———. 1995b. '"Being there": Proximity, organization, and culture in the development and adoption of advanced manufacturing technologies', *Economic Geography* 71: 1–26.

———. 1999. 'Negotiated path or "business as usual"? Ontario's transition to a continental production regime', *Space and Polity* 3: 171–97.

Gilmour, J.M. 1972. *Spatial Evolution of Manufacturing: Southern Ontario 1851–1891*. Toronto: Department of Geography, University of Toronto.

——— and K. Murricane. 1973. 'Structural divergence in Canada's manufacturing belt', *Canadian Geographer* 17: 1–18.

Glover, D., and K. Kusterer. 1990. 'McCain Foods, Canada: The political economy of monopoly', in Glover and Kusterer, *Small Farmers, Big Business: Contract Farming and Rural Development*. Basingstoke: Macmillan, 73–93.

Goodman, D., B. Sorj, and J. Wilkinson. 1987. *From Farming to Biotechnology*. Oxford: Blackwell.

Grass, E., and R. Hayter. 1989. 'Employment change during the recession: The experience of forest product manufacturing plants in British Columbia, 1981–1985', *Canadian Geographer* 33: 240–52.

Greater Toronto Area (GTA) Task Force. 1996. *Greater Toronto*. Toronto: Publications Ontario.

Green, M.B., and R.B. McNaughton. 1989. 'Canadian interurban merger activity, 1962–1984', *Canadian Geographer* 33: 253–64.

Hall, P. 1985. 'The geography of the Fifth Kondratieff', in Hall and A. Markusen, eds, *Silicon Landscapes*. Boston: Unwin Hyman.

Hamelin, L.-E. 1979. *Canadian Nordicity: It's Your North Too*, trans. W. Barr. Montreal: Harvest House.

Hanley, W. 1991. 'Tourism in the Northwest Territories', *Geographical Review* 81: 389–99.

Hardin, H. 1974. *A Nation Unaware: The Canadian Economic Culture*. Vancouver: J.J. Douglas.

Harris, R.C. 1987. 'Regionalism and the Canadian archipelago', in McCann (1987: 533–59).

Harvey, D. 1989a. 'From managerialism to entrepreneurialism: The transformation in urban governance in late capitalism', *Geografiska Annaler B* 71: 1–17.

———. 1989b. *The Condition of Postmodernity*. Oxford: Blackwell.

Hayter, R. 1997. *The Dynamics of Industrial Location: The Factory, the Firm and the Production System*. Chichester, UK: Wiley.

———. 2000. *Flexible Crossroads: The Restructuring of British Columbia's Forest Economy*. Vancouver: University of British Columbia Press.

——— and D. Edgington. 1997. 'Cutting against the grain: A case study of MacMillan Bloedel's Japan strategy', *Economic Geography* 73: 187–213.

——— and D. Soyez. 1996. 'Clearcut issues: German environmental pressure and the British Columbia forest sector', *Geographische Zeitschrift* 84: 143–56.

Helliwell, J.F. 1999. 'Canada's national economy: There's more to it than you thought', in H. Lazar and T. McIntosh, eds, *How Canadians Connect*. Montreal and Kingston: McGill-Queen's University Press, 87–100.

Hero, A.O. 1988. *Contemporary Quebec and the United States, 1960–1985*. Cambridge, Mass.: Center for International Affairs, Harvard University.

Hiebert, D. 1994. 'Canadian immigration: Policy, politics, geography', *Canadian Geographer* 38: 254–8.

Higgins, B. 1986. *The Rise—and Fall? of Montreal: A Case Study of Urban Growth, Regional Expansion and National Development*. Moncton: Canadian Centre for Research on Regional Development.

Hoberg, G. 1996. 'The politics of sustainability: Forest policy in British Columbia', in R.K. Carty, ed., *Politics, Policy, and Government in British Columbia*. Vancouver: University of British Columbia Press, 272–89.

Holmes, J. 1992. 'The continental integration of the North American automobile industry: From the Auto Pact to the FTA and beyond', *Environment and Planning A* 24: 95–119.

———. 'Restructuring in a continental production system', in Britton (1996a: 230–54).

Hutton, T.A. 1998. *The Transformation of Canada's Pacific Metropolis: A Study of Vancouver*. Montreal: Institute for Research on Public Policy.

Inglis, J.T., ed. 1993. *Traditional Ecological Knowledge: Concepts and Cases*. Ottawa: International Development Research Centre.

Jones, K. 2000. 'Dynamics of the Canadian Retail Environment', in Bunting and Filion (2000: 404–22).

——— and J. Simmons. 1993. *Location, Location, Location*, 2nd edn. Scarborough, Ont.: Nelson Canada.

Joseph, A., and P. Keddie. 1985. 'The "diffusion" of grain corn production through Southern Ontario, 1971–81', *Canadian Geographer* 29: 168–72.

Kerr, D., and J. Spelt. 1965. *The Changing Face of Toronto*. Ottawa: Information Canada.

Kneen, B. 1995. *Invisible Giant: Cargill and Its Transnational Strategies*. Halifax: Fernwood.

Knox, P., and J. Agnew. 1998. *The Geography of the World Economy*, 3rd edn. New York: Wiley.

——— and P.J. Taylor. 1995. *World Cities in a World-System*. Cambridge: Cambridge University Press.

Krueger, R.R. 1978. 'Urbanization of the Niagara Fruitbelt', *Canadian Geographer* 22: 179–94.

Leach, B., and A. Winson. 1999. 'Rural retreat: The social impact of restructuring in three Ontario communities', in D.B. Knight and A.E. Joseph, eds, *Restructuring Societies: Insights from the Social Sciences*. Ottawa: Carleton University Press, 83–104.

Lewis, R. 2000. *Manufacturing Montreal: The Making of an Industrial Landscape, 1850 to 1930*. Baltimore: Johns Hopkins University Press.

Ley, D. 1999. 'Myths and meanings of immigration and the metropolis', *Canadian Geographer* 43: 2–19.

Ley, D., D. Hiebert, and G. Pratt. 1992. 'Time to grow up? From urban village to world city, 1966–91', in Wynn and Oke (1992: 234–66).

Livingstone, D.N. 2000. 'Environmental determinism', in R.J. Johnston et al., *The Dictionary of Human Geography*, 4th edn. Oxford: Blackwell, 212–15.

Lösch, A. 1954. *The Economics of Location*, trans. W.F. Stolper. New Haven: Yale University Press.

McCallum, J. 1980. *Unequal Beginnings: Agriculture and Economic Development in Quebec and Ontario until 1870*. Toronto: University of Toronto Press.

McCann, L.D. 1980. 'Canadian resource towns: A heartland-hinterland perspective', in R.E. Preston and L. Russwurm, eds, *Essays on Canadian Urban Process and Form II*, Department of Geography Publication Series, No. 15. Waterloo: University of Waterloo, 209–67.

———, ed. 1987. *Heartland and Hinterland: A Geography of Canada*, 2nd edn. Scarborough, Ont.: Prentice-Hall.

——— and A. Gunn, eds. 1998. *Heartland and Hinterland: A Geography of Canada*, 3rd edn. Toronto: Prentice-Hall.

——— and J. Simmons. 2000. 'The core-periphery structure of Canada's urban system', in Bunting and Filion (2000: 76–96).

McIlwraith, T.F. 1993. 'The Railway Age, 1834–1891', in Gentilcore (1993: Plate 26).

McKay, P. 1983. *Electric Empire: The Inside Story of Ontario Hydro*. Toronto: Between the Lines.

Mackenzie, S. 1987. 'Neglected spaces in peripheral places: Homeworkers and the creation of a new economic centre', *Cahiers de géographie du Québec* 31: 247–60.

MacLachlan, I. 1992. 'Plant closure and market dynamics: competitive strategy and rationalization', *Economic Geography* 68: 128–45.

Maclaren, V.M. 1996. 'Redrawing the Canadian energy map', in Britton (1996a: 137–54).

McNiven, C., and H. Puderer. 2000. 'Delineation of Canada's North: An examination of the north-south relationship in Canada', *Geography Working Paper Series* 2000–3. Ottawa: Statistics Canada.

Mair, A., R. Florida, and M. Kenney. 1988. 'The new geography of automobile production: Japanese transplants in North America', *Economic Geography* 64: 352–73.

Manning, E.W. 1990. 'Presidential Address: Sustainable development, the challenge', *Canadian Geographer* 34: 290–302.

Mansell, R.L., and M.B. Percy. 1990. *Strength in Adversity: A Study of the Alberta Economy*. Edmonton: University of Alberta Press.

Markusen, A. 1996. 'Sticky places in slippery space', *Economic Geography* 72: 293–313.

Mather, C. 1993. 'Flexible technology in the clothing industry: Some evidence from Vancouver', *Canadian Geographer* 37: 40–7.

Matthew, M.R. 1993. 'The suburbanization of Toronto offices', *Canadian Geographer* 37: 293–306.

Mellinger, A.D., J.D. Sachs, and J.L. Gallup. 2000. 'Climate, coastal proximity, and development', in G.L. Clark, M.P. Feldman, and M.S. Gertler, eds, *The Oxford Handbook of Economic Geography*. Oxford: Oxford University Press, 169–94.

Merrett, C.D. 1996. *Free Trade: Neither Free Nor About Trade*. Montreal: Black Rose.

Michalak, W.Z., and K.J. Fairbairn. 1993. 'The producer service complex of Edmonton: the role and organization of producer service firms in a peripheral city', *Environment and Planning A* 25: 761–77.

Mitchell, B., ed. 1991. *Ontario: Geographical Perspectives on Economy and Environment*. Waterloo, Ont.: Department of Geography, University of Waterloo, Publication Series No. 34.

———, ed. 1995. *Resource and Environmental Management in Canada: Addressing Conflict and Uncertainty*, 2nd edn. Toronto: Oxford University Press.

Morrow, R.W. 1993. 'The Utilization of Trucks and Intermodal Systems in the Ottawa Airfreight Industry', MA thesis, Carleton University.

National Energy Board. 1994. *Canadian Energy Supply and Demand 1993–2010: Trends and Issues*. Calgary: NEB.

Natural Resources Canada. 1996. *The State of Canada's Forests 1995–1996*. Ottawa: Natural Resources Canada.

Nelles, H.V. 1974. *The Politics of Development: Forests, Mines and Hydro-electric Power in Ontario, 1849–1941*. Toronto: Macmillan.

Niosi, J. 1985. *Canadian Multinationals*, trans. Robert Chodos. Toronto: Garamond Press.

Norcliffe, G. 1994. 'Regional labour market adjustments in a period of structural transformation: an assessment of the Canadian case', *Canadian Geographer* 38: 2–17.

——— and J. Bates. 1997. 'Implementing lean production in an old industrial space: restructuring at Corner Brook, Newfoundland, 1984–1994', *Canadian Geographer* 41: 41–60.

North, R.N., and W.G. Hardwick. 1992. 'Vancouver since the Second World War: An economic geography', in Wynn and Oke (1992: 200–33).

Parker, P. 1997. 'Canada-Japan coal trade: An alternative form of the staple production model', *Canadian Geographer* 41: 248–67.

Peters, E.J. 2000. 'Aboriginal people and Canadian geography: A review of the recent literature', *Canadian Geographer* 44: 44–55.

Porter, M.E. 1990. *The Competitive Advantage of Nations*. New York: Free Press.

———. 1991. *Canada at the Crossroads: The Reality of a New Competitive Environment*. Ottawa: Business Council on National Issues and Minister of Supply and Services Canada.

Pred, A.R. 1965. 'Industrialization, initial advantage and American metropolitan growth', *Geographical Review* 54: 165–80.

Preston, V., J.N. Holmes, and A. Williams. 1997. 'Working with "Wild Rose I": Lean production in a greenfield mill', *Canadian Geographer* 41: 88–104.

——— and L. Lo. 2000. '"Asian theme" malls in suburban Toronto: Land use conflict in Richmond Hill', *Canadian Geographer* 44: 182–90.

Quarter, J. 1995. *Crossing the Line: Unionized Employee Ownership and Investment Funds*. Toronto: Lorimer.

Québec, OPDQ. 1991. *Profil statistique des régions du Québec*, 2ième edn. Québec: Office de planifiction et de développement du Québec.

Randall, J.E., and R.G. Ironside. 1996. 'Communities on the edge: a geography of resource-dependent communities in Canada', *Canadian Geographer* 40: 17–35.

Ray, D.M. 1965. *Market Potential and Economic Shadow: A Quantitative Analysis of Industrial Location in Southern Ontario*. Chicago: University of Chicago, Department of Geography.

———. 1971a. 'The location of United States subsidiaries in southern Ontario', in R.L. Gentilcore, ed., *Geographical Approaches to Canadian Problems*. Scarborough, Ont.: Prentice-Hall, 69–82.

———. 1971b. *Dimensions of Canadian Regionalism*. Geographical Paper No. 49. Ottawa: Department of Energy, Mines and Resources.

Rice, M.D., and R.K. Semple. 1993. 'Spatial interlocking directorates in the Canadian urban system, 1971–1989', *Urban Geography* 14: 375–96.

Robinson, J.L. 1969. *Resources of the Canadian Shield*. Toronto: Methuen.

Rose, D., and M. Villemaire. 1997. 'Reshuffling paperworkers: Technological change and experiences of reorganization at a Québec newsprint mill', *Canadian Geographer* 41: 61–87.

Royal Commission on the Economic Union and Development Prospects for Canada (Macdonald Commission). 1985. *Report*. Ottawa: Supply and Services Canada.

Rutherford, T.D. 1995. '"Control the ones you can": Production restructuring, selection, and training in Kitchener Region manufacturing, 1987–1992', *Canadian Geographer* 39: 30–45.

———. 1998. '"Still in Training?" Labor unions and the restructuring of Canadian labor market policy', *Economic Geography* 74: 131–48.

———. 2000. 'Re-embedding, Japanese investment and the restructuring of buyer-supplier relations in the Canadian automotive components industry during the 1990s', *Regional Studies* 34: 739–51.

Saarinen, O. 1992. 'Creating a sustainable community: The Sudbury case study', in M. Bray and A. Thomson, eds, *At the End of the Shift: Mines and Single-Industry Towns in Northern Ontario*. Toronto: Dundurn Press, 165–86.

Saku, J.A., and R.M. Bone. 2000. 'Looking for solutions in the Canadian North: Modern treaties as a new strategy', *Canadian Geographer* 44: 259–70.

Salisbury, R.F. 1986. *A Homeland for the Cree: Regional Development in James Bay, 1971–1981*. Montreal and Kingston: McGill-Queen's University Press.

Sancton, A. 2000. 'The municipal role in the governance of Canadian cities', in Bunting and Filion (2000: 425–42).

Sassen, S. 1991. *The Global City*. Princeton, NJ: Princeton University Press.

Savoie, D.J. 1992. *Regional Economic Development: Canada's Search for Solutions*, 2nd edn. Toronto: University of Toronto Press.

Saxenian, A. 1996. *Regional Advantage: Culture and Competition in Silicon Valley and Route 128*. Cambridge, Mass.: Harvard University Press.

Scholte, J.A. 2000. *Globalization: A Critical Introduction*. Basingstoke: Macmillan.

Science Council of Canada. 1986. *A Growing Concern: Soil Degradation in Canada*. Ottawa: Science Council of Canada.

Scott, A.J. 1993. *Technopolis: High-technology Industry and Regional Development in Southern California*. Berkeley: University of California Press.

———. 1998. *Regions and the World Economy: The Coming Shape of Global Production, Competition, and Political Order*. Oxford: Oxford University Press.

Seifried, N. 1989. 'Restructuring the Canadian petrochemical industry: An intranational problem', *Canadian Geographer* 33: 168–78.

Shields, R. 1992. 'The true north strong and free', in Shields, *Places on the Margin*. London: Routledge, 162–99.

Shrimpton, M., and K. Storey. 1992. 'Fly-in mining and the future of the Canadian North', in M. Bray and A. Thomson, eds, *At the End of the Shift: Mines and Single-Industry Towns in Northern Ontario*. Toronto: Dundurn Press, 187–208.

Simmons, J. 1991. 'Toronto's changing commercial structure', *Operational Geographer* 9, 4: 5–9.

Skogstad, G. 1998. 'Canadian federalism, internationalization and Quebec agriculture: Disengagement, re-integration?', *Canadian Public Policy* 24, 1: 27–48.

Slack, B. 1990. 'Intermodal transportation in North America and the development of inland load centers', *Professional Geographer* 42: 72–83.

Smit, B., ed. 1993. *Adaptation to Climatic Variability and Change*. Report of the Task Force on Climate Adaptation, Department of Geography, University of Guelph, *Occasional Paper* No. 19.

Smith, C.A. 1976. 'Exchange systems and the spatial distribution of elites: The organization of stratification in agrarian societies', in Smith, ed., *Regional Analysis*, vol. 2, *Social Systems*. New York: Academic Press, 309–74.

Smith, P.J. 1987. 'Alberta since 1945: The maturing settlement system', in McCann (1987: 351–99).

Smith, W. 1984. 'The "vortex model" and the changing agricultural landscape of Quebec', *Canadian Geographer* 28: 358–72.

Stabler, J.C., and M.R. Olferi. 1993. 'Farm structure and community viability in the northern Great Plains', *Review of Regional Studies* 23: 265–86.

Stallings, B. 1995. 'The new international context of development', in Stallings, ed., *Global Change, Regional Response: The New International Context of Development*. Cambridge: Cambridge University Press.

Statistics Canada. 1991. *Human Activity and the Environment*. Ottawa: Statistics Canada, Cat. no. 11–509.

———. 1994. *Canadian Agriculture at a Glance*. Ottawa: Statistics Canada, Cat. no. 96–301.

———. 1995. *Environmental Perspectives: Studies and Statistics, No. 2*. Ottawa: Statistics Canada.

———. 1997. *Census of Agriculture 1996*. Ottawa: Statistics Canada, Cat. no. 93–356.

———. 1998a. *Electric Power Generation, Transmission and Distribution*. Ottawa: Statistics Canada, Cat. no. 57–202.

———. 1998b. *Logging Industry*. Ottawa: Statistics Canada, Cat. no. 25–201.

———. 1999a. *Labour Force Update* 3, 2 (Spring). Ottawa: Statistics Canada, Cat. no. 71–005.

———. 1999b. *Canadian Agriculture at a Glance*. Ottawa: Statistics Canada, Cat. no. 96–325.

———. 2000a. *Canadian Economic Observer* 14. Ottawa: Statistics Canada, Cat. no. 11–210.

———. 2000b. *Labour Force Update*. Ottawa: Statistics Canada, Cat. no. 71–005.

———. 2000c. *Human Activity and the Environment*. Ottawa: Statistics Canada, Cat. no. 11–509.

———. 2000d. *National Tourism Indicators*. Second Quarter, 2000. Ottawa: Statistics Canada, Cat. no. 13–009.

———. 2000e. *Tourism Statistical Digest*. Ottawa: Statistics Canada, Cat. no. 87–403.

Steed, G.P.F., and D. DeGenova. 1983. 'Ottawa's technology-oriented complex', *Canadian Geographer* 27: 263–78.

Storper, M. 1997. *The Regional World*. New York: Guilford Press.

——— and R. Walker. 1989. *The Capitalist Imperative: Territory, Technology, and Industrial Growth*. New York: Blackwell.

Swift, J. 1983. *Cut and Run: The Assault on Canada's Forests*. Toronto: Between the Lines.

Tallow, P.M. 2001. 'Urban reserves: Canada's changing landscape', *Aboriginal Times* 5, 6 (Apr.): 16–28.

Taylor, G. 1961. 'Australia and Canada: A study of habitability as determined by the environment', *Professional Geographer* 13: 1–5.

Transport Canada. 2000. *Transportation in Canada, 1999*. Ottawa: Public Works and Government Services Canada.

Tucker, A. 1978. *Steam into Wilderness: Ontario Northland Railway 1902–1962*. Toronto: Fitzhenry & Whiteside.

Usher, P. 1998. 'The North: One land, two ways of life', in McCann and Gunn (1998: 357–94).

Vance, J.E. 1970. *The Merchant's World: The Geography of Wholesaling*. Englewood Cliffs, NJ: Prentice-Hall.

Ville de Montréal. 2000. *The Montréal Economy*, 4th Quarter, 1999.

Waddell, E. 1987. 'Cultural hearth, continental diaspora: The place of Québec in North America', in McCann (1987: 149–72).

Wallace, I. 1975. 'The containerization of traffic at Canadian ports', *Annals, Association of American Geographers* 65: 433–48.

———. 1977. *The Transportation Impact of the Canadian Mining Industry*. Kingston, Ont.: Centre for Resource Studies.

———. 1990. *The Global Economic System*. London: Unwin Hyman.

———. 1992. 'International restructuring of the agri-food chain', in I. Bowler, C. Bryant, and M.D. Nellis, eds, *Contemporary Rural Systems in Transition*, vol. 1, *Agriculture and Environment*. Wallingford, UK: CAB International, 15–28.

———. 1996. 'Restructuring in the Canadian mining and mineral-processing industries', in Britton (1996a: 123–36).

———. 1998. 'The Canadian Shield: The development of a resource frontier', in McCann and Gunn (1998: 227–67).

———. 1999a. 'Manufacturing in North America', in F.W. Boal and S.A. Royle, eds, *North America: A Geographical Mosaic*. London: Arnold, 141–54.

———. 1999b. 'Many lenses: Critical themes in diversification in the National Capital Region', in E.T. Jackson and K.A. Graham, eds, *Diversification for Human Well Being: Challenges and Opportunities in the National Capital Region*. Ottawa: Carleton University, Diversification Research Group Working Papers Series, 1, 15–31.

——— and R. Shields. 1997. 'Contested terrains: Social space and the Canadian environment', in W. Clement, ed., *Understanding Canada: Building on the New Canadian Political Economy*. Montreal and Kingston: McGill-Queen's University Press, 386–408.

Wallerstein, I. 1976. *The Modern World-System: Capitalist Agriculture and the Origins of the European World-Economy in the Sixteenth Century*. New York: Academic Press.

Wang, S. 1999. 'Chinese commercial activity in the Toronto CMA: New development patterns and impacts', *Canadian Geographer* 43: 19–35.

Warkentin, J., ed. 1968. *Canada: A Geographical Interpretation*. Toronto: Methuen.

Watkins, M. 1963. 'A staple theory of economic growth', *Canadian Journal of Economics and Political Science* 29: 141–58.

Weller, G.R. 1977. 'Hinterland politics: The case of northwestern Ontario', *Canadian Journal of Political Science* 10: 727–54.

———. 1994. 'Regionalism, regionalisation, and regional development in a university context: The case of the University of Northern British Columbia', *Canadian Journal of Regional Science* 17: 153–68.

Welsted, J., J. Everitt, and C. Stadel. 1996. *The Geography of Manitoba: Its Land and Its People*. Winnipeg: University of Manitoba Press.

Williams, G. 1983. *Not For Export: Toward a Political Economy of Canada's Arrested Industrialization*. Toronto: McClelland & Stewart.

World Bank. 2000. *World Development Indicators*. Washington: The World Bank.

Wynn, G., and T. Oke, eds. 1992. *Vancouver and Its Region*. Vancouver: University of British Columbia Press.

Yeates, M. 1975. *Main Street: Windsor to Quebec City*. Toronto: Macmillan.

———. 1991. 'The Windsor-Quebec Corridor', in Bunting and Filion (1991: 178–208).

# Index

Terms not found in the index may be covered in the Glossary.
Page numbers in **boldface** refer to figures and/or tables.

Aboriginal peoples, 21, 30, 41, 227;
    co-management of resources, 236; economic
    well-being, **237**; labour force, 149; land
    claims, 142, 145, 146, 149, 216, 234, 238; in
    Northern Canada, 230–9; real estate, 238; in
    rural regions, 138; self-government, 231, 233;
    traditional activities, 233; in urban centres,
    230–9; venture capital, 238
accommodation, 107; *see also* tourism
aerospace industry, 118–19
Agricultural Rehabilitation and Development
    Act (ARDA), 23
agriculture: BC, 125; crops, 133; government
    policies and subsidies, 129–33, 138–9; and
    European Union, 123; modern technologies,
    125; northern Ontario, 206; Nova Scotia, 187;
    and population, 92; Prairie, 47; Quebec, 203;
    and regional patterns, 133–7; southern
    Ontario, 10–11; supply management, 132–3;
    use of water, 47; US, 123, 132
agri-food industry, 125, **126**; *see also* agriculture
Agropur, 203
agro-rural regions, 138
air transportation, 166; airline regulation, 22;
    commercial, 172–3; hub airports, 172; and
    northern Canada, 173; Quebec, 197; routes,
    **173**; *see also* transportation
Alaskan oil drilling, 163
Alberta, 223–4; oil and gas fields, 152; Alberta
    Heritage Savings Trust Fund, 121, 223, 224;
    Alberta Research Council, 224
Alcan, 158, 203
Algoma Steel, 209
alienation, 22; western, 153, 191
aluminum, 53
amalgamation, municipal, 83–4, 202
'appropriationism', 125, 243
aquaculture, 188
Arctic regions. *See* northern Canada
Area Development Agency (ADA), 24
asbestos, 10, 203

Asia-Pacific region: and Canadian trade, 166;
    effect of economic crisis, 220
Association of Southeast Asian Nations
    (ASEAN), 6
Atlantic Canada, 179–90; corporate structure,
    37; fragmentation, 179–80; government
    policies, 23; high-technology industries, 121;
    regional challenges, 181–3
Atlantic Development Board, 23
Atlantic Groundfish Strategy (TAGS), 180
Atomic Energy of Canada, 209
auto industry, 11–12, 114–18; and cost factors, 117;
    effect of imports, 115; locations, **116**; and
    minerals industries, 148; suppliers, 118; *see
    also* Auto Pact
automation technology, 121; and minerals
    industries, 145–6
Auto Pact, 12, 29, 111, 114–15

'back office', 82–3, 243
base-metal industry, 141, 220, 235; *see also*
    minerals industries
Beauce region, 203
beef-processing industry, 137; *see also* agri-food
    industry
Bell Canada, 119
Berger Inquiry, 239
'big-box' retailers, 102, 103
bilingualism, 187, 207
biotechnology-pharmaceutical industry, 121,
    224
Bloc Québécois, 21
'blue-box' projects, 52
Bombardier, 88, 118–19, 204
'borrower circles', 238
'brain drain', 64, 186, 208
branch-plant economy, 11–12, 15, 65; in Toronto,
    85–6
British Columbia (BC), 215–16, 225–8; forest
    policy, 218–19; northern, 228; weather, 56

British Columbia Labour Relations Board, 144
Burghardt, A.F., 74
business services, 103–4

'Canada's Technology Triangle' (CTT), 120
Canada–United States Free Trade Agreement.
    See Free Trade Agreement (FTA)
Canada–US Auto Pact. See Auto Pact
Canadian Alliance, 21
Canadian Association of Single Industry
    Towns, 148
Canadian Forces bases, 27
Canadian Wheat Board, 132
CANDU reactors, 162
canola, 216–17, 221
Cape Breton, 23, 181; coalfields, 160–1; Cape
    Breton Development Corporation (DEVCO),
    23
capitalism, 4–5, 7–10, 60–2, 101
casinos, 38, 38–9, 90
census metropolitan areas (CMAs), 78, 80–2;
    and amalgamation, 83–4; economies of, 82–4;
    and high-technology industries, 120; self-
    government, 93; and specialization, 81
Central Canada, 191–210; differences between
    Ontario and Quebec, 195; as economic core,
    193; energy sources, 152; northern, 198;
    regional economic structures, 198–9;
    topography, 191
Chinese population, ethnic, 36; see also
    immigration
chlorofluorocarbons (CFCs), 51
Christaller, W., 73–4
'circular and cumulative causation', 62
cities: 'world', 74–6; see also urban centres;
    census metropolitan areas (CMAs)
Clergue, Francis, 11
climate: benefits of, 45–6; change, 53–6;
    constraints of, 234; extreme events, 53–6;
    northern, 45–6
clothing industry, 65, 87
coal industry, 50, 160–1, 162, 186, 215; Northeast
    Coal Project, 9
cod industry, 50, 180, 183, 184, 187
'colonialism, internal', 232–3
commercial service sector, 15

commodity shipments, 170–1
Common Agricultural Policy (CAP), 123
community economic development (CED), 180
'comparative advantage', 62
competition, inter-metropolitan, 90
competitive advantage, of urban systems, 91
competitiveness, 63; see also rivalry
computer industry, 119–21; see also high-
    technology industry
consumption, centres of, 89
Confederation, 9
consumers: and environment, 51–2; household
    spending, 37–8; needs of, 73–4
containerization, 171–2, 174
continentalism, 61
co-operative enterprise, 36–7
Co-operative Commonwealth Federation, 212
core region, 8, 193, 243; relations with periphery,
    61, 198
corporations, 7; headquarters, 79–80, 90, 202
courier and air-freight market, 176; see also
    transportation
CP Rail, 176; see also railways
Crow's Nest Pass Agreement, 22–3, 132, 169, 172,
    217, 221
culture, 36; investment in, 89; of Northern
    Canada, 233; and regional economies, 68

dairy sector, 133, 205
decentralization of routine work, 82–3
de-inking plants, 144
demand: linkages, 10–11; and service sector,
    100–1
Department of National Defence: contracts, 22;
    employment, 106; spending, 26
Department of Regional Economic Expansion
    (DREE), 24–6; designated regions, 25
determinism: environmental, 56; physical, 240
diamonds, 235, 236
distributive services, 102–3
diversification, 212–13
domestic passenger transportation, 168–9;
    airline routes, 173
Domtar, 203–4
drought, 53–4; see also climate

e-commerce, 103, 202

economic hierarchy, 59–60

economic theories, 60, 62

economy: branch-plant, 110; 'continental', 59; global, 59; 'homeland', 235–6; 'knowledge', 4, 89, 149, 185–6; post-staples, 110 (see also staples industries); underground, 238

ecotourism, 227

Eddy Match Company, 209–10

education, 105, 181; see also public services

electricity, 46, 156; deregulation, 164; and minerals industry, 146–7; supply, **159**

emissions reduction, 44–5, 51, 146, 163; see also pollution

employment: aerospace, 119; agriculture, 128–9; Atlantic Canada, 181–2, **182**; auto industry, 115; BC, 225–6; Central Canada, 194–6; in CMAs, 82; cyclical sensitivity of, 67; expanding, 67, 68; forest industries, 144; high-technology industries, 120; home-based, 83, 88; manufacturing, 114; Montreal, 86–9, **88**; Newfoundland, 183; Prairie, **214**; producer services, 103–4; Quebec, 199–202; service sector, 97; Toronto, 85–7

energy: alternative sources, **157**, 163; consumption, **157**, 157–8; prices, 163, 203

energy industries: alternative sources, 151, 163; Atlantic Canada, 182; Calgary, 224; environmental impact, 151; minerals, 141; nuclear, 162, 163; privatization, 163–4; and regional development, 160–2

environment, natural, 41; see also climate

environmental activists, 42

environmental determinism, 56

environmental non-governmental organization (ENGO), 216, 220, 235

equalization payments, 23, **24**, 241; oil and gas industry, 153

European Union (EU), 6, 123

exploration, 141–2, 145

exports: to Europe, 14; export-oriented sectors, 197, 215 ; non-traditional, 242

'fall-down', 219, 243

family-run enterprises, 181

farms, **129**; characteristics, 128–9; disadvantages for Canadian, 124; family-run, 124; incomes,

125, **127**; organic, 136; provincial differences, 128; in southwest Ontario, 206; types, **130–1**; see also agriculture

federal government: Atlantic Canada, 179, 189; and oil and gas industries, 153; and aerospace industry, 118–19; and agriculture, 124–5; support for research and development, 111

film industry, 225

finance, insurance and real estate (FIRE) sector, 104

financial services, 80–1

fishing industries: and cod moratorium, **184**; environmental impact of, 42; ocean, 50; and population, 92; Quebec, 204

food and beverages sector, 107

food-processing industries, 87, 183, 188, 205, 206; Prairies, 217–18

Fordist production values, 5, 11, 66, 244; transition to post-Fordist production, 111, 244

foreign direct investment (FDI), 15, **16**, 64

foreign investments, Canadian, 242

foreign ownership, 11

foreign visitors, 107–8, **109**

Forest Practices Code, 219–20

forest products industries, 11, 140–1, 142–4, 203–4, 206, 227; and activists, 42; in Alberta, 223; BC, 218–20; and climate change, 53; management, 47–9; 'market pulp', 140; New Brunswick, 188; restocking, 47; softwood, 6, 47, 141; stumpage rates, 142, 219; technological advances, 214

Forest Renewal Plan, 219

forests, **48**; management, 47–9; restocking, 47; secondary, 219

fossil-fuel consumption, 163; see also energy consumption

free trade, 6, 13, 29, 39, 241–2; consequences of, 112; with US, 190

Free Trade Agreement (FTA), 3, 31–3, 61, 117, 196; effects of, 208–9

freight transportation, 170

'frontier myth', 232

fruit growers, 136; see also agriculture

Fund for Rural Economic Development (FRED), 23

fur industry, 210

gambling. *See* casinos
Gander International Airport, 185
gas, natural, 156, 235; in Alberta, 223; reserves, 50; sales and movements, **155**; *see also* oil and gas industries
gas turbine technology, 164
gateway cities, 74; Edmonton, 224; in Prairie provinces, 212
General Agreement on Tariffs and Trade (GATT), 6
General Development Agreements (GDAs), 26
genetically modified (GM) foods, 136
global economy, 59
globalization, 4, 58–60, 241–2, 244; and environment, 46; and producer services, 104; and technology, 5
global urban system, 74
global warming, 163; *see also* climate; pollution
'Golden Horseshoe' (Ontario), 205
government: decentralization, 105; downsizing, 196; *see also* federal government; regional policy
grain industries, 216–17, 229; exports, 221; grain elevators, 217, 222; subsidy wars, 10, 217; transportation, 166, 216–17
Great Lakes, 51
'green technologies', 44–5
Greyhound Air, 227–8
Gross Revenue Insurance Plan, 221

Halifax, 174, 187
Harvey, D., 89–90
headquarters, corporate, 79–80, 90, 202
health services. *See* public services
Hibernia, 160, 183
high-technology industry, 12–13, 118–21, 203, 214; Atlantic Canada, 181; BC, 225; environmental impact, 51; Nova Scotia, 186–7; Ottawa, 208; Saskatchewan, 222
hog operations, 47, 137
home-based employment, 83, 88
'homeland' economy, 235–6
household consumption: differences in, 37–8; and environment, 51–2; *see also* consumers
hub-and-spoke districts, 69

Hudson's Bay Company, 236
Human Development Index (HDI), 238
hunting, 235
hydrocarbons, 235
hydroelectricity, 185, 194, 202–3
Hydro-Quebec, 164, 197, 202–3

immigration, 34, 36, 45; into BC, 216; into Montreal, 202; into Western Canada, 211
incentives, industrial, 24–6
Inco, 185, 221
income: in BC, 218; per capita in Quebec, **200**; personal, 80
industrial activity: incentives, 24–6; research on, 69; in urban centres, 68–9, 69–71; US, 11
Industrial Revolution, 8
information sector, 100
Innis, Harold, 60
Inuvialuit Development Corporation (IDC), 236
investment, Canadian direct, **17**; foreign, 15, **16**, 64, 242
Ipsco, 222
Irving family, 37, 181, 188
Isle Madame, 186–7

James Bay, 203
Japan, 6; and auto industry, 117; and Canadian coal supply, 162
'just-in-time' delivery, 117

'knowledge economy', 4, 89, 149, 185–6
Kondratieff waves, 8, 244

labour market. *See* workforce
labour productivity, **219**
labour relations, 66; and forest products, 144; in Ottawa, 208; and transportation, 171–2
'lean' production, 117
leisure-market services, 106
logging. *See* forest products industries
lumber, 6, 140; production, **143**; *see also* forest products industries

McCain Foods, 37, 181, 188
McKenna, Frank, 180

'macro regions', 59

Manitoba, 212, 220–1; floods, 53

manufacturing: Alberta, 223–4; Canadian-owned, 12; growth, 110; military, 118; Montreal, 87, 87–8; New Brunswick, 188; Ontario, 196, 207; overview, 112–14; Toronto, 85–6; and World War II, 9

Maritime Freight Rate, 23

Maritime Marshland Rehabilitation Act, 23

Maritimes. See Atlantic Canada

markets, national, government regulation of, 59

'Marshallian' industrial districts, 69, 70, 244

meat-packing, 218

megaprojects, 234

merchandise trade, 14–15; by commodity group, 14; by world region, 7

metropolitan areas, 69, 72–3; see also census metropolitan areas

Mexico, 117

Microsoft, 120

migration, 34, 189–90; interprovincial, 35; 'lifestyle', 216; out-, 34; into rural regions, 137–8

military manufacturing, 118; see also National Department of Defence

mineral resources, 50; and population, 92

minerals industries, 145–9, 206, 227; in BC, 220; environmental impact of, 140, 142, 145; and exploration, 141–2; and import duties, 148; jurisdiction over northern, 230; in Northern Canada, 234–5; potash, 222; property abroad, 147

mini-mill technology, 148

mining. See minerals

'modal split', 166; see also transportation

Montreal, 84, 87–9, 194, 197, 202; as gateway city, 198–9; and railways, 168; Stock Exchange, 84, 89

multiculturalism, 36

NASDAQ, 85

'national competitive advantage', 62–5

'National Dream', 168

National Energy Board, 156, 158, 160

National Energy Program (NEP), 153, 235

nationalism, economic, 8, 61

National Policy (1879), 19, 20, 62, 110

National Task Force on Environment and Economy, 44

National Transportation Act, 169, 172

neo-classical economic theory, 61

'neo-liberal' economic values, 5, 8

New Brunswick, 187–9; McKenna administration, 180; New Brunswick Power, 162

'new economy' industries, 86–7

Newfoundland, 183–6; groundfish stocks, 49

newly industrializing countries (NICs), 5, 65

newsprint, 140; recycling, 52–3

New York, 174

New York Stock Exchange, 85

Niagara Peninsula, 124–5

nickel, 185; see also minerals industries

Noranda, 204

nordicity, 232

Nortel, 88, 119; see also high-technology industry; telecommunications

North American Free Trade Agreement (NAFTA), 3, 6; see also free trade; Free Trade Agreement (FTA)

North American Industry Classification System (NAICS), 100, 101

Northeast Coal Project, 9

Northern Canada, 230–9; 'frontier myth', 232; megaprojects, 234; and public services, 105–6; and railways, 165

'norths, provincial', 231

Nova Scotia, 186–7

Nova Scotia Power Corporation, 186

nuclear energy, 162, 163

Nunavut, 233–4

office construction, 82–3

oil and gas industries, 9; Alaska, 163; crude oil production and movements, 154; imports, 152; prices, 151, 152–3; reserves, 50; service stations, 103; synthetic oil production, 223; in Western Canada, 211, 214, 223

oil-sands plants, 223

oilseed crushing plants, 218

Ontario: auto industry, 115, 118; eastern, 205–6; hinterland growth, 209–10; northern, 206–7;

Ontario Hydro, 158, 162, 164, 207; and Quebec border, 191–3; and Quebec politics, 205–6; southern, 207; and state intervention, 29; subregions, 205–7

orchard crops, 136, 228; *see also* agriculture

organic products, 136

Organization of Petroleum Exporting Countries (OPEC), 152

Ottawa region, 198, 207–8; high-technology industries, 119–20

out-migration, 34

outsourcing, 83; *see also* home-based employment

packaging materials, 140; *see also* forest products industries

Panama Canal, 9

Parti Québécois, 29

peripheral economies, 9, 11

personal services, 106

pesticide use, 47

petrochemical industry, 158–60; *see also* oil and gas industries

physical determinism, 240

pipelines, 152, 156, 170, 235

'pluriactivity', 109

polarization, socio-economic, 89; *see also* urban centres

political interests: and the economy, 19–20; and regionalism, 21–2; *see also* federal government; regional policy

pollution, 44–5; atmospheric, 51; effect on forest and grassland boundaries, 54; public response to, 51; water, 47

population: BC, 225–6; Canada, 45; and CMAs, 82, 90–1; density, 76–8; increase, 76; in Newfoundland, 185–6; Prairie, 212; rural regions, 137–8; Saskatchewan, 222; urban areas, 72–3

Population-Environment Process (PEP) Framework, 43, 44

port development, 174

Porter, Michael, 62–5

post-staples economy, 110; *see also* staples industries

potash industry, 222; *see also* minerals industries

potatoes, 136, 188

poverty, 80, 92

Prairies, 212–15; diversification, 212–13; settlement of, 45; weather, 53–4

Prairie Farm Rehabilitation Act (PFRA), 23, 212

Pratt & Whitney Canada, 88

primary metals industry, 141; *see also* minerals industries

Prince Edward Island, 187–9

privatization, 37, 145

producer services, 12, 80–1, 102, 103–4, 111, 244

production, 'lean', 117

productivity, labour, 219

'provincial norths', 232

public administration. *See* public services

public sector: Atlantic Canada, 181–2; Quebec, 194; Northern Canada, 234; Nova Scotia, 187; research and development, 121; and service employment, 100; spending, 89

public services, 104–6

pulp and paper industry, 9, 143–4; and recycling, 52–3; *see also* forest products industries

Quebec: agriculture, 125; alienation, 22; and Auto Pact, 115; clothing industry, 65; cultural distinctiveness, 30, 36, 193–4; and electricity, 156; and FTA, 32; Gaspésie, 204; political culture, 39; Quiet Revolution, 20–1, 197; recreation industry, 204; rural regions, 199; and state intervention, 28–9; subregions, 199–204

Quebec City, 199

railways, 19, 172; captive commodities, 175; and commodity shipment, 169, 174–5; congestion, 166; development of, 11, 168–9; expansion into US, 175–6; networks, 167; in northeastern Ontario, 206; in Prairies, 213; short-line networks, 172; unit-train shipments, 171

rain forest, coastal, 216; *see also* forest products industries

recreation industry, 53, 204; *see also* personal services, tourism

recycling, 10, 52, 53, 144

Reform Party, 21, 28

refugees, 6–7; *see also* immigration

Regina, 222

regional policy, 22–7; agriculture, 133–7; Atlantic Canada, 181–2; dismantling of projects, 28–9; effectiveness, 26; and neo-conservative values, 30–1; and railways, 169

regions: as key economic environments, 68–71; rural, 134–5, 137–8

regulation: airline, 22; of national markets, 59; theorists, 66

research and development, 12–13; and branch-plant economy, 110; producers, 121

resource-based industries, 3, 62, 63–4; additions to base, 180–1; in Alberta, 223; Atlantic Canada, 179; BC, 227; Ontario, 197; non-renewable, 10; pressure on, 46; renewable, 211; and transportation, 166–8, 169; *see also* staples

resource cycle, 46–7

retailing: 'big box', 102, 103; food, 103; Web-based, 102

rivalry, 63, 65, 90

roads, 166, 174; growth of, 168; in Atlantic Canada, 189

Royal Commission on the Economic Union and Development Prospects for Canada, 122

rural regions: population density, 137–8; typology of, 134–5

salmon, 50, 188, 227

Sarnia, 206

Saskatchewan, 212–13, 221–2; Saskatchewan Wheat Pool, 36–37

satellite platform districts, 69

self-employed professionals, 227; *see also* home-based employment

self-government, Aboriginal, 231, 233

services, leisure-market, 106

service sector, 73, 97–109; Montreal, 202; structure, **98–9**; supply and demand, 100–1

settlement, 19, 92

Sheridan College, 87

shopping centres, 102

'Silicon Valley North', 119

single-industry towns, 37, 66, 78–9, 148–9, 198

Social Credit Party, 212

social services, 104–6

soft drink producers, 53

softwood, 6, 47, 141; *see also* forest products industries

space sector, 118, 221

specialization: agriculture, 129; and CMAs, 102; high-technology industries, 120; in pulp and paper, 144

Standard Industrial Classification (SIC), 100

staples industries, 15, 46–51; development, 9–10; exports, 165; and railways, 174–5; 'staples trap', 10, 183, 186, 244; sustainability, 50; theory, 240

state-centred districts, 69

state intervention, 20; in Central Canada, 210; provincial, 20; in railways, 169; *see also* regional policy

St Lawrence Seaway, 170, 175

stumpage rates, 142, 219

sub-regional economies, 59–60

'substitutionism', 125

Suncor, 156

supply and demand, 101

'supraterritoriality', 4

sustainable development, 42–4; *see also* resource-based industries

Syncrude, 156, 236

tar ponds, 186

teachers, 105

technological advances, 5, 149; agriculture, 125; in Atlantic Canada, 183; clean industry, 51; and decentralization, 83; and foreign investment, 64; forest products, 143; and producer services, 103; and service sector, 100; transportation, 170–2

telecommunications, 119–21, 183, 187–8

territorial legislatures, 230

thermo-mechanical pulps (TMPs), 144

Toronto, 76, 83–4, 84–7, 193, 196; Stock Exchange, 84–5

tourism, 106–8, 187, 189, 215; Atlantic Canada, 183; BC, 227; distribution of visits, **108**; ecotourism, 227; Quebec, 204; *see also* personal services

trade flows: Canada-US, **32**, **33**; interprovincial, **30**, **31**

training, 209

Trans-Canada Highway, 174

transportation: domestic passenger, 168–9, 173; industries, 87, 88, 151, 165–76; air traffic, 166, 173, 197; commodity flows, 165; costs, 175; and environment, 176; networks, 22, 165, 172–4; and service employment, 103; and tourism, 107

travel sector, 15; *see also* tourism

trucking, 171, 175

truncation, 112, 245

underground economy, 238

unemployment. *see* employment

University of Waterloo, 120

uranium mines, 162, 222; *see also* minerals industries

urban centres: Atlantic Canada, 180; Canadian, 76–80, 77; economic specialization, 78–9; environmental impact of expansion, 42; exerting political pressure, 90; and industrial activity, 68–9; intermetropolitan competition, 90; size distribution, 79

urban-frontier regions, 138

urban systems, 73–6; alternative theories, 74; competitive advantages, 91; global, 74

US economy, and Canada, 13–15, 18, 65, 241

values, economic, 5, 8

Vance, J. E., 74; and settlement system evolution, 75

Vancouver, 74–6, 84, 215, 225

venture capital, for Aboriginal peoples, 238

visible trade. *See* merchandise trade

voluntary export restraints (VERs), 115

waste disposal, 52

waterborne movement, 170

waterfront redevelopment, 89

water supply, 46–7

wealth, 80, 100–1

weather, extreme, 45–6, 53–4; *see also* climate

Web-based retailing, 102

welfare state, 5, 31, 104

Welland Canal, 175

West Edmonton Mall, 224

Western Canada, 211–29; and FTA, 32; and policy-making, 228

Western Star Trucks, 228

wheat, 9; *see also* grain industries; agriculture

wholesale trade, 103

wind power, 163; *see also* energy sources

Windsor-Quebec City corridor, 76

wine industries, 136, 228

Winnipeg, 212, 220

wireless communications, 121, 224; *see also* high-technology industries; telecommunications

wood products, 140; *see also* forest products industries

work, routine, 82–3

workforce: bilingualism of, 187, 206; Norcliffe's analysis, 66–67; quality of, 4; supply, 67–8; training, 209

workplace flexibility, 209

'world cities', 74–6

World Trade Organization (WTO), 6, 39; and Auto Pact, 114

Wright, Philemon, 11

Yukon. *See* Northern Canada